THE
THIRD EARL
OF
SHAFTESBURY

THE
THIRD EARL
OF
SHAFTESBURY

❧❧

1671–1713

ROBERT VOITLE

Louisiana State University Press

Baton Rouge and London

Designer: Albert Crochet
Typesetter: G & S Typesetters, Inc.
Printer and Binder: Vail-Ballou Press, Inc.

LIBRARY OF CONGRESS CATALOGING IN PUBLICATION DATA

Voitle, Robert.
The third Earl of Shaftesbury, 1671–1713.

Bibliography: p.
Includes index.
1. Shaftesbury, Anthony Ashley Cooper, Earl of,
1671–1713. 2. Philosophers—England—Biography.
I. Title.
B1388.V64 1984   192 [B]   83-20365
ISBN 0-8071-1139-2

Frontispiece courtesy of the
National Portrait Gallery, London,
by permission of the Right Honorable
the Earl of Shaftesbury.

For

Bill and Clara Morris

Contents

Preface

The Shaftesbury Papers in the Public Record Office upon which this biography is chiefly based are a most remarkable collection. For the third Earl they provide us with a vast number of documents ranging all the way from his private notes to his published works. The chief problem with these papers is lack of continuity. For all the wealth of detail they provide, there are gaps which must be filled, sometimes indistinctly, from other documents. The papers do not enable a biographer of the Earl to treat in a fairly even manner as little, say, as four years of his life. Sometimes there is not only a day-by-day account of his activities but also the notation of his private thoughts on them; at another time there is lacking not only his thoughts but any notion of where he is and what he is doing.

One way of providing more continuity in such a situation is to go to the general history of whatever activity the subject is engaged in and work back to the individual. Many of the Shaftesbury Papers are organized on a basis which would make this possible. For instance we have a large number of orders from the Admiralty to the Earl as vice Admiral of Dorset, we have his own account of his wine cellar, we have his steward's account of his career as a rack-renter, and we have his own account of how he functioned judicially as lord of the manor. It would seem then that by looking into the history of the vice admirals, into the annals of the wine trade, into the changing meanings of the term *rack-renting*, or the history of the landlord as jurist, one should be able to provide more continuity and measure him against the norm for his day. As anyone who has tried this for someone born three hundred years ago knows, it does not work out well. These histories seldom involve enough detail to illuminate the subject's life, and the even more general statistical studies often fail to mesh with his career because of some geographical or chronological element. Sometimes one finds, rather surprisingly, that the nature of the activity was changing so rapidly during his time that it is difficult to find a niche into which the subject can be slipped.

Another problem is more easily resolved, so long as one stays constantly aware of it. Shaftesbury appears in the papers in many differing roles, not all of them consistent on the surface. A number of these involve postures that he consciously adopted in his daily life. All of us are forced to adopt personae in our lives, and some of us even relish doing so, as Shaftesbury did, but he was fulfilling a condition more necessary to his life than it is for most of us today. The times encouraged it—the patronage system, for instance; his rank in society encouraged it; he was an author, too, acutely aware that his effectiveness in manipulating his audience depended on it; and again, in the Stoic philosophy, where he gradually moved from theory into practice, masks were an absolute necessity, at least in the novitiate. Here the biographer has an advantage over the intellectual historian, because he must constantly be aware of when and in what role Shaftesbury is speaking. His problem is to see that all the various roles tend to coalesce. For a while I feared that they would not; at the end, though, they did for me, and I hope they will for my readers.

There is no attempt here to trace out the sources of Shaftesbury's thought, even if that were possible. Instead I try to see his thought evolving in response to the intellectual challenges of the day. Despite the fact that he is rightly viewed as a prophet of change, Shaftesbury saw himself as very conservative in most respects, as a disciple of the Ancients. Nor is there enough space for a neatly uniform treatment of his ideas. Where my investigations make possible fresh interpretations, these are argued. Where the discussions in the extensive literature are adequate, I content myself with summarizing his notions.

Perhaps there are fewer citations to well-known authors on Shaftesbury's ideas than there ought to be. Indeed, some authors from whom I have profited are listed only in the Bibliography. The reason it is difficult to cite them in the text lies in my very different mode of approach to Shaftesbury. Scholars who make solid contributions to the knowledge of his ideas can take the broad view, as Alfred

Owen Aldridge does, or use a narrower scope, as Esther Tiffany does, but perforce they must regard the text as all written at one time. As a biographer I am interested in the growth and development of his philosophy, so that instances specific enough to offer an opportunity for citation turn out to be rather rare. The twain simply do not often meet.

There is little here on Shaftesbury's literary collaborations. Indeed, I have sedulously avoided any reference to it except for obvious cases. The best a biographer can hope to do is to recover what was once known about his subject, and this material comes through in a fragmentary way. Since Shaftesbury made a great effort to conceal his collaboration from his contemporaries, the study of it involves a wholly different sort of evidence, that not simply concealed by the passage of time. It is legitimate to speculate on his collaborations, but this did not seem to be the place to do it.

I also wish it had been possible to discuss Shaftesbury's ideas always in the context of his life at the time, instead of placing the discussion of many of his notions in two separate chapters; for he very much lived the life of the mind. There are considerable difficulties in doing it any other way than I have done it. For instance, we do not know precisely when his *Inquiry Concerning Virtue* was written. How then is it to be tied to a specific year in his life? Furthermore, he was an anonymous author up until the very last years of his life. One of his books was printed without being actually published for several years, and two more very significant works were only published in the present century.

Of course we do know the order in which his works were written, and we know, too, that they reflect an evolving pattern of change in his thought over a quarter of a century. In many respects Shaftesbury was remarkably true to his ideal of constancy. Some of the transformations in him are merely a matter of growing up, but I have also tried to show how this pattern of change and his growing conviction of the validity of some of his own ideas affected his life from day to day.

The project has been supported by the Research Council of the University of North Carolina.

This book is indebted to the assistance of E. A. Alderman, Dora Beth, R. L. Brett, Giancarlo Carabelli, the late Rosalie Colie, Maurice Cranston, Günther Gawlick, Biaggio di Giovanni, K. H. D. Haley, Elisabeth Labrousse, Ted McVey, Horst E. Meyer, Mark Reed, Caroline Robbins, Louis Rubin, the late George Sherburn, Albrecht Strauss, and the late Giorgio Tonnelli. I also want to thank Samuel Boone for equipment enabling me to read difficult manuscripts expeditiously, and I want to thank my research assistants, Caroline Benton, Michael Kuczynski, and Jane Nunnelee, for their diligence. I am greatly obliged to Paul Betz for his fine editorial assistance.

For kind permission to use manuscripts, I wish to thank His Grace, the Duke of Rutland and the Right Honorable the Earl of Shaftesbury, the Bodleian Library, the British Library, and the Public Record Office. Transcripts of crown-copyright records in the Public Record Office appear by permission of the Controller of H. M. Stationery Office.

In England I am also indebted to the Trustees of the Broadlands Archives Trust, the Dorset County Museum, the Kent Archives Office, the National Portrait Gallery, the Royal Commission on Historical Manuscripts, and the Victoria and Albert Museum; in Amsterdam, to the Universiteits-Bibliotheek; in Naples, to the Archivio di Stato and its fine staff, the Biblioteca dei Girolamini, the Biblioteca Nazionale, and the Istituto Italiano per gli Studi Storici; in the United States, to the Harvard University Library and, for its continual helpfulness, to the Library of the University of North Carolina. Both the Earl of Shaftesbury and the Lady Lettice Ashley Cooper have been most graciously helpful to me. I also wish to thank the Earl for his permission to reproduce the portrait by John Closterman of the third Earl and an unknown attendant, perhaps John Wheelock. I have profited much from the wisdom of Dr. Esmond S. de Beer and his remarkable knowledge of the period. Adding to all the other debts I owe her in connection with this long protracted undertaking, there is no phase of the research or writing which has not benefitted from my wife's energy and common sense.

Abbreviations and
Notation Style

Manuscripts

BC	Belvoir Castle
BL	Bodleian Library
PRO	Public Record Office

Works by Shaftesbury

Char.	*Characteristicks of Men, Manners, Opinions, Times.* The second edition, corrected. (1714)
Ex.	"Exercises." PRO 30/24/27/10.
Inq.	*An Inquiry Concerning Virtue.* (1699)
SC	*Second Characters, or The Language of Forms,* ed. Benjamin Rand. (1914)
SE	*The Sociable Enthusiast: A Philosophical Adventure, Written to Palemon.* (1704?)
Mor.	*The Moralists, a Philosophical Rhapsody.* (1709)

All contractions are expanded. Brackets are used to enclose suggested emendations, words supplied for clarity, and occasionally, for translated material. Commas are added very rarely when necessary for clarity.

Unless otherwise noted, all dates are Old Style, but the year begins on January 1. All books cited are published in London, unless another place is specified.

THE
THIRD EARL
OF
SHAFTESBURY

⅃ I ⅃

Anthony's Early Years:
Education and Travels
1671–1689

Anthony Ashley Cooper, later third Earl of Shaftesbury, was born at
Wimborne St. Giles, Dorsetshire, on February 26, 1671. Typically
enough, there is very little to go on with respect to Anthony's first
decade. Indeed, the only really concrete piece of evidence we have is
a trifle which owes its survival to the tender feelings of a parent or
grandparent; it is a small bit of paper on which is written

ffor a stick	00 07 00
ffor a horn and whip	00 05 00
ffor a troup of geece	00 01 00
ffor a book with music	00 01 00
ffor a ribbon to tie the horn & stick	00 02 00
ffor a wrought box & ball	00 02 00

Turning it over, we read, "Mrs. Janes Bill for Babbles for Mr. Anthony at Hatfield, 0.18.0, August 25th 1672." On the other hand we
have a good bit of information about some of those who were close
to him in his early years: his father and mother; his grandfather
and his grandfather's wife by a later marriage; and John Locke
(1632–1704).

Anthony's father, also named Anthony (1651–1699), was heir of a
long line of Ashleys that have been traced back as far as the thirteenth century. For most of the time they were content to gather
property through purchase and marriage, but in the previous century
some of them had sat in Parliament; the family had risen from the
landed gentry to knighthood, and his great-grandfather Sir Anthony
Ashley (1551–1627) had been created baronet. Sir Anthony, a clerk
of the Privy Council in the reigns of both Elizabeth and James, was
the most striking member of the family during the sixteenth century and in many ways typifies the sort of versatility we think of as

Elizabethan. He was a soldier, an accomplished politician, a scholar who translated a Dutch treatise on navigation written in Latin, a philanthropist whose alms houses still stand at Wimborne St. Giles, and finally he was skilled in accumulating the means to philanthropy. He had no surviving male heir, so he used his prestige and wealth to assure that the eldest son of his daughter Anne and her husband John Cooper (d. 1631) from nearby Rockbourne, the orphan of a knight, would inherit by entail the Cooper lands and would be christened Ashley. Anthony Ashley Cooper (1621–1683), the future first Earl of Shaftesbury, was orphaned at age ten and his estate was plundered by law officers who stole much that John Cooper had not already spent in his profligate manner of living; yet there remained a substantial estate for him to pass on to his son and grandson.

The second Anthony Ashley Cooper is an enigma. He was the child of his father's second wife, born Frances Cecil (1632–1651), and was shortly the only surviving heir. From his early adolescence he suffered from some disfiguring malady, which promised him only a short and miserable life.[1] Many of his contemporaries knew what was the matter with him, but the details of private lives were then gossip, not history, and no one, not even Dryden, left us any specific information. Obviously, though, if the line were to be carried on, Sir Anthony had to find his son a wife quickly. After a failure in 1668, he did the next year succeed in settling for a match with Dorothy Manners (d. 1698), daughter of the Earl of Rutland. The Manners daughters seem to have developed early the reputation of being strong-minded women, defiant of male authority. In August 1667 Thomas Henshaw (1618–1683) wrote to Sir Robert Paston, later Earl of Yarmouth (1631–1683), "Lord Anglesey and Lord Ashley's son were plying their business at your cousins of Rutlands, and 'tis thought that each of them has by this time got a Tartar."[2] Every-

1. According to family tradition, a mercurial medicine was misapplied for a disorder he fell into at the age of fifteen; K. H. D. Haley's assumption in his *First Earl of Shaftesbury* (Oxford, 1967), 222, that this makes one naturally think of syphilis may be gratuitous. There were a number of mercury compounds in the seventeenth-century pharmacopoeia used for different diseases, though it is easy to understand why the rather defensive fourth Earl might feel caution was necessary and delete his reference to the family tradition.

2. *Seventh Report of the Royal Commission on Historical Manuscripts, Pt. I*

thing we know about the sisters of Lady Dorothy suggests they lived up to this reputation all of their lives. The considerable wealth of their family and its distinguished lineage—the Manners had been knights from at least the fourteenth century and earls for a century and a half—may account in part for this.

John Locke served as general factotum in the marriage. We see him traveling with young Anthony to Belvoir Castle, carrying a jewel from Sir Anthony to Lady Dorothy, and certainly he must have made many of the arrangements which his busy employer had no family to trust with. The third Earl was convinced that Locke actually chose Lady Dorothy for the match.

For the first year or two of her marriage we have a number of Lady Dorothy's letters to her mother. They reveal her as an unsophisticated—as she remained all her life—and thoroughly charming woman. Her first reactions to Exeter House in London, where she began her marriage after a wedding at Belvoir Castle, are a little mixed. Although the house is crowded and she and her husband have been given an apartment in the low-ceilinged Tudor section of the building, she extolls the elegance and convenience of the chambers, and her father-in-law has told her that in them she must always burn wax candles rather than the less convenient and smelly tallow variety, which were almost universal. Exeter House may not be as ancient as Haddon Hall nor as imposing as Belvoir Castle, but its master relishes magnificence and, moreover, the social life of London is rather overwhelming to a young woman who had been brought up in a great household but one far from the capital.

The happiness that seems to shine forth from almost every page of her letters from this period is difficult to characterize. Dorothy has a *joie de vivre* reserved to those who are pious, sincere, dutiful, and naïve and who embrace life with gusto, yet, though essentially sanguine, are reluctant to expect too much of it. Each new delight, great or small, is sufficient to the day, and it is savored as if it were the last delight. And all this joy is evoked in a very tense situation. Her first pregnancy has ended in a miscarriage a few months after the mar-

---

(1879), 531. From other proposed marriages for her among the Manners correspondence, it seems likely that Dorothy was older than Anthony.

riage and she continues to have difficulties, yet her responsibility becomes greater month by month. Lord Ashley's hopes were abundantly fulfilled, and John Locke's judgment well vindicated—two sons were born in the first thirty months of the marriage. Locke, the physician, seems to have watched over both of these pregnancies.

Dorothy Ashley's chief delight was her husband. Whatever the nature of his disabilities, they had led her not to hope for too much in her marriage. In a letter to her mother written a few weeks after the marriage she says, "For besides all, I finde that my happiness must increase, for I have a sober & serious good man to my husband, one who I never thought to be a foole, yet I could never (have) hoped to have found him what I daly se he is & will be, if he lives, as wise a man as any."[3] On her first wedding anniversary she writes, "From my serveing God I am just now come to doe my duty to your Ladyship & my Father who this day made me so happie in a most excellent husband."[4] And, a fortnight before the birth of Anthony, "Never was there more care had of any creature, as hath both Lord & Lady Ashley of me, both day and night, also am I never; till I am lay'd to sleepe; out of the eye; and tender care & kindness; of the affectionatest best husband that ever was."[5]

It seems very likely that his illness was degenerative. He was chosen for Weymouth and Melcombe Regis at the age of eighteen and attended Parliament, traveled about England, and for a short while at least was involved in business affairs. In the 1670s he must have become more and more a recluse on the family estates near Wimborne St. Giles—actually for the most part confined by his illness to the house, though he remained an M.P. for some time.

It had been arranged when Anthony was only four that as heir to the line he would be brought up by his grandfather, who was always very kind to his son, but felt that he could not trust him with this responsibility.[6] The logical place for little Anthony and his gov-

3. Lady Dorothy Ashley to the Countess of Rutland, n.d., in BC Add. MSS. 59, No. 2.
4. Lady Dorothy Ashley to the Countess of Rutland, September 22, 1670, in BC Add. MSS. 59, No. 30.
5. Lady Dorothy Ashley to the Countess of Rutland, February 5, 1671, in BC Add. MSS. 59, No. 32.
6. There is a document signed by Anthony's father on March 16, 1674—PRO

erness to live was at St. Giles's House, so that the first few years of his life were much like those of other small children, spent in the security of his family. When in 1676 the first Earl sold Exeter House and moved with his wife and servants to St. Giles's House until a suitable home could be found for them in London, Lord Ashley, his wife, and two more sons left St. Giles's, first for Haddon Hall, one of the seats of the Manners family, and thence to Martin, a few miles from Wimborne. Anthony was moved about some and eventually went to public school, but for at least three years his life probably centered on St. Giles's House, where often, since the Countess always followed the Earl about, he must have been alone in the great mansion, with only his governess and the servants for company. This was the first of many steps which tended to isolate him from the rhythms of the life of his class and eventually from fashionable society itself.

In all it was for nearly seven years, from 1676 to 1683, that he was the charge of one of the most puzzling of statesmen, his grandfather. It may not be true any longer that if you mention to an Englishman an interest in the Earl of Shaftesbury he will reply, "the good one or the bad one?"—the philanthropist seventh Earl or Anthony's grandfather, that consummate politician. K. H. D. Haley's definitive biography of the first Earl will eventually have its effect, but the whole issue is worth looking at briefly because the first Earl dominated Anthony's life, and not just for the period of custody. His ghost haunted Anthony until his death, shaping decisions large and small.[7]

The first Earl had many skills essential to the politician: he became a sagacious knower of men and was thereby able to move them to his will with his eloquence; he was witty and vivacious, quick on his feet, in short, a supreme manipulator. Whatever his part in the passage of the Habeas Corpus Act he had been a persistent supporter of parliamentary supremacy for a long time. He was also an un-

---

30/24/20/2—assigning the custody and tuition of Anthony and John to the Earl of Shaftesbury, but it is not certain when this was to take effect, for the document also contains the phrase "and the custody and tuition of all my other children which I shall have living at the time of my death" and it goes on to transfer all the real and personal estate belonging to the children to the Earl.

7. Much of this portrait is dependent on Haley's fine biography.

qualified supporter of religious toleration for Dissenters and he was equally intolerant of Catholicism, coming as he did from a Puritan background which stressed anticlericalism more than adherence to dogma; this must have been the most popular of his tendencies. Obviously he was intensely ambitious; yet with regard to wealth, he left the estate little better than he found it, certainly a below-par performance for his own generation of politicians and those to follow in the next century. In respect to power, as Haley points out, almost every time he shifted from one side to the other he either lost a position or the chance for one. His force of will was involved in his weaknesses as well as his strengths, and it causes one to wonder about the ability to develop such force and the ability to resist continual pain, as he had to until Locke directed an operation to remove an abscess in 1668. He could be ruthless at times, disastrously lacking in magnanimity, and fatally overconfident.

We may never be sure of the actualities with regard to the first Earl—who died five days before Anthony's twelfth birthday; however, for the grandson it was the memory that counted and this was solidly good. His biographer makes a good case for the first Earl's being sincere in the three principles I have mentioned regarding Parliament, Dissenters, and Catholics, and these views underlay Anthony's own political beliefs and he pursued them unrelentingly, sometimes unaware that the battle had in many respects already been won. But this would be only part of the story to close relatives, who always see the political figure differently from the pattern of strengths and weakness perceptible to the public. Here the private man dominates and everything we see is favorable. His letters to his son are very touching; they are benign and full of respect for the younger man. He also was continually kind and warm to his wife, his daughter-in-law, and his followers. This same affection they all felt strongly for him, and after his death toward his memory.

There is another factor which is harder to define. No official action was ever taken against the first Earl's family after his death, but there was a constant effort in the courts against them and the feeling evoked in its members by these cases was intensified when they found it necessary to sell part of the estate to pay off the first Earl's debts. Despite the polished manners Anthony early learned, he always felt apart from society, and the obvious corruption of many who were opposed to him tended to strengthen his confidence in his grandfather. He felt this when he first met the world at Winchester College, he felt it later in his dealings with the Apostate Whigs, and he was reminded of it continually until death. It is surely a simplification but in a way his whole life was an attempt to vindicate his grandfather, not simply to justify his principles, but to live a public life so exemplary as to counter the opprobrium laid on the first Earl.

There is no question about the first Earl's last wife, Margaret (1627–1693), sister of Henry Spencer, first Earl of Sunderland (1620–1692), who, though no relation to Anthony, became an almost archetypal grandmother to him. She was a deeply pious woman who maintained her household well and seems never to have been a fashionable person. Her earnest letters always have an appropriate touch of naïveté. Above all she was devoted to her husband, by whose side she stayed in the Tower of London—not a typical prison, but as it turned out not a healthy one for either of them. All the letters of hers we have from the period after his death are signed, "Mournefull M. Shaftesbury."

As we have seen, the first Earl used the polymath John Locke for any task that required high intelligence and integrity. His social finesse and medical skill had been of great service to the future second Earl and his bride; now it was Locke's turn to apply the theories he had developed as a tutor at Oxford to the education of Anthony. He left no plan but it is easy enough to guess from his later writings on the education of younger people the general pattern of his instruction to Anthony's governess, Elizabeth Birch. The list of books looks very much as it might if any teacher of the day were to set about training a child to grow up as a statesman and philosopher; what is distinctive about Locke's program is his methodology. He knows the ways of children, and parents, as only a sympathetic bachelor who has spent much of his life in other people's households can know them. Locke is convinced that any adult is largely the product of his *total* environment in childhood, and that to shape the adult that complete environment must be controlled, not just part of it.

7

The sort of discipline that Anthony experienced during his education in childhood shows how Locke put these principles into practice. Locke says that young children may need some discipline based on fear and awe. Up to a certain age, for example, they may for their own good have to be in awe of their parents, but as soon as possible this regimen should be replaced with one of love and friendship. "They love to be treated as Rational Creatures sooner than is imagined."[8] And it follows that they are soon to distinguish rational from irrational behavior in their parents and to revere the former as they contemn the latter. The principle of association operates powerfully in discipline, and a true love of learning will not be generated in a child who is continually "chid for his book." Nor should physical reward and punishment ever be used in teaching. Esteem and acceptance, signalized publicly, and, disgrace, administered in private, are far more effective than physical incentives, and they avoid the chief danger of the latter, which is that if physical pleasure is offered as a reward it tends to become itself the goal of the learning process, supplanting the higher ends it was supposed to further. In none of these suggestions regarding discipline does one sense that the pat formulas of a detached theorist are being applied, because everywhere Locke shows his awareness of the difficulty of maintaining a balance between restraint and freedom.

Especially significant for the future career of the man who came to be regarded as the inventor of the term "moral sense" is the attention Locke always gives to inculcating "good nature," which seems to be the principal ingredient of what is to him the first end of education, virtue. As practical guides to virtue Locke recommends Cicero, Puffendorf, Aristotle, and above all, Scripture, which can teach a man all he can learn through reading about how he should conduct himself toward others. Unremitting vigilance on the part of parents, governesses, and tutors is necessary, if the precepts are to bear any fruit.

Be sure to keep up in him the principles of good-nature and kindness, and encourage them as much as you can, by credit, commendation, and

8. John Locke, *Some Thoughts Concerning Education* (1693), 90.

other rewards that accompany that state: and when they have taken root in his mind, and are settled there by practice, the ornaments of conversation and the outside of fashionable manners, will come of themselves.[9]

Central to this process is Locke's profound awareness of the plasticity of young psyches. Those around the child must not be ill natured, for "you must do nothing before him which you would not have him imitate."[10] And one must always be on guard against tendencies which may develop into antisocial traits: especially watch children's conduct with "very young birds, butterflies, and such other poor things." "For the custom of tormenting and killing of beasts will by degrees harden their minds even toward men." "Children, then, should be taught from the beginning not to destroy any living creature unless it be for the preservation and advantage of some other that is nobler."[11]

We know too that Locke's method of teaching languages was used in Anthony's education, because one of the chief attractions of Elizabeth Birch as a governess was her command of Latin and Greek. Anthony himself has been traditionally supposed to have been fluent in Greek by the time he was eleven. Outlining his scheme to Edward Clarke (ca. 1650–1710), Locke says,

> Mine in short is this: to trouble the child with no rules of grammar at all, but to have Latin, as English has been, without the perplexity of rules talked into him. For if you will consider it, Latin is no more unknowne to a child, when he comes into the world, than English: and yet he learns English without master, rule or grammar: and so he ought Latin too, if he had somebody always to talk to him in this language.[12]

Locke's system of physical conditioning needs little comment because it is merely an extreme application of the precepts still to be found in some English texts on child rearing, the practice of which,

---

9. John Locke to Edward Clarke, September 1, 1685 NS, in Esmond S. de Beer (ed.), *The Correspondence of John Locke* (Oxford, 1976), II, 732–33.

10. John Locke, *Educational Writings*, ed. John William Adamson (New York, 1912), 55.

11. John Locke to Edward Clarke, February 8, 1686 NS, in de Beer, II, 773.

12. *Ibid.*, 775.

however sound in view of the climate, always arouses some as-
tonishment in visitors to Britain from more comfort-loving lands. It
is based on the logically attractive but thermodynamically unsound
discussion which ensued when a Greek asked a Scythian how he
could go about in midwinter with no clothes on. " 'How can you endure your face exposed to the sharp winter air?' said the Scythian.
'Because it is used to it,' said the Greek. 'Think me then all face,'
replied he!" [13] Accordingly, children are to be accustomed from infancy to spend as much time as possible at all seasons of the year in
the fresh air, wearing the lightest sort of clothing. And the elements
are to be helped along when possible: "I think that had I a daughter I
should order water to be put in her [shoes] when she put them on,
and have her feet well washed in cold water." [14] The rest of the precepts are largely concerned with diet, and anyone acquainted with
the eating habits of the upper classes in seventeenth-century England could not but applaud Locke's suggestions, which are generally in accord with the less quixotic pronouncements of modern nu-
tritionists. To these notions of Locke's, Shaftesbury owed much.
Without the love of temperance and the art of self-discipline which
Anthony learned so early, his dedication to his post in life would
have killed him sooner.

When we look at the third Earl of Shaftesbury in his maturity,
what traits of character seem to come in large part from his education as supervised by Locke? At least two. The first is his powerful
and disinterested love of learning which made him a supporter of
both struggling students and noted scholars and made him prefer the
life of contemplative study to all others and remain a student until
his death—a situation so out of place in his class that he was forced
to pose to his readers as a bantering dilettante, lest his erudition
scare them away. There was irony here of course. Locke, though he
would have been surprised to learn it, is now regarded as one of the
greatest Moderns of his era; Shaftesbury's studies led him to be a relentless supporter of the Ancients.

A second effect is that some of Shaftesbury's benevolism—in both

13. John Locke to Edward Clarke, July 19, 1684 NS, *ibid.*, 627.
14. John Locke to Mrs. Mary Clarke, February 7, 1685 NS, *ibid.*, 687.

his intensive private beneficence and in his published philosophy—must stem from Locke's intention to teach children "from their cradles to be tender to all sensible creatures." When the popularity of the moral, as opposed to the aesthetic, part of Shaftesbury's philosophy began to wane in the middle of the eighteenth century, it did so in part because the benevolism he preached had been fully accepted; and in spite of many reactions, goodness of heart is still the cardinal principle in popular moral notions. In the end, Locke's training had rather ironic results here, too, for when Shaftesbury turned against his master's ideas he did so largely because he thought Locke's whole philosophy would destroy true benevolence.

The day-to-day task of educating Anthony was from the first the responsibility of Elizabeth Birch, daughter of an ejected nonconformist divine turned schoolmaster, Samuel Birch (d. 1679). The first Earl seemed enthusiastic when Locke first mentioned her, and told him in November 1674 that as to paying for her he would not "differ upon any thing thats reason." The next summer we find her dining at the steward's table at St. Giles's House. Anthony must have first seen her, then, not long after his fourth birthday. Late in the same year Locke went to France for his health.

Presumably Elizabeth went on teaching Anthony until her father's death in 1679. Then there seems to have been some question as to whether she would take over his school in Shilton, Oxfordshire. The first Earl was much troubled by the whole business and in March 1680 resolved to take Anthony into his London house. But in August Locke, who had returned the year before, wrote to the Earl that although he had not been able to go to see Anthony at Mrs. Birch's school in Clapham, across the Thames, a Mr. Tanner associated with the school had been to see him and assured him that Anthony was well.

The time that Anthony spent at the school at Clapham ought to have been happier than the last period at St. Giles's House, despite the fact that these were troubled years for his family. He may have spent some of his holiday time at Wimborne St. Giles. Yet except when his grandfather and probably the Countess were living in various quarters in the Tower during July through November of 1681, Clapham was so close that he must have seen them occasionally.

Most important to a boy of ten, he now had a friend of his own age. In Locke's journals there is an entry "paid for 2 bows and six arrows for Mr Ashley & my Lord Fitzwalter." The friendship with Charles Mildmay, Lord FitzWalter (1670–1728), or Anthony's fond memories of it, seems to have continued on for some time. Another advantage of Clapham was that Anthony could see Locke, who seems to have visited him there regularly to watch over his progress and his health. Mrs. Birch remained close to Locke. On his return from France she may have been the one who made up shirts for him, and we also have a note in his journals indicating that she borrowed a French moral treatise from him in 1680. Beyond his obvious enthusiasm for his early education Anthony left no comments on Mrs. Birch.[15]

Late in November of 1682, after many weeks spent in hiding, the Earl of Shaftesbury slipped away disguised as a Presbyterian minister and sailed to Holland where he died two months later, the object of that sort of scorn which failure alone can evoke. This marked the end of an era for Anthony, as it did for so many others. On February 1 of the next year Lady Katherine FitzWalter (d. 1725) wrote to Thomas Stringer (1639–1702), who had been Shaftesbury's steward for many years: "I hope Lord Ashley [w]home I saw yesterday in health & mind must not part; my Lord is in great hopes he shall be under My Lady his Grandmothers care."[16]

It was not to be. In addition to a rivalry between his parents and the Countess Dowager for the affections of Anthony, the second Earl had his own ideas as to how his son should be raised. Furthermore, serious financial disagreements had soured the relationship between the two households. The first Earl left substantial debts to be paid off, and his wife was executrix. There was an argument as to whether these should be paid off from the entailed estate or by the Countess, who had been left with what turned out to be a competence, but little more. The second Earl and his wife suspected that she was

15. The relationship continued to be warm, however. Countess Margaret left her money for mourning clothes, and in 1696 when things were getting hard for her, Anthony gave her a handsome sum "to put her into a way of livelihood."
16. Lady Katherine FitzWalter to Thomas Stringer, February 1, 1683, in PRO 30/24/6B/405.

withholding important documents, perhaps in order to conceal that she was keeping some of the estate from them too.[17]

On the whole, Lady Margaret seems to have been treated unfairly in the matter. There is a draft of a letter from Locke, which we cannot be sure was sent, in which he castigates Lord Shaftesbury in tones which sound very strange to anyone accustomed to his letters to those very high above him in rank. Then there is even more conclusive evidence in a letter from William Montagu (1619–1706) to Dorothy Shaftesbury. As a sergeant-at-law and former attorney general he was certainly qualified to judge the facts of the case. His loyalty to Lady Dorothy and her family cannot be questioned, and his letters reveal him to be a just and wise man. After a meeting with Lady Margaret and Thomas Stringer, he writes

> My Lady Shaftesbury . . . made very kind expressions towards my Lord and Ladyshipp and the ffamily which I believe her to be very reall in, that I would faigne have a right understanding betweene you, which I hope to prevaile for when I can have the happiness to see my Lord and your Ladyshipp; ffor Mr. Stringer I cannot scarse apprehend so ill of him as your Ladyshipp doth, for . . . I . . . had very faire Answers of my Lady and Mr. Stringer.[18]

Lord Ashley's history for the months immediately following the death of his grandfather is summarized in the shaky handwriting of the second Earl on the flyleaf of one of his account books:

> 1682/3 Antho: came & his man at £16 the 8 of Feb:
> 1682/3 Antho: tutor came the 7 of March at £30.
> 1682/3 Antho: groom came the 10 of March at £5.
> 1683 the 6th of November my son Antho: went to Winton[19]

We know nothing of this tutor, but a good bit about Winchester College. If Henry Dalicourt (d. 1708), a servant of the Dowager Countess, is correct when he writes to Anthony, "I was very glad to hear . . . that you was to keep your Christmas at Winton not doubting but that your Lordship will be as merry there as you would a

---

17. A good bit of this is drawn from Haley, much of the rest from Esmond S. de Beer's splendid edition of Locke's correspondence.

18. William Montagu to the Countess of Shaftesbury, July 5, 1683, in PRO 30/24/45/i/2.

19. Memorandum by the second Earl of Shaftesbury, in PRO 30/24/19/2.

been at St. Giles," we can only be all the sorrier for Anthony; for Winchester most certainly fulfilled the expectations of Locke, who must have disapproved of his being enrolled there.[20] The teaching methods of the public schools were repudiated by Locke; he was certain, too, that the associations there would corrupt a well-bred youth. His attitude reflects the sorry state of some of the schools during his lifetime, and even ardent Wykehamists seem willing to admit that Winchester typified the situation; that it then had neither the eminence it earned in an earlier time, nor that which it now enjoys. One odd symptom of the decline is that it became customary during the seventeenth century for the wardens of its sister institution at Oxford to resign and become wardens of Winchester whenever the opportunity permitted: "In the whirligig of time the post of Warden of Winchester, which was intended by Wykeham to be only half as valuable as that of New College, had become the richer manger—perhaps because the Scholars of Winchester were easier to rob of their augmented commons than the Fellows of New College."[21]

It is unfortunate, perhaps, that Anthony's own comments on life at Winchester College during his day are among the few bits of personal testimony on the subject to survive, because they are most certainly biased. In 1689, discussing plans for the further education of his brother Maurice (d. 1726), who was fourteen years of age at the time, he says in a letter to his father,

> The seven improveing years of his life have been sacrificed at Winchester & all given up for Latten and Greeke and he is soe far from understanding the first, that he can neither make nor construct a sentence: besides that in any other sort of readeing he has no manner of tincture, nor as your Lordship saw can be brought to relish so much as a peece of Sir Walter Raleigh, or your English Cronicle, a Life in Plutarch, or any such plesent and Easie storie. . . . Besides that at Winchester I can tell your Lordship 'tis only those that studdie and are dilligent and scarcely they too Escape the Mother vice of Drinking, the Predominant of the Place; where the Punishment of it would be worse then insignificant amongst the Scholers, unless the reformation were made or began at least amongst the reformers; for whilst the example remayns amongst

20. Henry Dalicourt to Anthony, Lord Ashley, December 1683, in PRO 30/24/45/i/4.
21. Arthur F. Leach, *A History of Winchester College* (1899), 360.

the superiors, I leave anyone to Judge of what effects the Correction of it is likely to prove amongst the Youth.[22]

Later Anthony did compliment Winchester left-handedly as "one of the best" of the free schools, and it is only fair to point out that Maurice Ashley's translation of Xenophon's *Cyropaedia* continued to be reprinted for over a century after his death.

The young nobleman's bitterness is easily explained. The regimented communal life of a public school and the lack of privacy there were surely repugnant to him. The essentially solitary and withdrawn disposition of later years had already been in part formed when he went to Winchester at the age of twelve. For much of his childhood he had been separated from other children, from his parents, from his brothers and sisters, and, for that matter, from the affectionate grandparents whose ward he was. He entered Winchester several years after the normal age for doing so, the product of a scheme of education which today would be described as permissive.

From his relative seclusion, then, Anthony was removed and placed in a school where strong Royalist and High Church sentiments reigned. England had been agitated by four years of especially virulent political and religious controversies when the boy went to Winchester. Even had there been any disposition on the part of the masters and the boys, who were probably crueler, to forget that his grandfather, as the opponent of royal prerogative and the champion of true-blue Protestantism, had been one of the chief actors on the public scene, the Rye House Plot of June 1683 and the subsequent trials of the Whig leaders would have kept memories fresh and strong. The fourth Earl (1711–1771) in his biography of the third Earl recounts that at Winchester his father "was treated very indifferently by all except the schoolmaster . . . being often insulted on his grandfather's account, whose memory was very odious to the zealots for despotic power. His ill usage there made Winchester very irksome to him, and therefore he prevailed with his father to take him from thence."[23]

22. Anthony, Lord Ashley to the second Earl of Shaftesbury, July 1689, in PRO 30/24/22/2/p. 2.
23. *The Life, Unpublished Letters, and Philosophical Regimen of Anthony, Earl of Shaftesbury*, ed. Benjamin Rand (1900), xix. Despite the difficulties in using his edi-

There is no agreement among various scholars as to how long Anthony continued at Winchester. One version has it that he succumbed to the pressure almost immediately; another, that he persisted until 1688; and the fourth Earl, whose chronology is often weak, says that he left in 1686. The problem is complicated by the fact that all three brothers attended Winchester at one time or another during the period in question, and Christian names are not given in the rolls. For the statement that he left in 1683 there seems to be no authority; it probably derived from someone's wish to improve on a good anecdote. The notion that he was there until 1688 stems from the fact that the only Ashley listed on the roll for that year is prefixed by *Dus.*, for Dominus. Only Anthony should have been so referred to in this manner in 1688; however, he was in Italy when the roll was made up.[24] Anthony himself, then, must have left at some time during the months following the autumn of 1685, when the roll for that year was prepared. This is borne out by his appearances variously in London and St. Giles during the spring term of 1686, and by a letter of July 1687, from Daniel Denoune, Anthony's Scottish tutor, to the second Earl, where he speaks of his seventeen or eighteen months' acquaintance with the boy.

While Anthony was studying with Denoune, he must have lived much of the time in London, where he would have been near his grandmother. At fifteen he must have been well aware that his mother was jealous of his relationship with Lady Margaret, who after the first Earl's death seems to have focused on him all the warmth and tenderness she had felt for her husband. Even without

---

tions, Rand is still a most important source for Shaftesbury studies. The brief life he reprinted first appeared in Thomas Birch's *General Dictionary* (1734–41), where it was taken from British Library, Birch MSS. 4318. This was drawn in turn from PRO 30/24/21/225, the fourth Earl's original notes, which Rand often uses as his source. I will cite his *Life*, unless the additional material in the original notes makes them more cogent.

24. The prefix is either a simple mistake or it alludes to the noble birth of either of his brothers, John or Maurice. Actually the one year that all three brothers are recorded is 1685, when we have "Ld. Ashley, Mr. Ashley, med., Mr. Ashley, jun.," and since John was taken from Winchester and placed in another school, the Ashley who is referred to as *Mr.* in 1686 and the one called *Dus.* in 1688 must both be Maurice, who is said to have spent seven or eight years there. See Anthony, Lord Ashley to the second Earl of Shaftesbury, in PRO 30/24/22/2/p. 5. *The Winchester Long Rolls, 1653–1712* [Winchester] were meticulously edited by C. W. Holgate in 1899.

the controversy over funds between the two households, without the inevitable strain between the Countess Dowager and the Countess, who in the course of things deposed her, there would have been enough tension here to make Anthony very uncomfortable at times.

For her part, Lady Margaret, in her good-natured and rather naïve way, never could understand why there should be so much bitterness. Here is part of a letter in which she apologizes to Lady Dorothy for being forced to take Anthony into her own home:

> I assure you I aprihended him in an ill condittion when I sent for the Dr. to him, & the Dr. aggravated my fears with his expearinces of these Aguish feavers killing in 4 fitts, whear ther was less apearance then in him, or else I would not have given my consent for the Jesuicts powder, & that treatment required a quieater place then he was in; & I have reason to beleeve twas not his desier to be with me, & I am sure twas not my fondness to bring him to so ill a place, only proper because I knew not a quieter, & it is an infained truth, that if ever I was so selfish as to desier the conversation of those I loved, to there pregiduce, I have perfittly quitted it now, & can be as well plessed & truly content, to heare of ther well doing without seeing them.[25]

From Anthony's point of view things could not have seemed so simple. We have no way of knowing how deep his affection was for his mother. We do know that he had a powerful sense of duty toward her, that he felt held to her by a sense of filial piety that was at least as strong as the most demanding parent of the day could ask. On the other side was the very kind woman who had tried to be his mother in fact. Anthony's fondness for her was not, as we shall see, easily displaced.

Another adult to whom he had been very closely bound in childhood, John Locke, he was to see later in 1687, for the first time in four years. After those mournful six weeks Locke spent at St. Giles's House following the funeral of the first Earl, when he had to watch a new and uncongenial possessor take over the station and responsibilities of the leader whom he had served so long, he prudently went abroad. It seems certain that Anthony wrote to Locke during the long exile in Holland, but nothing about the correspondence has

---

25. The Dowager Countess of Shaftesbury to the Countess of Shaftesbury, St. John's Court, May 8, 1686, in PRO 30/24/19/13.

survived beyond a rather tantalizing reply of Edward Clarke in April 1687 as to why Anthony has not answered one of Locke's letters:

> The younge Gentleman (to whome I formerly delivered a Letter from you) came to mee the beginning of this Weeke and made greate Excuses for his not Keepeing his Word with you, and said that Hee had hitherto delayed Writeing to you, upon noe other reason but that of his Being from time to time ledd on with the hopes of Travelling abroad, and thereby haveing an opportunity to make His Personnall acknowlidgments to you for the Kind service you intend Him, and sayes Hee have now obtain'd his End. . . . I hope what Hee says is Reall and not a feign'd Excuse, but that a little time will shew the certainty of, and the Conversation you will have with Him will direct you to make a Better Judgment of Him then any thing I can Write concerning Him.[26]

Whether Locke was convinced that Anthony felt a reciprocal concern for him or not, Clarke seems to think that the younger man is insincere.

In July 1687 Anthony, Lord Ashley was ready for his grand tour; with him in addition to Denoune he took Sir John Cropley, Baronet (1663–1713), who was to become his closest friend. It is not known when they met, but considering the difference in their ages, probably after Ashley left Winchester. The Cropleys' considerable wealth seems to have come from commerce and the legal profession. Thomas Sclater Bacon is said by Ashley's son to have accompanied them. He is not mentioned in the initial letters or in Ashley's account of the *giro d'Italia*, but Cropley's name appears only once in the account, so Bacon may have joined the group after the letters were written. Ashley visited the exiled John Locke until early November, when they left for Paris. A good bit can be deduced about the early part of the tour, but until they reach Italy, almost a year later, little concrete evidence remains—only two warmly affectionate letters to Locke and letters of credit with endorsements proving where Ashley was and when.

The letters, both dated December 1687, tell us that Ashley has postponed beginning his "exercizes" until after the holidays, though Sir John has already begun with French and is studying with his master of the ventilabria. They have moved into a pension—"au Cha-

---

26. Edward Clarke to John Locke, May 13, 1687, in de Beer, III, 202–203.

teau Vieux dans la rue de St Andre des Arts." The plays are merely ordinary but Ashley knows that he will be ravished by the opera. He has bought only French books so far and must confess that he conforms better to the diet than to the manners. His first cousin, Lord Salisbury (1661–1694), a new convert to Catholicism, has come to see him, "but has, nor will Hardly Receive any Visit from me: which I find he resents." On the other hand, they have just received a message from the Envoy who, as promised, is taking them to Versailles.

Actually the letters to Locke tell us a great deal about the missing months. Ashley and Cropley had come to France like so many before them to complete their education. Anthony's age, sixteen on his next birthday, was about average, not that Sir John at twenty-three is too late, though Milton at twenty-nine was. In numerous accounts of the seventeenth century, the subject first settles in a pension, then begins his exercises. One might expect music, dancing, and fencing, but mathematics and the Classics were also common, and inevitably the serious learned much about French history and government. It also seems likely that Ashley began to collect books seriously in France. By his mid thirties he had built up two very fine libraries at Little Chelsea and St. Giles's House.[27] That the travelers started off with a serious intent is clear from the fact that they are accompanied not by a bear leader but by Denoune, who already had been Ashley's tutor for many months.

What Ashley learned without formal instruction in France may be difficult to measure; ultimately, though, it is surely the more important. Lord Salisbury had a right to expect a visit from Ashley. He was a kinsman; the English abroad were a coherent group; and he assumed that the noble blood they shared was more important than religious belief. What he failed to understand is the bitterness Ashley tasted at Winchester, and that he had just then come from visiting Locke, still in exile. One wonders what Locke might have done in his place. On the other hand, the Envoy is to introduce him at Versailles at the first opportunity. There is one record of the impression he made there. Fifteen years later the Queen of Prussia

27. For a sound study of the libraries, see Horst Meyer, "Ex Libris Shaftesbury: Die Bibliothek eines europäischen Aufklärers," *Wolfenbütteler Forschungen*, II (Bremen, 1977), 75–90.

(1668–1705), hoping that he would come to visit her at Lutzen-bourg, recalled from Versailles that "Milord Shaftesbury était tres joli garcon." Some urbanity was even granted those whom the grand tour ruined in all other respects. How much more it must have af-fected Ashley. It is hard to imagine him not taking advantage of an opportunity to learn the way of the world and its manners. Our ear-liest accounts of Ashley on his return, from the Stringers and Lady Masham (1659–1708), for instance, describe him as polished and affable. In France, too, he must have begun his study of wearing masks, masks assumed unlike most of those we wear, in a highly conscious fashion.

Of course there is a paradox involved. Ashley was from childhood until death an inveterate and relentless enemy of Louis XIV and his policies. He could separate French politics from French culture, however. Most of those on tour found much to object to in France—diet, food, manners, and so forth—yet, as J. W. Stoye points out, the grand tour went on even during the Commonwealth.[28] Whether the tour was a matter of need as it was in the beginning or finally just a fad, young Englishmen did go to get something not as easily avail-able at home, and if we look at Ashley's career to the age of fifteen, he had more need of it than most, no matter what pains were de-voted to his education. Paris was then the most splendid city in the world, and most of the serious travelers, tacitly or not, admitted this and profited from it.

After the grand tour of France comes the *giro d'Italia*. According to his letters of credit, Anthony must have headed south from Paris in August of 1688. The period spent there—over eight months—is typical for the time. The choice of a route into Italy was not to be made lightly. Early in the century it was customary to go overland because of the danger of piracy in the Mediterranean. Gradually, though, travelers began to sail or to go on muleback down the very dangerous corniche road to Genoa. The road might seem logical now. It was not, then; as Francis Mortoft says,

When wee were at Niece wee were told of the badnesse of the wayes, but no person alive can Imagine them to be so bad as they are, for wee

28. J. W. Stoye, *English Travellers Abroad, 1604–1667* (1952).

were forced to climbe up Rockes upon our Mules' Backes all the way for some 30 leagues together, and such terrible and dangerous wayes wee mett withal that it would make the stoutest man alive to tremble in passing them, It being indeed accounted by All Travellers absolutely the worst way in Europe.[29]

Use of the northern routes was complicated by the fact that they were most accessible when the heat and malaria in the south were worst. Ashley seems to have used the Mount Cenis Pass, which in his day involved going to Grenoble first. It was exhausting, but no route was easy, and as Joseph Addison (1672–1719) records, the new snow sometimes does not fall there until December. At no pass is the contrast between the transalpine land and Italy more dramatic.

He begins his diary with a carefully described panorama from a high point of the area around Turin, from the Alps sweeping around the town to the great plain of Lombardy stretching out to the north-west.[30] These broad landscapes are a feature of the diary; apparently Ashley liked to climb into steeples. In view of the use of natural landscapes as a source of inspiration in his *Moralists*, it would be interesting whether there is some anticipation here. Because of a missing page we do not know whether he remained at Turin or not. From there it took them two days to arrive at Milan, lying at "a poore place" and next at "a miserable village." The distance by auto-strada is only fifty-five miles, but constrained by the winding roads and somewhat by the rivers, they zigzagged back and forth for at least twice that distance, and this on horseback rather than in a coach. Ashley constantly paused to describe the fortifications they pass in this much-fought-over land, and he watches the Alps gradu-ally occupy less of the horizon as Lombardy opens before them.

29. Malcolm Letts (ed.), *Francis Mortoft: His Book Being His Travels Through France and Italy, 1658–1659*, Hakluyt Society (1925), 36–37.

30. Unfortunately his diary, PRO 30/24/21/240, begins with a page marked 2. What follows is a jumble of nearly forty pages of notes for a diary in a very fine and not too legible writing. Any full transcription would require a great deal of conjecture. Even though the various sides of a folded double sheet often bear no logical relation-ship to each other, his itinerary is fortunately typical, except for the return journey from Venice to Hamburg, where so many places have changed their names several times since 1689. With the aid of contemporary travel guides these have been worked out, though. The actual guides that Ashley carried were still in the library at St. Giles's House in 1750.

The visit to Milan characterizes very well the interests that drew him to cities all over Italy and will serve as a summary of them. On entering the city he first sees the "ruins of a Temple built by Maximian of 16 huge Corinthian columns"; then he admires the castle with its cannon captured from Louis XIII and lesser ones taken from Charles XII. Later, with a glance at the "houses thick, & filled with many shops & much manufactury," he goes to see the cabinet of curiosities belonging to Mr. di Satola. These collections, as in England, were a strange hodgepodge of whatever was richly made, very rare, aesthetic, or simply extraordinary—Ashley was later to become a virtuoso who focused his energies solely on the aesthetic. Thus in addition to a very large collection of fine paintings, he views "bables and follies, many curiosities: the monstrous birth, a mineral of crystal, diamonds, emeralds & gold, a curiously worked piece of marble of the tomb of Gaston de foy, fine [carvings] in stone, one [cut] in the stone called in italian nicolo, not of 2 inches long nor one broad, & the heads of Henry 8, Anna Bullen, Catherine and Edward the 6. 2 mandracks male & female, a great cabinet of lapis lazuli; agate &c." Ashley then climbs to the top of a church and describes another perspective—the Alps now filling only one part of the horizon. This was probably the cathedral, but characteristically he spends so little time within the Gothic structure that it is not possible to tell. Only paintings and sculpture attract him in such surroundings. He finds the books in the Biblioteca Ambrosiana mostly ill bound and he devotes some space to listing the paintings he admired in the Pinacoteca. He examines more paintings at the church of Santa Maria delle Grazie; but in the monastery there he dwells little on *The Last Supper*, "almost completely obscured." The architectural details of the Romanesque basilica of Sant'Ambrogio do strike him as very rich and fine, and are described in some detail. He also looks at the collection in the Palazzo delle Scuole Palatine, now dispersed, and at Santa Maria della Passione. What we have are hasty notes with no indication of how long it took him to do all of this, and without a break he is again on the road south to Parma. Modena is represented only by a list of paintings.

The trip to Bologna is much like what went before, ruins, fortifications, another steeple climbed. Only at Reggio Nell'Emilia is there a note of humanity, "idle Jews on their Sabath in their cloaks before their doors or in the Corners of the streets in Companies, the Red Ribbon in their falls."[31] Much of Bologna Ashley described as a "Handsome Pialzo," colonnaded streets abounding, then as now. Here, in addition to the usual, he admires the university and the collections of arms from the East. He provides us with still another perspective, possibly from St. Michele in Bosco, which he mentions. The wild country south of Bologna is described, but he seems glad to reach the fertile land and white houses above Florence.

The rich culture of Florence is sparsely enough described to raise some question about Ashley's note taking. He sees the Laurentian Library and the Chapel of St. Lawrence, the Armory, Santa Croce, Santissima Annunziata, the Duomo, and the Duke's collection at the Uffizi. The key I think is in the account of the last of these, where he describes only one picture or sculpture from each room. It seems likely that he is going to write home from Florence, and by keeping track of the rooms, and separate buildings visited, he would be able to refresh his memory from his guidebooks as he wrote, after the manner of John Evelyn (1620–1706). This would also explain why we have so little from Venice, where he stayed longest, nothing from Rome, and little from Vienna.

Leaving Florence, Ashley's party stopped the first night at Poggibonsi, north of Siena, the second at Torrenieri, and by dinner time the third day they arrived at the border of the papal states, where they plodded up the hill to Radicofani to dine at its renowned inn, which, Ashley remarks, pays six hundred crowns annually to the Grand Duke of Tuscany (1642–1723). Since they merely pass through Siena, the only large city on their route, Ashley spends most of his time describing nature. At one point he wonders whether man or nature is responsible for what he sees. "On our left a part of a Rock standing out in pieces crowded together like the lower parts of small trees cutt off. the Stones bending over like the ends of arches. it looks as if at first that it was not nature . . . had done it but when I looked more I believed it too hard for art." Near Aquipendente he finds "in the way a Bridg over one of those rivers and tho the streams

---

31. *Falls* probably refers to their collars.

be seldom otherwise than insignificint as they appear, yet in great rain or thaws in winter they come down from the Hills with an impetiouse current of vast waters." This is milder and much less eloquent than Evelyn's description of such a river, or for that matter Addison's. Travel writers of this period, say from 1640 to 1700, once removed from the works of man, can describe nature evocatively, the more so if what they describe is awesome—awe for them was more likely to be real than literary.

As I remarked, there is no account of Rome. Going south from there most travelers first remark the aqueducts, functioning and ruined—Ashley is no exception. Next they turn to the paradoxes of the land. In their minds would be the wealth of classical Rome surrounded by houses, market gardens, and orchards; before their eyes was a country plagued by disorder, extreme poverty, desolation of land—however rich potentially—and depopulation. As a constant reminder of the difference between past and present there was the Appian Way through the southern Campania, much of it then flooded and impassable, or, if built above ground, it was by then in ruins. Disorder preoccupied John Evelyn, who constantly worried about bandits on this leg of his journey; Addison, on the other hand, used the desolation for an attack on the Roman Church. There may be some justice in what he says about the administration of the lands, but certainly the shift from small holdings to large estates as wealth began to pour into ancient Rome had a decisive effect on agriculture throughout the whole area, and because silting of the rivers was so destructive, the effect was cumulative. As for the Pontine marshes, specifically, despite the efforts of many governments, they had to await the coming of Mussolini until they were finally drained. Ashley first sees the desolation below Velletri forty miles from Rome, and follows it with his farmer's eye as far as Terracina. The flooding is so bad in late November that he often is forced to keep to the foot of the mountains as he proceeds south. With his mind on the way water is managed at home in the valley of the Allen, he repeatedly sees nothing but simple neglect around him. For instance, "the Plain miserably let run to ruin being but in some places cultivated, the rivers overflowing it & the springs from the feet of the Mountains (which it sends forth all along it) choaking it for want [of] the keeping in repair the but few ditches that are necessary, must run into a bogg."

Ashley follows the familiar route from Terracina to Naples: Fondi, then Mola, now Formia, where he takes a felucca for a short visit to Gaeta; next he turns inland to Minturno, Cessa, and finally Capua above Naples. He seems to have more leisure than most contemporary travelers, and his accounts, at least here, are fuller. In addition to remarking the cultivation—or noncultivation—about him he has a good eye for perspective. He sees and records the actual contours of the land so well that one could take a topographic guidebook account of the trip from, say, Terracina to Capua and follow his path even without any of Ashley's place names. He and his party must have had a vetturino for a guide but, even so, they nonetheless managed to become lost one night above Cessa and found their inn by moonlight at three in the morning.[32]

Surely he saw more in this part of Italy than is recommended in the old three-volume Baedeker for Italy: Roman cities, temples, and houses without number, to say nothing of baths and grottoes; the tombs of Cicero and Lucius Plancus; the Monte Circeo; and numerous citadels, towers, castelli, and churches. Near Gaeta they see "Severale Galleys most belonging to the State of Genoa of which the Slaves were drawing in the oars and other businesses, as being to winter there." Near here, visiting a church built in a fissure caused by the earthquake on Christ's crucifixion, Ashley hears about further wonders and for the first time on the trip is indignant at what he considers foolish ignorance. Much of his constraint abroad must have stemmed from his strong distaste for flouting popular religious beliefs, no matter what he later said in his *Letter Concerning Enthusiasm*.

Below, at Cessa, the rough wine was not what Ashley would have expected "whereabouts the Vinum Falernum grew"; however, his party consumed large quantities of it and "the whole company more or less bore the effects of it all the next day & some longer." The scenes here must have been even more like what Piranesi was to en-

32. For a good account of the different guides available, see Esmond de Beer's edition of *The Diary of John Evelyn* (6 vols.; 1955), II, 315.

grave; massive pomp, beauty, and marvels of engineering in utter ruin in a region sparsely inhabited by a people who must have seemed very different from those responsible for glories past. It would not be difficult for Ashley to draw the inevitable conclusion, especially since he was to become a Roman Commonwealthman. One wonders how many Commonwealthmen of his time, born either 50, or perhaps 1,650, years too late, made the *giro d'Italia*, since they took quite seriously what was later to become a romantic and almost mythical vogue.

This passage also gives the reader a chance to judge how much Ashley depends upon his guidebooks as an aid in describing what he sees. Of course no account is free of this sort of influence. Ideally the traveler goes forth in the morning having already absorbed the information from his guidebook. What is more natural than that he should return to it to refresh his memory when writing the account during the evening? Despite the fact that the diary says so little about Ashley's companions, it has a great deal of freshness to it. When he could keep up with it, the diary is an account of what happened day by day, with the past tense covering no more than twenty-four hours. Often he begins a section with "this morning." There are also differences from guidebooks, especially in his account of the church in the cleft at Gaeta. On the other hand, though they are a startling sight, would he have mentioned the fields near Capua divided by vines growing on trees had they not been in his guidebook? Ashley, then, seems to use his guidebook as a stimulus, but for little more.

Ashley rode into a Naples, mourning, as Naples so often does. "Down the great one which we went in. Great Plenty—as I always found all days alike—of People mull the narrow streets. . . . pieces of timber from [one] side to the other above our heads to keep up the Houses which hung over. The Dominicans their Roots of their convent crack'd by the Earthquake. . . . The Jesuits front thick pointed comon stones. The Cubelo all fell in. 80 thousand crowns left by a woman to them towards the Repairs of their Church."[33] In this

33. The earthquake had occurred the previous June. The church is the Gesu Nuovo. The cupola is not yet repaired.

church Ashley saw paintings of his favorite Neapolitan artist, Luca Giordano, and the next day Giordano conducted him through his "renowned studio."

Like many of Ashley's notes on cities, this one is extremely compressed, though it probably involves more actual description than the accounts of either Evelyn or Addison. In cities he saw more and had less time in which to record it. Occasionally he leaves a blank for the name of a church, knowing that when he writes home his guidebook will recall it for him. A properly—and prudently—reverent attitude is maintained toward the churches and ceremonies, including a procession in honor of the patron saint of Naples, St. Januarius, and his remarkable miracle. Only in his graphic account of a visit to the catacombs is he openly skeptical of the accounts given him. Ashley admits that the catacombs are very old but he thinks that they were converted to burial grounds long after they were built. The earliest Christian decoration he can find has too much of the Gothic in it to be truly ancient.[34]

In terms of the space he devotes to describing it Ashley must have been most impressed by the Palazzo Real. He was also much interested in the Mole and its Lanterna. There is little room for wit in his style, but he does achieve it in his picture of the local aristocrats taking the air.

> What I learnt of the Neapolitans was that their nobility are by the zealous policy of the Spaniards all in great animositys, who are oblidg'd to use these courses to preserve themselves the power of this place through forces being not of more than 6 or 7 thousand men in the Whole Kingdome, & the people being always as ready as not to mutiny . . . indeed one would think by seeing them abroad that they were always [teasing] or Exciting their adversary, for nothing is more ordinary than to see one of 'em with a reasonable sword by their side when they are out of the Doublet & Cloak. & their man carrying a Tilter of a most unreasonably Big shell and Long Blade. & when with these by their sides & in their pumpes & Dublet and strait briches. tis but their putting on their Cloaks & they appear in an exact habbit.

34. For a discussion of the origins and seventeenth-century usage of the term, see de Beer's essay in Volume VI of Evelyn's *Diary*, 1–7. Ashley does speak of architecture as Gothic but fine. It is too bad we do not have his account of the Roman catacombs.

Probably the most effective passage in the diary is Ashley's account of climbing Vesuvius. He must have written these nine hundred or so words either on the night of his return or shortly afterward and never changed them. Addison continually enters into scientific speculations, so that the climb is hardly described. Evelyn is much better, but seems to stumble over his diction; and his allusions get in the way. In simple and forceful language Ashley vividly recalls the emotions most climbers of Vesuvius have felt.

As they begin their climb, Ashley marvels at how the natives clear their vineyards and build walls of lava; coming down he also wonders at their courage: "villages & a number of other little houses" built of lava which "may put 'em in mind of being Buried alive when they see the store has formerly served to others & may yet serve them for their grave stones." They ride up to the plain from which they can see the cone of Vesuvius and make their way across it through rivers of lava, dismount, climb for a half hour and gaze down in awe. "But the terriblest of all was to see in the Middle of this Bottom another Hill rising from it Exactly Round and prodigiously steep with in which was the Raging Mouth." At this sight some give up, but Ashley and others follow the guide, peering into fumaroles as they descend—"one wee looked into that was as round and strait in the Rock as the bore of a Cannon, but bigger"—until they reach the steep inner slope. Here Ashley describes an epic climb in which, although he had been warned, he falls behind. Suddenly he gets a "knock in the head by a Volley of Stones small and great" dislodged by a climber above him—"'twas a pain that nothing was so near recompensing as the Pleasure Every man conceived when he had gained the top." They walk around "the mighty precipice" looking into the mouth from every angle, but Ashley in his "tryal of going down a little way" further, burns his shoes and stockings. On the descent from Vesuvius he fantasizes that were he not worried about his clothes he could "slide down setting all the way."

It appears that Ashley left the *pièce de résistance*, the north shore of the Bay of Naples, until last and went from there directly to Capua and Rome. His party headed out of Naples on a road along the coast and soon entered the Roman Grotta Vecchia, about a third of a mile long, under the colline of Posillipo, as one must today, through a different tunnel in the soft tufa rock. On emerging from the tunnel into what his guidebook tells him is an arbor of fruits later in the year, Ashley theorizes that the vines running from tree to tree, as near Capua, must be responsible. He peers into the carbon-dioxide-filled Grotto del Cani, near which the guides kept a stock of dogs on hand, but there is some question as to whether the experiment of putting a dog in the cave was performed for him. He feels that ultimately it must be "efficacious" for the animal. It may have been, if the dog were quickly revived by the waters of the nearby Lago d'Agnano or, sometimes, by the air. Otherwise, as Evelyn noted, the results were fatal.

As was customary, Ashley used both horses and a ship to explore the area from Pozzuoli on the north shore of the bay down to Cape Miseno, then up the coast to Cuma. There is no space to summarize it all here, and it has been done often enough. Nor does it really matter whether he credited all the ascriptions—some he did not—for enough of them were genuine. It is hard now to conceive what it all must have meant to someone whose education was wholly classical. Here were the oldest Greek city in Italy, spectacular volcanic activity, and incredible beauty, "the Hills & the Vales producing the way as Pleasant to see as it was noble to Reflect on. 'tis no wonder . . . the Romans who in those times sought and understood Pleasures," chose it, of all they had from which to choose. Here Hercules labored and the sibyl sang. There were ruins of temples to all members of the Pantheon, homes of many of the emperors, the remains of vast public works, villas of statesmen, philosophers, and poets, the tombs of Virgil and many others. If we need any goal for Ashley's *giro*, this will do. Evelyn put it best: "There is not certainly in the whole World so many stupendious rarities to be met with, as there are in a circle of few miles which inviron these blissfull aboades."[35]

All that remains of the trip north is a single page beginning at Centino, about fifteen miles northwest of Orvieto and ending at the gates of Pisa. It may have been written several days later, perhaps on the ship to Genoa, because Ashley mentions stopping at places south of his starting point. The page is filled with descriptions of the

35. Evelyn, *Diary*, II, 352.

countryside, its wines that Ashley tasted, and of the agricultural conditions along the way. In Pisa he looks at the church of Santo Stephano dei Cavalieri and the statue of Grand Duke Cosimo, who founded the Knights of Saint Stephen, famous for crushing the Barbary Pirates. This has more meaning for him than for a modern tourist, because he also sees the knights themselves among the people of the town, dressed in black cloaks bearing red crosses. Next came a brief visit to the Piazza dei Miracoli, where he sees the tower similar to one he saw at Bologna, believing it, like many after him, to be "built hanging strangely," and then shortly they go through the Duke's hunting forests to Leghorn.

The next few days Ashley's party spends variously at Lucca, Pisa, Florence, and Leghorn. Ashley's republicanism is not yet fully developed; he spends more time on agriculture than government at Lucca, where the ambassador sent to see if they had arrived. In Leghorn, visited twice, he is chiefly interested in the Mole and their "Venice" built over the sea. This time in Florence he does climb the dome of the cathedral:

> a Noble sight besides a town fill'd with noble Palaces, Churches, & other Buildings. a Country of a Vast extent with a Multitude of Buildings of all sorts Lying so Pleasantly to the Eye & so amazing to my Consideration that I must esteem it as one of the finest sights I Ever Had. the North & South side of the town (which appear in a long Plain) is close Rounded with all those lesser Hills that are the Roots of the Greater Mountains. the other 2 sides Have a great length of Plain beside 'em especialy the West which is allmost to Loss of Sight.

On February 5, 1689, Ashley sailed from Leghorn for Genoa on a merchant-man of four hundred tons and thirteen guns commanded by Captain Picket. They had two days of fine sailing in a fresh breeze, close enough into the shore so that they could see "the long ridg of mountains full of pleasant Houses." The journey across northern Italy must have been very rapid or perhaps he was reluctant to repeat himself, having already described the Duchy of Milan. In any case they made slow progress over the mountains and spent the first night at Novi about twenty-five miles above Genoa. Near the end of this sheet the party is standing before the amphitheater at Verona.

The description of his long visit to Venice is very brief and, aside from a trip on the bay, the only excursion he describes is to Padua, to which he sailed, down the coast and presumably up the Brenta. Of the students of the renowned university he had only one comment, "No going after dark for 'em." He first visited and was suitably impressed by the Palazzo della Ragione and its vast hall. He then turned his attention to St. Anthony's, where he admired the lamps, the bas-relief life of the saint, "the Famous Madam Cornaro's tomb that was mistress of 7 languages that was lately gott up in white marble against one of the Great pillars,"[36] the candlestick, and Donatello's bronzes around the altar. They moved to Santa Guistina, where he thought the cupola fine and the art and architecture inside noble. Next they climbed a tower and saw the rich countryside around the town and, in the distance, Venice.

We do not know when Ashley found that it would be necessary because of the war to return to London via Prague and other eastern points, rather than by Marseilles, Toulon, and up the Loire as he had intended. Louis XIV was at war with the League of Augsburg before Ashley left Paris, but this was no bar, ironically, so long as James was king. News of the beginning of the interregnum in England in December 1688 or perhaps of James's actual departure from England early in January of 1689 must have been available when Ashley returned to Rome late in that month. All of this might explain the erratic pattern of his travels, his rapid return from Rome to Venice, his missing the major cities of north-central Italy which are on most itineraries. Of course he spent more time in Venice than anywhere else in Italy, but there was still plenty of snow awaiting him when he set out late in March for Vienna.

Ashley's scheme for avoiding the war—and more important, the possibility that he would fall into French hands—looks rather drastic, but there is the likelihood, which increases as one contrasts his diary with the gloomy tone of the one letter which has survived, that he considered the whole trip as something of a lark. Who might not at his age? In any case his scheme for going along the Gulf of Venice, almost to the borders of present-day Hungary, continuing north to Vienna, northwest to Prague, and finally to Dresden, Berlin,

36. Elena Cornaro Piscopia, Ph.D. (d. 1684).

and Hamburg, seems to be the only way he could in the very early spring, when the Alps were impassable, avoid both France and the states on its northern border.

The trip began romantically enough. They left Venice by moonlight in a piolla with five rowers through canals and the sea for about forty miles to Caorle. The next day they skirted the coast again, went into the Laguno di Marano and up the river to Cervignano in the lands of the Emperor, whence the following day they proceeded in post chariots across Friuli. Ashley thought this the finest agricultural land he had seen—a land sheltered by mountains on the north, "all cultivated and planted with vines in as great order with as much beauty & with greater care than even either in Lombardy or Campania," the populace "all mighty courtiouse & ready to serve you."

The fine country continued beyond Gorizia on what is now the Yugoslav border. Ashley notes that "the language here among the common People [is] Sclavonick." The party had found it necessary to change from chariots to post horses as they proceeded into the Julian Alps, which run roughly parallel to the Yugoslav coast. Ashley, always conscious of timber and thinking of England, France, and Italy, marvels as they proceed through the snow how huge pines fall and are simply left there. He describes the ascent as at least as severe as that of Mount Cenis, yet they are soon in a flatter area at Logatetz (Dolenji Logatec), where they put up at a foul inn—"the People looking out of the little windows as out of the portholes of Vessels. almost wild in these mountains. the children and most of the people almost naked." Their food stinks of garlic worse than in Italy. The next day they reach a river where they board "2 Boats joyn'd together, each made with 3 pieces of timber" and sail to Lauback (Ljubljana), the capital of Carniloa, where they find German spoken and "a fine inn, . . . contrary to expectations excellent Bread, wine & oil."

In the morning they ride out to the east crossing the Sava in double boats, this time each boat made of one log. They travel toward Zyla (Celje) in the province of Styria through foothills and plains; the posts were very long and sometimes covered at a footpace, but, as Ashley remarks, the horses were better equipped than those they had been accustomed to in Italy. At Zyla the next morning he is de-

lighted to find a number of inscriptions, which "were certain dem-
onstrations to one that this had been the seat of some Considerable
Roman colony." The party heads for what Ashley calls Malpootz,
which must be Maribor (Marburg) on the banks of the Drava. All the
rivers were brimming at this time of year and the party deplored the
flimsiness of "the scurvy wooden bridges," "as dangerous as if one
went on roling pins, round little timbers being the only covering
which are so slightly fasten'd together that one expects 'em to run
under one & let one fall thro. thus are all the Bridges hereabouts."

From Maribor the party headed north across another range of hills
and the border of modern Austria toward Gratz (Graz). As they rode
up the valley of the Mur the going improved; Ashley speaks of their
riding in four-wheeled chariots to Willdagen (Wildon). Gratz, the
chief city of Carniola, Styria, and Carnthia, delighted Ashley—a fine
town of solid and beautiful architecture, a powerful citadel against
the Turks, and with handsome women. He spends a lot of time describing the art in "the Palace of Prince Ek-en-berg 2 miles out the
town. Ekenberg signifies a corner of hills, the situation of this house
is his title." They may have rested a day there; in any case, Ashley
was practicing his German.

From Gratz Ashley started out in the splendor of a coach and eight.
Since he mentions the river Mur we can assume that he continued
north up its course until it joins with the Murz Tal, then turned
northeast toward Vienna, following this river toward its source in
the chain of mountains thirty-five miles southwest of the capital.
The journey to Newstadt ought to have taken at least two days, but
we do not know where he slept. At most times of the year the road
was good. In April the grain fields of the bottomland were flooded;
he complains of this and their food, or lack of it: "our diet onely
bread with sometimes & egg or 2 but the wine was pretty good." Apparently they continued through mountains in the coach because he
mentions "Ice, snoe, oxen hired & our way cutt before us." At the
top of the pass they can see Newstadt some fifteen miles ahead of
them. The mountaineers are goiterous and Ashley offers an explanation: "the People over all these Mountains Past & where they have
the Rivers from the Mountains, as in Italy from the Alps and Ap-
enines . . . have . . . swell'd throats, the common people Drinking in

33

necessity of their drouth & Labour of those snowy melted filthy waters." The descent was even more precipitous. Once down, they found the road clear and Vienna lay before them.

There is surprisingly little chauvinism in Ashley's diary. His chief problems are, I suppose, the elements; roads are bad and inns are bad but never exactly because they are where they are; there are very few bad people either; and remarks like those on the strength of garlic in the Slovenian mountains or the students in Padua are surprising because they are so rare. Yet the diversity of life he encountered left him no more opportunity for naïveté. One can only conclude that he is a genuinely open-minded traveler, what the average parent of the day must have hoped his son would be.

Vienna struck him with awe. There are the usual catalogs of jewels and art objects, yet he also remarks that most of the shopkeepers speak French. With a glance ahead to London's nocturnal dangers, he remarks on how well the streets are lighted at night. Most of all, the court of the Emperor Leopold I (1640–1705) impresses him: the hundreds of chamberlains all working at once; the Emperor riding through town and "wherever he goes the Princes walk on foot before his Coach"; "the little King of Hungary with his Court apart with great Majesty"; and "the Assembly's nobler than any Court in . . . Appointments & dress, full of Princes and Princesses dress'd out always in their jewells."[37] Finally, he saw the preparation for war, "all the Great men & officers in the Emperor's service were there mett alltogether from all parts to Advise and to receive instructions."[38]

Reluctantly, Ashley's party left Vienna April 19, went down the Danube for a while, and then over the plains into Moravia, where they found devastation: "Remains of pain and work on the faces of all. the Houses which had once been allways fair, depopulated extremely. weemen without stockins or shoos." Typical of the era, all this had been accomplished not by the enemy but by friendly troops: "Here it was that the Polish armie pass'd and repass'd in their return from their succour of Vienna where they did no other

37. Joseph I (1678–1711), crowned King of Hungary in 1687, Emperor from 1705.
38. Anthony, Lord Ashley to the second Earl of Shaftesbury, Hamburg, May 3, 1689 (marked os but actually ns), in PRO 30/24/20/229.

34

service but to help off the biggest part of the Plunder."[39] They "spared sword and fire: but everything they carried away, devour'd, or destroyd. Little good they did all the seige to have render'd this . . . desirable to Popery." The journey from Vienna to Prague through Moravia, then Bohemia, took seven or eight days according to Ashley's letter to his father, and this is one section where we have no day-to-day account, for obvious reasons:

> for our lying wee had been pretty well wean'd from Beds before wee gott to Vienna: but afterwards clean straw grew a delicacy & wee were Contented . . . every Night to lye promiscuously among the rest of the Creation, the tame beasts of Cottage: & I assure you my Lord when a Barn or a Cockloft was found for our nights lodging wee thought ourselves fortunate that night.

The sheer mass of buildings in Prague, where he spent two days, affected Ashley strongly—"the Long Strait Stone bridg that leads over the Multa, 24 mighty High arches," the Emperor's palace—and he spends a page describing the architecture in this "one of the biggest cities" he had ever seen. On the other hand, he was depressed to find that there were now two thousand Jesuits in the once Protestant capital. The road from Prague to Dresden lies principally in the valley of the Elbe with only a diversion over a range of mountains. They went nearly to Dresden, and found the Elector of Saxony (1647–1691) had retired for the waters to Derplitz in Bohemia. They followed the court there, and then went back again to Dresden, where most of Ashley's description deals with the various arms they saw, mainly wheel locks, but one gun had "a thick old barrall no bigger than a pistoll, the first fire arm seen there: fire brought by rubbing 2 thongs backwards & forewords."

None of this sounds like someone in a hurry to get home, nor does the fact that as they moved on toward Berlin they took a byroad heading east toward the river Spree, avoiding the main road through Leipzig. Although they came across some white bread now occasionally, conditions were still poor: "the miserable Bitter bear, sower Bred, no wine crop, hardly flesh or anything wee could find . . . the

39. From the letter just cited, which is the only one surviving of the many he must have written to parallel the diary.

People stoning all strangers & taking us for french men very ill natur'd too." Ashley is struck, nevertheless, by the beauty of the countryside and its intensity of cultivation, so that we have a procession of descriptions of rich valleys which becomes monotonous. We "came down into a delicate Vale that lay att length before the hill opposite to us, broad, open and finely manurd, full of clover. Fruit Trees in the fields."

One thing not made clear in the diary we can now see from the parallel letter: Ashley had been regularly visiting the courts as he went along his path, just as he visited Versailles at the beginning. This was why he went into mourning in Vienna and why he followed the court of the Elector of Saxony back into Bohemia. These visits both trained him and polished his skills. In any case, Berlin crowned his journey. It is for

> the Electour of Brandenbourgs court that since I have spoke of places I should, speaking rather but a word on all the Rest, have reserved a side for this: where Greatness & Goodness meet to such a degree in the Persons of the Electour, and His Princess, where with so much Policy, Power, Martial Discipline & temper & amidst such splendour & Magnificence, there Reigns so much justice, sincerity, & Vertue in a manner I thought unknown att a Court. It may very well indeed come into Composition with any Court of Europe after Versailles for State & Majesty.

Later on in a letter to the second Earl, Ashley remarks that "the Electour was Extreamly kind to me, he had me att his table with him the 3 days which he kept me there above the one single day I had design'd for the Place."[40]

What came later was largely anticlimax. During the trip down, again, largely the Elbe, Ashley spends all of his time just recording the movement from one principality to another. When he wrote his father from Hamburg on May 3 NS, he had already waited there for one post hoping to hear of a convoy going directly to England, but on the fourth he began what he supposed to be an eight-day journey to

---

40. Presumably a four-day visit. The Elector is Frederick (1657–1713), son of the Great Elector, who had died the previous May. Ashley had met the Electress in Paris.

Amsterdam. It could not have taken so long. In a letter of May 3, 1689 os, his aunt, Lady Chaworth (1632–1700), writes from London to her brother, Lord Roos (1638–1711), later first Duke of Rutland, that Lord Ashley, newly returned, and his mother dined with her that day.[41]

41. Lady Chaworth to Lord Roos, May 3, 1689, in BC Add. MSS. 7, No. 90.

⥤ II ⥢

Lord Ashley:
The Fervency of Youth
1690–1698

For the years immediately following Lord Ashley's return from abroad there is no detailed journal such as he kept while traveling, but there are enough letters and other papers to give us a good idea of what he was doing and of his state of mind during this period of his life. His time and energy were largely taken up with family business for some time after he arrived back in England late in the spring of 1689. Perhaps we should first look at these activities, for the stresses which they imposed upon a youth of eighteen explain some of the singularities of the mature man.

Now, for the first time Anthony became a real member of his immediate family. The new experience cannot have been pleasant. This we can see from the amount of time he spent with the Countess Dowager in London and at Ivy Church, the residence of the Stringers, where she kept rooms. At his age one is likely to be especially intolerant of the weakness and bad humor of the chronically ill, and St. Giles's was a house of sickness. Lady Dorothy was soon grievously ill, and the eccentric Earl was apparently bedridden. Moreover, there were six brothers and sisters ranging from three to seventeen years of age to be looked after. And, although the Earl still held the purse strings and had the final say in family matters, any responsibilities that called for much energy, for worldliness impossible to that recluse, now fell to Anthony.

His chief problem was his brother John (1672–1692), a year younger. John's education had not been a success, and it had been necessary to transfer him from Winchester to another school. In any case, according to Anthony the gentlemen commoners at the public schools of the day were subject only to the laxest sort of discipline, and it is no wonder that with an invalid father John grew up aim-

1691, the two brothers set forth in a small boat for the man-of-war, which was anchored some twenty-five or thirty miles down the Thames from London, and Anthony records that "the wind & tide being strong against us att Gravesend, wee were forc'd to take another boat thence to the ship that lay in the Hope with 2 more men in her."[4]

Finally there is a short note signed by the rector of a church in Bridgetown, Barbados:

> These are to Certifye to all whom it may Concerne That the Honorable John Ashley Cooper Esq: was buryed on the second day of April One Thousand Six hundred Ninety and Two in the Parish Church of St. Michael aforesaid as appeareth by the Register Book thereunto belonging.[5]

He may well have died of one of the pestilential fevers which often swept through the West Indian fleet in those days, but there is no way of telling, for this is the last mention of John in the family papers.

Why devote so much space to a brother whose name never again appears in the Shaftesbury Papers? Those papers which survive the accidents of time have a special authority, because we know that the matters they deal with were considered important by Ashley. By the same reasoning we will also lose papers which he considered too personal, but given the powerful sense of family common to his rank, his handling of material relating to John suggests that it falls into a third category. It is more a matter of he himself wanting to forget it. He would like to sweep it under the rug but cannot. Brother John is like Sister Frances. I was only able to find the date of her death by a real stroke of luck. For another reason, Anthony preferred to forget her too. We never will know exactly how Anthony felt about John, though one would like to think that the avuncular smugness of his youth was replaced by sympathy, perhaps even by a sense of guilt at having sent him to his death. John's significance is proved then by his absence from the record. Anthony was haunted by him until he died too. This we will see.

Anthony had better luck with his brother Maurice, who seems to

4. Account, Anthony, Lord Ashley, August 1691, in PRO 30/24/47/30.
5. April 11, 1692, in PRO 30/24/45/i/22.

have been enrolled in Winchester College when he was just past his seventh birthday, and was still enrolled there when Anthony returned in the late spring of 1689 and brought up the problem of what to do with him. To realize that the subject of intense discussion had just turned fourteen is to sense the difference between rearing children then and now, because Maurice is seen as having drifted so far in one direction that if he is not deflected immediately his whole life will be ruined. The Earl and his Countess are just as much concerned as Anthony. Whatever may be said of the second Earl's slowness of wit as he grew older, he was a most devoted father, absolutely determined that his sons have the best possible sort of education. During a period when the family fortunes were ebbing, no costs were spared on Anthony's grand tour; John's sad career must have been very expensive; and Maurice was to be treated the same as Anthony. More important than the willingness to spend the money was the second Earl's concern for his sons and his involvement with them, however confounded he may have been by the various pressures to do one thing or another.

According to Anthony the crisis in Maurice's education is twofold. When Anthony left for the Continent in 1687 Maurice had a "perfect good nature," a "trusty, sincere, plain dealing disinterest," and a "benign bookish temper"; on his return he finds him all changed, fallen in with bad companions and their habits, and grown lethargic, too. Secondly, his education at Winchester has not really prepared him for anything. All of this the eighteen-year-old Anthony relates to his father in a very long and sometimes pompous, always prolix treatise on the education of the younger sons of nobility. It is so rich in detail that one wonders why neither father nor son perceived the irony of the son's being the authority, though perhaps they did. In any case it reveals what Anthony feels his position in the family is; it reflects the moral stiffness common to his youth, and his feelings that all things must be spelled out in absolute clarity for his father.

A younger brother who is to find a place in the world must become a

> gowns man or a sword man: under the first denomination come all that have a dependencie on or relation to either Law or divinity: under the other all that have the same regard to the Court, or Camp, which have

soe neere a relation to one another, that whatever need the first stand in of the other; in the other there is little success to be expected in matters of advancement; but by means of the first: and a good souldier shall doe but little in raising himselfe if he be a bad Courtier. . . . The expencive Education of an Academic is . . . distructive and ruinous in regard of all other education I have named, Schooles first & then University & Inn's of Court are the beaten roads of those Advancements . . . And for Lattin: besides the Accomplishment of a Gentleman, it is absolutely necessary to every considerable Station & almost every office (except . . . in the Camp) . . . this one single easie pleasent Language has been the stumbbling Block in my Brother's fourtunes: & this must be got over by my Brother Maurice or he must [take] after my brother John and apply either to Sea Servis or to Marchants affaires.[6]

The only solution, then, is for Maurice to be sent abroad where he will be removed from his present companions and where his governor will have more authority than would be possible to him at home. Daniel Denoune is the ideal tutor, and Utrecht the most suitable place, because it is pleasant, healthful, and cheap, the people genteel and the university inspiring, and because Denoune is very familiar with it, having taken his doctoral degree there.

The Earl and Countess must have accepted Anthony's plan, but shortly there arrived in London letters from both the Earl and his steward, Williams, announcing a new plan to put both John and Maurice under the tutelage of Denoune. Anthony replies to his father's letter in what can only be described as a cold rage. He left the two letters with Denoune, as he says, "without any mention from my-self of any thing" and received from him the answer that Denoune could not undertake in good conscience any project so bound to fail. Anthony goes on to say,

I have acquited myselfe entirely of my whole duty both as to God and Man in this case and to justifie my selfe to any rationall part of Mankind. . . . Such is my misfortune that where I desire not ever to produce my reason it would appeare and availe, and where I now offer it and only beg for success to it, to avert the evill that may throw me into the necessity of such an Appeal, there I have at last learnt to dispare of having any.

6. Anthony, Lord Ashley to the second Earl of Shaftesbury, St. John's Court, July 1689, in PRO 30/24/22/2/pp. 4–5.

Twice he makes this threat: "I finde myselfe reduced to the necessity of declareing to your Lordship that I cease to act in theire concerns otherwise then as one that is obliged to be according to his
duty the executor of what his ffather and Mother should comand
him to doe in any case."[7]

Maurice and Denoune went abroad without John. Whatever the
merits of the decision about the trip, Anthony must have borne
much of the responsibility for it and with what ensued, and it perfectly illustrates what we can see of the young man's character at the
time: in theoretical matters, a tendency toward a dogmatic rigidity,
as in the first version of his *Inquiry*; in practice, powerful affections
at work.

When Maurice and Denoune were at Vevey on Lake Geneva near
Lausanne, Denoune came down with a tertian ague, probably malar-
ial. Either the lassitude induced by the fever or the fact that he himself had medical training made him hesitant to take the Jesuits' powder, until the fever grew intense and began to affect his eyesight. The
fever struck again in the middle of the summer, but the powder
enabled them to pursue their journey into Germany, where they
met either by design or accident an old Huguenot acquaintance of
Locke's, Dr. Lewis Pau (d. 1709), who accompanied them to Rotterdam. Pau was not able to do much for Denoune, and the disease also
began to affect his mind. Anthony was greatly distressed and persuaded Pau to write Locke for advice. When Maurice and Denoune
arrived in London in March 1692, Anthony rushed Denoune to St.
Giles's House. The last notice of Denoune among the Shaftesbury
papers is a record of some payments by Williams to him in 1694
and 1695.

Daniel Denoune had a profound effect on Maurice and Anthony.
Of the slow-starting Maurice he made a very sound Greek scholar,
and, while there were many other influences on Anthony, no one
who reads of his deep affection for Denoune or who senses the erudition, so carefully masked in his works, can doubt that three years

7. Anthony, Lord Ashley to the second Earl of Shaftesbury, n.d., in PRO 30/24/
22/2/pp. 9–11.

with the young Huguenot physician were the equal of any education he might have received at Oxford or Cambridge.

While Anthony was struggling to get his brothers' lives on a safe course, the marriage of his parents—both around forty—began to collapse. The growing rigidity of the second Earl's opinions must have been a problem for some while, but they did not threaten his marriage until the Countess became seriously ill in 1690. Her sister Grace, Lady Chaworth (d. 1700), then wrote to the second Earl, very humbly:

> I have bin terrified with hearing how my poore dear Sisters health is Impared, that the most ill distempers have so prevailed upon her former strongh Constitution, that they shew themselves Sometimes in paraleticke, Sometimes in Convulsive, Sometimes in Hystericke Signes; as Appeares in her fainting fitts, Cardiacke passions, lamblenesse &, too Sure Evidences of these Malignant diseases. Whereupon I humbly Supplicate your lordships goodnesse to urge & presse her to come Instantly to London to Consult with her old Physitian Dr lower, who knows her Constitution & hath formerly by Gods blessing bin so fortunate in her recoveries of health; before these Miserable diseases get such a dominion in her that we loose such a valuable a relation.[8]

Richard Lower (1631–1691), who had been Locke's teacher at Oxford, was one of London's most eminent physicians.

From St. Giles's House came the reply that Lady Dorothy could not be moved because her illness had affected her mind, a statement which the Manners family regarded as merely "a salve for their intollerable usage." Lady Chaworth, speaking of the possibility of her insanity, says, "she poore soule so far from, by Gods Mercy, that those most sorrowfull bleeding letters to me are the best she ever sent to me, & full of most pious and Calme Christianity."[9]

Lady Chaworth wrote monthly, and her brother, the Earl of Rutland, added his voice. Lord Shaftesbury, finally consenting, seems to have feared that some effort might be made to estrange her com-

8. Lady Chaworth to the second Earl of Shaftesbury, March 22 (1690?), in PRO 30/24/45/i/14.
9. Lady Chaworth to the Earl of Rutland, April 15 (1690), in BC Add. MSS. 7, No. 96.

pletely from him. He writes to Lord Rutland that she is getting good care at St. Giles's House, but if "I may from your Lordship be assur'd that in her much altered condition (which the violence of her late distempers have left her in) shee may have that care taken of her there that shee may not doe herself any prejudice or that it lie in the power of ill people by whome she may be influenc'd (in her unsteady condition) to draw manifest inconveniencyes on mee and my family, I shall not in the least oppose itt."[10] Lady Dorothy's sister Elizabeth, Countess of Anglesey (d. 1700), and perhaps Scrope Howe (1648–1712), later Viscount Howe, and husband to still another sister, Lady Anne, seem to have come to take her away from St. Giles's, where it is likely she did not return until the year before her death, seven years later.

So far no disfavor seems to have befallen Anthony; this situation, however, was not to last. Lady Dorothy finally settled at Haddon Hall, one of the Manners' estates, and in 1691 the Earl of Rutland sought to get £400 a year from the Earl of Shaftesbury so that she could have a degree of independence. Considering the terms of the marriage settlement, the amount seems reasonable enough, yet Shaftesbury is indignant. He writes to Montagu: "My house has always been open to Dorothy & shall always be so, but to make the offer you suggest would own myself the Transgressor—most of the world knows the contrary."[11] As Montagu put it in a letter to Rutland, "My Lord I am the more troubled that as by faire means nothing is like to be done, so all compulsory means his Lordship will endeavour to avayd, by offering to receive her Ladyship and desire her coming to him." Others have tried to intervene and, worse yet, Anthony refuses even to try, as Montagu points out: "Both myselfe and wife have often spoken to Lord Ashley to interpose in the behalfe of his Mother, but he pretends it is not fitt, him to medle

10. Lord Shaftesbury to the Earl of Rutland, April 1, 1690, in BC MSS. 20, No. 71. Many of these letters are noted in the Rutland volumes of the Historic Manuscripts Commission, but without any text being given. They are marked "on domestic affairs."

11. The Earl of Shaftesbury to Edward Montagu, October 5, 1691, in BC MSS. 20, No. 94.

between his father and Mother, and upon pressing peremptorily re-
fuseth to do anything in the business."[12]

This refusal of support was then still another grievance for Lady
Dorothy to hold against her husband. Another yet is Williams,
Shaftesbury's steward. Here her suspicions of perfidy seem to have
been justified. An analysis of his accounts for a period of three and a
half years reveals an obvious deficit of around a thousand pounds,
and much more could be concealed behind individual entries. In a
memorandum book, now at St. Giles's House, John Wheelock
(d. 1719), the able retainer of the Countess Dowager, who became
Anthony's steward, recorded in 1702 the report that Williams got between seven and eight thousand pounds during his tenure of fourteen years. Wheelock was not a rumor monger, and if the tale is true,
this was a huge sum to mulct from an estate where the gross income
was less than five thousand pounds a year.

As if the difficulties within the family were not enough, it was
still under attack from without. This situation had developed before
the flight of the first Earl; his death did not end it, but it continued to
worsen through the short reign of James II. Even James's abdication
did not put a halt to it, for legal processes are not so easily halted,
and the enemies of the family could see all too clearly that the second Earl was very weak and had few friends at Court. Most of the
burden of this fell upon Anthony, who had not yet reached his twentieth birthday.

His woes with Cranborne Chase illustrate what the family suffered. In his day the Chase consisted of about forty thousand acres of
pasture and woodlands in a tract three or four miles wide and ten
miles long running northeast and southwest. Wimborne St. Giles
lies only a few miles to the south, so that the various landown-
ers and their tenants who lived within the Chase were fairly close
neighbors of the Ashley Cooper family, who as owners of the Chase
since the time of the first Earl had rights to the very large herd of
deer which the Chase supported, but they were proprietors of only a

12. Edward Montagu to the Earl of Rutland, December 31 (1691?), in BC Add.
MSS. 13, No. 189.

relatively small portion of the lands and buildings in it. The possibilities for conflict of interests were thus virtually limitless.[13]

The conflict between the proprietors of the Chase and the other inhabitants of the region seems to have been more or less continuous from the beginning; but whereas the earls of Gloucester had been frequently accused of being high-handed in their administration of the Chase, by Anthony's day innovations in agriculture, various other changes social and economic, and the general attrition of a once-powerful set of laws and customs had clearly shifted the balance of power. The illegal hunting of deer became a form of knight errantry among some of the more substantial men of the district. In bands of from four to twenty, they sallied forth after dark with dogs, nets, and quarter-staves, dressed in an especially developed sort of armor consisting of a long, heavily padded canvas coat called a jack, topped by a deep hat made up of wreaths of straw as in a beehive, reinforced sometimes with iron rods. When the hunters stood their ground, as they sometimes agreed beforehand among themselves to do, bloody battles with the keepers could ensue. At some stage a specialized weapon was adopted, a vicious flail-like club called a swingel, which was a fair match for the hangers carried by the keepers, if the hunters could keep the battle to the more open areas where their weapon could be used most effectively.[14]

During Anthony's childhood and while he was abroad, the second Earl appointed rangers to watch over the declining herd of deer, which still ran into the thousands, and granted the "walks," as the subdivisions of the Chase were called. Yet the Chase was not part of the entailed estate and seems to have been left to his grandmother, with the remainder to Anthony. It was the only considerable piece of property which he had any hope of inheriting before his father's death. Thus he took over the management on his return, and very soon heard that some of the neighbors were burnbeating a section of

13. From papers at St. Giles's House. The general account of the Chase is taken from Volume III of John Hutchins, *The History and Antiquities of the County of Dorset* (4 vols.; 1861–70), and from the 1886 facsimile edition of William Chafin's second edition of *The Anecdotes and History of Cranbourn Chase* (1818).

14. Examples of the costume and weapons can be seen in the extremely interesting and informative collection of the Dorset County Museum in Dorchester.

common land in the Chase just north of the village of Sixpenny Handley, rendering it unfit for deer. Burnbeating was a process for preparing moor or fallow land so that grain could be grown on it. A layer of turf was pared off and burned, the ashes being spread so as to manure the soil, or, if the turf would not burn, it was carried off. Perhaps the burnbeaters were encouraged to convert the common into grain land by the Corn Bounty Act of 1688, which set a bounty of five shillings to be paid for each bushel exported when the domestic price fell below forty-eight shillings. Their motives are not mentioned in these letters from Anthony to Thomas Stringer, but Anthony's rage and frustration at the infringement on the Chase is obvious enough.[15]

In the first letter Anthony has already made a strong declaration in regard to burnbeating and wants to proceed vigorously against the offenders, "for fear that which is nothing els in me but caution of doing anything that may appear hard or severe tho justifiable be construed by them as distrust of my own Cause & least they take that to be my fear of them which is nothing but my Care of 'em." He feels sure that if he arrests the workmen and shows that he is in earnest, the neighbors will come to some composition. Stringer, on the other hand, has counseled delay and wants the second Earl to have recourse to his privilege as a peer, which suggests that some counteraction is under way, since the various privileges of the nobility at law were then largely defensive in nature. In the next letter, Anthony reports the visit of a peacemaker from Handley:

> Sir Harry Butler has been just now with mee, with the speciouse name of Accommodation: and Profession of Good Neighborhood: two such things as should carry respect with them in any Mouth: & which I must take more care then of any Weapons that they bee not turn'd against mee: & that therefore are such as may, however made use of, demand a truce: tho when searched; may bee found to have been but the deceiving bottom of an Unjust Peace.

Sir Harry points to precedents for the burnbeating within the bounds of the Chase and wants to try the case "att Common Law or els (which he says he had rather) referr it to two Councell on Each

15. All of the letters cited here have the common designation PRO 30/24/21/229.

Side, & upon their disagreement to a Fifth Person." This seems fair enough, but actually if Anthony agreed to trying the case in one of the common-law courts he might be giving up an important advantage. He is able to take action in one of the courts proper to his father as lord of the manor, most suitably in the Chase court, which was intended to deal with such offenses. In another place, Anthony remarks that it is symptomatic of the general decline of the rights of the owner of the Chase that the neighbors are trying to undermine the authority of the Chase court. During the tenure of the previous owner, the Earl of Salisbury, there is said to have been a room set aside in his manor house at Cranborne as Chase dungeon for offenders against the animals or the vert, the cover and food of the deer.

In a third letter Anthony says that he has brought quite a few neighbors over to his side and that they admit his rights, but, apparently, their numbers were not sufficient, for in the last two letters, dated in November and December from London, he still talks of seeking new ways to retain his Chase rights and to punish his enemies. The November letter is hopeful in some respects. The attorneys in the Handley matter intend to lay the action at the King's suit, because of some rent reserved or "otherwise frame some interest in the King," that it may be brought "into the Exchequer where there is a fresh president that will decide the thing for us most advantageously."

The letter that Anthony writes in December ends the series pessimistically. He has not written sooner because he has been "so entangled perplex'd & tormented in a Crowd of affairs the greatest part of which have been drawn upon mee by the malignity of some most inveterate Enemy's." One alternative after another has proved of no avail in the matter of the Chase. The workmen can be jailed but there is no hope of charging them with riot, because, although they confess a sufficient number of accomplices, three were not seen together at one time by the keepers. There is no rent reserved for the King, so the action cannot be laid his suit. "Many, & but too many reasons dishearten" him from having recourse to Parliament. There is one final hope. They have been to consult with Sir Francis Winnington (1634–1700) about the possibility of an injunction in Chancery, but first Anthony wants some hint from Stringer of the character of Winnington, who professes to a wish to help Anthony on his grandfather's account.

The family is at the same time involved in a lawsuit over the "great gunns," a project for developing a weapon that would fire several shots at once, in which his grandfather and Prince Rupert (1619–1682) had invested. Now, this case has been lost to enemies through deceit; and lost with it are some of his prospects, since this also was one of the properties in the first Earl's personal estate which was willed to his wife:

> My great aggravation of concern is that what injury they have done us here has been struck through the reputation of my Grandfather, for the sly but most partiall Charge that Holt their Councell in the habitt & seat of a Judg, gave to the Jury; & the wise Honest Verdict that those Blades gave in: was grounded all & meerly on that reasonable beleif of the Princes, My Grandfather's, & Sir T. Chichley's having made a fraudulent deed. a supposition that could scearce have bore even in the worst of the late times. but patience is that Honest men must learn if they expect to live but tolerably happily in this world of knaves & fools.[16]

The family is involved in still another lawsuit, which comes on Tuesday in the court of the Duchy of Lancaster at Westminster. Perhaps it will turn out well.

Most of Ashley's enemies are members of the Court party, and he is certain that even those neighbors who have joined against him in the controversy over the burnbeating in the Chase were egged on by local Tories, the "men of interest." After the Revolution many of his grandfather's old adherents in the Country party had come into office, but no government which included men such as Sir Edward Seymour (1633–1708) and, worst of all, as president of the council, the Earl of Danby (1631–1712), was likely to be very sympathetic to the family of the first Earl of Shaftesbury, or to his heir who was trying to find a place for himself in the world. Furthermore, it is evident from these letters that, in the period immediately following this essentially conservative revolution, the very intensity of the reaction to the name of Shaftesbury somehow outweighed the effect of the shift in the balance of power, so that many Tories and some trimmers

16. Sir Thomas Chicheley, M.P. (1618–99).

focused on the memory of Anthony's grandfather all the residues of those savage hatreds which had burgeoned in the final years of the reign of Charles II.

It seems likely that Anthony was candid when he said in 1690 that this turmoil in his family affairs was not the reason he refused to stand for Parliament. The first Earl of Shaftesbury during his long career had been a powerful, sometimes the most powerful, politician in the West Country. Obviously his invalid son could never amount to much in this respect, and he did not, in fact, hold a seat in the House of Commons after the summer of 1679. In any case, the political climate was not particularly auspicious for a new start during the final years of the reign of Charles II or during his brother's brief season upon the throne, but in 1689 circumstances were again favorable, and an able-bodied, intelligent, and apparently personable member of the family had arrived at an age where he might be expected to serve the cause in the House of Commons, for there was yet no barrier to the seating of a minor son of a nobleman. Whig politicians did so expect, and when new elections were imminent during the winter of 1689–1690, Anthony returned to St. Giles's from Wiltshire, where he had gone for the purpose of discouraging some gentlemen from promoting his interest toward a seat in Parliament, only to find that the same thing was happening at Weymouth in Dorset. He protested to Mr. Taylor of Weymouth that his decision not to stand at this time came not from any lack of zeal to serve his country, but because his supporters did not know him well enough. In writing to Sir John Morton (1627?–1699), who was chosen for Weymouth in the subsequent election, Anthony is more candid: It is not enough to be confident of his own good intentions; he must also be sure of his capabilities for office, and those whom he serves must believe in him, too. Were these latter conditions satisfied, he would not permit other considerations to intervene—his urge to improve himself, his desire "of gaining greater experience by still looking on" and the need to attend to those "disorder'd concerns" of his own family.[17]

17. Anthony, Lord Ashley to Mr. Taylor, February 16, 1690, in PRO 30/24/22/2/ pp. 14 and 15; Anthony, Lord Ashley to Sir John Morton, February 14, 1690, in PRO 30/24/22/2/p. 13.

It appears, then, that in this first confrontation of the three forces which were to dominate his existence—political obligations, his intellectual and literary career, and his personal affairs—politics lost out, yet lost not at all because Anthony lacked idealism but in some part at least because his idealism was counterweighed by a bitter distrust of the people he must serve if he were to act on his aims. On one side we have his burning desire to vindicate his grandfather, coupled with a set of idealized principles distilled from the first Earl's practices and inculcated by Locke; on the other, his feeling that an ingrate populace had repudiated their champion. That he is speaking of this when he implies in his letter to Morton that the public lacks confidence in his capability to serve is clear from the way he talks about his grandfather in a letter that he wrote to an unknown correspondent the previous autumn:

> It is a very great satisfaction to me to finde that every private person is not infected with the baseness of the Publick; but that there are those who will make a profession of gratitude. . . . For how he preferr'd the publick even to himselfe & every thing that was deare to him the latter parte of his life proved, & his family, and I (who was as you say what he loved most) that feele, can wittness: and how he is repay'd such debts let an Age Judge that shall be worthier & wiser then this; that may do their Bennefactours & themselves more Justice.[18]

Anthony feels justly that the first Earl had sacrificed the family's fortunes to his political aims.

His refusal to stand does not mean that he turned his back on politics. During this period Anthony is usually in London while Parliament is in session, so that it is likely that he was very busy with politics before he stood and was chosen for the seat at Poole vacated by the death of Sir John Trenchard (b. 1649) in 1695. For instance, in a letter written early in 1693 William Popple (1638–1708) tells Locke that Anthony intends to visit his old mentor at Oates as soon as Maurice is well "and the public Busyness of the Parliament is over."[19]

18. Anthony, Lord Ashley to [?], St. John's Court, August 10, 1689, in PRO 30/24/22/2/p. 12.
19. William Popple to John Locke, March 2, 1693, in BL MS. Locke c. 17, f. 205–206.

Actually the only glimpse we get of Anthony's political ideas at this time is in his letters as one of the Lords Proprietors of the Carolina Colony. In 1663, Anthony's grandfather and General Monk (1608–1670), along with the Earl of Clarendon (1609–1674) and five others, were granted a strip of land bounded on the north by the colony of Virginia and on the south, approximately, by the present borders of Florida, and extending westward to the Pacific, or the South Seas, as it is called in the charter. This document made the eight men feudal overlords of this immense tract, and the governmental structure it set up was modeled, like that of the Maryland colony, on the County Palatine of Durham.

Except for his grandfather, all of the original Proprietors had long and faithfully served the Royalist cause. If a grateful Charles was trying to reward them, however, his attempt went completely awry. Instead of powerful, they found themselves vexed and frustrated; instead of wealth, their reward was crushing expense. There is no evidence that the Ashley Cooper share had yielded any net profit up to the time the third Earl died, half a century after the charter was granted, and some of the other shareholders must have had similar experiences.

Ashley had much more of a stake in the muddled affairs of the Carolina Colony than historians have realized. Since Maurice began attending meetings of the Proprietors around the time of the second Earl's death in 1699 and shortly thereafter was styled a Lord Proprietor in official documents, it has been assumed that Anthony never was a Proprietor but merely served as his father's deputy during the latter's lifetime, after which the share somehow passed to Maurice. The truth of the matter seems to be that the second Earl is the one who was never a Lord Proprietor and that the small part that he took in affairs of the colony was in the role of Anthony's guardian. This is clear enough from a letter that the secretary of the Proprietors, Samuel Wilson, wrote to the second Earl in 1683, about a month after the death of the first Earl, in which, after telling him that he is preparing copies of the constitutions and a description of the colony for father and son and after begging the Earl to inform himself, Wilson says, "Your Lordship hath it in your power as Guardian to (and with my Lord Ashley's Consent) make whome you please a landgrave."[20]

The colony was troubled by so many problems by the time Ashley returned from abroad that it is possible to describe only those which vexed him most. In the first place there was no stable body of law for the colony. When the colonists were finally willing to accept the first set of "Fundamental Constitutions" drawn up by Locke, the Proprietors had twice felt it necessary to supersede them. Again, there were simply not enough people, nor sufficient capital, nor even enough potential nobility to set up an elaborate feudal system in Carolina. And even the servants who were adventurous enough to come over in indentures were unlikely, once there, to enroll themselves perpetually as leet men. The establishment of a stable agricultural economy on the coastal plain was necessary, but there was a shortage of labor willing to work in such a climate. Despite every effort of the Proprietors to keep settlers on the coast and away from the Indians, many colonists were attracted by the prospects of wealth to be gained in the hinterlands without any onerous tilling of the soil, by the eternal dream of mineral wealth, the much more solid prospect of trading profitably with the Indians for furs and such, or by the still more lucrative practice of trading the Indians themselves and thus relieving the labor shortage too.

The Proprietors, not the Crown, were responsible for the defense of the colony, but they had to enforce the Crown's policies whether they were for the good of the colony or not. Failing to follow royal policies could lead to *quo warranto* proceedings to cancel the charter, as had been done during the reign of the pro-Spanish James. Then, there was the problem of the Huguenot immigrants for whom the Ashley Cooper family wanted to find a new home. That these people were exceedingly thrifty and industrious seemed all the more reason for the established colonists to oppose them. Finally, as to the

20. William L. Saunders (ed.), *The Colonial Records of North Carolina* (10 vols.; Raleigh, N.C., 1886–90), I, 342. This can be confirmed in the largest group of documents relating to the Proprietorship; in every paper where any reference is made to the Ashley Cooper share between the death of the first Earl and that of the second, the Proprietor of the share is described as Anthony, Lord Ashley. If historians of the subject have not been aware that this courtesy title could at this time refer only to the second Earl's heir, we can be sure that those who made out the documents were.

matter of the governorship to which Anthony refers, by this time it had become too complex to explain in detail. Very briefly, James Colleton had been appointed governor of the southern part of the colony in 1686 but he soon proved incredibly autocratic and in 1690 committed the fatal blunder of declaring martial law. When the Proprietors heard of this, they immediately acted. As usual, they were too late, for it took almost a full year for news to come from the colony and for the Proprietors' orders then to return. One wonders how many colonial problems in America were aggravated by the communications problem, which some historians tend to overlook. In this case, Seth Sothell (d. 1697?), who had purchased the share of the Earl of Clarendon and had been governor of the northern part of the colony until the irate populace drove him out, appeared in Charles Town and was welcomed as the new governor, though the Proprietors had already appointed another.

It is at this point in the confused affairs of the colony that we have some evidence of the part played by Ashley, who had been attending the meetings of the Proprietors since the order deposing Sothell from his post in North Carolina had gone out in December 1689. One of the chief complainers about conditions under Governor Colleton had been an early settler, Andrew Percivall, who had been manager of St. Giles's Plantation for the first Earl of Shaftesbury. Percivall had been writing to the Proprietors for at least a year when, in May 1691, Ashley received a plea directed personally to him and replied in one of the longest and most passionate letters he was ever to write. We are fortunate to have it; the few letters that survive from this period tend to be coolly formal and brief.

At the beginning of his letter to Percivall he declares, I have "in me soe much desire and Love to perfect Retirement and other wise too haveing been soe involved, against my wish, in such troubled Affaires att Home, as would have made to have shun'd all other Buisness, and avoideing any Engagement Here, which yet notwithstanding the Danger of this Court has thus drawn me too."[21] He acts now in the business of Carolina not from self-interest, only from "an Un-

21. Anthony, Lord Ashley to Andrew Percivall, May [27], 1691, in PRO 30/24/22/2/p. 24.

moveable Principle of Duty" to mankind. Ashley is as sincere in the idealism as he was in the cynicism.

The whole letter on Carolina and, indeed, most of his early thinking on political and moral philosophy can be interpreted in terms of these not always compatible idealistic and cynical impulses of his personality. Of course, it is the common thing to find the young idealist at odds with the way the world is being run; the ingredient which jars here, and which we still less expect to find in the earliest systematizer of an ethic grounded on the ultimate goodness of man, is Ashley's cynicism about human nature. He is convinced that the greatest part of mankind is corrupt.

Certainly, Ashley feels that the South Carolinians in particular are corrupt. There is a good bit about Indians in the letter to Percivall and, doubtless, some primitivism, but though the savages are noble enough, it is obvious that Ashley points to this nobility to shame the South Carolinians, who with their civilized advantages should be nobler still. Speaking of Sothell's taking over the governorship he says,

> Immediately upon the Change arrived in your government . . . there was an Incursion made into theire Country where open Hostillity has been Comitted by which the Indians have been drawn togeather & drawn downe upon us. Who ever have been the Authors of this May the Curse of God and Man, as they deserve, light on them. . . . And may that greedy Persuit of unjust spoyle & Rapine, That thirst of Blood, of Muthering enslaving of Torture and Inhumanity which they have showne and which they thus have taught this Innocently Ignorent Poore and Harmless People; may it bee all Acted and Executed upon themselves. . . . Shall Wee call ourselves Civiliz'd People & those Barberouse to whom wee have been thus Learning and Teaching all this Treachery Barbarity, by acting it to such a degree on them?[22]

The bitterness of the diatribe on the mistreatment of the Indians, which goes on at this rate for two closely packed pages, is intensified by the great difference in rank between the writer and the object of his wrath.

Ashley further says that the best sort of state would be run by rational and disinterested men in whom "those Stations ought only to oblidge to an Exactor Justice & Stricter care and Concerne for the

22. *Ibid.*, 29–30.

Interest of their ffellow-Creaturs, with less regard to theire own." It must not reflect those "Disgracefull & Unseemly Meane and Vulgar Popular & Mischeivouse ways & uses of Government" which have been seen in Carolina. Above all, it must be a government of order established on a base of recognized and universally accepted laws. For this reason all the controversial issues raised by parts of the fundamental constitutions must be settled as soon as possible. Only then will the individual liberties which are their purpose and for which he is willing to fight be assured:

> If any of Yee . . . Represent to me, what should, what may or can bee don for the Interest of the Country, for the takeing of what greivances may Lye on Itt, and for the support of such a Government as may best Secure to every man his Naturall Rights, His Property His Enjoyment of the Lawfull ffruits of his own Labour & Industry, and his ffreedom from Injury and violence. This I will doe my Part vigourously to promote and Establish and where I cannot; I shall ffreely acquitt my selfe by openly chargeing those who obstruct and who are found to bee the Hindrance.[23]

Later, when Ashley enters practical politics, we see him supporting various policies, sometimes for reasons too intricate to be discerned at this distance, but the idealism evident here is never lost. As for the cynicism which we can see in every other line of this youthful letter—the frustrating conviction that human nature must forever prevent any substantial fulfillment of the ideal—Ashley later became much more optimistic about human nature in general, but he showed little sign of changing his early notions of the nature of man as a political animal.

Andrew Percivall could have considered himself fortunate had the letter ended as it began. After writing these first ten pages, Ashley put the letter aside, intending to add any fresh thoughts which might occur to him and conclude it when the sailing of the ship for Carolina forced him to seal it up. On May 27, however, the news arrived in London that the deposed Colleton had been ordered to put up a bond of ten thousand pounds to secure that he left the colony, and if he did not provide the bond he was to forfeit five thousand

23. *Ibid.*, 25, 28–29, 26.

pounds, to be raised by seizing his estate.[24] Since Colleton's whole estate was apparently insufficient to satisfy the fine, much less to provide security for the bond, it was obvious what must happen to all of his property under this act of the Parliament at Charles Town.

Ashley's reaction to this news was to add to his letter nine pages of still more intemperate prose. Is this why you ask me to devote my time to your interests? Is this why I did so? Is it for this that I resolved to protect you? Are these the means that you afford me? And on and on. The Lords Proprietors are by this act determined to abandon the constitutions and govern by means of the very broad powers granted them under the terms of their charter. Unless Percivall is willing to change his ways and to forsake these desperate men he will soon find himself the victim of power, and Ashley will do nothing to aid him.

One can understand why Ashley became so emotional. The political tradition to which he fell heir involved a strong theoretical distrust of excessive bail, based on years of practical experience with Stuart monarchs; his own grandfather had been more than any other man responsible for the Habeas Corpus Act, and it was also obvious to Ashley that the bill which Sothell had persuaded the South Carolina Assembly at Charles Town to enact was precisely the sort of device by which he had enriched himself as governor of North Carolina.

The letter Ashley wrote a few days later appointing as his deputy Stephen Bull, a member of the "Lords' Party," which fell from power when Sothell evicted Colleton, also enables one to see the rash letter to Percivall in a better light. He tells Bull quite plainly that it was "the ffoolish avarice Rashness and ill Management and Proud Carridge of the 'Lords' Party'" which started the trouble in the first place, and he warns them that when they again come to power they must break the disastrous cycle of "Revenge and Rage against one an other." He also praised the Huguenots at some length, saying that he has heard that Bull's faction have been responsible for making the French Protestants fear that their estates "for want of Naturalization" will not be inheritable. The Lords intend to bind and oblige

24. Alexander S. Salley (ed.), *Commissions and Instructions from the Lords Proprietors of Carolina to Public Officials of South Carolina, 1685–1715* (Columbia, S.C., 1916), 18–21.

themselves further in any way that is necessary to assure this right of inheritance and retain these valuable settlers.[25] Beyond the fact that the Proprietors beseeched Ashley himself to accept the governorship of Carolina in 1694 and he refused because he was too much occupied with family affairs, we have no more details of the part he played in the affairs of the colony.[26]

Turning from Lord Ashley's political ideas during these years following his grand tour to look at the intellectual and literary side of his life, we find that little evidence has survived of the activity which must have occupied more and more of his time as he managed to escape from family problems, and what we do know is best described by discussing his relationship with John Locke; for Locke's ideas shaped his own by attraction or repulsion; many of his friends were Locke's; and the surviving scraps of his philosophical correspondence from this time were directed to Locke.

In some respects it was a rather strange friendship; Locke was fifty-six and Ashley only eighteen, and to judge from their published works, their habits of thought were quite different. Yet, both were devoted to intellectual pursuits; in politics, their ideals and practical principles were identical; and they shared memories of life in the first Earl's household and a loyalty to his memory. Some of the letters make unpleasant reading—we have only Ashley's side of the correspondence—because the younger man so frequently apologizes for neglecting the older. He often begs forgiveness for not writing more or at greater length; at Wimborne St. Giles he wishes he were

25. Anthony, Lord Ashley to Stephen Bull, June 1, 1690, in PRO 30/24/22/2/ pp. 43–47.

26. He did faithfully participate in the Proprietors' deliberations until his trip to Holland in the summer of 1698, when Maurice took over as deputy and not long after became a Proprietor in his own right. The account of the affairs of Carolina in the preceding pages is drawn in part from William Rivers, *A Sketch of the History of South Carolina to the Close of the Proprietary Government* (Charleston, 1856), which includes a valuable appendix of documents, and from Edward McCrady, *The History of South Carolina* (New York, 1934). It is well to consult the original documents, which are not especially numerous. For the period during which Anthony was active in the government of Carolina a good selection of these is to be found reprinted in the already cited *Colonial Records of North Carolina* and *Commissions and Instructions* and in *Records in the British Public Record Office Relating to South Carolina*, intro. by Alexander S. Salley (5 vols.; Atlanta, Ga. 1928–47).

in the city with Locke, or, when Locke goes to live with Lady Masham, Ashley yearns to be with him at Oates in Sussex, but business is too pressing in London.

Yet it is easy to discern behind Ashley's sometimes bantering tone that a strong affection exists between the two men. In 1689 he says to Locke, "Convince others by your Writings that you know the Growth, the Motions and the distempers of the mind: I, for my Part, by this Experience shall stedfastly hold, that that part of man is better Known to You, then ever the Body has been to our Professours of Anotomy or Physick; or Els you must have some very strang and peculiar ascendant over mee."[27] This last theme Ashley often pursued, as when, after a visit to Oates at Christmas in 1691, he addresses Locke at great length as a sorcerer presiding over an enchanted castle:

> O sage et Puissant Enchanteur! Je vous conjure de ne me plus tenir dans vos Enchantements a present que je suis dehors de vôtre Chateau, et ne Souffrez plus que Je me vois Tyrrannizé par ce Degout que J'ay presentement pour le monde ou Je suis rentré et pour touts mes anciens Plaisirs: Ce qui ne me vient que de L'Idée imparfaite de ces Plaisirs surnaturelles que vous m'aves fait eprouvé dans ce Chateau, et qui mesme presentement que J'en suis si Eloigné me Suit Incessamment et ne me laisse jamais en repos a Jouir paisiblement de ces Divertissements du monde. . . . Voyez dont a quel Etat vous m'avez reduit![28]

The amiable relations between the two during this period were occasionally threatened by problems arising from the annuity which the first Earl had granted Locke in 1674. This was one of those arrangements which ought never be entered into, for it represented neither an outright gift nor a business transaction. Locke paid in £700, and his income of £100 was secured by a small property which

27. Anthony, Lord Ashley to John Locke, Ivy Church, October 11, 1689, in de Beer, III, 709.
28. "O wise and powerful sorcerer! I implore you not to hold me in your enchantments while I am outside your home, nor tolerate it any longer that I am tyrannized by the disgust which I feel presently for the world to which I have returned and for all my old pleasures: Those which evoke only an imperfect notion of the supernatural pleasures which you have made me experience in that home, and which even now when I am so far away, follow me incessantly and give me no rest to enjoy the pleasures of the world. . . . See then that state to which you have reduced me." Anthony, Lord Ashley to John Locke, London, December 31 [1691], *ibid.*, IV, 350.

had been in the family for centuries, Kingston Farm in southeastern Dorset, now presumably swallowed up by the suburbs of Bournemouth. This was a very handsome return, even in an era of high interest rates, and, as so frequently happens in such cases, the donor tended to regard it as a gift and the recipient as legitimate earnings from his invested money. Kingston Farm was part of the jointure of the first Earl's third wife, so that upon his death the Countess Dowager rather than the son assumed the payments.

Locke had not examined the farm to see whether it was sufficient security for his money, and as the years passed it proved not to be. The net income from the farm dropped below £80 in the 1690s, and to make things worse, the second Earl had charged some building costs to the Countess Dowager's income from her jointure, which was supposed to yield her £1,450 per annum but by 1690 had dropped to £1,200. In 1692 the Countess was advised that the best thing would be to throw Kingston Farm into Locke's hands and let him worry about it. This, she was told, she had a perfect right to do, and it is unlikely that she had a copy of the original agreement, which would have told her the contrary. She must have sensed, however, that Locke had no wish to become a farmer, and she determined instead to improve the property so as to increase the income, deducting the taxes from Locke's £100 to defray the costs of the improvements. Assuming wrongly that the farm was to go to Locke if he outlived both Anthony and herself, she felt that he could have no objection to this scheme.

In the meantime, Locke was also thinking about the future of his annuity but along different lines. The Countess was now elderly, and if something should happen to Anthony, he would eventually be dependent upon the bounty of John Ashley, whom he did not trust. Because the farm was becoming less profitable, the thing to do was to have the agreement reaffirmed and the security increased by more property. The sums involved were quite substantial to a person in Locke's situation, and he had some reason to be uneasy because of the informal way in which he had invested his £700 twenty years before. Yet the situation was made all the more painful for him because he suffered from a species of fiscal hypochondria.

Since Anthony was to come of age on February 26, 1692, the moment seemed opportune to press for a new agreement—though, actually, there is no evidence that Anthony's financial situation improved when he came of age. Thus in March of 1692 Locke appealed directly to Anthony in the terms which he knew were most likely to affect the young man. "Among the things that I have Lov'd best in this world, the two that I allwayes preferr'd to the rest, were, My Lord your Grandfather, and Quiet." And after describing the terms of the annuity agreement, he goes on to say, "But your Lordship is not ignorant, That it has been under deliberation, and Advice has been given, That instead of receiveing an Annuity, I should bee made a Farmer; I wish my Lord your Grandfather had been by to have hear'd it."[29] Anthony immediately tries to placate him: "You have now a Full assurance of what ever you could have assurance of before, and that your security is as Good for what ever my Grandfather in the Name of his Family has signified a Promise of. During my Life therefore and whilst I am master of any Proportion of what was his, You have that to your Intrest that is Equivalent to what you could have; were he (as I wish him) alive." He goes on to add that, should he die without ever possessing more of his grandfather's estate than he does at present, he would not be able to control the disposition of Locke's annuity after his own death.[30]

These well-intentioned but very cautious words were not calculated to soothe the anxious Locke, and he began to fret even more when it seemed that the Countess was going ahead with her plans. In May, Locke finally wrote an indignant letter to her steward, John Wheelock, bidding him show it to his mistress, and he also gave Clarke careful instructions for the conduct of an interview with the Countess. This got results: the rather startled Countess accepted his version of the original agreement, she agreed to pay for a farmhouse which Wheelock had just built presuming Locke would pay for it, and she promised to make up the deficit in the income from the farm. Locke yet had no increase of security and apparently con-

29. John Locke to Anthony, Lord Ashley, March 11, 1692, *ibid.*, 412. Locke mentions £800, but according to BL MS. Locke c. 19, f. 114 he paid £700.
30. Anthony, Lord Ashley to John Locke, March 26, 1692, in de Beer, IV, 24.

tinued to worry about it until Anthony, who had inherited the estate of the Countess on her death in 1693, was able to assure him that Kingston Farm would be improved to be sufficient security. Irregular payment of the annuity remained to vex Locke until the end of his days. His account books show that he was always paid, but when Anthony began to sacrifice his fortune in the Whig cause, the payments were often very late. The first Earl must have seen the annuity as binding Locke closer to the Ashley Cooper family; the effect was for the most part just the opposite.

Until the summer of 1690, when Locke fled to Oates in search of fresher air and quiet, he and Ashley must have engaged in many philosophical discussions. Ashley found the charms of Locke's company and conversation at times irresistible, but even at eighteen he was able to see quite clearly where the philosopher's ideas were leading. Just a fragment remains of their earliest debate. When Ashley arrived at Locke's rooms at Mrs. Smithsby's in Channel Row, Westminster, one day in the autumn of 1689, only to find his old teacher abroad, he wrote out for Locke his own side of the argument, a continuation of a thesis which he had been developing in a discussion the day before. Ashley's arguments are more remarkable for their ingenuity than for their persuasiveness; more interesting is the question he and Locke are arguing and the general position which the disciple took.

In his *Essay Concerning Human Understanding*, which was in the press at the time and went on sale three months later, Locke was able to carry on a dispassionately empirical analysis of the processes of thought, because he rigorously limited his discussion to thinking and avoided any bypaths which might lead into areas which were the subject then of violent theological controversy. Probably the most dangerous of these areas concerned the relationship of matter to thought or spirit. Locke assumed the independent existence of thought, but he did not seek to prove it: "I shall not at present meddle with the physical consideration of the mind; or trouble myself to examine wherein its essence consists; or by what motions of our spirits or alterations of our bodies we come to have any *sensation* by our organs, or any *ideas* in our understandings; and whether those ideas do in their formation, any or all of them, depend on matter or

not."[31] And later he remarks that some say "they cannot comprehend a *thinking* thing, which perhaps is true: but I affirm, when
they consider it well, they can no more comprehend an *extended*
thing."[32] In his letter to Locke, Ashley takes the materialistic position and tries to prove that, on the basis of some of the assumptions
which were shortly to appear as foundation stones of the system developed in the *Essay*, there is no need at all to assume the existence
of immaterial thought; that thinking can be explained à la Hobbes in
terms of matter and motion.[33] It is unlikely that he is anticipating
his later Stoic materialism—which he never argued. The point is
that Ashley disliked the moral implications of Hobbesian materialism as much as Locke feared being associated in any way with its
theological implications. He posed as a Hobbist here merely to dem-
onstrate what he was not to state openly until some years after his
mentor died, that Locke's empirical psychology was no less dangerous to morality than Hobbes's materialism.

Another of Ashley's philosophical letters to Locke, written in
1694 near the end of this period of closer association, seems even
more prophetic when read in the light of his mature opinion of the
empirical psychology, and more important, it gives a glimpse of Ashley's motives and aspirations at a time when he was probably com-
posing *An Inquiry Concerning Virtue or Merit*. Usually he apologized for writing from the country. In 1691 he said, "I perceive from
the beginning of my Letter hetherto, I am hedg'd in with a Style
meerly Clownish Rude and Barberouse; infected with the Practice of
Life and Objects I have continually before mee Here, where I have
now been a longer time, to my sorrow, then ever since I knew my
self."[34] In 1694, however, Ashley seems to have a change of heart.
The pressure of business lessens that spring and he goes to Dorset
and stays there for a very long period, not because family concern
demands but so that he can study undistracted by city life. There is
some proof that he was at work on the *Inquiry* at this time in his

31. John Locke, *An Essay Concerning Human Understanding* (2 vols.; Oxford,
1894), I, 26.
32. Locke, *Essay*, I, 409–10.
33. Anthony, Lord Ashley to John Locke [August 1689], in de Beer, III, 666–71.
34. Anthony, Lord Ashley to John Locke, August 10, 1691, *ibid.*, IV, 305.

refusal to offer Locke a quid pro quo for a copy of the second edition of the *Essay Concerning Human Understanding* which the latter had sent him: "I who am never very well satisfied with what I speak; should be verry sorry to be Oblig'd for an Agreable Present made mee, to Return so Bad a one as a Bundle of such Thought as mine, and an Essay of my own, of such a Genius, such Invention, such a Style as mine—I Find, if I goe on, I shall Doe as bad as what I pretend to be displeas'd with."[35]

In September, after again coyly refusing to impart the results of his studies to Locke, he does tell what he hopes to do and why:

> Itt is not with mee as with an Empirick, one that is studdying of Curiositys, raising of new Inventions that are to gain credit to the author, starting of new Notions that are to amuse the World and serve them for Divertion or for tryall of their Acuteness. . . . Descartes, or Mr Hobbs, or any of their Improvers have the same reason to make a-doe, and bee Jealouse about their notion's and DISCOVERY'S, as they call them; as a practizing Apothecary or a mountebank has to bee Jealouse about the Compositions that are to goe by his name. . . . [F]or my part: I am so far from thinking that mankind need any new Discoverys, or that they lye in the dark and are unhappy for want of them; that I know not what wee could ask of God to know more then wee doe, or easily may doe. the thing that I would ask of God should bee to make men live up to what they know; and that they might bee so wise as to desire to know no other things then what belong'd to 'em, and what lay plain before them.

And, later,

> What I count True Learning, and all wee can profitt by, is to know our selves. . . . Whilst I can gett any thing that teaches this; Whilst I can search any Age or Language that can assist mee here; Whilst Such are Philosopers and Such Philosophy, whence I can Learn ought from, of this kind; there is no Labour, no Studdy, no Learning that I would not undertake.[36]

In putting morals first, in opposing ethics to physics and metaphysics, in his confidence that all man needs to be moral is to apply sound psychology and a few clear and simple principles, Ashley is

---

35. Anthony, Lord Ashley to John Locke, May [28, 1694], *ibid.*, V, 66.
36. Anthony, Lord Ashley to John Locke, September 29, 1694, *ibid.*, 150–51, 153.

the true prophet of the era which was to come to England. Locke by now had fallen more into the habit of suggesting the Bible to those who wished him to erect a moral system on rational principles. One would give a great deal to know what he really thought of Ashley's brave aims.

Though Locke must have realized by this time that Ashley's thoughts were diverging from his own, the two men almost always agreed as to what sort of friends they liked best. In the spring of the year before, the wife of William Popple had a dream which her husband thought would interest Locke. In a church like that at the Temple, four men soberly attired rise up and talk the minister out of his pulpit. She knew immediately who they were: philosophers, such as Locke, Lord Ashley, John Freke (1652–1714), and Benjamin Furly (1636–1714). The dream does not tell much of what the philosophers said beyond speaking of morality, truth, and reason but it does emphasize in another way a decisive influence of Locke on Ashley; so many of the men who shaped his thought in conversation and by letters were introduced to him by Locke, and their influence, usually pro, sometimes con, persisted after Locke's death in 1704.

In politics Locke's friends Sir John Somers, later Baron Somers (1651–1716), Sir Walter Young (ca. 1653–1731), M.P., and John Freke, the radical politician, must have shaped the young man's opinions. In ideas there were, for instance, William Popple, Edward Clarke, and other members of the clubs that Ashley joined. There was also a substantial group of people of Huguenot or Dutch background: Paul d'Aranda (1652–1712), a merchant; Benjamin Furly, merchant and polymath; Jean Le Clerc (1657–1736), scholar and editor; and Philip van Limborch (1633–1712), the Remonstrant author and editor. On the fringe was John Toland (1670–1722), who knew many of these men. The best thing Toland could do was to stay in a city for a while and then leave quickly while he still had good friends and strong recommendations, which he had a knack of acquiring, only matched by the rapidity with which he lost them. For most of these people, Freke and Toland for example, we have few remains of their association with Ashley. Many of the others got to know him later, so that only two need to be mentioned here, Furly and Popple.

Ashley's most steady correspondent for his whole life was Furly.

He was introduced to him in Rotterdam in 1687 when Furly was fifty-one and he only sixteen. William Penn (1644–1718) probably introduced Locke to Furly, in whose house the philosopher was lodging when Ashley visited him at the beginning of his grand tour. Furly was an altogether remarkable person. An Englishman, he had been converted to Quakerism and had emigrated at an early age to Holland, where he soon manifested the business acumen which seems typical of the sect, and he became a comparatively wealthy man while yet young. His radical religious notions had caused some controversy among the Quakers at one time, but by the time Ashley met him these notions had mellowed considerably. His political ideas remained radical, however, as can be seen by comparing Locke's more conservative remarks on William Penn's frame of government for his new province with those of Furly, who apparently had a substantial influence on the document in its final form.[37] Ashley had no need to go to Holland to learn about republican sentiments; more important to him were Furly's unusual talent for friendship, his philanthropy, and, above all, his learning. In his house with its famous library, Ashley found entrée into a circle of Continental intellectuals, which, although centered in tolerant Holland, spread its influence widely over Europe. In his youth he had two opportunities to spend much time with Furly: on his grand tour and when Furly visited England in 1691. No more than a letter or two survives from that era, though there may have been many. The period of real closeness between the men was to come later after Ashley's second visit to Holland.

From frequent allusions in his letters it is clear that Ashley saw more of another merchant friend from this time of his life, William Popple, nephew of the poet Marvell. Popple had begun his career in London, moved to Bordeaux sometime after 1661, and perhaps in 1668 returned to London, where he was later secretary of the Dry Club, which Locke founded in 1692.[38]

37. Maurice Cranston, *John Locke* (1957), 261–62, 281.
38. A thoroughly definitive essay on Popple is Caroline Robbins' "Absolute Liberty: The Life and Thought of William Popple, 1638–1708," *William and Mary Quarterly*, 3rd ser. XXIV (1967), 190–223.

Since Popple's philosophical and theological notions are available to us in his *Rational Catechism* (1687), in his letters, and in the preface to Locke's *Letter Concerning Toleration*, which Popple translated in 1689, it is useful to see whether he had any influence on Ashley's earliest writings. There are some resemblances. Popple shares Ashley's cosmic optimism and his despair over man's irrationality and inhumanity from which Christianity has not succeeded in freeing him. Popple is, like Ashley, primarily a moralist, and he also feels that self-interest is best served if each man prefers the public good. And something like Ashley's *moral sense* may be involved in Popple's belief that there exists an "inward Law in the Hearts of Men, with regard to the General Good."[39] All these notions were very much in the air, however, when Ashley began his philosophical meditations, and although he has much more in common with Popple than he does with Locke, one is more impressed by the radical differences in attitude than by the resemblances of ideas. For all of his heresies Popple seems genuinely religious. He is distressed by atheism and retains some faith in revelation, in the supernatural generally and in a future life in particular. Like his grandfather, Ashley early realized the necessity of keeping up an appearance of religious orthodoxy, but there is no evidence at all that he ever shared Popple's sentiments on these matters. He is described in part, at least, in one of Popple's letters to Locke on Deism and lack of faith:

> They talk big of Virtue and Morality. But when they lay all the grounds of both Virtue and Morality onely in the good-nature of particular persons, or in the fear of the Magistrate's Rod, I fear their Superstructure will be very tottering. And what makes me fear this, is because I see plainly the Youth of this Age build all upon that Foundation. . . . even Irreligion is a sad Sanctuary from the Mischiefs of Superstition.[40]

After 1694 the correspondence between Locke and Ashley, which had never been voluminous, becomes sparse and perfunctory, and Ashley no longer receives complimentary copies of Locke's books, though many of their mutual friends still continue to do so. There is

39. William Popple, *A Rational Catechism* (1687), 62.
40. William Popple to John Locke, January 16, 1696, in de Beer, V, 519.

no evidence at all that the mutual affection which they felt for each other ever waned, but the intellectual rapport between these two men gradually dissolved.

II

From all signs Lord Ashley was very busy during the years from 1695 to 1698, but he saved only a few letters, attracted little gossip, and preserved no records, so that all we have are some details of his public career as an M.P. and the account of the most important event of his private life at the time, his decision that however painful it might be to him he must intervene in the dispute between his parents.

Of his father's career as a member of the House of Commons, from November 1695 to July 1698, the fourth Earl says that he "persevered in the same way of acting, always heartily concurring in every motion for the further securing of liberty; and though these motions very frequently came from people who were of a differently-denominated party in politics, yet he was never for refusing any proposal that he apprehended to be beneficial to his country, and was always for improving the present opportunity, forming his judgment of things by their own merits, and not by the quarter whence they came."[41] We know from Ashley's later behavior that he must have been a hard-headed and effective politician, but it is true that ultimately the source of his energy lay in principles, not in party loyalty or self-aggrandizement, as even many of his enemies came to admit before he died.

There is one group with which Ashley can be associated, the Old or Country Whigs, more particularly those who had an admiration for the Commonwealth and for its theorists, such as James Harrington (1611–1677) and Henry Neville (1620–1694).[42] By this time he probably knew Walter Moyle (1672–1727), M.P., writer, and student of classical government, and the political economist Charles Davenant (1656–1714), M.P. But his closest friends among the group were Robert, later Viscount, Molesworth (1656–1725), a longtime

41. Rand, (ed.), *The Life, Unpublished Letters, and Philosophical Regimen*, xxi–xxii.

42. See Caroline Robbins, *The Eighteenth-Century Commonwealthman* (Cambridge, Mass., 1958), for a complete study.

M.P. and author of *An Account of Denmark* (1694), and John Toland.

Molesworth may be forgiven if in the years just before his death he tended to exaggerate the nature of his early friendship with Ashley, who by that time had become the subject of a remarkable popular adulation. Molesworth owned to have "taught the incomparable Shaftesbury," and he was "proud enough of having been not only so intimate with that great man, but to have had a hand in the first forming of his mind to virtue."[43] Yet Ashley admired *An Account of Denmark*, which was not in print until December 1693, for some time before he became acquainted with its author, and when he did that acquaintance "was only upon publick affairs."[44] In this case he was certainly Molesworth's disciple, but the personal friendship came over a decade later, after they had been separated for a long while. And so far as Toland is concerned, the history of his relations with Ashley will add little luster to his rather tarnished personal reputation, but he was a man who believed strongly in freedom of thought, which he often asserted energetically and defended with great courage.

The trouble with Ashley's being a Country Whig is that the character of the Whig party gradually changed from 1689 on. The Country Whigs found that the bulk of the Whig party were moving toward the Court and that the Tories seemed more and more to represent the Country element. These changes are discussed in *The Danger of Mercenary Parliaments* (1698?), which was drawn up by Toland, presumably from Ashley's ideas. The author was "fill'd with golden Dreams not only of bare Security for our Estates and Lives but of inexhausted Affluence of all manner of Blessings a Nation is capable of enjoying, but tho' we have dream'd the Dreams, yet have we not seen the Visions." Instead of the visions, perversions are seen everywhere.

Who can enough lament the wretched Degeneracy of the Age we live in? To see Persons who were formerly noted for the most vigorous As-

43. William Wishart, citing Robert Molesworth in a letter to him, November 7, 1723, in *HMC, Various Collections*, VIII, 366. Robert Molesworth to John Toland, June 25, 1720, in *A Collection of Several Pieces of Mr. John Toland* (2 vols.; 1726), II, 461–62.

44. Lord Shaftesbury to Robert Molesworth, January 12, 1709, and February 21, 1709, in *Letters from the Right Honourable the Late Earl of Shaftesbury, to Robert Molesworth, Esq.*, edited with an introduction by John Toland (1721), 26, 28.

sertors of their Country's Liberty, who from their Infancy had imbib'd no other Notions than what Conduc'd to the publick Safety, whose Principles were further improv'd and confirm'd by the Advantages of a suitable Conversation, and who were so far possess'd with this Spirit of Liberty, that it sometimes transported them beyond the Bounds of Moderation, even to unwarrantable Excesses; to see these Men, I say, so infamously fall in with the Arbitrary Measures of the Court, and appear the most active Instruments for inslaving their Country.[45]

According to Ashley's later recollection he was saved from becoming a Tory only by the fact that in the late winter and spring of 1695 a number of Tory leaders were in trouble over a whole series of corruptions. It is likely that he is making his role seem more dramatic than it actually was, as most men sometimes do. Earlier or later, the High Church bias of the Tory party would have been utterly intolerable to him.

One might normally turn to the authorities to clarify Ashley's position at the beginning of his political career, but in this case they are less useful to the biographer than expected. With the Glorious Revolution of 1688 a complete change in English political thought began. We know where the change was heading—toward the general pattern of Whig and Tory beliefs of, say, the period 1710 to 1720—but we do not know how fast it moved. Nor do we know, granting that the new party structure is only developing, how much it means to call an M.P. of this period a *Whig* or a *Tory*. How accurately does the terminology predict how he will vote when confronted by a specific issue in the House? Naturally the further back we get toward the Revolution, the more vigorous the controversy becomes and here, as in so many scholarly disputes, the argument has moved from those simplifications, beloved academically, to a realization that any situation wherein the human mind and heart—and their motives—are involved is likely to be complex.

Now we are beginning to see more clearly the pattern of transition in political parties during the most confused period, up to the death of King William in 1702. Studies such as Henry Horwitz's astute and undogmatic *Parliament, Policy and Politics in the Reign of William*

45. John Toland, *The Danger of Mercenary Parliaments: With a Preface, Shewing the Infinite Mischiefs of Long and Pack'd Parliaments* (1722), 8–9, 11.

III have brought much light to a situation which will never be completely clear, but it is important to realize that Ashley, who was all too well aware of the transition, never took any part in it. To borrow a sentence from another writer who has clarified much, B. W. Hill in his *The Growth of Parliamentary Parties, 1689–1742*, "the absorption of Old Whigs by the Tories, and the conversion of the latter to the idea of opposition, were not achieved overnight or without difficulty." Ashley was never absorbed, and no matter whether he voted with the Tories or the new Whigs, no matter how intricate the practical political situations he became involved in, he remained from 1695 to his death, as he was before, an old parliament Whig.[46]

When Sir John Trenchard, William's secretary of state and M.P. for Poole, died in the spring of 1695, Ashley stood for the seat as a Whig and was returned on May 21, a little over a fortnight after what turned out to be the last session of this Parliament had ended. He was returned again for the same seat the following November and first took his place in the House on November 21. From this time until his death he consistently fought for toleration for Dissenters, for parliamentary authority, and against measures which might lead to a Catholic hegemony in Europe.

As we shall see, application of these principles required a great deal of finesse. For instance, England was at war with France for most of his adult life, and since the Crown was nominally in charge of foreign policy, his loyalty to it depended largely on the zeal with which the war was pursued. Or consider the matter of the various oaths and abjurations in support of the Crown. We do not know whether in 1696 he signed the association to proclaim William the king, yet it seems certain that he must have. He did vote in favor of the abjuration oath earlier in the year, even though it was supported by the Court party. To Ashley this must have seemed most reasonable. He was a supporter of parliamentary authority to be sure, but these bills dealt with the possibility of the return of James. What better time to be a Williamite? Principle, not party, was involved.

When he did begin his career as M.P., he did so with a momentum

46. For Ashley and his associates, see Henry Horwitz, *Parliament, Policy and Politics in the Reign of William III* (Manchester, 1977), 216, and B. W. Hill, *The Growth*

which is proof enough that he had been busy with political affairs for some time. Soon after Parliament was summoned, he was deeply involved in promoting a measure restricting prerogative, the Bill for Regulating Trials in Cases of Treason. This law was to guarantee the defendant the right to defense by counsel and of subpoena. There could be no indictment but by the oaths of two lawful witnesses. And, among other provisions, the bill also set up a three-year statute of limitations on the crime of treason. Obviously, since the trials of Algernon Sidney (1622–1683) and Lord William Russell (1639–1683) were still fresh in the minds of the Whigs, such a bill would have a great appeal to them. At that time, however, the chief beneficiaries of such a law were likely to be Jacobites, and the bill seems to have been passed with the same strong Tory support which it had received when introduced unsuccessfully in the previous Parliament.

Late in 1695, or perhaps in January of the following year when the bill was again debated in Commons, this time with a rather unpalatable clause attached to it by the House of Lords, there occurred an incident which gave rise to the only anecdote of the young Ashley that contemporary historians seem to have preserved for us. His son tells it best:

My father prepared a speech, which those, to whom he showed it, thought a very proper one upon the occasion. But when he stood up to speak it in the House of Commons the great audience so intimidated him that he lost all memory, and could not utter a syllable of what he intended, by which he found how true Mr. Locke's caution to him had been, not to engage at first setting out in an undertaking of difficulty, but to rise to it gradually. The House, after giving him a little time to recover, called loudly for him to go on, when he proceeded to this effect:—"If I, sir, who rise only to speak my opinion on the Bill now depending, am so confounded that I am unable to express the least of what I proposed to say, what must the condition of that man be who is pleading for his life without any assistance and under apprehensions of being deprived of it?" The sudden turn of thought (which by some was imagined to have been premeditated, though it really was as I mention

___

of Parliamentary Parties, 1689–1742 (1976), 66. Neither Anthony nor Maurice is labeled as to party on the basis of the division lists published by Professor Horwitz, Parliament, Policy and Politics, 338–57.

it) pleased the house extremely; and it is generally believed, carried a greater weight with it than any of the arguments which were offered in favour of the bill which was sent to the Lords and passed accordingly.[47]

Most students of English history are aware of the ironic aftermath. While Parliament was deliberating the bill, a group of Jacobites were, with King James's blessing, plotting to assassinate William near Turnham Green, a mile or so north of the Thames, where he often passed Saturdays on his way from the palace in Kensington to his deer hunting in Richmond Park. As Bishop Burnet (1643–1715) recounts it, "the conspirators were to be scattered about the green, in taverns and alehouses, and to be brought together upon a signal given. They were cast into several parties, and an aide-de-camp was assigned to every one of them, both to bring them together, and to give the whole the air of a military action."[48] The plotters were betrayed, however, and most of them taken. Years later, Toland cited the subsequent trials as a vindication of Ashley's argument before Commons that the bill would offer no loopholes through which genuine traitors could escape.

Shortly after the Treason Bill was passed, Ashley writes Thomas Stringer:

> We have got a bill to be engrossed, which lays an incapacity on the Elector (as the late passed act does on the Elected) in case of corruption, meat, drink, &c. and which obliges the knights of the shire to have £500 a year, or the inheritance of it, as freehold within the county, and a burgess £200 a year somewhere at least in England on the same terms. You cou'd, I believe, scarcely imagine with yourself, who these are in the world, or who they are in the House, who oppose this, and all other such bills as this, might and main.[49]

47. Rand, *The Life, Unpublished Letters, and Philosophical Regimen*, xxi. This anecdote has been given to Charles Montagu, later first Earl of Halifax (1661–1715), by some modern writers, because it is cited in his *Memoirs* (1715), but the earliest printed account of it that I have come across is in Abel Boyer, *The History of King William the Third* (3 vols.; 1702–1703), III, 117. Because there it is told of Ashley— though Boyer thinks he is the son of the first Earl—and also because Locke in January 1696 inquires about a notable speech of Ashley's which he has heard of (see *The Correspondence of John Locke and Edward Clarke*, ed. Benjamin Rand [Cambridge, Mass., 1927], 436), the fourth Earl must be correct in assigning it to his father.

48. Bishop Gilbert Burnet, *History of His Own Time* (1838), 623.

49. Anthony, Lord Ashley to Thomas Stringer, February 15, 1696, in *Letters of the Earl of Shaftesbury* (1750), 157–58.

The bill he speaks of is called the Qualifying Bill or, more commonly, the Bill for Regulating Elections, and Ashley's enthusiasm for a measure which would in effect restrict the franchise and permit only the affluent to sit in the House has led modern commentators to apologize that his republicanism was not more tinged with democracy. Rather we should be more than astonished if at that time a man whose inheritance involved membership in a very select group at the top of the social structure—there were then about 160 temporal peers—were anything but thoroughly aristocratic in his political and social thinking, however his grandfather may have manipulated the populace for political advantage. Personal considerations aside, it seemed but common sense to Ashley and his friends that poorer men are more easily corruptible than rich ones. The Qualifying Bill was principally intended to prevent the Court from further building up its influence in Commons, and William's vetoing of the bill is some proof that he thought it would do what its supporters intended.

The last major House of Commons debate in which Ashley seems to have been involved, over the standing army, typifies his whole career. The war which had been waged against France almost from the beginning of William's reign had been a formidable impediment to the efforts of those who, like Ashley, believed in the sovereignty of Parliament. After the war came to an end in October of 1697, Parliament seized the bit and that winter voted to disband the army, keeping under arms only a quarter of the soldiers William had hoped to retain. Ashley's position against the standing army was, like every other position he took in the House of Commons—according to what records we have—thoroughly consistent with his principles.

At some time during his service in Parliament in 1696 or 1697 Ashley first felt the strangling grip of the asthma which was to shape his life thereafter. According to his son, it was fatigue from his parliamentary duties which brought on his respiratory troubles. This tradition was established at least by 1705, when Christopher Pitt (1663?–1723), an eminent physician of Blandford—about ten miles southwest of Wimborne St. Giles—and father of the popular poet of the same name, wrote in a report that before he was in the House of Commons, my Lord had a firm, healthy Constitution: He had been allways Regular in his eating & drinking: his Drink was generally Water; his Diett simple without high Sauces, He observ'd allso the same Regularity as to going to bed and Rising. But when in that House, he constantly attended the Service of the House by day, and was late at Night at the Committees in a close room, with a Croud of People, where he was often carry'd into an eagerness of Dispute, he contracted such a Weakness of Lungs, as to bring on a Convulsive Asthma, which seiz'd him with that Violence, as to be a perfect Orthopnoea; by which he became very weak, and by the frequency of the fitts his sight has been extremely impair'd. His Lordship found no Advantage from any Medicines used for his Asthma; but he finds the smell of Sea Coal, the Smoak of Tobacco etc. will constantly occasion a return of it; so is he free from it, if these last mention'd Evident Causes are avoided.[50]

Making it the easier for Ashley to decline to stand again after the Parliament was dissolved in July 1698 was the constant criticism of him for his lack of party spirit. He did not give up until he had to, but these reproaches had haunted him from the beginning. Three months after he took his seat, he wrote to Stringer: "You wou'd hardly believe that your poor friend, that now writes to you, has sentence (and bitter sentence too) every day passing upon him, for going, as you may be sure he goes and ever will go on such occasions as these; whatever party it be, that is in, or out at court, that is in possession of the places, and afraid of losing their daily bread by not being servile enough, or that are out of places, and think, by crossing the court, and siding with good and popular things against it, to get into those places of profit and management."[51] The political heir of the man regarded as the archfiend of all Whiggery by the Tories could hardly expect any gratitude when he sided with them, as his principles often led him to do; at the same time this behavior made the Whigs mistrust him, even when he agreed with them. Obviously there is some truth in Toland's account of Ashley's predicament:

He so heartily expostulated with such as he met of those *Apostate-Whigs*, he oppos'd all of them so much by his Interest in and out of

50. May 13, 1705, in PRO 30/24/20/100. *Orthopnoea* is a form of asthmatic attack during which the patient can breathe only in an upright position.
51. Anthony, Lord Ashley to Thomas Stringer, February 15, 1696, in Shaftesbury, *Letters* (1750), 158.

Parliament, and so livelily represented the treachery and baseness of the Measures they were following, that they cou'd not endure him. They gave out that he was splenetick and melancholy; whimsical and eaten up with vapors: whereas he was in reality just the reverse, naturally chearful and pleasant, ever steddy in his Principles, and the farthest in the world from humorsom or fantastical. But becoming an Eyesore to them, as being an eternal reproach upon their conduct, they strain'd their inventions to turn his best qualities into defects. They gave out that he was too bookish, because not given to Play, nor assiduous at Court; that he was no good Companion, because not a Rake nor a hard Drinker, and that he was no Man of the World, because not selfish nor open to Bribes.[52]

As the years go by the animus of Lady Dorothy Shaftesbury seems to be deflected from the Earl and turned toward Lord Ashley. After all he had not intervened to get her financial support, and she now seems to feel that the increasingly feeble Earl has become merely the pawn of his son, though as Anthony learned from bitter experience, his father's will became more intense and inflexible as he grew older. In addition the Earl grew increasingly secretive about his affairs, so that no one but he and Williams seemed to know what was going on at St. Giles's House.

John's tragic death could not have helped the relations between Anthony and his mother. A childhood portrait of John reveals a very handsome boy whom one cannot see without the vivid impression that he is someone's pampered darling. It seems likely that Lady Dorothy's affections became strongly fixed on her second son after her firstborn was taken from her to be raised in her father-in-law's family. Of course it was the second Earl who in desperation first decided to send John to sea. When Anthony finally concurred, he did so so strongly that the Earl, who had again changed his mind, probably under pressure from the Countess, was forced to send John off.

The attitude of the Countess toward Anthony by 1695 is epitomized in a letter to her brother the Earl of Rutland referring to his expected grandchild: "my affectionate love to my kind Sister. I begg, I pray, the Lady Katherine may have a better sone then I have or

52. Shaftesbury, *Letters . . . to Molesworth*, viii.

none, I pray God." She flatly refused to permit him to come to Haddon Hall—a considerable journey—in order to pay his respects to her. That winter he apparently asked for and got the support of some of her relatives, his "Aunt" Montagu and Lady Dorothy's sisters, Lady Anglesey and Lady Chaworth—but to no avail.

Anthony must have become desperate early in 1696. This is the only explanation for the utterly tactless letter he wrote to his mother then:

> Had itt been my misfourtune to have been led into a behaviour ever soe unbecoming me or to have given you never soe just an occasion of offence, yet the consideration of that early tyme my fault must have been committed in; When I knew my selfe soe little, and was of an age soe little able either to Judge or to Act right; this and the Proofs your Ladyship has since had of my intire Submission, and Willingness to doe any thing that may regaine mee your ffavour, my earnest desire to mend what ever has been amiss and to attone for what ever you may have judged me guilty off or that I have fail'd in. All this together with the applycation that has been made for me by all those here whom I have the Happiness to be related to through you & who have had the goodness all of them to plead my cause for me. This I say, I might have expected, would have been of sufficient weight to have enclin'd your Ladyship towards me, and have gain'd for me if not kindness and forgiveness at least some thing in answer to that sincerely Dutyfull & humblest application I have been soe long makeing to your Ladyship.

Ashley goes on that, since he is not at all conscious of doing anything which justly might offend her, he finds her lack of charity astonishing: "I must submitt to what God pleases. I thank him that He has been soe mercifull as to make me sensible what it is to bee a Son, and what I am to doe as such. I trust in him that Hee may one day also give you the Heart of a Mother, and restore me to the good will and Blessing of a Parent."[53]

Anthony was young enough that he did not despair for long. In April, he sought an ally at Haddon Hall, the Earl of Rutland, who had not been favorable to his cause. Anthony's feelings are essentially the same as before; he is willing to go to great lengths to bring about a reconciliation, but he must remain impartial. He does reveal

---

53. Anthony, Lord Ashley to the Countess of Shaftesbury, beginning of 1696, in PRO 30/24/22/2.

one of the pressing reasons why he continues to struggle for a change of heart in his mother:

> If nothing from me is able to prevaile with her to think of her ffamily, Yett the case of my Sisters I should hope might, who as to their coming up in the World and what is necessary in that respect are Destitute of all Manner of assistance & support, and can only receive it from my Mother or some of Her Relations, I for my own part having no other service in my power to doe them besides what Relates to their Four-tunes in which I have done & shall doe my Best.[54]

Shortly after this Ashley learned the reason for his uncle's coolness toward him. When Lady Rutland had been traveling through Dorset, Shaftesbury had refused to entertain her at St. Giles's House, and her husband believed that Ashley, who was actually in London at the time, was responsible for this dismaying insult. According to the customs of the day any peer would have had a claim on Lord Shaftesbury's hospitality, but to refuse a lady of her quality, and a close relation, to boot, was absolutely unthinkable. He wrote to his uncle,

> Could I my Lord have sett aside My Respect to your Lordship & ffam-ily; itt surely had been impossible for me to have comitted any thing like that of being the occasion of my Ladys not being entertain'd at St. Giles. besides the honor I have of being related as I am to my Lady, and what the sence of it would have carried me too, there was certainly enough besides to have kept me from such a Rudeness: and either I doe not know my selfe att all, or it has not been amongst my Faults to car-rie my selfe with soe little Breeding towards Quallity, and least of all towards Ladys. If my ffather be soe much of a Different Charracter from me as in shuning all Company whatsoever, to Decline what my Ambi-tion would have made me to have Courted; my misfourtune will be allowed the greater: Nor is this the only thing in which I am made a sufferer by my ffathers Malloncholy Temper and Industrious Avoidance of all Company.[55]

Lord Rutland was won over, but he failed to mollify his sister.

Although Lady Dorothy was in poor health, she knew precisely what she wanted from Anthony, and she was prepared to go to the grave unrelenting, if he did not both accept the blame and intervene

---

54. Anthony, Lord Ashley to the Earl of Rutland, April 9, 1696, in BC MSS. 21, No. 127. Also in PRO 30/24/22/2.
55. Anthony, Lord Ashley to the Earl of Rutland, June 1, 1696, in PRO 30/24/22/2.

with his father in domestic matters. In the fall of 1696 her equally stubborn son finally accepted the necessity of giving her what she wanted. He says,

> I begg you would forgive mee that, soe well as other things, and whatever in my Youth I may have offended in before I came to Years of Discretion or to that sence of my Duty to you which I thank God I now have. Had I had formerly at those Years the same serious sence which I now have of what that Duty is, I am confident I should have prevented your falling into displeasure with me, And never have given you the least of those Occasions. They are now what I heartily Mourn for, And call God to Wittness that if ever I become so Happy as once againe to bee restored to your Favour and affection, I shall count itt above all I can gain in this world.

He goes on to say,

> Itt may I hope bee some proofe of this to Tell your Ladyship that I have don all I am able with my Father, and I have constantly spoke with all the earnestness that became mee in your Interest. I now know and am satisfyed that there is no servant nor any thing of that Nature which Hee would not part with on the account of seeing you. I obtained itt from him Yesterday that hee would give me leave to write to your Ladyship and present his Love and service, with my own Duty.[56]

Lady Montagu soon informed Anthony that humbling himself and intervening with his father in the matter of Williams had borne fruit, and the next month he received an invitation to wait upon his mother at Haddon Hall. It was February before his political concerns permitted him to journey to Derbyshire. Lady Dorothy describes his visit in a very touching letter to her husband:

> Our Dear'st Childe Ashley hath demonstrated his Duty & Love to so Great a degree by Comeing on Wensday to see his Mother, he being 26 years old and haveing write me soe Many Extraordinry Submissive Letters, I cannot rest till I have given your Deare Lordship an account of it & if God permitt I will not be long before I wait upon your Lordship at St. Giles, if the Bearer can but get this Letter safe into your Deare Lordship's hands. It has been a great griefe to me many years to see my selfe & Children Commanded & Slighted by an unworthy servant. . . . I know it is troublesome to your Lordshipp to write & begg

56. Anthony, Lord Ashley to the Countess of Shaftesbury, October 10, 1696, in PRO 30/24/22/2.

you will order our very Bad servant Williams to Get him out of St. Giles walls. When I know that is done I will sett out towards you & my poore Girls the next day affter; If your Lordship doe not Like of my comeing by London I will hire a Coach & Come Cross the Country, I having a worthy Doctors promises to come with me in my Coach, he haveing bine my Doctor since I came hither & says he hops to bring me safe into your Arms.[57]

Lady Dorothy's offer to come directly to Dorset, sick as she was, instead of proceeding down the high roads to London and thence by way of the normal routes via Guildford and Winchester, or through Basingstoke, would in the 1690s indicate a great determination to get to St. Giles. It also reflects Shaftesbury's obsession against wives or daughters even visiting London, a disposition Anthony was to inherit. She did take the easier route through London.

Much of the blame for alienating his mother and keeping her from his father and the family must fall on Ashley. In his defense it can be said that he felt strongly that both he and his mother owed his father a fundamental obedience in all things. Whether it was followed or not matters little, for it was then a central principle of filial piety. It should have been clear to him, though, that this principle had become a convenient legalism in the case of his father, who had become too helpless and irrational to lay claim to it—witness the case of the steward, Williams. Ashley was imprudent and afraid of being involved in a frustrating situation. He must have known that any time he wished to have his way in this nasty and distracting business of family affairs, all he had to do was stamp his foot firmly enough.

However much or little Ashley was at fault, it is doubtful that he ever had cause to regret his disheartening and arduous struggle to win his mother back. The accounts of Williams run to April 8, 1697. The night of the eleventh, the Countess wrote to her husband from Haddon Hall, "My Last [letter from you] my Deare Lord much supris'd me. Tom coming allmost at my Bedtime, & Honest Matchett Bringing your kinde Noate for my journey & returne if God Gives Life. I will not stay above a weak, only to rest my selfe, for now Judas

<hr>

57. The Countess of Shaftesbury to the Earl of Shaftesbury, Haddon Hall the 26th, in PRO 30/24/22/1/22.

is Gone, had I winges surely I would soon come."[58] Later in the month, Ashley awaits her arrival in London so that he can escort her to St. Giles's House. The following November he goes to Charlton, Kent, with Sir William Montagu in order to consult with her sisters about a new attack of illness. And the next year, on the fifth of July, Lady Dorothy Shaftesbury was buried at Wimborne St. Giles.

58. The Countess of Shaftesbury to the Earl of Shaftesbury, April 11, 1697, in PRO 30/24/22/1/24.

⊱ III ⊰

Rotterdam
and Little Chelsea
1698–1699

Before the end of the month in which he buried his mother, July 1698, Lord Ashley was in Rotterdam at the house of his friend Benjamin Furly. He was in a hurry to flee the tension of political affairs and the illness it had brought upon him. Respiratory disease, oddly, focused his energies, and without his illness he might not have accomplished enough to be the subject of a biography. His problem was not too little energy but too much; as Locke said of him, the sword was too sharp for the scabbard. Everything in life he pursued with such zeal and sincerity that he could have ended up doing too little of anything with sufficient intensity. Now he has been forced into taking the retreat he had longed for.[1] In Rotterdam, after deploring how his own fondness for the world has made him the plaything of men and of circumstance, he says, "At length thou hast retir'd. Thou art again in possession of thy self & mayst keep so; being to come as it were, into a new World, free of former Engagements & Tyes, unless of thy own accord voluntarily &, officiously thou renew'st them, & art willing to begin where thou left'st off" (Ex., 64).

It is ironic that Ashley, absorbed in the movement of ideas, should have chosen Holland as the scene of his retreat, because nowhere in Europe could he have found greater intellectual ferment, nowhere more men who were likely to draw him away from Stoic self-

---

1. Ex., 162. There is a persistent tradition that this was his third trip to Holland, that he made a visit incognito in 1691. See, for example, William I. Hull, *Benjamin Furly and Quakerism in Rotterdam*, Swarthmore College Monographs on Quaker History, No. 5 (1941), 101. The only basis for this assumption seems to be a letter from Ashley to Furly in June of 1691 announcing his intention to make such a trip. Yet every month from June through December we can, on the basis of his correspondence or his attendance at meetings of the Lords Proprietors, place him in England. In December he visited Furly at Oates.

examination into the delights of thoughtful and learned conversation. Perhaps like so many of us, Ashley was wishfully confident of the power of change of place, or perhaps he felt that by putting the North Sea between himself and his family and political associates he would be more isolated than in, say, a quiet country retreat in England. He did forbid all of his family and friends to write unless they had been specifically authorized to do so.

In any case, the Netherlands in its golden age was bound to be distracting, for in 1698 conditions for learning and independent thought were even more favorable than they had been when Descartes decided to work there seventy years before. Holland was the publishing center of Europe; it was blessed with fine universities and schools nourished by an active and rigorous tradition. During this period three important journals were established which gave Holland a still greater part in the distribution and interchange of ideas, and Ashley came to know the editor of all three. Most important was the Dutch spirit of toleration, for many of the men with whom Ashley became friendly were foreigners enjoying its bounty, especially the Huguenots who had fled after the revocation of the Edict of Nantes. Ashley was drawn to them by the same political principles which led his family to favor their cause in Carolina. He found among them a number of free spirits who attracted him regardless of their religious and philosophical convictions.

Rotterdam was a pleasant, bustling walled town of about 30,000 people, roughly triangular in shape, and moated all around by canals and rivers. One English traveler who arrived two months before Ashley was impressed with the great quay running the full length of the side facing the broad river Maas, and the New East Indian House and fine merchants' homes built upon the quay—signs of the rapidly growing prosperity of the city during the last decades of the century. A contemporary engraving shows an abundance of trees; the typically tall and rather narrow houses; taller still, and sprouting right among the rooftops, the masts of innumerable ships docked in the canals and basins which interlaced the town and were reached through water gates in the walls; and the whole scene surmounted by the towers of several churches within the city and the sails of windmills around the perimeter.

There were few houses anywhere like that of the remarkable Furly. Ashley did not live there throughout his stay, as has always been assumed, but it was the center of his life in Rotterdam. When he arrived Furly was deeply concerned with Anglo-Dutch affairs in relation to France, and he and his friends were not only able to appeal to Ashley's delight in intellectual conversation; they also aroused his strong sense of political duty, which he had hoped to put to sleep by flight.

The most notable of these friends was the great Huguenot writer Pierre Bayle. Ashley's son, believing that his father first met Bayle in 1703, refers to him as Lord Shaftesbury instead of Lord Ashley in this anecdote, which one hopes is true:

> Being determined not to be interupted in what he principally went thither to follow, Studying & that in the most private manner, he concealed his name pretending to be only a Student in Physick. In that character he became acquainted with the celebrated Mr. Bayle with whom he soon grew intimate. But a little before his return to England, being willing to be made known to him by his real name, Mr. Bayle was invited to dinner by a friend to meet My Ld. Sh——ry. Mr. Bayle calling upon my father in the morning, on his pressing him to stay a little longer, "I can by no means," said Mr. Bayle, "for I must be punctual to an engagement where I am to meet My Ld. Sh——y by appointment." The second interview as may be imagined occasioned some mirth at first. After that they renewed their professions of mutual esteem to each other which rather increased than lessened their intimacy for the future & they corresponded frequently together after my father's return till Mr. Bayles' death.[2]

From the eighteenth century on, a good bit has been said regarding the relationship of the two men, and it may be useful to compare their intellectual positions when they first met. Most scholars seem to have assumed that two men of strong views would not be drawn together unless they shared many ideas, and without the ideas of one rubbing off to some extent on the other—in this case, those of the older and established Bayle on the younger man. Some of the parallels commonly pointed to are the thesis that an atheistic society can be morally superior to a misdevoted one—which appears

2. PRO 30/24/21/225.

in *Pensées diverses sur la comète* (1682) and in the *Inquiry*—their attitudes toward religious enthusiasm, the notion that ridicule is the best weapon against folly, and their opposition to certain phases of religious orthodoxy of the day. Given Ashley's preoccupation with the company and the books of what he called "free writers," it is hard to conceive that he would not be influenced or at least confirmed in some of his views by a contemporary whose prose was so toughly logical, so trenchant and erudite.

Turning from specific ideas to general attitudes and habits of thought, we can see that Ashley and Bayle do share a plot of ground which permits intellectual sympathy to flourish. If they disagree, as they do in so many things, they speak the common language of that ground and, unlike so many who argue, understand the real nature of their disagreements, no matter how irreconcilable these may be.

Although it would have been out of character, Coleridge might just as well have divided all thinking men into metaphysicians and moralists. Ashley and Bayle are both moralists. Ashley became a moralist as the reverent disciple of certain classical philosophers; Bayle's chief impulse in the same direction was his pious Huguenot upbringing. The result is the same: they see all too clearly and tormentingly the disparity between Christian ideals and Christian practice. They conclude that orthodox religion as it is practiced is impotent to make man better morally. It is no wonder then that both Ashley and Bayle despise error just as vigorously as the detached pursuer of truth for its own sake—whether the error is bred of superstition, enthusiasm, or, simply, lack of respect for the moral significance of truth.

The moralist, because he often seems more concerned with the consequences of what men believe to be true than with truth itself, is in one sense far more pragmatic than the metaphysician. In Ashley and Bayle, however, the pragmatism is very limited because they are both men of exceptionally strong principles. One thinks of the humiliation and the frustrations which his loyalty to principle cost Ashley during his political career, of how he refused to shift like most with the wind, so that often he sailed on with difficulty and almost alone. In Bayle's case it is difficult to choose from the instances small and great which come to mind: his refusal to write, after the custom of the day, what would have been a very lucrative dedication of his monumental *Dictionary*, or, earlier, after his dismissal from his professorship on account of enmity toward him and his ideas, his courageous acceptance of straitened circumstances, because the new leisure would enable him better to get on with what was his real vocation in the world. Sometimes the two men hold to similar principles for different reasons. Ashley's devotion to freedom of conscience and toleration stems from his political heritage; in Bayle its origin is deeply religious. But more important for their friendship than common principles is the fact that their ideas and their lives are strongly undergirded with principles as such. Men of real though differing principles can often talk; when, to either of them, the man whose principles are merely rationalized expediency will seem to speak another language.

Once we grant that Bayle and Ashley are both moralists with an exceptional regard for principles, that they are very studious, though in different ways, and that they share a deep love of learning and of letters, their intellectual dissimilarities stand out so clearly that only a niggler would search for more parallels. Men of active minds usually seem alike as we learn more about them, and these two have diverged radically with the progress of scholarship. Once it was easy enough to lump them together as freethinkers. Now, students of Bayle are as much interested in what he believed as what he did not; his fideism is taken into account along with his Pyrrhonism.[3] On the other hand, study of Ashley's aesthetic theories and analysis of his published works in the light of his personal Stoicism reveal him as far more sophisticated and systematic than he has been thought to be, but hardly in a manner which Bayle, the enemy of metaphysics, would approve. If one seeks to reduce the divergence between Bayle and Ashley by a very simple formulation of the sort to which I have confined myself, it would seem best to say that with respect to

3. Contrast two good books published thirty years apart: Howard Robinson's *Bayle the Sceptic* (New York, 1931) with Elisabeth Labrousse's monumental *Pierre Bayle* (2 vols.; The Hague, 1963–64), and see also, for example, K. C. Sandberg's "Pierre Bayle's Sincerity in his Views on Faith and Reason," *Studies in Philology*, LXI (1964), 74–84.

both man and his world Bayle is resolutely pessimistic and Ashley essentially optimistic.

What Elisabeth Labrousse calls "le profond pessimisme anthropologique de Bayle" is wholly contrary to the underlying spirit of Ashley's thought, as contrary to it as Hobbes's notion of man to which Ashley replied, or that of Mandeville, who replied in turn to him.[4] It is true that in 1698 Ashley was less sanguine with respect to mankind than he became later. The early letters to Locke, the haughty Stoic scorn for the *idiotai*, or laymen, revealed in the "Exercises," the intensely bitter passages in the *Inquiry* which were to be expunged when he prepared the final edition—all testify to this. Yet underlying Ashley's disgust is man's complete failure to achieve anything like his real potential. It is no longer fashionable to look on Ashley as facile, but he retains the expectation and Bayle does not. The crucial difference is between a blend of old idealism and new optimism on one hand and the Calvinistic assurance of depravity on the other.

Their attitudes toward the universe as a whole diverge just as radically. According to Ashley's own scheme of classification, outlined in the *Inquiry*, he himself is a perfect Theist, believing the cosmos is ruled by one benevolent deity. There can be no real evil, then; evil is merely an illusion resulting from our too limited point of view. More subjectively, what we call evil subsists only in those external circumstances to which we ought to be indifferent, and the virtuous man, one who has properly turned his desires and affections within, is automatically freed from its tyranny. One can imagine how Bayle, the cosmic pessimist, might react to this sort of theodicy. At best, Bayle's religion would fall into one of Ashley's moderately reprehensible subcategories as a mixture of theism with daemonism.

Because both men deplore the prevalence of superstition, hypocrisy, ignorance that acts like authority, and cant in contemporary religion, it is possible to overlook the fact that Ashley's heterodoxy is much more comprehensive than Bayle's; indeed that those elements of his Calvinist heritage which Bayle retains are what Ashley con-

4. Labrousse, *Pierre Bayle*, II, 603.

temns the most in orthodoxy. This truth is further obscured because Ashley's task is essentially positive, whereas Bayle's is in a sense negative, and he is the more obviously skeptical and is far more outspoken. For all his heterodoxy, the compound of doubt and faith in Bayle's religion is closely related to one of the great traditions of seventeenth-century Protestantism, a tradition particularly strong in England. Ashley, though in practice he may seem as pessimistic as Bayle, is remote from all this. In his theism there are few doubts, no real mysteries, no evil, no need for a redeemer.

The fact is that the young Ashley constantly sought out freethinkers. He was speaking facetiously but nonetheless truly when he wrote to Pierre Desmaizeaux (1673–1745) in 1701, "I have a generall Acquaintance (as you very well know) with most of our Modern Authors and free-Writers, severall of whome I have a particular influence over."[5] This involvement with a great number of diverse intellects must have been important to the development of his ideas. The closer an individual was to the old orthodoxy, the guiltier Ashley felt and the less likely he was to acknowledge any debt to him. Thus he exclaims in Rotterdam, "Amongst those that are celebrating superstitious rites, what would I have? Why seek Familiarity with These? can I make my self what they are? Can I reconcile my Opinions to theirs? if not, why do I affect this Intimacy? their Principles & mine are opposite as the Antipodes. I have the utmost contempt for theirs: and they for mine; as far as they know any thing concerning them" (Ex., 124). Among the freethinkers he was more tolerant, but he was always aware of the gulf that divided all of them from himself: "What tho' he be one of the better sort, that seem to philosophize? What if he be a Believer in a certain way? What if he be an Atheist? Yet these, as different as they are amongst themselves, are yet in harmony & agreement with one another, in respect of what they are towards *me*" (Ex., 133). These of course are therapeutic remarks from the Stoic Ashley, and must be read as such. He may well have had Bayle in mind when he wrote them, but as we shall see he wrote his

5. The Earl of Shaftesbury to Pierre Desmaizeaux, St. Giles's House, August 5, 1701, in British Library Add. MSS. 4288, No. 98.

finest tribute to Bayle after the man died. There the fact that this relationship transcended the others is clear enough; there we can see the exhilarating nature of the relationship and its genuine warmth.

Ashley also made other friends in Amsterdam. It must have been through Locke that he met Jean Le Clerc, who later told him, " 'Tis not without a singular Pleasure that I remember the time when being in Holland some Years ago in my House we discours'd about the antient Greeks and the reading of their Books. 'Twas with Delight I heard You deliver Your self very differently from what is usuall with Persons of Your Rank. . . . You . . . affirm'd that the Grecians were more civiliz'd and more polite than we ourselves; notwithstanding we boasted so much of our improv'd wit and more refin'd manners."[6] Le Clerc, a Genevan by birth, was an Arminian minister, who became a professor in the seminary at Amsterdam. His literary output was prodigious. He wrote at least sixteen theological treatises, edited both ancient and modern authors, translated, among others, works of Ashley and Locke, and composed numerous histories, biographies, and philosophical works. He spent thirty years of his life as an editor of three successive cosmopolitan journals of letters and scholarship. If his writings are not especially profound, he was an exceedingly useful citizen of the international republic of letters. The friendship was mutually advantageous: Ashley became Le Clerc's active patron, and Le Clerc, in turn, by early spreading Ashley's gospel made a significant contribution to the latter's strong influence on Continental letters and thought.

Another of Locke's Arminian friends in Amsterdam with whom Ashley became acquainted at this time was the important Dutch theologian Philip van Limborch, who was also a professor in the seminary. Although no record of the meeting survives among the Shaftesbury Papers, the correspondence between Limborch and Ashley and Ashley's annual subsidy to Limborch began after this trip to Holland. A much more substantial theologian than Le Clerc, Limborch was one of the most influential proponents of Arminian doctrines in his era.

6. Jean Le Clerc to the Earl of Shaftesbury, n.d., in PRO 30/24/27/23.

It would be pointless to tabulate the various politicians and merchants whom Ashley met in Rotterdam. Those whose correspondence is useful will be cited later. They do represent, however, another distraction from the goal which Ashley had set for himself. For a number of years after this he was deeply involved in Anglo-Dutch politics—especially as an apologist to the Netherlands for Parliament. One can sympathize with the difficulty of his task: to explain the confusing workings of a centralized state to the citizens of a state where the government was decentralized and even more complex.

Ashley tried to protect himself in Rotterdam from the intrusion of a milieu well suited to destroying whatever apathy he might painfully achieve. Every time he opened his green vellum notebook he could see set down in the opening pages an appendix entitled, "Meeting with people." As I have remarked before, Ashley, at his writing desk or in company, was a man of masks. Sometimes he wore them to conceal the vast difference he sensed, despite his gregariousness, between himself and others; often they are protective; when he is writing they often assist him in saying precisely what he wants to say and assure that it gets the most favorable reception. This appendix to the "Exercises" is fascinating because it reveals just how systematic he hoped to be at the age of twenty-seven in shaping the persona behind which he hid himself: "And first as to COUNTENANCE: that this be suitable. and remember how much depends on it; how instantly a Chang here is follow'd by an absolute Chang of the Mind. And hence it is that Mimickry & Imitation in speech is at all times very dangerouse. . . . How monstrouse all this, when even [a cheerful countenance] as yet befits thee not?" That is, when he has not yet proceeded far enough with the Stoic thought that he dare be cheerful, lest he lapse into the wrong kind of joy.

> In the second place as to Action & Gesture, that this be in the same manner Chast; and leave that other open, loose, independent boisterouse way. But then thou must also leave the same Subjects, the same Designs, the same Ends; & be a New Man, serious, slow, doubting, indecisive; neither a Reformer nor an Entertainer of the World. . . .
>
> And in the third place, observe the Tone of VOICE *Pronounciation* & *Accent*: for this will be no little help. Remember Him of whome it was said that he spake not any word higher than another. Remember

therefore: Neither the Flashy, Suddain, Precipitant Way: nor the Animated: nor the Loud: nor the Emphaticall: But the Still, Quiet, Backward, Soft, Deliberate: so as to be rather remiss & Life-less than Lively in that other manner.

Now Remember SIMPLICITY. No Graces of Speech: no Repartees or Sharpness of Witt: no Raileries, Ironyes or Mockeryes: no Narrations of a certain kind. . . . no Adding, Diminishing, Palliating, Alleviating, Aggravating, Exagerating, Flourishing, Embellishing, & (as He call'd it) *Paraphrazing*. what is this but *Lying*? Thus Extolling, Decrying, Urging, Declaiming, Expatiating, Figures, Metaphors &c: How abhorrent from Simplicity! how repugnant to thy Rule, Law Character! (Ex., 3)

The guilt-ridden often admonish themselves not to do again what they never have done in the first place, but here there would be little point in Ashley decrying anything to which he is not himself susceptible. Even in his more morose twenties he must have had his grandfather's way with people. In a later addition to the appendix he makes one of his very rare references to the man whose memory was such a powerful force in his life: "And Remember the treacherouse Pleasure: *reviving, chearing, entertaining*, moving, *affecting, imprinting*: Imitation of Gd F———Pernitiouse! Ruinouse! All this cutt off. no Pleasure in pleasing: none in being hearken'd to: none in amusing astonishing: no, nor profiting—What *Profiting*? (Wretch!)" (Ex., 3).

The fourth Earl says that Ashley had twelve months to enjoy the way of living he had taken up in Rotterdam; actually, he came back after only nine months, his contentment abandoned because of the importunings of his family and friends. In the "Exercises" he describes the way a true Stoic should react to the demands of the world—though he fears that he cannot live up to the ideal:

Whilst I find it to be my Part in the world, to live, as now, a more retir'd sort of life; to learne withall what I can from the Antients; I will continue in this, chearfully & contentedly. If Greek be a help; I studdy Greek; and this, tho' I were now but beginning, & at the age of the first Cato. If any better part be given me, I accept it. If all Books are taken from me, I accept that too, & am contented. If He who plac'd me here, remove me elsewhere (let the Scene chang to Asia Africa, Constantinople, or Algiers) I am contented. If there remain, there, any part for me to act, that I can act decently & as a Man, 'tis well: if there be none such given; I know my summons; & leaving all others thought and Care, I bend my Mind wholly towards my Retreat: and this, thankfully & joyfully. (Ex., 81)

Acting a part is better than retreat because it fulfills the ideal of *koinonia*. If it is less pleasant, the mature Stoic ought to be indifferent to external circumstances anyway, for to repine against them is to accuse Providence.

Thomas Stringer, who after thirty years remained devoted to the family and their causes, is one of those who implore Ashley to take his place in the world again. His letter is worth quoting at some length because of its candor, and because it spells out clearly some of the facts of Ashley's existence and some of the various emotional pressures under which he lived most of his life. On March 27, 1699, he writes:

I have had many struggles with my selfe about writing unto your Lordship, thinking it look'd a little neglecting in me, not sometimes to write to a Person I am soe highly obliged and doe soe truly honour & love, but on the other hand, considering your obscure retirement did seem to forbid all Correspondence (except from those you have pleased to Licence) I have hetherto (out of respect & duty, tho with great unwillingnesse) forborne to be troublesom, And only contented with hearing by others. I doe not doubt but your Lordship had very good Reasons to satisfye your selfe for leaving your native Country, but those being concealed from your ffreinds, Your Enimies have very much interpreted your journey to your disadvantage, both in relation to the publick & your private concerns. You know the world doth always Judge by what doth appeare & not upon the measures we make to our selves & reserve in our own breasts. . . . My Lord you are under the observation of many eyes. . . . Reputation & honour should be dearest unto you & the greatnesse of it doth not arise from what a man is in himselfe but as he Stands & Acts with relation to his Country. . . . And it is never to be obtained by a private or retired Living, but whosoever quits the World will be forsaken by it. God Almighty hath blessed you with a ffortune & ability suitable to your quality for which you must be accountable. And soe it is a duty to put your selfe into such a post as may be most usefull to the System you belong [to]. As that Exelent book (the inquiry Concerning Virtue) lately published by an Anonimous Author doth admirably well explaine it is worthy every mans study. And if you will consider & duly apply it I dare say it will alter your thoughts in that particular.

As for the private concerns of your ffamily, though you are at that distance it is certainly known & as openly discussed that every thing is acted in it by your direction. And your not being on the place to heare, see, & judge your selfe makes many mistakes Lye hard upon you. The conduct about your sisters produces different effects from what was thought on. The three who were permitted to visit theire relations & others are returned with a Character & have settled a Correspondence with theire Aunts and others whereby they have ffrequent intelligence of transactions in London with the opportunity of supporting theire own credit & depressing theire sister & whoe is complained off for affronting both the Rutland & Mountagu ffamilys by refusing to returne theire visits or paying them any respect which I heare is very highly resented. And that she lyes under the weight of soe many reproaches as I am well assured (from what I have observed of her temper) she will want the Strength of minde to bear them. . . . The truth is here are such things published by letters & discourses as I feare will becom barter for the printers, if not timely prevented.[7]

Stringer may sound too much like Polonius, and his intense concern with appearances ought to repel a young man who is at the moment meditating upon the moral realities of his situation in the world. Yet, no better engine could be devised to breach the walls of Ashley's self-imposed isolation. He knows his own potentialities. His political zeal and his skill in handling people have already been demonstrated. Moreover, the remnants of the political machine which his grandfather built up in the West still persist. Nor can he deny that capacity implies responsibility, as Stringer reminds him, before capping the argument by acidly citing Ashley's own Stoic exposition of each man's duty to serve the whole in the recently published *Inquiry Concerning Virtue*. Stringer fails only to invoke the family motto, *Love, Serve*.

As to reputation and appearances, they are to Ashley in the best way a lifetime preoccupation. He recognizes them as one of the longest and strongest levers that the practical politician has to do his work with. On a more philosophical level, he has already discovered that if one is to live as a Stoic in the everyday world and not be thought self-righteous, insufferably proud, and possibly subversive,

7. Thomas Stringer to Anthony, Lord Ashley, March 27, 1699, in PRO 30/24/44/77/f. 5–5v. Capitalizations are normalized.

some sorts of masks are necessary. So long as his significant actions never run counter to his underlying principles, he can see no wrong in masks, no wrong even in a natural religionist adhering minimally to the forms of an orthodoxy which in truth he regards as little better than paganism. Indeed, masks provide the modern Stoic with the best of both possible worlds—privacy and moral growth in the one and the opportunity to be a more effective force for good in the other. Emotionally, too, Ashley has been hypersensitive about his family's reputation ever since that shocking awakening when at the age of twelve he left the milieu of the family and found himself treated as a pariah at Winchester College on account of his grandfather. Nothing must hinder his effort to rescue his family's name and the memory of his grandfather from slander.

It is not altogether clear as to what has gone seriously awry in the "private concerns" of the family. Three of the sisters have been permitted to run the risks of a visit to London—their father, remember, so feared the city's dangers that he would not permit his wife to journey there even to seek better medical treatment—and they have returned not corrupted, but improved. The recalcitrant fourth sister should be either Frances (1677–1706) or Elizabeth (1681–1744); they inherited much of the strength of will and natural independence of the Manners women—the same aunts who were offended. Whatever gossip is referred to, the prospect of such public trading in the family name would be most painful to Ashley.

Stringer must have observed that Ashley was sometimes quite gregarious, sometimes almost reclusive in his longing to get away from human society. It is unlikely that he knew how complex were the motives behind this peculiarly reciprocal motion in regard to the world and how closely they were bound up with the young nobleman's idealism. Ashley replies to Stringer in the "Exercises": Occasionally, he is satisfied with Seneca's convenient reasoning that the greater world can be better served in isolation: "O, Folly! as if it were not apparent that if thou but continuest thus, & art able to persevere, thy Example alone (when thou least regard'st it) will be of more service than all thou canst do whilst thou retain'st thy selfishness." Also, he fears that the evil of the world will rub off on him, "Thou would'st serve thy Country, right. But consider withall & ask thy self, would'st thou willingly be perjur'd, would'st thou be fals, would'st thou lye, flatter, be debauch'd & dissolute to serve it?" (Ex., 70).

More practically, he knows his own mind well enough to admit that the inevitable gap between ideals and realities may cause such a revulsion, that more harm than good will result. He is one of those persons who can work for a cause with great gusto—up to the point where he finds he must compromise, or where someone compromises him:

> In a little while some new Matter will appear; something striking, astonishing, overpowering, from Family & Relations, from a Sett of Friends, from the State, or some new Nationall Revolutions; immediately as an Enthousiastick thou art snatch'd away: Duty is alleg'd & Morality pleaded. then Hinderances come; & ill success, Disappoints, Disturbances. the Mind is at a loss: Providence is accus'd: and all within disorder'd. Where is now that former Disposition? Where is that Benignity towards Mankind, & that generouse affection towards the Ruler & Soveraign? (Ex., 81)

There must have been other appeals for his return—Locke later congratulates himself on having a part in bringing Ashley out of retirement—in any case, our philosopher overcame his scruples, and Stringer's next letter, just over a month later, is addressed to him at Red Lion Square. He did not have long to rejoice at his success in bringing Ashley home, for shortly thereafter he heard some disquieting rumors:

> I am exceedingly transported with joy to heare you are soe safe & well arrived at London, which makes me thus hasty to be troublesome. It being the happyest news to me that hath these many yeares reached my eares. And though some persons talk that you intend suddenly to returne into Westphalia whether severall are already gone & others goeing, with whom you are to spend your time in a Platonick & retir'd life, confining virtue only within the Shades of the Chestnut Groves. Yet I hope better things from the Grandson of one of the greatest & wisest, as well as the best of men. It is impossible for me to believe that a person of such early ripenesse & worthy Principles who hath already set his hand to the plow & perform'd such eminent services for his Country, should now turn back or sink soe low in dispaire as wholly to desert his duty unto it. And, like Poeticall Lovers, delight in nothing but Shades & Woods at a time when his partes & abilities is most

wanted to serve the publick. If all others should be of that minde, what would be the consequence? And how far the examples of great men may influence is dangerous to think off. What if we live in an age wherein vice & corruption doth abound? Our History tells of former times much like unto it. And yet by the helpe of worthy Patriots England hath hetherto been preserved. And whoe knows what disappointments an industrious & diligent Application may at this time effect. I am sure it will be the Glory of those (both in present & future ages) whoe in such a time of Generall desertion shal be fixed & steady in their Endeavours to save a perishing Kingdom.[8]

We hear no more of the fantastic Westphalian Arcadia, so that there is no way of telling whether Ashley really did consider living out on such a scene the sort of dialogue which he later described in his *Moralists*. In any case the obligations which drew him back to England turned out to be pressing enough to keep him there for a long time. Very few documents have survived for the year 1699, but almost every one relates in some manner to Ashley's rapidly increasing burden of responsibilities. He can no longer evade the truth that, in addition to his demanding political heritage, he has become master of estates not yet inherited and of his family, a term which in his situation extends to the lowliest stable boy.

As a practical example of why Ashley should not even dream of arcadian retreats, Stringer brings up again the offer which has been made for the hand of the nineteen-year-old Lady Dorothy (1679–1749). The negotiations are interesting—one hopes they are not typical of Ashley's numerous experiences of this kind, but we cannot know because in none of the other cases have many details survived. The suitor is one Richard Butler, who apparently lives in chambers in one of the Inns of Court. A relative, Mr. Gervoise, "often mentioned the Lady with such a character as induced the other to make this offer. And at the same time gave him to understand that he was refused to court her." This, Stringer comments, "I only take to be a genteel Excuse because I never heard he ever made any proposall that way." By the end of May the dowry has been settled tentatively at £6,000 and Stringer is confident this will be satis-

8. Thomas Stringer to Anthony, Lord Ashley, May 5, 1699, in PRO 30/24/44/77/f. 10–10v.

factory to Butler. The sum is large considering the family's circumstances at that moment, though not impossibly so, yet it seems the larger because the prospective bridegroom turns out to be less prosperous than was thought. The £12,000 he has spoken of is not actually in his hands, though he does have a thousand pounds a year. A few days later, Stringer, who is the sole intermediary, feels assured enough of the success of the negotiations that he urges Ashley to show the correspondence to Lady Dorothy, who presumably knows nothing of all this. Unfortunately, Ashley does so, only to be informed on the tenth of June that Butler's relatives are now pressing him "not to sink below £7,000." Stringer decides to let matters rest while the prospects of the match work on Butler, but in a few weeks the latter overplays his hand, even to the point of being brusque in his insistence on the new sum, though he seems to have been unprepared for the reaction of Ashley, who then just as brusquely announced that he wished to hear nothing more of this particular suitor.[9]

Apparently, poor Lady Dorothy was unprepared for this outcome, too. The unhappy Stringer begs Ashley to permit her to come to Ivy Church: "I have wrote her Ladyship some short account of his rude behavior in it, but if I could but see her I believe I can convince her that she hath an happy deliverance." Perhaps he was more practiced in the art of consolation than his well-meaning but sometimes blundering wife Jane, who, apprehensive of slander like so many who had some connection with the fortunes of the first Earl, tells Ashley how happy she is to realize that "twas only theire cunning to get more mony & not that any malitious account of your family had been the occasion of so miraculus behavior; which I must own was my greatest dread." Ashley must have reflected that more such experiences might well lie ahead in the life of a man blessed with four sisters.

No sooner were the negotiations for Lady Dorothy's hand thus unhappily concluded than Locke brought up the matter of Ashley's own marriage. By 1699, the subject must have been considered a number of times, though the letters surviving refer to only two earlier occasions, the first when Ashley was sixteen. On March 17,

9. All of the relevant correspondence is in PRO 30/24/44/77.

1688, the second Earl wrote to his stepmother, Margaret, the Countess Dowager, to ask her if she would approach the widow of William, Lord Russell, Lady Rachel (1637–1723), to find out if a match could be made for her youngest daughter, Catherine (1676–1711). As Lady Margaret said in her reply, such a match would be an "inexpressable advantage" to the family. The Russells were immensely wealthy, and the coupling of the two names would brighten whatever hopes the Earl had for Anthony's career in politics. Catherine's father, who had been executed by Charles in 1683 and who with Algernon Sidney was the last English aristocrat to die for his political opinions, was to be a Whig hero for generations, and his father received a dukedom, in part as compensation.

The Countess, however, was unsuccessful:

> Upon the furst opertunity, I acquainted that Excelent person my Lady Russell with your desiers to me; (& my owne wishes & indeavers to the utmost shall be added, even to the stratening my self in a great degree) She received your Lordship's expretions with great servilety . . . of your good will, in desiering to have any alliance with her, for which she returnes your Lordship her hearty thankes, but assures me she will not harken to any propositians, so as to ingage for her till she has attained more yeares, but be absolutely free, in all considerations.[10]

Lady Russell had good reason to demur. Apparently Catherine's sister at an early age had received a proposal too attractive to refuse, and her mother did not want to commit Catherine's future by a betrothal at the age of twelve. The Earl may not have known that the child was this young, but her youth seems to have given the Countess Dowager no pause. When she was eighteen Catherine wed Ashley's first cousin, Lord Roos, later second Duke of Rutland (1676–1721).

In 1696, James Tyrell (1642–1718) proposed to Locke another match for Ashley, a young woman whose present fortune was "£16.000, besides some Jewells, £200 per annum Inheritance after the death of her Mother, and the blessing of an old rich Grandmother with whom she lives, & is able to give £5000, or £6000 more when she dies; and it is likely she will doe it, because she is very

---

10. Margaret, Dowager Countess of Shaftesbury to the Earl of Shaftesbury, March 24, 1688, in PRO 30/24/22/1/23.

fond of her."[11] It is not certain whether matters went any further, but Locke probably did tell Ashley about the proposal.

In 1699, when a Mrs. Berkeley suggests an even more opulent candidate to Locke, he writes Ashley that

> there is a yonge Lady Handsome well-natured well bread discreet with a great many other good qualitys which I think your Lordship would like, whose mother can make her worth twenty thousand pounds. besides this there is but one yonge man betwixt her and an estate of three or four thousand pounds a year. This is writ to me out of an Esteem of your Lordship and with a designe that I should tell it you: And therfor if I were lesse a servant to your Lordship than I am it would not be fit I should let it die with me. What the meaning of it is your Lordship needs not have explain'd to you. But what answer you will think fit I should returne that I must expect from you.[12]

Ashley did not long reflect on the merits of this offer, nor is it likely that he sought more details, for although Locke is in London and Ashley in Dorset, within ten days of writing, Locke has his answer and he poignantly replies:

> My Lord,
> How much soever the world wonders that you doe not marry it is certain that you are the best judg when that ought to be, and therfor I shall not enter into the matter. Only I beg leave of your Lordship to say, (what, if he were alive, I should say to your Grandfather, and perhaps more too) that such offers are not to be met with every day. I take this liberty because I can assure your Lordship that you are not at all mistaken when you think I am concerned for you. I have not much to hope or expect in this world, But should be very glad if in the small remainder of my life I might have the oportunity to serve you in any businesse that might be usefull and acceptable to you.[13]

Locke and other friends of the family had good reason to worry over Ashley's failure to marry. He was now twenty-eight, and his once robust constitution had been weakened by illness. His only surviv-

---

11. James Tyrell to John Locke [June 1696], in de Beer, V, 651. Tyrell, who was an intimate friend of Locke, translated and published in a modified form Bishop Cumberland's *De legibus naturae* (1672), which must have influenced Ashley when he came to write his *Inquiry*.
12. John Locke to Anthony, Lord Ashley, August 5, 1699, in de Beer, VI, 665. I am indebted to Dr. Esmond S. de Beer for some of the details of this incident.
13. John Locke to Anthony, Lord Ashley, August 15, 1699, *ibid.*, 670.

ing brother was likewise unmarried, and, though only twenty-three, must have already revealed that he had little inclination to become a man of affairs. The second Earl was still in his late forties, but he was in such a sorry state of health that there was no possibility that he would remarry and father more children.[14]

Ashley had already given his answer to all suggestions that he marry and father children to carry on the line. He wrote in Holland:

> Is it no longer in the power of any Chance whatsoever to raise any contrary affection, or to interrupt the course of That which carryes me with the Whole of Things, & makes me to be unanimouse with Deity? If it be otherwise; it is in vain to plead Nature, & say, I lament & grieve: but I am *Naturall*: This is the Part of *a Father*-Wretch! . . . What hast thou to do with *Nature*? What pretence of being *Naturall*? . . . But all other Creatures are thus affected towards their Young—And are all other Creatures, therefore, sensible of that other Relation? Were they made to consider Nature as thou dost? Were they brought into the World to contemplate the order of It & recognize the Author & Supream, joyn themselves to Him, & assist in his Administration & Rule? Were they made Free, un-hinderable, invincible, irrefragable, as to that Inward part? . . . If not; what should they follow but that other affection, which, with respect to them, is Naturall? (Ex., 116–17)

Here is the Stoic, standing arrogantly aloof from a world populated by *idiotai*, but it is also a young man longing desperately for tranquillity and for freedom from the world which had crushed his grandfather, a young man unwilling to give any hostages to fortune or to the mankind he mistrusted. Yet Locke's second letter must have in some degree accused Ashley and continued to do so, for this letter is one of the very few he ever annotated: first, with a fragmentary quotation, "freed from those pursuits of vulgar men; may best ... ... the secrets of the Gods"; and then at some later date he

14. The second Earl was, moreover, an only son, and, one might think, succession technically would fall to the only brother of the first Earl of Shaftesbury, George Cooper, of Clarendon Park, Wiltshire, or to his descendants. Cooper, if he was still alive at this date, would be at least seventy-five years of age; his eldest and perhaps his only son, George, must have been near fifty and was childless. Later, when the third Earl, as yet childless, wrote his own will, he must have known that the Cooper line had died out, or he simply ignored it, because after assuming that the estate would go to Maurice if still alive, or to his sons, if he had any, he then leaves it first to possible male heirs of Dorothy and then of Elizabeth.

scribbled in red chalk, "/selfish/then how; now not." The hiatus is Ashley's.

Whether or not he had opportunity for contemplation, Ashley seems to have spent most of his time in the months following his return from Holland in the relative seclusion of Wimborne St. Giles. In September, Sir John Cropley writes begging him to return to the world: "Methinks my Ld. continuing so well you might come see yr friends . . . the society is well & always have yr remembrances." The letter reveals that Cropley had been enough in touch with his old friend during recent months to be influenced and perhaps amused by Ashley's Stoic notions. This is interesting, because in the "Exercises" Ashley always speaks of his own conversion as something very private which sets him apart from other men; he intends to teach only by the example he will set. Cropley, an account of whose splenetic and melancholy behavior has reached Ashley's ears, also says:

> Tho you may laugh at what I tel you. if I have had sp[l]een it has been on this subject: the plain imperfection and weaknesses I too plainly discern in myself. for I see tis evident no happiness can be come att but by a subjection of passions. which is a subject I have but early enter'd on & what is worse make slow proficiency in. I am certain in my determinations of a happy state yet by ill habits have but an ill prospect of getting in to it. how to remove hope and fear, and yet to think it strongly necessary as I doe is not only difficult but disquieting. I see clearly every thing that departs from that rectitude or reason nature has given to make him happy by so much as he wants of it, but so much wide is he of his intended happiness.[15]

The two men by this time had been close friends for at least twelve years, but in part because the friendship was so close that they spent much time together and thereby had the less need to correspond, this is our first glimpse of Sir John. Nothing we shall learn of him hereafter will show that he made much progress into Stoicism.

In Holland Ashley had dreamed of having a house of his own in London, "*a private Retreat*: a studdy: Gardening: *Planting*." Then his Stoic persona asked himself "Is this Philosophical?" On his re-

15. Sir John Cropley to Anthony, Lord Ashley, September 1, 1699, in PRO 30/24/20/11.

turn his longing for retreat and love of possessions soon won out over philosophy, and he bought a property from the Bovey family. This house in Little Chelsea is worth pausing to consider because it is the only one where we know what alterations Ashley made to suit his own needs and tastes. No matter how much conventional evidence they may collect, most biographers are sorely aware that they lack much of the evidence by which they daily judge their own contemporaries. How often we depend upon the surroundings in which a man lives and how seldom does the biographer of someone born, say, before 1750 have any real notion of these surroundings, much less a Strawberry Hill, by which to form an opinion of him.

Ashley had a practical reason for seeking new lodgings in London. One side of him had always been drawn to city life and his duties in Parliament would offer him little choice in the matter anyway. After the household in St. John's Court was broken up in 1692, on the death of Margaret, the Countess Dowager, letters to Ashley are directed to Devonshire Street, near Red Lion Square. This square, now a quiet backwater surrounded by the taller buildings of important thoroughfares, lies a few hundred yards north of Lincoln's Inn Fields and on the other side of High Holborn. Ashley was able to look up Devonshire Street—it ran north from the square—and out over open country to the village of Hampstead. It is likely that green fields spread to the east and west, but directly south the city was built solidly down to the river. Thus any wind which was at all southerly would bring the dreaded smoke down upon him and according to contemporary accounts London may have been smokier than it is today. Furthermore Parliament met during the colder months.

Little Chelsea, on the other hand, was a small village, a few dwellings strung out along Fulham Road, over three miles from the center of the city. Near the banks of the Thames to the south stood some great houses but the area round about was largely parks and open fields. Ashley's new home was on the south side of Fulham Road on the present site of St. Stephen's Hospital. The grounds must have included the whole block now taken up by the hospital and perhaps more. The house had been built in 1635 by Sir James Smith and was sold to Ashley by the heirs of his widow. From Ashley's hands it passed to the chronicler Narcissus Luttrell, then to his relatives, the

Wynnes, and, finally after being purchased in 1787 by St. George's Church, Hanover Square, it served many generations of the parish poor as a workhouse. In the early years of the present century, topographers refer to the building as still standing.

A woodcut made before the house was put to these humble uses reveals a long, narrow rectangular building of four stories in an austere seventeenth-century style. The main part of the building has a simple gable roof and a large chimney at each end—it must have presented an imposing facade over the wall which separated it from the road. According to Daniel Lysons, it does not appear that Ashley "pulled down Sir James Smith's house, but altered it and made comfortable additions, by a building, 50 feet in length, which projected into the garden. It was secured with an iron door, the window shutters were of the same metal, and there were iron plates between it and the house to prevent all communication of fire of which the learned and noble Peer seems to have entertained great apprehensions. The whole of the new building, though divided into a gallery and two small rooms (one of which was his Lordship's bedchamber), was fitted up as a library."[16] This library wing had a notably beautiful ceiling and on the back a balcony, from which a staircase led down to the garden.

The interior seems to have impressed visitors as elegant and efficiently comfortable. In 1707, Isabella, Lady Wentworth (d. 1733), was invited there by Shaftesbury's housekeeper and described the visit to her son Lord Raby, later Earl of Strafford (1672–1735):

My daughter Wentworth carryd me yesterday to Chelcy to see Mrs. Skinner, whoe is with Lord Shasbary not as a sarvent but as a freind. She was to see me and invyted us to walk in the Gardens, prommisseing me I should not see my Lord, but he sent to her to know whoe we wear, and came to us and showed us his gardens and all his ingenious contryvencis in his hous, gave us fruet and french wyne and sack, and Tea, and spoake very hansomly of you, and hee is com to see me at Twittnam. I am in lov with him, and alsoe with his wey of living, it is very delightfull; he is very obliging and has a mighty ingagin way, but he loocks as if he was very short lived, which is pety. Was he twenty years older and I as many years younger, I would lay al the traps I could

16. Daniel Lysons, *The Environs of London* (4 vols; 1792–96), III, 628.

to gett him . . . he is one that I could sooner be in lov with then any-
body I ever yett see, his youmore and myne are soe alyke. . . . he man-
agis his hous, and many of his affairs very lyke you, and is neet in his
person lyke you.[17]

A century and a half later, Mrs. S. C. Hall could still see some of
those features of the house which had delighted Lady Wentworth:
delicately carved staircases "whose neatly cut spiral banisters . . .
give the house altogether a Flemish formality and preciseness," rich
stucco work, and on the oak with which the interior was finished, an
abundance of panel paintings, even on the strips above the door. A
painting over the fireplace, executed on the panel, represents a group
of classic ruins and statues in the taste of William the Third. If his
fine house had to become what it did, the charitable Ashley might
have been pleased that one of the inmates told Mrs. Hall that "she
liked to look up at that bit of a picture, when she was sick-a-bed; it
took away the notion of a work house."[18]

The gardens were laid out as regularly as the house. There is abundant evidence in his plans for the gardens of St. Giles's House of
Ashley's love of horticulture, and apparently he practiced it here, for,
if Lyson's source is correct, he "was very fond of the culture of fruit
trees, and his gardens were planted with the choicest sorts, particularly every kind of vine which would bear the open air of this climate."[19] The whole was surrounded by a high wall interspersed with
alcoves. In the south wall was constructed a summerhouse, from the
second story of which one could look out across the fields to the
Thames. Here Locke is supposed, erroneously, to have written part
of his *Essay*. There were other such curious traditions associated
with the house: the "Chancellor's closet," for example, and it is very
doubtful that, if Addison wrote any *Spectators* there, he did so while
Ashley was its master. One becomes more tolerant of the foibles of
popular historians as he becomes better acquainted with the blun-
ders of professionals, but it is not too much to hope that one tradi-

17. Lady Wentworth to Lord Raby, July 8, 1707, in *The Wentworth Papers, 1705–
1739*, ed. James J. Cartwright (1883), 59–60.
18. Anna Maria Fielding Hall, *Pilgrimages to English Shrines* (1850), 195, 196.
Mrs. Hall was something of an expert, and there is no reason to doubt her description
of the paintings as of Shaftesbury's day.
19. Lysons, *Environs of London*, III, 628.

tion, at least, is authentic, that the great parliamentary hero John Pym lived in the house during the Civil Wars.

Those ingenious contrivances which seven years later charmed Lady Wentworth must have been installed over a period of time, but the rebuilding of the house in Little Chelsea is the first tangible sign we have of Ashley's career as a virtuoso. From 1699 on, he becomes more and more the virtuoso, a fact which affects his writing as much as the pattern of his life. This trend is confirmed by two letters written to Ashley from Italy by John Closterman, who must have already painted portraits for Ashley and was to paint still more.[20] Some twentieth-century critics would not approve Ashley's choice of a portraitist; this, however, must reflect some changes in taste over the intervening years, for the artist had a distinguished clientele: the King and Queen of Spain, Queen Anne, the families of the Dukes of Marlborough, Rutland, Argyle, Queensbury, and Chandos, and among commoners, John Dryden and Henry Purcell.

From Florence in August of 1699, Closterman writes that he can find no master well-qualified enough to execute two statues according to Ashley's instructions. In Rome a while later he has no better success. Most artisans are busy with commissions for the Jubilee year, and, anyway, Roman taste and workmanship have sadly fallen. Perhaps the figures—which accompanying sketches reveal to be Justice and Prudence, one with scales and fasces, the other holding a snake and a hand mirror—would be best carved in England according to drawings which can be made in Rome. Then Ashley could have the pleasure of supervising the work, and he, Closterman, the privilege of a long visit to St. Giles's House where they could "hourly" have their "thoughts together." Since on his return he did make an extended stay with Ashley, it is possible that he had done so before and already helped shape the young virtuoso's tastes. Surely, either the two men's inclinations are quite similar, or the artist knows what his patron wants to hear. The true models for all modern artists should be, of course, the Ancients.[21]

Ashley's virtuosoship is symbolized by the folly tower he had

20. Closterman's dates are given variously as 1656–1713 and 1660–1711. He was born in Osnabrück, Hanover, and emigrated to England in 1681.
21. John Closterman to Anthony, Lord Ashley, Florence, August 19, 1699 NS, in

built about this time atop a hill, a short ride from St. Giles's House. It was restored in the early part of this century, so that one can get a good idea of what it must have looked like then. Envision a perfectly square tower, covered with a stuccolike material, two stories high with a short brick chimney at each corner. Above this a reddish-tiled, hemispherical cupola, with eight metal ridges on it, which spring from its base to where they all come together at the top and are surmounted by a ball. As one mounts the short hill toward it, the family crest can be seen in high relief in the stucco. Inside there is a single room where Ashley's servant awaited his call. A simple stair-case leads up to the brighter study above, whence it is said one can see the Isle of Wight on a clear day.

Even though his father may have been alive when the tower was built, there must have been many rooms in St. Giles's House where Ashley could find enough solitude for study and meditation, with-out this extravagance; so that it became for him the image of the self-indulgent vanities of the world, to which he felt, as a Stoic, he was too much drawn. Its stubby shape appears sketched in his note-books—along with his symbols for St. Giles's House, his involve-ment with gardening, the home in Chelsea, and so forth—when he rails against his own worldliness.

That during his most intensely Stoic phase Ashley should be turn-ing into a virtuoso is one of those paradoxes which are the basic modules of his personality. As on so many topics in the "Exercises," we may hear only one Ashley talking, but the other one, who is drawn so strongly to what is being railed at, is never far away:

> What miserable Subjects are those in which thou hast been so long busied & taken up, & which have left such Impressions behind? *a neat House: Garden: Seat: Apartment: Pictures: Trees: Fabricks: Modells: Design & ordering.* Remember to distinguish. Is it to please thy self, stand by, alone, look upon this, & admire it? Or is it that Others may? What Others? Consider only *Who;* Are they the common people who repine at it, & justly? are they the Rich, who are Rivalls in these mat-ters, & see with Envy & Detraction? are they Men of Business & Em-ployment: they have no relish for things of this kind, & admire some-

---

PRO 30/24/45/i/25–26; to the Earl of Shaftesbury, Rome, before Easter 1700, in PRO 30/24/21/230.

thing else, which is in there own way, & what they are used to. Are they therefore a few friends for whome all this is reserv'd? O, Folly! is this the way of serving them? are these the studdyes in their behalf? Remember also this: that by so much as they are better People, so much the less have they any admiration of these matters. (Ex., 95, 104)

No passage could better show the dangers of taking much of what is said in the "Exercises" at face value. The novice must shun these objects of the virtuoso's enthusiasm because they place him in the power of external things and subject him to the whims of others, and because they distract him from the main task of becoming a moral enthusiast, a moral virtuoso. Later on in the notebooks, Ashley is more prone to admit that the pursuit of worldly beauty has its place, however inferior—that underneath the analogy between the two sorts of virtuosi lies the truth that they are both pursuing a beauty which, though highly imperfect in one instance, yet springs from a common source. By then he felt secure enough in his Stoicism to dwell on this.

All of the letters that have survived for Ashley in 1699, except the first one, are either to or from St. Giles's House. The indenture for the leasehold of his Chelsea house was not signed until the beginning of October and, as we have seen, many alterations were needed. He had other reasons for staying on in Dorset, in any case—first, the family land and its people. There is no reason why a well-run estate ought not be able to run along for quite a while with no more attention than the second Earl was able to give it, but this estate, in addition to having been plundered so long by Williams, must have been poorly staffed, and all that the paragon of stewards, John Wheelock, could do in the short time he had been there would not suffice to make it run without a master. As we shall see, this is defining the Earl's role very narrowly. He was, or ought to have been, the chief representative of law and order over thousands of acres of land. No doubt others filled the need, as they did on a number of estates. This could only mean, though, that for some years the safety of law and the hope for an orderly life had been only intermittently achieved and fulfilled in this part of the world.

Another reason for Ashley to remain at home was his father's health. The second Earl's unexpectedly long, painful life came to an end on November 2, in his forty-seventh year. Shaftesbury preserved some of the replies to his letters telling the family of his father's death. Few of the writers can find the heart to praise. Oddly, the Earl of Rutland is most pained by the death of his "Brother Shaftesbury" and says "it will be a great satisfaction to me to see you all before I follow your dear Father and Mother." Of all the writers of letters of condolences in the family, he had the most life left. Despite his evident sympathy, the letter could not have been altogether pleasant reading for Anthony. In a typically stiff-necked way he took pains to point out that he had heard from Lady Russell and others of his brother-in-law's death at some time before his nephew's letter arrived at Haddon Hall on the fourteenth, or before.

Only one letter of condolence from outside the family was kept, from William O'Brien, third Earl of Inchiquin (c. 1666–1719) in Dublin. The records show that the Earl took his seat, rather tardily, in the House of Lords about the same time Anthony became a member of Parliament, where it is likely they met since they held similar views. The letter is interesting because it reveals what sort of attitude Anthony must have maintained publicly toward his father despite their differences. Inchiquin says that he never met the second Earl but he knows that as a father "he was a very Kind one to you & the good nature & tenderness I always perceived in you towards him, assures me that your looseing him is an affliction to you."[22]

One hopes that Anthony in retrospect felt just the way Inchiquin thought he would, for it is difficult for an outsider not to feel compassion for the second Earl of Shaftesbury. His weaknesses were less of his own making than is the case with most people, and though Anthony could not know of Lady Dorothy's touching letters to her mother about her young husband, he must have reflected on his father's real concern for bringing up his children properly. In one respect, too, the second Earl would have been no disappointment to the first. Seven children: a distinguished son to carry on the name, a translator of Xenophon whose work was to last a hundred years, and the two longest-lived daughters, both mothers of families distinguished in the West.

22. The third Earl of Inchiquin to the Earl of Shaftesbury, November 13, 1699, in PRO 30/24/45/i/27.

❧IV❦

The Patterns of
Shaftesbury's Earlier Thought
1691–1703

The general principles of Shaftesbury's political thinking in the 1690s can be inferred, but until 1698 there is no indication of what direction his philosophical ideas had been taking since his debates with Locke early in the decade. In that year, with his publication of *Select Sermons of Dr. Whichcote*, the patriarch of the Cambridge Platonists, we get some glimpse of the results of Locke's tutelage, of years of intensive reading of the Ancients and the Moderns, and of the effects of his association in the years immediately previous with liberal thinkers in general, and with some who were then considered more than liberal—Socinians, Deists, and Quakers.[1]

Twelve sermons, filling 452 pages, were selected from two manuscript volumes which Shaftesbury owned. The first six are a series dealing with the foundations of Christianity, natural and revealed; and the second group treats diverse subjects. At the end of his preface, Shaftesbury remarks that since Whichcote preached only from brief notes, the versions from which he must print are incomplete transcripts by those who heard the sermons, but that every addition which has been necessary to complete the text is marked with an asterisk and italicized; he was to become even more concerned with good editing later. A holograph note in one copy of the edition says that the actual editing was done by the Reverend William Stephens (1647–1718). Shaftesbury often employed others to do such chores for him, but in this case at least the annotations on the manuscript appear to be in his own hand. The manuscript also reveals that the sermons are from very late in Whichcote's life, 1678–1680; and

---

1. Bishop Benjamin Whichcote (1609–1683). The manuscripts of his sermons are PRO 30/24/24/16 and 30/24/24/17.

more interesting, it suggests how the sermons became available to Shaftesbury, for one of the two manuscript volumes is inscribed "Tho. ffirmin his book." Thomas Firmin (1632–1697), a Quaker merchant and Socinian, whose philanthropy made him perhaps the most notable practical exponent of Whichcote's principles, had been the friend of the first Earl of Shaftesbury, and through him had developed his strong friendship with John Locke. Whether or not Firmin's death the year before accounts for the timing of Shaftesbury's publication of the sermons, it was opportune, because the public seems to have been receptive—five additional volumes of Whichcote were published during the decade following.[2]

There is no irony in the fact that Shaftesbury's first publication should be an introduction to a volume of sermons. First, the sermons are from the hand of a Latitudinarian whose Platonism he admires, a man who preached the right sort of religion. Secondly, we should keep in mind Shaftesbury's own concepts of who should believe what. For his servants, for his farmers, for the great mass of mankind there is no hope except by earnest and continued attention to the moral dictates of religion from the earliest age. Even if these people escape from superstition born of ignorance, Shaftesbury admits that the fruits of self-interest—greed, laziness, and dishonesty—are likely to dominate. The paternalism of the system of which he is a part, and his own hopes, may encourage him to give them a second or a third chance, but often, he knows, they will fail anyway. Even among the better favored who have special opportunities or education to help them to turn out right, there is always the danger of backsliding—witness the letters he was later to write to Henry Wilkinson, Arent Furly, and Michael Ainsworth. Only the very few who through intensive reading of the ancients have come

2. S. W. Singer relates an anecdote that when Shaftesbury found the Dowager Countess reading a manuscript sermon by Whichcote, he asked her why she bothered when so many by others were already printed. She replied that she could find none in print so good as Whichcote's. The anecdote may well be true, but it tells us nothing about the source of Shaftesbury's manuscript. The sermons he published are from a book obviously bound when Firmin owned it. In the anecdote, unbound sermons are referred to, and the Countess, of course, died in 1693. See Notes & Queries, Series I (June 15, 1850), II, 33–34.

to love virtue for her own sake may not need religion. Still fewer are those who, like Shaftesbury, are able and qualified to follow Stoicism.

According to the introduction, the sermons are published to confute Thomas Hobbes, who has substituted for whatever good affections man may have "*only one Master-Passion,* Fear, *which has, in effect devour'd all the rest, and left room only for that infinite Passion towards* Power after Power, Natural *(as he affirms)* to All Men, *and never ceasing but in Death.*" Have there not, Shaftesbury asks, been enough replies to Hobbes in the previous half century? Yes, indeed, but too many of Hobbes's opponents have played right into his hands. "*Had not the Poyson of these Immoral, and (in reality)* Atheistical *Principles been diffused more than 'tis easie to imagine . . . we should, perhaps, where Morality was concerned, have heard less of* Terror and Punishment; *and more of* Moral Rectitude *and* Good-Nature."[3] In reaction to Hobbes, those who disagree with him have sought to buttress revelation and the spirit by stressing the certainty of reward and punishment in a future state, thereby basing religion on Hobbes's notion that the nature of man is wholly motivated by fear and self-interest. But fear alone is no better basis for religion than it is for morals, for ultimately both religion and morals must be founded on love.

If the same industry had been applied to the correction of Hobbes's "*Moral Principles, as has been bestow'd in refuting some other of his Errours, it might perhaps been of more Service to Religion, in the Main.*"[4] While some of Whichcote's own disciples and other Latitudinarians did concern themselves with the basic ethical implications of Hobbes's system, Shaftesbury is correct in complaining that most of the protest concerned other matters: the philosopher's politics and, above all, the implications for religion of his materialism. The extreme sensitivity of so many of Hobbes's contemporaries regarding his denial of the existence of the spirit, in particular, leads one to suspect that their objections were not altogether theoretical. In theory, a material deity might be acceptable, but who in practice

3. Benjamin Whichcote, *Select Sermons of Dr. Whichcot[e],* A5, A5v. The preface is unpaginated.
4. *Ibid.,* A4v.

could calmly give up all hope of an afterlife, or for that matter even bear to have that hope questioned?

The reason Shaftesbury is equally sensitive with respect to the tendency of religionists to defend the existence of the spirit at the expense of human nature—"*as if Good-Nature, and Religion, were Enemies*"—is not so easily understood today. Judging from the letters which he wrote to Locke when he was coming of age, Shaftesbury was a moralist from the very start of his mature life, and a moralist may not expect much of humanity, but he must have some sort of ideals by which to measure and condemn it. The governess whom Locke had sought out for the four-year-old Anthony laid a good foundation on which his later masters must have built well, for he grew up with a firm confidence in the rational ideals of the classical age, especially as typified by Cicero and by the Stoics. The best hope of maintaining these eternal and immutable verities independent of revelation was through the still vital tradition of natural law, for by the 1690s a point of equilibrium had been forever passed, and the world view which had enabled earlier English humanists to fuse these ideals with Christianity was fading away.

Today there is some debate over Hobbes's exact position on natural law, but to many of its seventeenth-century proponents there was no question that he was attempting to substitute for it positive law—the law of the magistrate, for instance. Good nature is involved because those writers who were most influential on English notions of natural law based its existence upon the social inclinations of man, not actual but potential. No matter how much man may have fallen away from his potentialities—his true nature— there remains within him some spark of affection for his kind, parallel to that which he feels for his close kindred. Natural law is, then, for Samuel Puffendorf (1632–1694), and for Bishop Richard Cumberland (1632–1718), the law of human nature—as it had been earlier for Hugo Grotius (1583–1645), "*naturalis juris mater est ipsa humana natura.*"[5]

This is in accord with one of the prime meanings of *natural* and *nature* in the seventeenth century, yet we persistently misunder-

5. Hugo Grotius, *De juri belli ac pacis libri tres* (Washington, 1913), f.5v.

stand it because perforce we see nature either romantically or scientifically. Consider the absurdity of Whichcote's hoary injunction "follow nature," which, instead of being a sternly moral invocation of the whole classical code of ethical conduct, now seems to suggest that he wants us to go back to the woods à la Rousseau or, conversely, to become the sort of automaton subject to external laws that we appear to be when viewed from the artificial perspective of the detached scientific observer, biologist, or psychologist. To interpret *natural law* in this latter fashion, is to behave very much like those who attempted to codify the observations of early economists into a body of law analogous to that which used to govern Newtonian physics. To the seventeenth-century humanist, *nature* was *human nature* or it referred to a general system of which man is an integral part and, more important, the mirror, or microcosm of the whole. Thus Shaftesbury points out that in making man utterly selfish, Hobbes not only destroys the basis of ethics in man, but casts doubt as to the goodness of creation and of God, in whose image man is made.

Of course, there is a danger in making Hobbes too much the scapegoat. For years attention was paid to what positive effects his philosophy had; now that the negative influence of his thinking is being recognized it is easy to see Hobbes as shaping by indirection the whole structure of Restoration ethical and religious thought, and the general outcry of his contemporaries against him makes this more plausible.[6] In truth, Hobbes described perhaps too effectively currents which were already running strongly but covertly when he began to write, and thus the resentment against them was focused upon him, just as Shaftesbury himself came to be regarded as the father of sentimental morality in his own century. In a universe which was coming to be regarded as a machine composed of atoms and susceptible to empirical study, a chasm had opened between matter and spirit and it was inevitable that someone should give voice to a growing sentiment that the best solution was to assume that matter alone counted.

6. For a balanced analysis, see Samuel I. Mintz, *The Hunting of the Leviathan: Seventeenth-Century Reactions to the Materialism and Moral Philosophy of Thomas Hobbes* (Cambridge, 1962).

Certainly, one of Shaftesbury's chief impulses in seeking a humanistic basis for ethics independent of revelation owes none of its momentum to a reaction against Hobbes. Conventional religion as he conceives it offers little or nothing on which to ground a moral system, and unless he can find some other basis, there will be no morality at all. One wonders how readers of the preface to Whichcote's *Sermons* could have missed the irony in lines like these, especially since they are followed ultimately by the remark that Whichcote never esteemed his own sermons worthy of publication:

> *Amongst those many Things which are made Publick; it may be thought, perhaps, of* Sermons; *that they are, of any other, the least wanted; and for the future, least likely to be found wanting: since to that rich and inexhaustible Store, with which the Learned and Orthodox Divines of* England *have already furnished us, there is daily fresh addition, from worthy and able Hands. Neither have we cause to fear a Cessation in this kind; or that so great a Blessing is likely to fail us, for the future; having such security, not only from the unwearied Zeal of present Divines (of whom we may always hope a worthy Succession) but, from the just esteem which the Publick never fails to shew, for such pious Discourses: Upon which account, we find that many of these are every day made Publick; and as it were, forced into the World; not withstanding the great Modesty of their Authors, whose Humble Thoughts, and devoutly resigned Affections, lead them not towards Eminence, and Advancement in the World.*[7]

He goes on to remark archly, "*It is certain, that we must not ever imagine, nor can it enter into a Mind truly Christian, that because we see not an apparent Change for the better in the Lives of Christian Professors; that, therefore all* Preaching *is ineffectual.*" Then Shaftesbury touches lightly on the strange paradoxes that Englishmen are no more prone to ethical behavior than their neighbors and, indeed, that Christians in general "*are said to be rather inferior in this respect, to the Civilized People, whether Pagan or Mahometan, lying round them.*"[8] From this dangerous ground he turns to the attack on Hobbes, a safer opponent for the skeptic.

Although in his choice of sermons Shaftesbury was true to his edi-

---

7. Whichcote, *Sermons*, A2–A2v.
8. *Ibid.*, A2v–A3. Note *Civilized*; Ashley is no primitivist.

torial ideals in giving a rather full picture of Whichcote's thought, including much that it is unlikely he himself could have agreed with, the *Sermons* offer useful commentary on Shaftesbury's own ideas because they define more precisely some of the points in the preface and develop their implications. When one looks at the actual ideas behind the writings he discovers virtually nothing, at least in the later Whichcote, that is exclusively Platonic. Central to his system is a deity who is good and thereby beneficent, though neither he nor his actions are in the naïve sense scrutable. Holiness consists in praise and imitation, "in substance, *our Imitation of God in his Moral Perfections, and Excellency of Goodness, Righteousness and Truth.*"[9] As in *Paradise Lost*, praise has no savor of merit if the praiser is forced into it; man's will must therefore be free. He has truth to guide him to actions in imitation of God's goodness, the truth of first inscription, and revelation, which was given to man to offset the ruin of the former truth in the Fall.

The last is thoroughly orthodox, of course—witness the contemporary Theophilus Gale (1628–1678) in his *Court of the Gentiles* (1669): "Man by reason of his fall being greatly *wounded* in his *Intellectuals* and thereby disenabled to *contemplate* that *Natural Wisdom, objective light,* which shines in the *book of Nature;* it pleased Divine Wisdom to send forth a book of Grace, a more resplendent and bright beam of Divine Revelation." Yet, as might be expected, Whichcote does not always seem faithful to the doctrine.[10] Often, the book of Grace does not seem to shine more resplendently and we must presume that the wound which man received in his intellectuals was rather superficial, for, as Shaftesbury was fond of remarking, heathens many times act better by light of nature alone than Christians do with the assistance of revelation; "they speak and act so as to shame us."

In referring to this as truth of *inscription*, Whichcote does not seem to be thinking of innate ideas. He does use the world *connatural* to suggest a power which develops, though obviously he is not thinking of conscience in the usual sense of the world. Some-

---

9. *Ibid.*, 351.
10. Theophilus Gale, *The Court of the Gentiles: or A discourse Touching the Original of Human Literature* (4 vols.; 1671–78), I, 7.

times he speaks of a sense of right and wrong, and on other occasions of an instinct parallel to that natural to animals. Perhaps the traditional symbolism of light, also used by the very different Gale, best describes how reason works according to Whichcote, whose "Candle of the Lord" illuminates the data acquired through the senses and reveals the moral and spiritual truths involved in it. However vague the epistemology, the greatest truth and the most faithful imitation of God is, again and again, charity.

Anyone so steeped in Greek and Roman classical thought as Shaftesbury was would also find much purely classical to attract him in Whichcote's sermons; thus, reason is continually stressed instead of will, and, though reason is often ineffective, it will embrace truth clearly presented. Neither sin nor punishment is attributable to God, for the greatest punishments have their existence within the mind, just as surely as the greatest sins are conceived there. Conversely, Paradise or, at least, virtue's greatest rewards also lie within. Whichcote also stresses both the value of the contemplative life and the importance of rising above the intrusions of external circumstance.

Finally, the vigor and conviction of Whichcote's sermons—transmitted at second hand—triumph over all the inherent repetition, loose organization, and awkwardness of expression. Whichcote speaking from his pulpit must have been justly celebrated, and much of his appeal surely derived from his clear-eyed and compassionate manner. For all his idealism, he saw plainly how far off the mark most men must fall, yet toward them he always shows the same tolerance and benignity he preached.

II

Shaftesbury says that he published Whichcote's sermons because he felt that they were a more effective antidote to the poison of Hobbes than anything most clergymen had to offer; his own first book is best understood as directed against John Locke. Ten more years were to pass before he would reveal even in his private letters his bitter reactions to the moral implications of *An Essay Concerning Human Understanding*. When he does show how he feels, the violence of his emotions is startling, no matter how much he professes admiration for his old teacher in most other respects. In 1709, he writes to his protégé Michael Ainsworth that " 'twas Mr. Lock that struck the home Blow (for Mr. Hobb's Character, and base slavish Principles in Government took off the poyson of his Philosophy). 'Twas Mr. Lock that struck at all Fundamentals, threw all *Order* and *Virtue* out of the World, and made the Very Ideas of these . . . *unnatural* and without foundation in our Minds."[11]

To understand Shaftesbury's attitude toward Locke's philosophy it is necessary to see the younger man as he sees himself in the preface to Whichcote's *Sermons*, as a preserver of the moral wisdom of the past, not as an innovator nor as he is commonly seen today, as one of the earliest and most eloquent of a group of benevolists and sentimental moralists. In this first book, *An Inquiry Concerning Virtue, in Two Discourses* (1699), Shaftesbury does alter, subtly and pervasively, the basis of the traditional humanistic moral idealism which he had absorbed during years devoted to classical studies, but his attention is focused on preserving the system itself and perhaps he does not perceive alterations which seem so patent to our hindsight. He does not see them because others have been preparing the way for half a century and because of that wondrous way man has of willy-nilly disguising the mutations in his patterns of thinking by dressing them in the same terminology that clothed the old. When one looks at Shaftesbury's methods of defending the humanistic moral ideal in relation to the contemporary intellectual milieu, they take on that aura, perhaps specious, of inevitability which seems to characterize the ideas of so many influential writers—Locke himself, for example. What Shaftesbury does may seem quite natural for the times, but this does not detract from the achievement, nor does it divorce him from the cherished tradition, distant from us, which was ever present in his own mind.

Locke is more dangerous to the tradition than Hobbes because he subverted it both in man the microcosm and in the macrocosm. "*Order & Virtue*" are in a sense synonyms, or, more precisely, one is best expressed in terms of the other. Man is part of the cosmos yet a mirror of it, because he shares faculties with all of animate nature

---

11. Lord Shaftesbury to Michael Ainsworth, June 3, 1709, in PRO 30/24/20/143.

from the lowest to the highest. He follows nature or fulfills the ideal of his nature when he orders all these faculties harmoniously. Thus virtuous, he in turn fulfills his purpose in serving the larger system around him, which also has implicit in it an ideal of harmonious order. This concept is highly idealistic, to be sure, but it is not facilely optimistic. The superficial optimism which characterizes much eighteenth-century thought evolved when it had been forgotten that the perfection involved in the natural order is ideal, not actual.

Foremost in Shaftesbury's mind when he accuses Locke of destroying the evidence of moral order in the nature of man is the latter's devastating attack on innate ideas in the first book of the *Essay*. The question is "not whether the very philosophical Propositions about Right and Wrong were innate[.] But whether the Passion and Affection towards Society was such: that is to say, whether it was natural and came of it self, or was taught by Art, and was the product of a Lucky Hit of some first Man who inspir'd and deliver'd down the Prejudice?" Unless some tendency, however faint, toward the good of the whole is universal in men—the "social affection" of the writers on natural law such as Hugo Grotius and Richard Cumberland—there is no natural basis for relating individual conduct to some sort of eternal and immutable moral principles; yet in destroying the *consensus gentium* Locke seems to rule out any such tendency. Moreover, Locke's proneness in later life to stress, as he does in his *Reasonableness of Christianity* (1695), that men should obey the moral law because of "unspeakable rewards and punishments in another world, according to their obedience or disobedience," seemed further to deny the social nature of man by making morality wholly a matter of self-interest.[12]

In *The Reasonableness of Christianity* Locke refers continually to an eternal, immutable standard of right with respect to the nature of things, but here Locke's doctrines are from Shaftesbury's point of view just as destructive as they were of the foundations of morality in the human psyche. In the first place, Locke implies that God is the author of this immutable eternal law, an implication which

---

12. Lord Shaftesbury to General James Stanhope, November 7, 1709, in PRO 30/24/22/7/p. 11; John Locke, *Works* (9 vols.; 1824), VI, 122.

Shaftesbury will not accept. The Cambridge Platonists rejected voluntaristic ethics as strongly as they rejected the God of will worshiped by their theological opponents. Secondly, even though he admitted the existence of an eternal law, Locke became less and less willing to grant that it is rationally available to man. Early in his career he had written a treatise on the laws of nature without ever publishing it. As late as 1690, in the *Essay*, he states that "moral rules are capable of demonstration: and therefore it is our own faults if we come not to a certain knowledge of them." Yet he persistently refused the pleas of his friend William Molyneux (1656–1698) that he draw up a treatise of morals according to a mathematical method, replying finally that did "the world want a rule, I confess there could be no work so necessary, nor so commendable. But the Gospel contains so perfect a body of Ethics, that reason may be excused from that enquiry, since she may find man's duty clearer and easier in revelation than in herself."[13] He explains to Molyneux that he is tired and can better use his time and energy in other tasks; from *The Reasonableness of Christianity* it is clear that it is his conviction of the weakness of human reason which deters him.

Lastly there is Shaftesbury's belief that "Virtue according to Mr. Lock, has no other Measure Law or Rule, than Fashion & Custome."[14] Unlike the churchmen who reacted so violently to the apparently relativistic statements in the *Essay*, Shaftesbury knows that Locke is speaking of what men *call* virtue, that Locke admits an absolute standard of morality, the will of God; he is troubled, nonetheless, by the pessimism in Locke's suggestion that the natural law is either unavailable to or utterly disregarded by man. Shaftesbury is not altogether fair to Locke, for the latter's tendency to stress revelation and the certainty of rewards and punishment in a future state springs from his belief that, from a practical point of view, if most men are to act morally they must have some simple and clear rules to obey, and some powerful incentives to ensure that they do obey them. On the other hand, Shaftesbury, like some of the Cambridge Platonists, was trying to steer a course between the Scylla and Cha-

13. Locke, *Essay*, I, 65; John Locke to William Molyneux, March 30, 1696, in *Some Familiar Letters Between Mr. Locke, and Several of His Friends* (1708), 144.
14. Lord Shaftesbury to Michael Ainsworth, June 3, 1709, in PRO 30/24/22/143.

rybdis of naturalism and fideism, in a world where confidence in the humanistic natural moral order and its guidance was fast waning, and it is easy to see how, for him, Locke's ideas involved both perils, the worst of Hobbes and the worst of the theological doctrines advanced to counter Hobbes.

Shaftesbury's strategy in the *Inquiry* is to ask first "How far Virtue alone could go; and how far Religion was either necessary to support it, or able to raise and advance it," an approach which enables him to respond at the beginning to both the naturalistic and fideistic arguments against the humanistic ethic; but before he can consider this question he must define atheism and virtue. The definition of atheism turns into a highly schematized analysis of all religious systems on the basis of the sort of order they presuppose in the universe. Men may not be able to discern the final causes of particular events or the ultimate ends toward which they tend, but everyone must assume that either all is for the best or that it could have been better. According to the first of these assumptions there can be no ill toward the whole; such a situation implies design; and design implies a ruling intelligence, in this case a good one, and, accordingly, Shaftesbury calls this belief Theism. If, on the other hand, there is real ill in the universe, it can arise by chance, which implies the absence of order, or by design. He who chooses the first explanation is an Atheist; and he who admits any real evil and yet believes in design and a ruling intelligence is to some extent a Daemonist. Shaftesbury goes on to consider some of the various combinations which can occur: by his definition Zoroastrianism would be a mixture of Theism and Daemonism; the Roman religion would involve Polytheism, Polydaemonism, and Atheism. Elaborate subdivisions are largely a smoke screen which veils but thinly the real point of this section of his *Inquiry*: as it is everywhere implied in the book, followers of Calvin are in reality Daemonists. Shaftesbury also makes the point that Daemonists, instead of worshiping the good itself, chiefly worship to forestall evil. It is clear too that those opponents of Hobbes who, unlike the Calvinists, grant man a measure of free will yet stress that he must make prudent use of this life so as to evade eternal torment in a future state are also in a large degree Daemonists.

Obviously, Shaftesbury was a Theist by 1698 and, it is likely, had been one for some time. It is not so much what he says in this first section of *An Inquiry Concerning Virtue*, as what he fails to say, which makes this clear—his situation is similar to that of Locke, who wrote *The Reasonableness of Christianity* ostensibly to prove that Christ was the Messiah and in the end was attacked as a Socinian because of what he failed to say about Christ. Thus, the absence of any reference to Christ, to sin, to the spirit, and his persistent tendency to see Theism as something apart from the various contemporary manifestations of orthodox Christianity leave no doubt as to Shaftesbury's affiliations. The analysis of religions in the *Inquiry* provoked so little hostile reaction because it forms such a small part of a book which had a very limited circulation, and because Shaftesbury was content at this stage to appear as what Sir Leslie Stephen calls a constructive deist, one who attempts a positive synthesis, rather than making a skeptical analysis of miracles and the like.[15]

It is true that the theologically disreputable Pierre Bayle (1647–1706) had made a great deal of the independence of morality from religion and he may have influenced Shaftesbury, but the clearest parallel to Shaftesbury's three categories is in the preface to Ralph Cudworth's (1617–1688) *True Intellectual System of the Universe* (1678), where this Cambridge Platonist makes a similar distinction into Theists, Atheists, and Immoral Theists. Cudworth was so incredibly prolix that he did not live to publish the section on the last group, but it is obvious that he considers the Calvinists as chief among the Immoral Theists of his own day.

Having declared himself a Theist, Shaftesbury in the next section proceeds to define virtue in terms of that cosmic order which is the Theist's chief article of faith. The cosmos is made up of a vast collection of systems or natures, inanimate, vegetable, animal, and human, which together comprise a universal nature. Every creature has a good or end, and this good we usually define in terms of the creature's relation to the system or species to which he belongs. For the good of an individual creature to be described wholly in terms of its

15. Alfred Owen Aldridge found only one printed reply to Shaftesbury's first work. See "Shaftesbury and the Deist Manifesto," *Trans. American Philosophical Society,* n.s., XLI (1951), p. 371.

relation to itself, the creature would have to exist in complete isolation, as no creature does. Real evil in such a cosmos—as opposed to the evil of a creature with respect to his particular system—would be defined in terms of the relation to the whole, or universal nature, whose workings are not scrutable: and, in any case, the Theist believes that real evil does not exist.

An action may result in benefit, but we do not call the creature who performed it *good*, unless it proceeded from his own good nature, his good affections. A person subject to convulsions cannot be bad during a seizure then. A creature securely bound up and restrained from action cannot be considered good, any more than one who is constrained only by fear of punishment. Moreover, purely occasional or casual actions or affections do not determine whether a creature is good or bad, and some affections, such as the desire for self-preservation, are good in moderation and harmful if they become excessive, so that it is the balance or temper of the affections which makes us call the creature good or evil. A good creature is "such a one as by his Affections or natural Temper, is carried *primarily and immediately*, and not *secondarily and accidentally*, to Good and against Ill" (Inq., 25).

At a certain point in his discussion Shaftesbury stops speaking of creatures and begins talking of men. The distinction which he then introduces is his most celebrated contribution to ethics. We may sometimes call an animal vicious on account of its bad temper but conversely we never call it virtuous, reserving that term exclusively for human creatures, and the fact of the matter is that calling an animal *vicious* is just a manner of speaking, for an animal can be moved by a good or bad temper to good or bad actions, but man is the only moral creature. He is moral because he is rational and accordingly has the power of reflection. He responds not only to external stimuli, as a lioness may to the plight of her cubs, but responds and approves goodness itself, good acts and good affections:

> In a Creature capable of forming general Notions of things, not only the sensible things that offer themselves to the sense, are the objects of the Affection; but the very *actions* themselves, and the *affections* of Pity, Charity, Kindness, Justice, and so their contraries, being brought into the mind by reflection, become objects; as even that very thing it self of

a good and virtuous Life, or the Part of a good and virtuous Creature, having thorow good Affection, or intire good Affections: so that, by means of this reflected sense, there arises another kind of Affection, which is towards the very Affections themselves that were first felt, and are now the subject of a new feeling, when either they cause a liking or aversion. (Inq., 27)

This affection—which is drawn to acts or emotions beneficial to the whole and repelled by harmful ones—Shaftesbury identifies with natural affections toward one's species, the "social instinct" of the natural law philosophers. Thus, as for them, the basis for his ethics is the moral nature of man.

The *modus operandi* of the sense of right and wrong—or, as he was to call it later, though sparingly, "moral sense"—seems clear enough. A man sees an action and it is brought into the mind, where reason "readily discerns the good and the ill towards the Species or Public," and if the man has a well enough developed sense of right and wrong he will be drawn to the good or repelled emotionally by the bad. If his sense of right and wrong is undeveloped or distorted, he will not have the appropriate reaction, but Shaftesbury believes that there is a spark of social affection in all men. He finds it impossible to believe that there is any man who when he "comes to be try'd by rational Objects, as of Justice, Generosity, and other Virtue, have no inclining Affection, no kind of *liking* towards these, or *dislike* towards what is on the contrary side cruel, horrid, base, villanous, or the like" (Inq., 43). To refer to it as a *sense* of right and wrong is, then, only a manner of speaking; though it may involve sense perception, as it does when the moral activities of others are being judged, the moral sense is basically an activity of rational reflection and emotion. That Shaftesbury called it a sense is probably due to Locke's habit of referring to reflection—"that notice which the mind takes of its own operations"—as an "internal sense," for, especially in the first version of the *Inquiry*, Shaftesbury is very careful to stick closely to the psychological principles outlined in Locke's *Essay*—however much he may diverge from its author's pessimistic view of human nature.[16] Obviously, the sense of right and

16. Locke, *Essay*, I, 68–69.

wrong was conceived to circumvent Locke's interdict upon innate ideas and it does so with considerable success.[17]

There are two principal reasons why the mechanics of Shaftesbury's sense of right and wrong have been so little understood in our own day. Although we owe many debts to Locke, we no longer instinctively think of the mind's operations in his terms, whereas it is a real novelty to find an Englishman in the century after the publication of the *Essay* whose unvoiced presuppositions regarding the human mind are not solidly based on the principles outlined in that book. Only in the last twenty-five years have the implications of the fact come home to us, for it is not long since historians of ideas were uncovering traces of Locke's "influence" with all the naïve glee of Little Jack Horner. Secondly, Shaftesbury himself contributed to the confusion by rephrasing his description of the moral sense in the much more widely read second edition in such a way as to make the mechanics appear more complicated, even if he may not have intended anything different from what had appeared in the first version.

Despite the fact that almost all of his contemporaries read the second version, most of them must have had little difficulty in understanding precisely what Shaftesbury meant. Bishop Joseph Butler (1692–1752), for instance, was a moralist of a different persuasion and tried to introduce a principle of authority and obligation into the sense of right and wrong, which was utterly incompatible with Shaftesbury's moral outlook, yet Butler could see clearly enough what it was he was trying to modify, and the similarity to the original is striking:

> Brute creatures are impressed and actuated by various instincts and propensions: so also are we. But additional to this, we have a capacity of reflecting upon actions and characters, and making them an object to our thought: and on doing this, we naturally and unavoidably approve some actions, under the peculiar view of their being virtuous and of good desert; and disapprove of others, as vicious and of ill desert.[18]

17. There seems little doubt of the debt to Locke. For instance, the *O.E.D.* cites Locke's *Essay* as the first example for *reflection* used in Ashley's sense.

18. Bishop Joseph Butler, "Dissertation of the Nature of Virtue," in *Works*, ed. Samuel Halifax (2 vols.; Oxford, 1820), I, 431.

Actually, it is the dissimilarities between Shaftesbury's "sense of right and wrong" and the innumerable contemporary analogues which are most significant. Typical of the vagueness of these concepts is Henry More's (1614–1687) "boniform faculty" to which he frequently alludes yet never defines with any precision. With more precision the popular theologian John Scott (1639–1695) in his *The Christian Life* (1681) speaks of the "natural Sense of Good and Evil which springs from the Frame and Nature of our Affections." There is a connection between this characteristic vagueness and the fact that most such writers are seldom satisfied with one means to moral knowledge independent of revelation and usually postulate several. The greatest preacher of the day, John Tillotson (1630–1694), seeks security in four modes of knowing our moral duties independently of revelation: first, he says, "by a kind of natural instinct, by which I mean a secret impression upon the minds of men, whereby they are carried to approve things as good and fit, and to dislike other things, as having a native evil and deformity in them." Then he goes on to compare this moral faculty with natural affection as Shaftesbury does.[19]

This tendency toward vagueness and toward multiplying the means to moral knowledge represents a groping for new epistemologies to replace those outworn and no longer tenable as the basis of ethical systems. Such tendencies are most often seen, logically enough, in those who like Shaftesbury oppose Hobbesian materialism but are unwilling to accept either Calvinism or an outright dependence upon reward and punishment in the hereafter as alternatives.[20] The roots of their difficulties go back much further than Hobbes, and they involve something more than the decline of faith in the intuitive powers of reason and in innate ideas, which never were accepted in some circles. Since the mid sixteenth century a tendency had been growing to make psychology the study of processes of thought scientifically observed, just as anything in the world of accident might be. Since first causes were ruled out accord-

19. John Scott, *Works* (2 vols.; 1718), I, 201; Bishop John Tillotson, *Works* (10 vols.; 1820), V, 281–83.
20. See my "The Reason of the English Enlightenment" in *Studies on Voltaire and the Eighteenth Century*, XXVII (Geneva, 1963), 1735–74.

ing to this method, psychology came to deal with *mind*, rather than with *soul*, which was interrelated in a complex fashion to a moral and spiritual universe. The divorce of the mind from the universe is virtual in Locke, but the crisis caused by this transition began at least half a century before the publication of his *Essay*, and it was compounded by a parallel breakdown in psychological terminology which makes it very difficult now to tell what the average writer on the subject is saying.

Unlike other proponents of the sense of right and wrong, Shaftesbury depends upon only one means of moral knowledge, building his whole ethical system upon it. More significant, although some modern scholars have been confused as to what he meant by his sense of right and wrong, Shaftesbury clearly defined it in terms understandable in his own day, instead of resorting to the fuzzy generalities so characteristic of the other writers. And he defined it in terms of the psychological system which was to shape English presuppositions about the human mind for a long time to come—that of Locke, the same system which put an end to the easy epistemological assumptions involved in the "boniform faculty" and similar notions. No doubt the fact that Shaftesbury was not a cleric, as were almost all of the other writers who were seeking a new basis for morality, gave him a wider audience. The easy style in which the *Inquiry* was recast for its appearance a decade later in *Characteristicks* also helped, as did the rank of its author. Indeed, half a century later, when the notions involved had become so commonplace that it was difficult to imagine anyone buying a book in order to read them, one sour opponent of Shaftesbury's ideas declared that the nobility of its author was the sole reason for the book's remarkable popularity, which carried it into edition after edition up to the middle of the century.

Having defined religion and virtue to his satisfaction, Shaftesbury is ready to proceed to some more or less foregone conclusions regarding the relation of one to the other. The best procedure is to determine the impact of religion on virtue, since he assumes the latter can exist independently of the former. In three ways only can virtue be harmed: by the sense of right and wrong being destroyed, by its distortion, or by opposing emotions which hinder its working. Shaftesbury has already declared his belief that there is some spark of the moral sense, however faint, in every man's breast, so that he is unwilling to admit that it can be completely eradicated. Distorted it can be, though—not by atheism which as nonbelief does not constrain, but by superstition and ill religion, which he defines as belief in a deity not wholly good. Thus the moral sense can be corrupted by faith in a lustful Jupiter or in a vengeful god who punishes those who do not sin and those whose transgressions are slight, or by faith in an unjust god who plays favorites after the manner of the Calvinistic deity with his election and reprobation. Faith in a beneficent deity who is worshiped out of love, not fear, can, however, greatly strengthen the moral sense.

With respect to the possibility of opposing affections being raised, Shaftesbury takes up in turn the effects of belief in a deity of power, in a nonbeneficent deity, and in no deity. The attempt to ground true morality upon fear of punishment or hope of reward in a future state is self-defeating because it strengthens selfishness, the opposite of natural affection. Shaftesbury is willing to concede, though, that the inducements of reward and punishment may drive more violent passions out, which if they remained in control might obstruct the moral sense. He was also ready to grant the classical moralists' confidence in the force of habit, and he is willing to admit that continual right action upon the wrong motives may lead one eventually to act upon the proper ones. Yet how much more effective is perfect theism, which inculcates love and where confidence that all is for the best breeds resignation in the face of adversity? Atheism cannot do this, for one can always complain of the tyranny of chance, even though it is futile to do so. Furthermore, how is a love of the whole to be nurtured where there is no whole, where the atheist's chaos reigns, "So that the chiefest security, the perfection and the highest degree of virtue, must be owing to the belief of a God" (Inq., 81).

Shaftesbury seems wholly sincere in coming to this conclusion, but his terms must be understood only in the manner he intends them. If the belief in a conventional deity who rewards and punishes his creatures according to their merits promotes morality, it does so largely because men are slaves to habit, which may eventually counteract the selfishness this species of piety inculcates. Shaftesbury's deity, like Whichcote's, from whom he seems to derive, is completely benevolent and punishes no one. Whatever hells men suffer, they themselves create. There is, however, a significant difference between Shaftesbury and Whichcote, which, though fundamental, is only implicit, not stated outright. Christ figures seldom in either writer, but Whichcote's sermons continually display the preacher's own love of his benevolent Christ and his desire to emulate him. Shaftesbury's love is for the harmonious whole which implies the existence of a deity and in implying somehow makes that existence unnecessary, for once it is believed that there is a universal order in which all things happen ultimately for the best, the essential part of Shaftesbury's theistic credo has been fulfilled, and what remains to be performed is an act of logic and not an act of faith.

In the second book of his *Inquiry Concerning Virtue* Shaftesbury considers "how any one may have reason to imbrace Virtue, and shun Vice." It is no accident that he chooses to divide his book here, for in doing so he emphasizes the difference between being virtuous and enjoying the resultant happiness. One must be virtuous first and the other will follow, and virtue sought solely on account of its by-products could never be virtue. Motive is primary in his ethical system, not the results of an action. Of course, any act which is beneficial to others or to the whole is *good*, but he who does it is not virtuous unless he acts upon the proper motive, love of the whole or of others, which is virtue itself. A horse as well as a man can do beneficial acts through fear of punishment or hope of reward. This distinction is basic to the Stoic philosophy in which Shaftesbury had steeped himself, and some of his modern interpreters, failing to discern this, have seen in Book II the evidence that Shaftesbury was a hedonist or a utilitarian, or that he based morals on emotional satisfaction, as was common enough later in the century. One could hardly be further from the truth.

Moralists have dwelt on the advantages of being virtuous since the beginning of time, and however rationalistic he might be in theory, the practical moralist has always been forced to speak in terms of the emotions, so that even though Book II makes up the largest part of the *Inquiry*, we need not expect to find anything very fresh in it. Reason, as we have seen, has its role in the moral sense; here it has no place, and the discussion is wholly given over to the "oeconomy of the passions." All emotions are divided into three classes: "1. The natural ones towards the Kind, or which carry to the good of something beyond the privat System. 2. Or the self-ones, which carry to the good of the privat System, as towards self-preservation, self-nourishment or support, self-defence, or repelling of injury. 3. Or such as are neither of these, and neither tend to any good of the public or privat System" (Inq., 88–89). The first of these, Shaftesbury admits, can be too strong, just as it is possible for the second to be too weak and the third wholly absent. Usually, however, the case is far different, and it is this situation to which Shaftesbury now addresses himself.

He begins with the natural other-regarding affections. Happiness consists of pleasurable experiences, and, as can be demonstrated by hoary arguments, mental pleasures are far superior to physical ones. The greatest mental pleasures, in turn, either involve the natural affections directly—friendship, for example—or they proceed from them as does the delight one takes in the pleasures of others or in a sense of well-merited esteem. Natural affection confers other benefits, too. Virtue as a practical matter derives from a balance of the various affections, or good temper. If the natural affections are deficient, disharmony will result and with it perturbations which will render the individual incapable of pleasure. So, too, with the intellect. The reflective man is capable of the greatest pleasures in this world, but it is just he who is most susceptible to having the necessary calm disturbed by sensations of guilt, if in the past he has acted with too little natural affection. Finally, enjoyment of natural affection is involved in the physical pleasures of this world, for interior though these pleasures are, they are best enjoyed in company.

Shaftesbury could have devoted less space to proving the disadvantages of having the self-affections too strong, or of possessing any of the unnatural ones. Love of ease becomes sloth, desire of what sustains life becomes greed—thus, each of the prudential virtues becomes, in excess, one of the deadly sins. And these self-affections in excess make up the bulk of the third class, the unnatural ones. One need only add malice, envy, sadism, and a host of sexual perversions to the catalog. For anyone who assumes that Shaftesbury's ethical notions are the product of an easy optimism concerning human nature, the latter sections of the *Inquiry* will come as a shock, for he details the unnatural passions with all the fervor of those fire-and-brimstone preachers from whom in theory he is so far apart. All the bitterness of those years since he returned from his grand tour seems to be distilled into these pages, and he exhibits a theriophilia that reminds one of Montaigne. If one wishes to see creatures living according to nature one had best look to the beasts, the bulk of whom exhibit notable social instincts, while "Man in the mean time, vicious and unconsonant man, lives out of all rule and proportion, contradicts his Principles, breaks the Order and Oeconomy of all his Passions, and lives at odds with his whole Species, and with Nature: so that it is next to a Prodigy to see a Man in the world who lives NATURALLY, and as a MAN" (Inq., 99).

Some years later in *The Sociable Enthusiast* Shaftesbury tells us that the *Inquiry* was intended for a specific audience, the doubters. He sees the audience of any writer on religion as divided into three groups: atheists, agnostics, and believers. Only the magistrate can deal with the outright atheist, and there is little doubt that Shaftesbury would have the flagrant ones dealt with. At the other end of the spectrum, the threat of hell fire, though miserably ineffective, is all that the common man of religious bent has to keep him in line and the social structure stable. What then to do with the doubter or agnostic? Most apologists are busy defending the Christian faith in general and refuting innovation, and they have little to say to him. Only reason will appeal to the doubter, for how can he be moved by reward and punishment who has no strong belief in them? This is why in the *Inquiry* the normal order is inverted, why the author argues rationally from virtue to religion, instead of the opposite.

Shaftesbury's achievement in his *Inquiry*, especially as it appeared in final form a decade later, was largely as a popularizer of the ethics of emotion, or sentiment as it came to be called, but much of the book's popularity was owing to the original and opportune way in which it blended old tradition and new thought to serve the needs of the time. There was nothing new about making morality dependent upon goodness of heart; English Latitudinarian divines had been doing this for several decades. Nor can the fact that Shaftesbury and these divines resorted to the emotions per se be explained as a reaction against Hobbes, the Puritans, or the Stoics. Though Hobbes's methods are rationalistic, his ethics are not. As Shaftesbury realized, the difference between Hobbes and the Latitudinarians is not a matter of reason versus emotion but rather a question of which emotion, fear or love, lies at the heart of morality. As for the Puritans, the popularity of such works as *A Treatise of the Affections or the Souls Pulse, whereby a Christian may know whether he be living or dying* (1650) by the Puritan William Fenner (1600–1640) or the often translated *Use of the Passions* (1649) by the French Augustinian J. F. Senault (1601–1672) indicates that those most opposed to the Latitudinarians were not uniformly rationalistic. A better case could be made with respect to the Stoics, but at least one Stoic, Shaftesbury himself, could see no fundamental opposition involved.

The truth seems to be that in many diverse camps the emotions were becoming more and more highly regarded. Reason, which had become *reasoning*, a process instead of an agent or faculty, may have turned into a more effective instrument for studying nature, man, and society, but it was no longer so noble. The pronouncements of the older divine faculty had an authority lacking in mere process, and they were based on data unavailable to a process depending wholly on the senses. There were doubts, too, that a process could initiate and carry through right action. If one contrasts Spenser's or Milton's confidence in the moral effectiveness of rational choice with Pope's figure of reason as the compass needle in the gale of passion, it can be seen how feeble reason had become in all attributes but the cardinal task of pointing to one kind of truth. In his *Inquiry* Shaftesbury took the classical injunction to follow nature and put it partly on an emotional basis when reason as then understood could no longer completely sustain it. The work of defining virtue as goodness of heart had already been done for him. His real contribution was the sense of right and wrong, which legitimized the ethics of sentiment by providing it with a plausible epistemology on a Lockean basis and gave it authority by relating it to the nature of things, through the spark of natural affection he believed to reside in the hearts of all men.

In his life of his father the fourth Earl of Shaftesbury says that the 1699 version of the *Inquiry* was surreptitiously taken from a rough draft, sketched when his father "was but twenty years of age. He was greatly chagrined at this, and immediately bought up the whole impression before many of the books were sold. . . . The person who treated him so unhandsomely he soon discovered to be Mr. John Toland, who made this ungrateful return for the many favours he had received from him."[21] It is unfortunate that we must rely upon the fourth Earl's account for information on so many circumstances of his father's life because the biography he wrote is based almost equally upon documents—some of them now lost—and upon not overly reliable family traditions. As a result it is difficult to distinguish fact from fancy when reading the sketch, and this passage is no exception.

As Locke suspected, Shaftesbury seems to have been at work on some sort of essay as early as 1694, so that his son may not be far off in giving a date for the work.[22] Furthermore, the indiscreet Toland was fully capable of taking this manuscript and publishing it against his benefactor's wishes. He apparently stole a manuscript of Giordano Bruno's from the library of Anthony Collins (1676–1729) and had it printed for his own profit. Later he distressed the fourth Earl's mother by publishing some personal correspondence relating to her marriage. Finally, although the *Inquiry* does appear in a bookseller's advertisement long after Shaftesbury should have finished buying them up, it is a book of very great rarity, which does lend some credence to the story of his buying up copies.

As it so often is in the description of the publication of Shaftesbury's works, there is another side to the story. We can discount the fourth Earl's calling it "a rough draft" when it was not. Toland was to him the betrayer of personal matters his mother would have preferred to keep private, and even his father might have used the term to describe an earlier work so discordant with the tones of *Characteristicks*. The problem is that Shaftesbury did not drop Toland as we might expect, if he was as indignant as his son suggests. Obviously some of Toland's charms were already tarnishing by 1699, but he was still useful. He collaborated with the Earl on another work

21. Rand, (ed.), *The Life, Unpublished Letters, and Philosophical Regimen*, xxiii.
22. Lord Ashley to John Locke, May 28, 1694, in de Beer, V, 65–66; September 8, 1694, V, 123–35; September 29, 1694, V, 150–54.

in 1702 and his pension was last paid in 1703. Furthermore, in 1701 Shaftesbury seems quite happy to learn that Pierre Desmaizeaux is translating the *Inquiry* into French and plans to send a copy to Pierre Bayle.

We simply do not have enough solid evidence to make a judgment. All we can be sure of is that there is some degree of truth in Shaftesbury's later statement that the original publication of the *Inquiry* was "contrary to the author's design." It never pays to read at more than face value the words which he chooses so carefully when speaking of his literary career, but he always seems to avoid any outright lying on the subject.

III

Shaftesbury began to write his Stoical meditations during his retreat in the Netherlands during 1688 and 1689. They are unique because he never intended them for the eyes even of his close friends; they are remarkable as the finest examples of purely Stoic thought since Marcus Aurelius wrote down his own meditations. The manuscript fills two medium-size volumes, well bound in vellum, which today still keeps the rich green tint of which Shaftesbury was fond. Under a number of headings, such as "Deity," "Mankind & Human Affairs," "Self," and "Natural Affection," are grouped thoughts which he began to record on this trip and continued to enter until the final year of his life, though they are much sparser in his later years. Since the entries are carefully dated, it is easy to determine that they are not random reflections but, rather, were made during periods of retirement from public affairs and, sometimes, from both family and friends, as on his second and third trips to Holland.

At first glance there does not seem to be much system to the entries: several pages of meditations on, say, "Passions" will end with a reference to a page number below, where after a number of pages devoted to other topics, "Passions" will again be taken up, but shortly one is again referred ahead; and, most puzzling, interspersed among the pages which intervene will be brief entries from later periods. On analysis, however, it is clear that in setting down his reflections, Shaftesbury was his usual systematic self. He wrote his thoughts on a given topic into the book, sometimes transcribing them from a rough draft, until he had said all that he had to say on that matter at the moment. Then, turning to the first opening where there was writing on neither page, he dealt with other ideas, repeating the procedure each time he changed subjects. When he came back to a given topic, he normally went to the two facing pages where he had ended his last discussion of it, filling the pages out before going on to the first available blank page.

From all this it is evident that we have a running, though not continuous, record of Shaftesbury's philosophic meditations over a fifteen-year period, thoughts written down roughly when they occurred to him and not altered later to suit the changes in his own attitudes. These meditations—all in Shaftesbury's hand—could not be recopied by an amanuensis, as were so many of his writings, because even the philosophical attitudes expressed in them he wished to keep secret. That makes them even more fascinating, because, philosophical or not, many of the reflections come from that inner core of the conscious personality which not many men reveal to anyone. All in all, in these books we find a man who would be recognized by few if any of his friends and, certainly, by none of that larger audience who thought that they saw the man revealed in his widely popular published works.

Ignoring the title that Shaftesbury gave them, "ΑΣΚΗΜΑΤΑ," or "Exercises," Benjamin Rand, the editor of these reflections, called them instead a *Philosophical Regimen*, perhaps because he felt that the original name made them seem too unsystematic and tentative. Obviously, they are not a methodical philosophical exposition, such as *An Inquiry Concerning Virtue*. What Rand seems to have had in mind was something like the *Encheiridion* of Epictetus, a set of fixed rules for the practical application of philosophy to everyday life. Now Shaftesbury was in the habit of compiling rules and resolutions of this sort. In fact, there are some tables of them at the beginning of the first volume, but the meditations which he began in Holland clearly are what he called them, "Exercises." They are much closer in nature to the *Meditations* of Marcus Aurelius, analogous to religious meditations—self-examination, morally therapeutic and, in a sense, devotional in purpose. We need not expect, then, his "Exercises" to be consistent, after the manner of the *Encheiridion*, because often a specific truth will be overstated in order to counter a specific failing. And they will be far more personal, for it is reasonable to assume that sometimes those traits of character and habits which Shaftesbury most deplores will be those to which he himself is most prone. There is a fair amount of Greek strewn through the pages, but the bulk of it is drawn, with accuracy, from the works of Epictetus and Marcus Aurelius.

These Stoical meditations are best discussed under three headings: *physis*, *ataraxia*, and *koinonia*, which can be rendered broadly as *nature*, *apathy*, and *community*. Each of these can, in turn, be considered as relating to the craving for order: *nature*, order in the universe; *apathy* or impassiveness, order in the individual; and *community*, order among men. In a very real way, Shaftesbury saw his mission as seeking order in a world which was becoming increasingly disorderly. As we have seen from the *Inquiry* and from his preface to Whichcote's *Sermons*, Shaftesbury regards the orthodox religionists, especially the more enthusiastic and Augustinian sectaries, as little better than Manichees; the disciples of the newly rehabilitated Epicurus are reviving the ancient atomism, and scientists, no matter how pious, in attempting to explain the physical world are destroying a larger order. By denying the symmetrical parallelism between this larger, cosmic order and the nature of men, Hobbes had threatened the social order and the community of mankind; and Locke had disrupted the moral order by his persistent use of relativistic arguments in his *Essay*. In a narrower frame of reference, Shaftesbury's personal universe, bounded by the political situation on one extreme and the fortunes of his family on the other, had been disorderly and hostile ever since the death of the grandfather. It is not too surprising, then, that he turned to the Stoics, who in their own time had sought stability in a world which seemed to them too much dominated by atomism, by enthusiastic religious irrationalism, by hedonism, and by the vicissitudes of political and social flux.

Most analyses of Stoic thought began with a discussion of *physis* or Nature, even though this aspect of the system is secondary to and perhaps derivative from potent ethical impulses. Shaftesbury's "Exercises" are typical; the ethical notions, though primary, appear doubly paradoxical unless seen in the framework of his cosmological and religious ideas. First we will take up what Shaftesbury's cosmos shares with most ancient systems: an organic nature. Then, we will turn to what is distinctively Stoic: the underlying materialism of his universe, the rigorous yet beneficial necessity, and the possibilities for freedom in such a universe. He insists on necessity and freedom; the materialism, however, is only suggested by indirection. Yet the materialism is essential to make the system function, and Shaftesbury's oblique approach to it is derived from Epictetus and Marcus. Finally we will consider just how pious he is, confronted by such a universe.

The best text with which to begin a discussion of Shaftesbury's notion of the cosmos is an injunction of his favorite authority on the subject, Marcus Aurelius, who like most Stoics says that one must constantly strive to "think of the Universe as one living creature, embracing one being and one soul; how all is absorbed into the one consciousness of this living creature; how it compasses all things with a single purpose, and all things work together to cause all that comes to pass, and their wonderful web and texture."[23] This quotation is especially apt because it refers to the cosmos as *thou*, not *it*. If we need a model or pattern to help us understand the workings of something exceedingly complex, almost instinctively we tend to think of it, even though actually alive, as some sort of machine or mechanism. Men who seek order in a world where the only really complex entities are living things think differently. Neither surrounded by machines nor sympathetic to the scientific and mechanical habits of thought which were spreading ever more widely in his time, Shaftesbury quite naturally considered the cosmos in the ancient manner as a living organism. Unless we grasp this important difference between his and our presuppositions there is little hope of understanding his ideas. To this notion there need be added only Shaftesbury's conviction—derived more from Epictetus than Marcus—that this "consciousness of the living creature" is rational and beneficent.

Very much in the vein of Marcus Aurelius is Shaftesbury's re-

23. Marcus Aurelius, *Meditations*, trans. A. S. L. Farquharson (2 vols.; Oxford, 1944), I, 67, 69. The *Meditations* will be cited from the more literal and easily available translation of C. R. Haines in the Loeb Classical Library except in cases where,

peated insistence on the closely knit interdependence of all parts of the cosmic hierarchy:

> The Elements are combin'd, united, & have a mutual dependance one upon another. all things in this world are united. for, as the Branch is united & is as one with the Tree; so is the Tree with the Earth Air & Water which feeds it, & with the Flyes Worms & Insects which It feeds. for these are made to it. and as much as the Mold is fitted to the Tree, as much as the strong and upright Trunk of the Oak or Elm is fitted to the twining & clinging Branches of the Vine or Ivy; so much are the leaves, the seeds, the fruits, of these Trees fitted to other Animalls, and they again to one another. All holds to one Stock. Go farther: & view the System of the bigger World. See the mutuall dependance, the relation of one thing to another; the Sun to the Earth, the Earth & Planets to the Sun; the Order, Symmetry, Regularity, Union & Cohaerence of the Whole. (Ex., 16)[24]

He even toys with Marcus Aurelius's notion of a universal sympathy:

> *To sympathize*, what is it?—To feel together, or be united in one Sence or Feeling—the Fibers of the Plant sympathize. the Members of the Animal sympathize. and do not the heavenly Bodyes sympathize? why not?—Because we are not consciouse of this feeling—No more are we consciouse of the Feeling or Sympathizing of the Plant: neither can we be consciouse of any other in the world besides that of our own. If however, it be true that these others sympathize; then the World, & the heavenly Bodyes (more united, & more harmoniously conspiring together than either the Plant or Animal-Body) must also sympathize. If there be a sympathizing of the Whole, there is one Perception, one Intelligence of the Whole. If that, then all things are perceived by the Intelligence. If so, then there is one all-knowing, & all-intelligent Nature. (Ex., 23−24)[25]

Only when Shaftesbury, following Marcus, contemplates the universe in order to enforce the triviality of those concerns upon which men exhaust their energies and their time does a modern perspective appear:

> View the Heavens. See the vast Design, the mighty Revolutions that are perform'd. Think in the midst of this Ocean of Being, what the

as here, literalness leads to awkwardness, or where Farquharson's definitive Greek text differs from that of Haines.

24. Compare, for example, *Meditations*, 29.
25. Compare *Meditations*, 151.

Earth & a little part of its Surface is; & what a few Animalls are, which there have being. Embrace as it were; with thy Imagination all those Spaciouse Orbs; and place thy self in the midst of this Divine Architecture. consider other Orders of Beings, other Schemes, other Designs, other Executions, other Faces of things, other Respects, other Proportions & Harmony. (Ex., 26–27)

So far there is little to distinguish Shaftesbury's universe from a number of ancient cosmologies which persisted into the Renaissance. The great interdependent chain of being was common property, and those Ancients who did wish to see the universe as orderly were likely to see it as a living organism. The Stoic cosmology was chiefly distinguished by its materialism, and overtly or not, perhaps reluctantly, Shaftesbury does seem to accept this persistent phase of Stoicism in his "Exercises." He sedulously avoids dualism in all forms, and there is no sign at all that he believes in an afterlife. The spirit is absent. Furthermore, he seems to adhere to the conventional Stoic theory of causation, which is meaningless without materialism. As is the case with many Stoics, it is impossible to understand Shaftesbury's concept of deity without positing some sort of materialism.

The dogma that matter is penetrable distinguishes the Stoic's materialism from Epicurean atomism on one hand and Shaftesbury's pantheism from that of Spinoza on the other. Everything is material, even sense impressions. Thus, in a heated horseshoe both heat and iron are bodies, temporarily interpenetrating one another. When the Stoic speaks of his deity as a breath, *pneuma*, or species of fire everywhere present in the cosmos, he is not using the words as a dualist might, as metaphors to describe an unmaterial substratum. Fire, which is most often associated with deity, differs qualitatively from air, water, and earth, just as they do from each other. Deity may also be eternal, and the rest of the universe subject to flux, but this has no bearing on materiality, which is universal. The dependence of Stoic materialism upon the ancient theory of the four elements and on theories of vision which were rapidly becoming obsolete may be another reason why Shaftesbury does not stress it, even though he accepts corollary dogmas.

He never refers to his deity as "God," perhaps because the word has anthropomorphic connotations for him; instead, he speaks of a "Presence," "Deity," "The Nature of the Whole," "Eternall & Infinite Mind," or an "Intelligent Principle." We can tell much about his deity from the fact that he considers all of these terms exactly synonymous. In a sense, Nature is his god, but *nature* must be understood as *physis*, as the principle inherent in every thing which makes it act as it does or, at least, ought to. Each living thing has a nature: "Thus even in Plants, & Seeds, every particular Nature thrives & attains its perfection if nothing from without obstruct" (Ex., 22). If all organisms, vegetative, animal, and rational, possess such a nature, he argues, the Cosmos, which is obviously an organism too, must have such a nature, and the nature of that whole is the deity.

Above all, the nature of the whole is intelligent. In arguing this point, Shaftesbury makes one of his few allusions to contemporary philosophers. Although the "Exercises" represent a very strong reaction against some seventeenth-century currents of thought, at first glance the book might well appear to be written by some third-century disciple of Marcus Aurelius. Shaftesbury seems to have Ralph Cudworth in mind when he ridicules the suggestion that the nature underlying the whole is "itself meerly Vegitative & Plastick, like that of a Tree or of a Foetus" (Ex., 16). Cudworth was unable to accept a deity remote or cut off from the material world, Epicurean or Cartesian, yet he felt that to require God to act directly in everything that occurs "would render Divine Providence Operose, Sollicitous and Distractious."[26] Accordingly, Cudworth proposed that a vegetative principle or soul pervades the physical world—a nature, which, though it possesses neither intelligence nor sensation, has an ordering function which can account for the regular motions of matter. To this notion, Shaftesbury replies, if this is so, "then it could have produc'd only things of the same species . . . if there be in the Univers Being of another kind, that is to say such as have perception and intelligence; by what should they be produc'd unless by a like Nature? . . . therefore the Nature of the Univers is intelligent" (Ex., 19).

26. Ralph Cudworth, *The True Intellectual System of the Universe* (1678), 149.

Finally, Shaftesbury's deity is a Presence, everywhere immanent, and all-perceiving. His concept of deity is, then, no less exalted than that of the Cambridge Platonists, who may have influenced his ideas of God, and like them he contemns the anthropomorphic tendencies among orthodox religionists of the day almost as strongly as he abhors Epicurean atheism:

> Dost thou, like one of those Visionaryes, expect to see a Throne, a shining Light, a Court & Attendance? is this thy Notion of *a Presence*? and dost thou wayt till then, to be struck and astonish'd as the Vulgar are, with such appearances & Shew?—Wretched Folly!—But if without all this, He be *here*, actually present, a Witness of all thou dost, a Spectator of all thy Actions & privy to thy inmost thoughts: how comes it that thou livs't not with Him, at least but as with a Friend? (Ex., 92)

Cudworth, in a similar connection, quotes Xenophanes: "If Oxen, Lions, Horses and Asses, had all of them a Sense of a Deity, and were able to Limn and Paint, there is no question to be made, but that each of these several Animals would paint God according to their respective Form & Likeness, and contend that he was of that shape & no other."[27]

If deity is eternal according to Stoic dogma, Cosmos is not; it is constantly in the throes of flux. Both Epictetus and Marcus Aurelius see the process as cyclic, each revolution terminating in a conflagration, after which only the fiery substance of deity persists to begin the work of creation anew. The influence of these doctrines, which the earliest Stoics derived from Heraclitus, can be seen in Shaftesbury's cosmological notions. Sometimes the flux seems to him pernicious, a species of cosmic rot. Marcus is often morose but seldom does he look upon the world as darkly as Shaftesbury does in this passage from the "Exercises":

> Consider the number of Animalls that live & draw their breath; and to whome belongs that which we call *Life*, for which we are so much concern'd: Beasts: Insects: the swarm of Mankind sticking to this Earth: the number of Males and Females in copulation: the number of Females in delivery: & the number of both sexes in this one & same instant expiring, & at their last gasp: the Shreeks, Cryes, Voices of pleasure, Shoutings, Groans; and the mixt Noise of all these together.

27. *Ibid.*, 136.

> Think of the number of those that dyed before thou wert, & since: how many of those that came into the World at the same time & since: and of those now alive, what alteration. consider the Faces of those of thy acquaintance, as thou saw'st them some years since: how chang'd since then! how macerated & decay'd. All is Corruption, & Rotteness: nothing at a stay; but continued Changes & Succession renew the Face of the World. (Ex., 77)

Of course this is a therapeutic meditation, serving the same purposes as Marcus' rhapsodies on the *ubi sunt* theme. Nevertheless, coming from the pen of a twenty-seven-year-old it should be sufficient warning against hasty judgments as to what cosmic optimism means to a Stoic.

Most of the time Shaftesbury does regard the flux more optimistically, though never with any expectation of lasting betterment. He often longs for an England as civilized as ancient Athens, yet

> what tho' it were Greece? How long should it last? must there not be *again an Age of Darkness? again Goths?* and shortly, neither shall so much as the Name of *Goths* be remember'd: but the modern as well as the ancient Greeks & Italians be equally forgot. . . . Such is the State of Mankind. these are the Revolutions. The Tree sprouts out of the Ground; then grows; then flourishes a while: at last decays & sinks, that others may come up. Thus Men succeed to one another. thus Names & Familyes dye: and thus Nations & Cityes. what are all these Changes & Successions? what is there here besides what is Naturall, & Familiar, & orderly, & conducing to the Whole? (Ex., 48–49)

Unlike the older Stoics, he seldom looks beyond the repetitious cycles of human affairs to speculate upon the workings of the flux in the Universe as a whole. The world must either undergo a perpetual succession of cataclysms, or, if it is not eternal, it will perish altogether someday. If the flux in human affairs is beyond the control and therefore beyond the proper concern of the virtuous man, how much more remote from his concern is the resistless change in the physical universe itself.

In the notion that change—which may seem to bring about so much natural evil—is at best good and at worst indifferent there is involved the Stoic dogma to which most people are least likely to assent, the triple paradox of a world in which rigorous necessity, beneficent providence, and free will coexist. Some features of Stoicism are softened in Shaftesbury's system, but not the traditionally rigid determinism. Every living thing would perfect itself according to its nature were it not for interference from without; the one nature which cannot be interfered with from without is the nature of the whole, which "can act nothing against Itself: and what is best for Itself, Itself surely best knows" (Ex., 86).[28] In some respects this is rather like believing in an afterlife; the believer is not likely to be confuted, now or later—either he is right, or if not he will never know he was wrong about the matter.

Narrowing the focus, it is possible to argue also that whatever happens ultimately benefits mankind, that individuals do not accept this only because they cannot see the situation of their own kind in broad enough perspective: "But this is not *best for Men*—how know'st thou this? Know'st thou all former ages of Men, & all to come? the connection of Causes, & how they operate? the relations of these to those? the Dependence & Consequences? how it shall be with Mankind at one time and how at another?" (Ex., 86). Hypothetically, if he had to choose between the good of the whole and the good of mankind, the former would be preferred. Speaking of flux, he asks,

> But what if it were *Ill for Mankind*; is it therefore *Ill for the Whole*? or ought the Interest & Good of the Whole to give way, be set aside, or post-pon'd, for such a Creature as Man, & his affaires? are the Laws of the Univers on this account to be annull'd, the Government of the Univers subverted, & the Constitution destroy'd? for thus it must be, if any one Cause be remov'd: and thus the Whole (which is one Concatenation) must necessarily be render'd imperfect, & hence totally perish. (Ex., 86–87)

But Shaftesbury is convinced—more by faith than reason, it seems—that the choice between the good of the whole and that of mankind need never be made. The deity of the "Exercises" is just as beneficent as that described in Whichcote's *Sermons* and *An Inquiry Concerning Virtue*—in this Shaftesbury followed Epictetus more than Marcus Aurelius or any other Stoic. Providence and necessity are, then, one and the same. This act of faith is all the easier for

28. Compare *Meditations*, 263, 265.

Shaftesbury because he accepts the corollary Stoic dogma that physical evil has no reality. External goods, like external evils, are illusory; the only real and lasting good is a virtuous mind, the only genuine evil, a vicious one.

Nothing could better illustrate the essentially paradoxical nature of Stoicism than the fact that Shaftesbury also insists that the human will is free. Occasionally he refers to *Chance*, but he is thinking subjectively rather than cosmologically; from the individual's narrow point of view there is little to distinguish an inscrutable determinism from complete indeterminism. Marcus uses *Chance* in the same way, to refer loosely to the daily succession of events beyond the individual's control—*Fate* in seventeenth-century terms. However, when he or Shaftesbury cries out, as they often do, "Providence or Atoms," there is never any question in our minds as to what side they are on. Epictetus, more careful in his choice of words, avoids the term *Chance*.

No, it is freedom, rather than necessity, which is limited. Man has no control over his actions, only over his moral nature, or purpose, and this is rational, so we can say, in effect, that only reason is free. Furthermore, this freedom is hypothetical and ideal. To achieve it fully the individual must become totally independent of external events, of the world's joys as well as its sorrows; his reason must have mastered his desires and aversions so that they are turned wholly within and have fixed on the proper objects. All men have a potential for freedom, but no men are free. The Stoic sage does not exist and never has. Epictetus, the most self-sufficient of the great Stoic teachers, knew this: "Show me a man who though sick is happy, though in danger is happy, though dying is happy, though condemned to exile is happy, though in disrepute is happy. Show him! By the gods, I would fain see a Stoic!"[29]

Some of the theoretical justification of this potential for limited freedom in a deterministic universe becomes clear if we compare microcosm and macrocosm. What is subject to necessity in the cosmos is not the inherent rational Nature of the whole but the body or

---

29. Epictetus, *Discourses*, trans. W. A. Oldfather, Loeb Classical Library (2 vols.; 1946), I, 367.

matter of the universe, which is interpenetrated by this material, governing Nature. So, too, in man the body and the irrational parts of the soul are subject to causality, but the reason is free because it is part of the same substance as the Nature of the Whole. Indeed, though personality does not survive, this part of the person is immortal and at death returns to the general stock. Man can become free because he partakes of the divine Nature, but actually to achieve freedom he must successfully imitate God, the being who cannot be interfered with from without.

To speak so often of deity in discussing Shaftesbury's Stoic cosmology raises the question of just how much genuine religious sentiment there is in his meditations. His ancient Stoic predecessors differed greatly from one another in piety—though both of the Stoics he admired the most were deeply religious in their own ways. The great difficulty in accepting Shaftesbury as devout lies in the nature of his deity, who varies all the way from the cold abstraction of the *Inquiry* to the Presence just described, who resembles the personal deity of Epictetus. Yet even the Presence seems paradoxically remote when Shaftesbury speaks *of* the deity, never *to* him. Eventually he did pray directly, but in our first impressions his deity resembles the God of Gatsby's world in Fitzgerald's novel, where from an abandoned billboard the two huge eyes of Doctor Eckleberg stare vapidly out across the land. At one point Shaftesbury asks himself ironically, "What would you have,—a Voice?"

Shaftesbury is poignantly aware that his is a different religion which draws on very few of those aspects of human nature which breed and nourish devotion.

> Is it not a thing monstrously preposterouse to be fully & absolutely convinc'd that there is a Deity & of the highest Perfection; that He superintends all things, sees & knows all things & is present every where; and yet at the same time to be so little affected by such a Presence as to have more regard even for the commonest human Eye? What can be the meaning of this? where dos this Mistery lye? (Ex., 103)

Not only does the orthodox Christian have much to mediate for him; his deity is a mirror of powerful human impulses, who, instead of reflecting an ideal and unattainable good, is actually empathic.

The Vulgar have an Idea of *God*: they have Ideas also of *Good*, of Excellent, of Noble, Admirable, Sublime. Now, they for their part, unite these Ideas & joyn those of this latter kind to the Idea of their God. therefore, that which they count Good they ascribe to him. thus they give him a Will such as our own; Passions such as their own; Pleasure like that of their own; Reveng, as delighting in Reveng; Praise, as loving Praise. . . . Correct the Vulgar Idea. Divest the Deity of all which we esteem Happiness & Good: take from Him what we Reckon Power, what we extoll as Great & Mighty: and what remains? what must be the Effect? where can Piety be? where Adoration, Reverence, or Esteem? (Ex., 118–19)

The fault, Shaftesbury believes, lies not with his concept of deity, but with himself. It remains for him to be made over in the image of his god; when he sufficiently reveres the good, he will sympathize and his sense of communion will be no less strong, his devotion no less enthusiastic, than that of the orthodox who have made God in their own image, or, rather, in the image of their worldly desires.

The knowledge that he is yet a beginner makes Shaftesbury consciously avoid direct prayer and other conventional patterns of devotion. He fears that he has not wholly purified himself of his old notion of deity and that he may endanger his conversion by contaminating his new concept if he returns prematurely to any of the forms by which he worshiped the old.

Consider the Age: vulgar Religion: how thou hast been bred: and what impressions yet remaining of that Sordid, Shamefull Nauseouse Idea of Deity. Consider in the case of any good Motion & Affections that way; what affinity they have with vulgar Prayers & Addresses to Deity, and what a wretched effect this has within, when any thing of this kind mixes, or whilst so much as the remembrance of those other Feelings remain. Therefore if thou wouldst praise, magnify, worship & adore aright; wayt till other Habits are confirm'd. (Ex., 100)

This seems odd, perhaps, yet it is a dogma of Epictetus and others that the novice must purify himself within and achieve a considerable degree of freedom from the concerns of his former world before it is safe for him to return to certain outward forms and duties, however commendable they may be.

This intense awareness of conversion is one of several aspects of his meditations which mark Shaftesbury as genuinely pious and devout in his own way. Another is his attitude toward the orthodoxy of the day, even if we grant that Shaftesbury, nobleman and public moralist, has special reasons for wishing to see popular religious forms preserved, as did Marcus the emperor. Personally, Shaftesbury regards these forms as grossly superstitious, but he will not tolerate any tampering with the faith of those who subscribe to them; as in the *Inquiry*, he feels that there are worse things to be feared. We wonder whether he has some of his freethinking associates and perhaps his own conduct in mind when he says,

> What a wretched kind that is which we call *free talking* about matters of Religion & the Established Rites of Worship. . . . What dost thou teach them in this other way, but Impiety & Atheisme? how dost thou appear to them but as one Sacrelegiouse & prophane? as indeed thou art, on this very account. for, what greater Sacrelege is there than that which removes the Notions of Deity out of the Minds of Men and introduces Atheisme? . . . If Modern Superstition disturb thee; be thankful that it is not Indian & Barbarian; that [there] are not Human Sacrifices; that they are not Druids. (Ex., 120–21)

Finally, as evidence of Shaftesbury's piety, there is the whole tenor of his meditations on deity. Of course when we take the opportunity to peer behind the facade of Shaftesbury's Deism, we may not expect to find a Pangloss or a Square lurking there, but neither are we prepared for what we do find—one who is almost devoid of facile optimism and bears many of the doubts and scruples of the more fervent of his orthodox contemporaries, one who, despite a measure of Stoic pride in his attitude toward the unconverted, maintains a posture of reverent humility, as when he reproves himself, "Wretch! Consider: What art thou thy self & Whence? Where dost thou inhabit? in whose City? under what administration? Whence dost thou draw thy Breath? at Whose Will & by Whose Donation hast thou receiv'd this Being, & art now at this moment sustain'd? Dost thou not consider, that by thus deserting Him . . . [thou] art thy self, an Unnaturall Son, an ill Subject, an ill Creature?" (Ex., 116).

The order without can only be realized and truly venerated by the man who has achieved order within: "By despising outward things we become strong & firm in the opinion & conception of Deity"

(Ex., 99). According to Epictetus this state of internal order fundamental to Stoicism, *ataraxia*, or, apathy, can be attained by laying
hold of those things that are within our control:

> Of things that are, God has put some under our control, and others not
> under our control. Under our control He put the finest and most impor-
> tant matter, that, indeed, by virtue of which He Himself is happy, the
> power to make use of external impressions. For when this power has its
> perfect work, it is freedom, serenity, cheerfulness, steadfastness; it is
> also . . . the sum and substance of virtue. But all other things He has
> not put under our control. Therefore we also ought to . . . lay hold in
> every way we can upon the things that are under our control, but what
> is not under our control we ought to leave to the Cosmos, and gladly
> resign to it whatever it needs, be that our children, our country, our
> body, or anything whatsoever.[30]

This strain of thought came into early Stoicism because of the influence of the Cynics; though always present, it did wane, but then during the first century A.D. it again gained strength and, perhaps due to
the situation in the Empire, continued to flourish. Shaftesbury's cosmology is drawn largely from Marcus; in seeking the path to self-
sufficiency he takes as his guide Epictetus, the most Cynic of the
great teachers of the school.

The impulse to order is basic to all phases of Stoic thought, but
inner consistency is sought chiefly for the freedom and tranquillity
it promises: without, freedom from the power of other men and
from the tyranny of circumstance, and, within, a tranquillity won by
directing the emotions so that they serve virtue rather than perturb
the mind. Epictetus greatly reveres the first of these goals; *freedom*
appears much more often on his pages than in the works of other
Stoics. This is to be expected, for although we know little of his life,
it is clear from what Arrian has recorded of his words that his actual
manumission by his master was but a pallid symbol of the spiritual
liberation which he had achieved for himself by philosophy and self-
discipline:

> I have been set free by God, I know His commands, no one has power
> any longer to make a slave of me, I have the right kind of emancipator,

---

30. Epictetus, *Discourses, Fragments*, II, 445.

and the right kind of judges. "Am I not master of your body?" Very well, what is that to me? "Am I not master of your paltry property?", Very well, what is that to me? "Am I not master of exile or bonds?" Again I yield up to you all of these things and my whole paltry body itself, whenever you will. Do make trial of your power, and you will find out how far it extends.[31]

Shaftesbury also yearned for deliverance from the intrusion of others. In a sense, his deep longing for retirement is typical of his times; the Sabine farm of his favorite poet, Horace, had long provided a setting for the English dream of escape, as it was to continue to do. And if Shaftesbury's trip to Holland was merely preparatory to a more profound retirement than is possible by change of place, the currents of English subjectivism which were to reach some sort of confluence in Berkeley had been flowing for some time and in channels so diverse as the poetry of Suckling—"'Tis not the meat, but 'tis the appetite makes eating a delight."—and the *Sermons* of Whichcote, as when he maintains that Hell is a state of mind. Yet Shaftesbury had personal reasons for feeling that his life was an island on which others insisted on trespassing. Whether he wanted to or not, he had learned all through his childhood the pains and pleasures of separateness. By his early twenties he had made some fast friends, but his letters to Locke reveal that he had become one of those persons who never will lose his sense of isolation.

And, actually, by his late twenties he felt the same way about the men he met with socially. Thus he meditates in his "Exercises" not long after arriving in Holland: "Thou hast engag'd, still sallyed out, & liv'd abroad, still prostituted thy self & committed thy Mind to Chance & the next comer, so as to be treated at pleasure by everyone, to receive impressions from every thing, & Machine-like to be mov'd & wrought upon, wound up, & govern'd exteriourly, as if there were nothing that rul'd within, or had the least controul" (Ex., 64). Apparently he did renew his ties, because later he writes,

> Remember still, what thou art to them; & they to thee: and how it
> must be when any occasion shall chance to show this opposition. how
> will they like to be thus thought of? how treat the person who has

31. Epictetus, *Discourses*, II, 367.

these thoughts? What is this but naturall Enmity cover'd over? . . . [Remember] the Fight, Enmity & Opposition of Principles; what it is that is plac'd as a Gulph between us. remember Hipocrisy, Imposture, Imposition, Intruding: Who *They* are; and What *I my Self am*. that we now talk to one another mask'd, & in disguise. that I take not Him for Him; nor he Me for Me. He pleases himself with a Specter: and I, my-self with another Specter. (Ex., 132–33)

Even when we make allowances for the fact that the meditations are devotional, not confessional, these words reveal a remarkable desire for aloof isolation and independence. The hypocrisy and imposture he upbraids in the above passage are in a sense his own.

Obviously, freedom in the Stoic discipline cannot be separated from tranquillity, for the latter is enjoyed only by those who have freed themselves from the tyranny of external impressions. One can free oneself from others by running away from them—as Shaftes-bury may have intended when he went to Holland—but not from chance, from which only emotional calm gives escape. But the events which can disturb our tranquillity are more numerous and some-times of a different order from those that bear directly on our free-dom. The imagination and the emotions can in concert produce monsters far more devastating to tranquillity than anything that malignity can conspire at, or chance let fall. Furthermore, whatever guilt the Stoic may feel when he allows malice or bad luck to per-turb him, it is nothing to what he feels when beset by a perturbation for the most part self-generated.

There is not enough information about the young Shaftesbury to enable anyone to decide whether he often became extravagantly emotional. His behavior in the matter of the Chase was certainly in-temperate; one of the letters to Carolina was written in a consuming rage; and there is sometimes a rather cool and steely obduracy evi-dent in his relations with his family, which, since it does not proceed from any observable principle, can appear to be the outcome of some resolution made in the heat of passion. Yet, he is more often remark-ably dispassionate for one so young, and these incidents merely add some welcome coloring to a portrait which can have few flesh tones before 1698. In any case, when we finally have a chance to look more directly at what is going on behind the facade, Shaftesbury reveals a typically Stoic preoccupation with the force of the passions. He strives to keep in mind the scene from the *Aeneid* where, entreated by Juno, Aeolus pierces the side of the mountain with his spear, letting forth the fury of the winds upon the ship of Aeneas and his companions:

> The same as to the Passions. think often of this Picture for tho' poet-icall, what can be more exact?—*Eurus, Notus, Boreas*—thus Anger, Ambition, Desires, Loves—eager & tumultuouse Joys, Wishes, Hopes, transporting Fancyes, extravagant Mirth, Airy-ness, Humour, Fan-tasticallness, Buffoonery, Drollery when once any of these are let loose, when once they have broke their Boundaryes & forc'd a passage, what ravage & destruction is sure to follow? and what must it cost ere all be calm agin within? (Ex., 74)

This longing to be free of the despotism of passion is traditional; what is out of place is a very powerful sense of sin which seems to have carried over from his early religious training. Loss of control almost always arouses remorse in the Stoic. Marcus continually re-proves himself, but shows no guilt so intense as can be seen in his English disciple:

> Know therefore, that when thou return'st to the same objects; if pres-ently thou art seiz'd after a certain manner; if thou admitt the least de-gree of that former Commotion & art tempted into the least feeling of that sort; all is lost, thou art over-power'd & can'st no longer command thyself. Remember what thou carriest in thy Breast: remember those former inflammations & how suddainly all takes fire; again, when a spark is got in. remember *the Fuell* within, & those unextinguish'd Passions which lye as but in the Embers. think of that Impetuouse, furiouse, impotent Temper, & what trust is to be given to it. This too remember, that as in certain Machines that are fast'ned by many Wedges, tho' they be made ever so compact & firm by this means, yet if one Wedge be loosen'd, the whole Frame shakes: so with respect to the Mind, it is not meerly in *one* Passion that the mischief is receiv'd, but in *all*. (Ex., 64–65)[32]

This passage can be better understood if we consider the practical steps the novice takes to begin his journey and how he progresses in his everyday life down the road to freedom and tranquillity. Shaftes-

---

32. The reference to a particular passion so perturbed Benjamin Rand that he si-lently eliminated it from his *Philosophical Regimen*.

bury usually follows the guidance of the *Encheiridion,* or *Manual,* of Epictetus, the systematic epitome by Flavius Arrianus of the wisdom of his master which he had recorded in the *Discourses.* The heart of the method is the proper management by reason of each external impression to which Epictetus bids us say, "You are an external impression and not at all what you appear to be!" The student is to examine whether the impression has to do with the things which are under our control or not: "And if it has to do with some one of the things not under our control, have ready to hand the answer, 'It is nothing to me.'"[33] To do this effectively one must drastically reduce the number of vagrant ideas which enter the mind, and the best way that is accomplished is by keeping the attention occupied with morally fruitful ideas. A wandering habit of mind is thus very dangerous, as Shaftesbury constantly reminds himself in the "Exercises": "Remember therefore this δόγμα [dogma] and to have it present in all trifling, fond, dallying, wand'ring, floating Seasons. Remember that all this while, I am tempering, sharpening, pointing the wrong & destructive *Visa:* whilst for want of use, the others loose their Edg, grow dull, unweildy, & unmanageable" (Ex., 96). One of the chief ways of handling forcible and insistent impressions is to apply to them the process of inversion—rather like the children's game of seeing how many words in a sentence, from a song, say, can be replaced by antonyms—"the wresting of them from their own naturall and vulgar sence into a meaning truly Naturall & free of all delusion & imposture" (Ex., 112). Sometimes an impression can be countered by placing it in a different perspective, usually one which belittles man and his affairs: "Remember also that of Marcus, to *look down as from on high &c:* A city; a Rumor of People; A nest of Mites; the Swarming of Insects—How, when the Tree is shaken? . . . Where are the solemn Brows, the important Reproofs, the Anger or Mirth?" (Ex., 42). Often, they turn the *ubi sunt* theme upon themselves, especially Marcus Aurelius: "A little while and thou wilt have forgotten everything, a little while and everything will have forgotten thee."[34]

---

33. Epictetus, *Discourses, Encheiridion,* II, 485.
34. Marcus Aurelius, *Meditations,* 173.

It may not have been very difficult for Shaftesbury, who was temperamentally ascetic and detached, to turn away from the concerns which engross the bulk of mankind, but, as a novice Stoic, Shaftesbury must also turn his back on concerns of lasting value and importance whenever they distract him from his task of inner reformation, whether they involve the pursuit of truth, the urge to improve man morally, or socially and politically: "By the suspension of the ὄρεξις [yearning] & vigorouse use of the ἔκκλισις [aversion]" even these legitimate concerns can be driven from the mind until it is again safe to become involved with them. The method is essentially the same as is used with wealth, pleasure, power, and so forth—depreciation—yet the arguments often sound specious and forced. They illustrate once more how many of the Stoic dogmas are actually therapeutic and valid only in their impact on the learning novice.

Five years before, for example, Shaftesbury had been deep in a continuing series of hairsplitting epistemological and ontological controversies with his master; now he cries out, in specific reference to Locke's theorizing,

> What is this to *Me*? What am I the wiser or better? Let me hear concerning what is of some Use to me. Let me hear (for instance) concerning *Life*, what the right Notion is, & what I am to stand to. that I may not, when the spleen comes, cry *Vanity*! and at the same time complain that Life is *short & passing*. For why so short; if not found sweet? Why do I complain both ways? Is Vanity mere Vanity a Happiness? Or can Misery pass away too soon? This is of moment to me to examine. This is what is worth my while. If I cannot find the *agreement* or *disagreement* of my *Ideas* in this place; if I can come to nothing *certain* here; what is all the rest to me? What signifyes it how I come by my *Ideas*, or how I *compound* them; which are *Simple* and which *Complex*? If I have a right Idea of Life now at this moment, that I think slightly of it & resolve with myself that it may easily be layd down; teach me how I shall remain in this opinion. (Ex., 90–91)

Though the mood may be temporary, these words accurately picture how far he has diverged philosophically from Locke by 1698 and what direction his thoughts are now taking.

Shaftesbury may have turned away from abstruse philosophical speculation by this time but he was all his life an ardent moralist, so that it seems most ironic that during this novitiate he must have no interest in whether the rest of the world acts well or badly:

> That another Person's Mind should be in health, is no more necessary to my own Mind, than it is necessary to my Body, that any other should have his Body in the same disposition. If I am dissatisfyed & troubled that any *part* of the World is Vitiouse, I may as well be dissatisfyed that any *one person* in the whole world should be so. In short. Either my Good is in certain outward Circumstances; or in a Mind and Affection. If I grieve that any of those around me are not as I would have them to be; then my Good is in outward Circumstances: if so; how is this Vertue? (Ex., 54)

The antidote which Shaftesbury usually applies when faced with this dilemma is as old as Stoicism itself, the idea of cosmopolis or the world city—the dogma that because all men share the divine reason or *logos* they are brothers in a larger community of mankind. Shaftesbury, Marcus Aurelius, and Epictetus all cry out, though in differing tones, "I am a citizen of the world." This notion of cosmopolis is to some degree transformed in middle and later Stoicism, but many of the early more Cynic teachers used it to depreciate traditional values and human concerns, including the strong Greek loyalty to the *polis* or city-state, and Stoics of all times are likely to turn to it, as Shaftesbury does, when tranquillity becomes all important to them. Readers of Seneca know that whenever he tires of the tensions and arduous commitments involved in his services for the Emperor and longs for his quiet retreat, he is likely to argue that he can serve far more men and better serve them by philosophizing in retirement. Thus universalism becomes the helpmate of individualism, which is one of the better illustrations of the paradoxical character of Stoic thinking.

All of this may seem a demanding regimen for even the most zealous Stoic to follow while going about his daily affairs, and, though Shaftesbury feels that he has been able to achieve some degree of apathy during secluded periods, he realizes that a return to social life is likely to lose him all he has gained in solitude. The Stoics well know that concern for the opinion of others is the most difficult of all weaknesses to wipe out and that the Stoic novice is peculiarly vulnerable because what is going on inside of him is likely to make him appear an odd fellow. Shaftesbury draws from Marcus and Epictetus a series of corrective reflections for use when he feels that the pressure of opinion is making him swerve from his course, and he memorizes a corresponding series of key words, one to trigger each of the reflections. The word *calamity* is to suggest the following train of thought: "They laugh at the Habit, the Posture, Place, Countenance. shall this disturb? But were it another case (a Loss of Fortune, of Friends; a Melancholy or Concern about a dying Relation or a Sinking Publick) this would then be otherwise; there would be little regard to this or to anything they could say." The words *Robbers and Common Women* bring to mind the question "How do Robbers, Debauchees, & the Common Women? But, These are not asham'd of ill actions And, shall they be unhurt by the Report of others that are Vertuouse; whilst Thou art inferior to the Reproaches of those who are Ignorant & Vitiouse?" *Children and Idiots* reminds him that since he is not perturbed by the ill opinion of these creatures, why should he be by the opinions of those who, morally speaking, are in the same class. *The world and its Inhabitants* brings on the *de contemptu mundi* theme, and God admonishes him that there is a more important judge passing on his behavior: "Why, Man! is there not a Greater Presence than all this?" (Ex., 41–43).

And, though it may involve a certain amount of deception, the apprentice may have to protect himself by use of a persona—a "fixed stamp of character," Epictetus calls it—which he can perfect when he is alone and display in company. The adept will need no mask; an entirely different person, he presumably has no need for rules either, which is why it is misleading to read the *Encheiridion* as the description of a Stoic—the personal Epictetus as he appears in the pages of *Discourses* is a more accurate portrait. Finally, if there is no other way, the novice must take that advice of Epictetus which Shaftesbury followed in going to Holland: "Flee from your former habits, flee from the laymen [idiotai], if you would begin to be somebody some time."[35]

The ideals of tranquillity and independence which the Stoic

35. Epictetus, *Discourses*, II, 109.

teacher promises are universally attractive. From another point of view the Cynical phase of Stoicism has something to offer even more attractive to many men, for, if a feeling of mastery is the measure of one's success in attaining power, Stoicism is a philosophy of power. The traditional arrogance does not spring wholly from a consciousness of belonging to an elect: "The good man is invincible; naturally, for he enters no contest where he is not superior. 'If you want my property in the country,' says he, 'take it; take my servants, take my office, take my paltry body. But you will not make my desire fail to get what I will, nor my aversion fall into what I would avoid.'"[36] He is not humble, because he possesses that ideal power, that power which Milton's Satan could not attain because he was corrupt.

Even from the point of view of the layman or outsider, some aspects of Stoic individualism are quite attractive; most of us applaud self-knowledge, self-discipline, and the sort of devotion to virtue which never seeks or expects reward. Yet it must be admitted that this phase of Stoicism is more likely to appear meritorious to the practitioner than to the spectator. The Stoic may believe he is following nature or imitating God, but these relations are not obvious to the onlooker, to whom it may seem that the philosopher is merely sacrificing human ties and the obligations which they involve in order that he may satisfy his own selfish desires for peace, quiet, and personal sanctity. Or if the onlooker is willing to admit that the Stoic is not selfish and is genuinely seeking a higher good, he may also suspect that the lesser good most likely to be sacrificed for the higher one will somehow involve his own personal welfare. Add to this the fact that although the devotee feels that in suppressing all his emotions he is cultivating his true—rational—nature, to most it will appear that he is dehumanizing himself. All this makes it clear why Shaftesbury went to such pains to conceal the fact that he aspired to be a Stoic.

As soon as one is well persuaded by the Stoics that a principle such as following nature or the necessity of tranquil self-sufficiency is a

36. *Ibid.*, 47.

basic dogma of the school, the next thing he had better do is to look around for the inevitable paradox. In the case of *ataraxia*, there is not far to look, for the third fundamental axiom of Stoicism is *koinonia*, or the fellowship of mankind—not an abstract ideal but an injunction practical and peremptory. As Marcus Aurelius puts it, "Delight in this one thing and take thy rest therein—from social act to go on to social act, keeping all thy thoughts on God."[37] He is, of course, in some degree exceptional. The creed of each Stoic reflects his own pattern of emphasis among these three basic axioms, and certainly Marcus stresses *koinonia* more vigorously than any other major Stoic. The man himself was not only devoutly loyal to the traditional Roman personal and civic virtues, he was truly magnanimous and deeply compassionate. During his reign Marcus Aurelius erected but one temple, to Beneficence.

Yet social duty is increasingly emphasized by most Stoics from the first century B.C. on, and it is a logical development from their passion for order, not an accretion. When the individual achieves *ataraxia* he is following nature because he is imitating the order of the whole. *Ataraxia* and *koinonia* do not seem so contradictory when they are juxtaposed to the Epicurean's world in which the whole is dominated by a chaotic atomism and mankind lives in disorderly selfishness. When Epicurus wished "to do away with the natural fellowship of men with one another," Epictetus says he would have liked to be there to ask, tauntingly, "Why do *you* care, then? Allow us to be deceived. Will you fare any the worse, if all the rest of us are persuaded that we do have a natural fellowship with one another, and that we ought by all means to guard it? . . . Man why do you worry about us, why keep vigil on our account, why light your lamp, why rise betimes, why write such big books?"[38] The tranquillity which Epicurus sought in retirement was so austere that the Stoic's concern for *koinonia* is one of the best ways of distinguishing his retreat from that of the Epicurean.

Men are universally brothers because each of them shares in the divine reason which permeates the universe. More important, rea-

37. Marcus Aurelius, *Meditations*, 133.
38. Epictetus, *Discourses*, I, 373.

son functioning in the same general way in all men will cause them to acknowledge their community of interest—even if some of them do so unwittingly, as in the case of Epicurus rising betimes to write big books. Every man, then, possesses a social reason—*politikos logos*, Marcus calls it—analogous to the social instinct which causes many species of animal life to band together. As we have seen in the *Inquiry*, this faculty which binds men together is usually called *natural affection* by Shaftesbury; it is emotional rather than rational, and it thus resembles even more closely the instinct of animals. When he fears that remaining tinges of his former Christianity are causing him to doubt "*Man's being Sociable by Nature*," he asks himself, "Are Bees, Ants & even all Creatures that do but herd, allow'd Society; & man deny'd it? . . . Consider, therefore, how great must be the Power of those former Impressions to marr & corrupt?" (Ex., 101).

In the writing of the great Roman Stoics a typically austere and remote image of the ideal predominates; it is in their lives that the influence of the notion of *koinonia* is best seen. They may be austere, but very seldom are they removed from the world and its concerns in order to perfect themselves and contemplate the whole in tranquillity. At one extreme we have the greatest of emperors, the world's most important public man for nineteen long, wearying years; at the other, Epictetus, a slave who was nonetheless a renowned and active teacher, and, between these extremes, his disciple Arrian, who became a colonial governor and general, Seneca, Musonius Rufus, very much a public figure, or Panaetius of Rhodes, one of the fathers of Roman Stoicism and a wealthy man of the world.

Furthermore, Stoic teaching depended much upon the use of exemplars, and the figures they chose for what amounted to near deification also reflect this other side of the creed. Diogenes, admired by some of the more Cynic writers such as Epictetus, is about as close as we can come to the stereotype of the detached sage. We can easily forget that Socrates was a senator, magistrate, and soldier, but the Stoics who revere him never do. Ulysses is another wise man, and Cato of Utica was especially revered in the early decades of the Empire, but the greatest of all Stoic heroes is Hercules—later,

Shaftesbury was to write a whole treatise interpreting a painting of him which he had commissioned. There is no real paradox in the choice of very active men as exemplars of virtue, because ultimately the ideal wise man is active. The novice must withdraw; his concern is with freeing himself of his old habits and developing tranquil self-sufficiency. In the adept, however, *ataraxia* and *koinonia* coalesce; he has so ordered himself within that he serves the greater order of mankind naturally and without fear of the world's intrusion upon him. Social action is at once the proof and the fruition of his virtue.

This suggests the general nature of the answer to the most perplexing question about Shaftesbury's Stoicism: Why, when he has written what was to become the most influential book in the history of the ethical movement which made morality dependent upon good affection toward one's fellow men is there so little attention given to *koinonia* in his meditations? Students of Shaftesbury have had several choices of what to do with the ideas that appear in the "Exercises." They have tried to fit them into the general structure of his thought, treating them as little different from the ideas they find expressed in the works which he intended for the public. This approach does not work very well. An alternative is either to ignore the Stoicism or, conversely, as in one rather brilliant attempt, to ignore some of what was published and interpret the remainder as essentially Stoic. In any of these methods there are a good many pieces left over when one is finished. The analyst's situation is rather like that of an archaeologist who when trying to reconstruct a building from its ruins comes across in the heap a totally different sort of stones which do not seem to fit in with the materials he has been using. Assuming that all the materials come from one specific era, as is the situation here, he can attempt to fit and mortar the whole heap together into one structure, or he can ignore the new sort of fragments, or, perhaps, tear down what he has already built and start over with the new materials alone. In the case of Shaftesbury's ideas, it is necessary first to acknowledge that the fragments come from two edifices different in function, then to proceed with the rebuilding of both, and finally, to relate one structure to the other.

In relating the "Exercises" to the *Inquiry*, function is all important. Shaftesbury is in a sense reversing the normal order of procedure on the road to sagedom. After discussing the methods by which a young man can attain *ataraxia*, Epictetus says, "Then, when he has worked his way through this first field of study and mastered it like an athlete, let him come to me again and say, 'I want, it is true, to be tranquil and free from turmoil, but I want also, as a god-fearing man, a philosopher and a diligent student, to know what is my duty towards the gods, towards parents, towards brothers, towards my country, towards strangers.' Advance now to the second field of study; this also is yours."[39] Despite the occasional harshness of the first revision of the *Inquiry*, Shaftesbury is already the "Friend of Man" when he comes to seek the tranquil self-sufficiency which Stoicism promises him. There is no need to rehearse the rules of benevolence; what is necessary is intensive, heightened meditations—exercises, which will turn him away from all considerations other than the harmony of his own soul, which may even turn him away temporarily from any feelings of charity.

When one singles out ideas from the "Exercises" and the *Inquiry* for comparison they look as if they ought to be congruent, but somehow they are not. The treatment of deity provides the closest parallel, yet in the "Exercises" Shaftesbury is largely concerned with affirming the cosmic nature of the deity and the essential harmony of the universe so governed by it; the disjunctive syllogisms of the *Inquiry* are directed against the atheist and against the god of wrath and revenge, the daemon, worshiped by some of the orthodox. The concept of natural affection is vital to both works, though it is interpreted divergently, in the meditations directed to the deity, and in the *Inquiry* to mankind. In most cases these differences can be reconciled in terms of function—the ideas often look as if they ought to be congruent because they are the same ideas, only seen differently. The two halves of a mussel's shell are the same color and texture and involve the same families of curves, yet they never can be superimposed. Treated as mirror images and put together properly, they do make a whole. So, too, do the "Exercises" and the *Inquiry*, when we stand back from them: contemplation of Nature and the search

39. *Ibid.*, 347.

for *ataraxia* intensively stressed in the one, *koinonia* in the other—all three primary concerns of the Stoic come together in the two books. This is not to suggest that the *Inquiry* is essentially Stoic; the fellowship of man is too much a matter of emotion and it is carried too far for even Marcus to accept. The *Inquiry* for all its ancient roots is modern, just as surely as the "Exercises," despite some modern touches, is ancient.

The *Inquiry* is a polemic work intended to convince a large audience that man is ultimately beneficent and that Locke's ideas do not mean a broadly based, humane morality must be abandoned, that one must now choose between relativism and a wholly biblical ethos. The "Exercises" on the other hand is a private work, therapeutic in the same way that many seventeenth-century metaphysical religious poems are—by repeating certain loaded, corrective axioms one changes one's own views in the process. It could be useful to a necessarily small group of Stoic novices—Stoicism is not for everyone—but even in this case the evils it intends to correct are those which Shaftesbury sees predominant in his own heart.

If the "Exercises" are ancient, just how true are they to their originals? The aspect in which Shaftesbury diverges most from his masters is in his attitude toward the emotions. Neither Epictetus nor Marcus is as indurately rationalistic as we commonly think the Stoics are—and certainly not so emotionless as their English and French admirers of the seventeenth century thought them. Both philosophers tolerate emotion in the man who can properly use reason to manage impressions, because they can be confident the emotions will not flare into passion and perturb him. Affections which are subordinate to reason are in a sense rational, and if when Epictetus refers to a favorable emotion like love it seems a rather cool and aloof emotion, there is fervor enough in Marcus' injunction that we must love all men as brothers. The basis of the Stoic brotherhood of man is clearly rational, however, and natural affection between the kin and the social instincts of the animal kingdom are used only as analogies to explain the *politikos logos*, which depends upon each man's reason acknowledging that reason is divine and common to all men, bonding them one to another. In the "Exercises," Shaftesbury uses *reason* much less than his predecessors, and the significance of this becomes clear when we realize that for him the bond that unites men, the higher "natural affection" which he longs to develop in himself, is more emotional than rational. What lies behind this significant change in the basis of Stoicism is obvious; Shaftesbury is the child of his own century, and, as the *Inquiry* shows, by 1698 he was very well aware that the movement culminating in Locke had stripped *reason* of its more remarkable intuitive powers, mechanized it, and tarnished its divinity. It was no longer a divine faculty of the mind but merely one of the mind's powers, *reasoning*.

In conclusion, then, the "Exercises" are remarkably true to the spirit of later Stoicism, and in most respects Shaftesbury varies no more from his masters than each Stoic is bound to vary from every other. Because he is mainly concerned with achieving tranquillity and self-sufficiency for himself, the difficulties he would encounter were he to enter into other regions of philosophy which interested the Stoics are masked. His dependence upon the affections would raise problems in a system so rationalistic, no less perplexing than if he were to speculate more largely on the Stoic deity in an age when men could no longer credit the particular sort of materialistic physics upon which the concept was based. Shaftesbury must have been aware of his dilemma; he often remarks poignantly in the "Exercises" on the impossibility of reviving true classical philosophy in his time. Although he could not re-create their system, he did have an appreciation of the Stoics and he set down their essential moral wisdom. This is his achievement.

V

Lord
of the Manor
1700–1702

The land which Shaftesbury inherited upon the death of the second Earl lies principally in the northwest corner of Dorset. If one imagines an equilateral triangle made up of nine- or ten-mile sides with the northernmost face running roughly east and west, most of the family land would lie within it. The northeast corner of the triangle lies in Wiltshire; the northwest corner is crossed by the hills of Cranborne Chase, now sold to pay part of the debt left by the first Earl. Most of the land within the triangle is low and rolling, and in the summer assumes an unbelievably lush greenness. The estates are drained by the river Allen, which runs south to Wimborne Minister, where it joins the Stour. In Shaftesbury's day, something less than half the land where his property lay like patchwork was cultivated; the rest was covered with woods, downs, and small villages. This is the land which Thomas Hardy so richly described, old when the Romans settled there. The Badbury Rings lie just south of it, and around Whichbury in the northwest a relief map shows all sorts of earthworks whose purposes have been long since forgotten. Yet despite centuries of cultivation the land through careful husbandry had grown richer as the ages passed and Shaftesbury was to leave it richer still.

St. Giles's House lies midway in the southeast side of the triangle. Only the east facade now bears any resemblance to what the third Earl knew. Built by his grandfather, the house is faced in pink stone. The front, about seventy feet across, is cut by a heavy eave line at thirty feet, surmounted by three huge chimneys. All is symmetry. Six large windows and the central door are repeated in the seven windows of the second story, the central of these windows being more ornately framed to match the door below it. The decoration is restrained: the door has a bow-shaped canopy above it, all of the windows are keystoned, and large quoins run up the sides. From this narrow facade springs a long and rather loose structure running westward, much of it built since the third Earl's day.[1]

We know even less about the interior of the house as it looked then. The high-ceilinged great rooms on the ground floor face east and the third Earl's bedroom was over one of these on the south corner, where it received the most light. All the rooms were centered around an open court—a winter dining room, the formal dining room with drawing rooms, the withdrawing room, the cedar room, nurseries, and chapel. There is no way of determining the exact number of bedrooms, but the third Earl's will reveals that there were at least forty beds, most of them double. The bedrooms were largely on the second floor, in the garrets, and in the second floor of the various service buildings attached to the house. The finer bedrooms were sumptuously decorated. Shaftesbury's will mentions "six peices of History of Jupiter," "four hangings of sylvan scenes, four peices of the history of Hero and Leander." It is possible to rate the bedrooms simply by the quality of fabric used in the upholstery and hangings. Thus the best rooms are done in damask, red and green. Further down come kitterminster stuff, then serge, drugget, and finally, just old stuff. The walls of the great rooms were filled with portraits of the family and its relations, the Spencers, the Manners, and others. Giving a more somber air to the formal dining room were three pieces of the history of Moses and four of the history of the Apostles. Overall, the house must have been very impressive because even before all of the third Earl's improvements his grandfather here entertained Charles II.

Attached to the main house and running westward were the various rooms devoted to serving the home, which, since the whole establishment was self-sustaining, must have numbered fifteen or twenty. There was a parlor for the servants, a steward's room, and a

1. The tenth Earl has removed much of the western end in order to return the house to the way it looked in the first Earl's day.

smoking room. The bake house had a separate room for boulting the flour. The kitchen and pastry room formed a separate complex, with sculleries and wet and dry larders. There was a malt house, a brewery which also produced cider, and cellars for storing the product. A wash house, ironing room, dairy, storerooms, still house, and stable complete the house. Only the still house needs any explanation. It had nothing to do with liquor in the modern sense—for some reason neither spirits nor wine appear in the will, though cider and beers are carefully totaled up. The still room was rather the source of flavors and scents for the house, of extracts and essences used in both cooking and medicine. The still house maid used the mortars and pestles, alembics, sieves, and scales to produce from the gardens and orchards such flavorings as rosewater and almond paste, in addition to all sorts of medicinals. She also had charge of the coffee- and tea-making equipment. Shaftesbury's instructions to his servants reflect the constant apprehension of fire necessary until the present century, so that it is no surprise to find that a "fire engine" and pumps are always ready to protect the whole establishment.

Shaftesbury gave specific instructions for visitors to the house when he was absent, and these rules give us some idea of what was done when he was present. For farmers and tenants his servants are to charge the household accounts a shilling a day, for common men or relations of under-servants, sixpence.

But if any Gentlemen's Steward or Head-Servent, or other of the better rank dines with you, I allow 2s. or 1/2 a crown, or what more a Head you think fitt to charge, & Wine when you think fit to call for Wine. & take notice, no other Person is to be entertain'd at either of the Tables, but who is so charg'd & allow'd for. If any of the Gentlemen be so kind at any time as to call to see you, or to enquire after me, or if they bring any Freind to see the place, let them allways be offered a botle of Wine; and lett Jonathan & the House-Maid & the Gardiner be allways ready to wait on them, Within & Without-doors, with all civility & respect. If there come any People from Pool or Weymouth; let them be kindly entertain'd on account of mine and my Brother's obligation to them on account of the Publick. If there come any Strangers that have the countenance of Gentlemen (especially if Forreignors that are travelling) let them in the same manner be civily received, & if occasion require at anytime, let them be offered a Bed & what conveniency the House affords: taking their names down, to acquaint me with it, & that I may know them.[2]

We even have a notion of the kinds of food the family and guests at St. Giles's House consumed. The typical upper-class meal of the day was, of course, simply meat and more meat. Except for Friday, the first course of dinner always included beef—boiled, stewed, or roasted. Along with this, puddings and also a lamb or veal pie, or perhaps asparagus, or pigeons and bacon, or a calf's head. There would also be a fish course, for which veal and bacon could be substituted. The second course always began with at least two joints of mutton, lamb, or veal. The second serving was generally pigeons, though lobsters could be substituted on Friday. There followed two or three servings: usually an apple pie, a tart, or sweet breads; a salad or asparagus; and finally still another joint or perhaps rabbits, ducks, or chickens.

Supper was a lighter meal. Almost invariably it included both asparagus and a salad. There was also the inevitable joint, though sometimes cold meat was served. A separate course of chicken or pigeons was also served, though bacon and eggs or poached eggs could substitute. And supper also included a course made up of leftovers: lamb or veal hash, a lamb's head, calf's foot, cold ham, or tripe. Turkeys, geese, partridges, pheasants, and venison were also served in season. All of this is taken from a sample menu prepared, one assumes, by Shaftesbury himself, since he wrote the rest of the family book in which it appears.[3]

We also know the wine Shaftesbury drank during and after his meals, although the sample list for 1707 which he entered in his directions to his butler raises some questions, too. The list looks like this—Shaftesbury in his usual systematic way also lists the number of bottles drunk each day, where, when, and by whom—but these figures are a sample of the stock on hand:

Greek wine	712
Red Port	42

2. The Earl of Shaftesbury to Henry Dalicourt, February 7, 1700, in letter inserted in Family Book, PRO 30/24/22/3.

3. PRO 30/24/22/3, p. 109. Asparagus could even then be forced in frames.

Pale wine	287
Old Red	198
W: wine	24
Langedock	44
Sack	30
Palme	1cs
Old Hock	6
Rhennish	12
Madera	5
Tent	4
Mum	156
Cyder	168
Best Claret	44[4]

From his tabulation of how much wine was consumed daily at St. Giles's House, it is clear that some bottles were kept over until the following year, but most wine bottles were then more spherical than cylindrical, making proper storage—bottles laid side-by-side—impossible. It is not easy to estimate how long a bottle with a dry cork might keep.

As our look at Shaftesbury's farming practices will show, it is an illusion to assume that because so many institutions of the past from our point of view seem to have been changing slowly, all or even a major part of the milieu of an individual from that past was altering in the same leisurely manner. No better example of this truth could be pointed to than the state of the wine trade in Shaftesbury's day, and it hardly needs to be emphasized that this was of greater importance then than now, since for a member of his class almost all that it was desirable, or safe, to drink either had been boiled or was alcoholic.

4. That there is so little French wine and that Greek wine heads the list reflect the state of the trade. Greek wine is, at least, Mediterranean in origin, and should have been red and dry. Many of the others are self-explanatory. Pale wine is likely a sherry. Old Red is either port or French. Palme is a Canary. Tent is Spanish—heavy, dark, and of low proof. Mum is a beer brewed in Brunswick. All books on the subject deal with the London wine trade, whereas Shaftesbury's wine came only 25 miles or so from Southampton, where the imports may have differed. André L. Simon's *Bottlescrew Days: Wine Drinking in England during the Eighteenth Century* (1926) and the third volume of his *History of the Wine Trade in England* (3 vols.; 1909) have been useful, as has H. Warner Allen's *A History of Wine* (1961), though his figures are not always to be trusted.

England was, during the seventeenth century, a beer and wine drinking nation. For example, the allotment of wine to British sailors has been estimated at a third of an imperial gallon a day. There is so much controversy over wine in the later seventeenth century that it is difficult to pick a date when consumption began its permanent decline. The year 1667, when Colbert prohibited the importation of English goods, would be as good a date as any. From then on there was a steady war of commerce, punctuated by military wars during which the English prohibited the import of French wine. Charles II banned French wine, James reinstated it, and William and Mary both raised the duty on it and at times banned it. By the 1690s, as Richard Ames points out in his *A Search After Claret* (1691) and *A Farewell to Wine* (1693), it was very difficult to find a glass of what Englishmen had been accustomed to drinking.

England did turn to Portugal for wine after the Methuen treaty of 1703, but the Portuguese had not then the facilities to produce either the quantity or the quality needed. As a result, by 1707, when Shaftesbury compiled his list of wines, London was already on its way to becoming the gin capital of the world. In 1714 two million gallons of the poor man's drink were distilled; in thirty years the distillation had increased tenfold. The Earl's own cellar confirms again what we have seen since he first set up housekeeping in Chelsea. However austere his philosophy and moderate his habit of living, Shaftesbury's daily life involved a substantial measure of physical enjoyment and deliberate connoisseurship.

There remains a tablebook to give us a notion of who ate this food and drank this wine at Shaftesbury's board. It gives a full account of the entertaining at Chelsea, but since it begins in mid-December of 1700 and ends the following September, the record for St. Giles's House is incomplete. In December Shaftesbury's brother Maurice and his sister Dorothy and her husband Edward are there for most of the month. A number of guests are local political associates: Sir James Ash (1660–1733), George Lewen, mayor of Poole, and Sir Nathaniel Napper. There are clergymen: his own chaplain Mr. Horsey and Samuel Stillingfleet, nephew of the Bishop of Worcester. In January there are Mr. Churchill, the bookseller (Awnsham, presumably [d. 1728]); the Hoopers for the rest of the month; and every night, too, Mrs. Percivall.[5]

The book must have been kept by a domestic who moved with Shaftesbury because the Chelsea entries go on without a break, though the Chelsea house had a different staff. It makes one wish we knew more of Shaftesbury's life in London. In addition to Shaftesbury's immediate family and his close friends Sir John Cropley and Thomas Micklethwayte (1678–1718), the list includes the names of most of the powerful politicians whom Shaftesbury would be likely to invite to dinner—Lords Somers, Spencer, later Sunderland (1674–1722), Pembroke (1656–1733), Townshend (1674–1738), Mr. Robert Harley (1661–1724), and many lesser figures. There are four persistent figures: Dr. Chamberlayn, probably John (1666–1723), a physician and author and continuer of his father's *The Present State of England*; the Reverend William Stephens, Shaftesbury's literary collaborator; Adam Franke, a correspondent of Shaftesbury's regarding Dutch affairs; and Sir John Cope. There are old friends of Shaftesbury's, Lord Mordaunt (1681?–1710); Gilbert Burnet, Bishop of Salisbury; Sir Walter Young; and Dr. Pau. There was a Tory nobleman, Lord Kent (1671–1740), and a Whig peer, Lord Ross (maybe the one b. 1656?–1738). Perhaps the most amusing entry is "Lord Fetchwater." The keeper of the diary, who may have been John Howard, Shaftesbury's manservant, is not too literate, though no one can be accused for mispelling a name when even the best writers used a freehand phonetic method. This is doubtless Shaftesbury's childhood friend, Baron FitzWalter.

All is quieter after the return to St. Giles's House; the Hoopers, the other sisters and their companion, Mrs. Pack, and frequently Maurice stayed there. Dr. King and the Bishop of Salisbury also dined, and Dr. Pau, who was there for most of the summer. Three of Shaftesbury's chaplains, Horsey, Gane, and Clerke, dined, as well as the Reverend Mr. Sutton. Arent Furley (d. 1712) arrived to spend a week. Significant for Shaftesbury's growing interest in art was the

---

5. Probably a relation of the first Earl's old retainer in Carolina. Shaftesbury's will shows that she had deposited a substantial sum with him.

arrival of the Dutch painter John Closterman for a long visit. The diary ends on September 24.

On becoming an earl, Shaftesbury's first thoughts were not of power or pleasure, but of the awesome responsibility. Now he was for the first time master of the family estate:

> Behold an other *Age*! (for so it may be call'd) another Face of things, another Scene, another Period of thy Life. Go back to what it was lately, a year or less than a year since. Are not all the Views chang'd? Family, Friends, Father, Brother, Sisters. some allready gon out of Life, remov'd, chang'd: Others in another manner chang'd, & in a way still of further Chang. New Ages, New Seasons of Life, new Companyes, new Opinions, new Pursuits, new Passions. all is under chang. all is chang.[6]

There is no precise way of estimating the rent roll at this time, but if we add the estate inherited from his stepmother in 1694 to that of the second Earl it comes to about £4,500. This would appear to be a favorable situation for a young nobleman to succeed to, yet there are complications. Williams, the Earl's previous chief steward, and ostensible cause of Lady Shaftesbury's flight from St. Giles's House, had of course been stealing from the estate, and even though he repaid £700 on leaving, substantial arrears remained. It seems doubtful that there was much improvement in the return from the estate until the effects of the third Earl's management from 1700 to 1703 appeared.

Again, Shaftesbury can live on two or three hundred pounds a year abroad and he continually complains of expenses at home, yet he can spend with a lavish hand. The £1,500 his Chelsea house cost him was likely the smaller part of the cost of buying it, rebuilding the house, furnishing it, and setting up an elaborate garden. St. Giles's House had for a long time received little attention and Shaftesbury immediately set about making it an estate worthy of his rank. There is no real paradox here. His ability to live cheaply abroad is due to a remarkable flexibility of spirit. He can live like a philosopher if he wishes to, or he can live as a virtuoso and an earl. On one

---

6. Written at St. Giles's House in December 1699, in "Exercises," 143.

side Stoicism, on the other responsibility to his family, to his country, and, personally, to his cultivated tastes, a need to do things right whatever the cost. Furthermore, Shaftesbury actually expanded his political activities after entering the House of Lords. There is no way of telling how much it cost him to reverse temporarily political tendencies in the Southwest during 1701. We know that his impecunious brother paid out £700 in his own efforts to assist Shaftesbury.

He also had to provide for Maurice and four sisters some sort of financial competence. Maurice had received the proprietorship of North Carolina—no bargain—before Ashley went to Holland in 1698. On his father's death Shaftesbury made over Purton to Maurice and promised him the rent from the Holborn Estates. Together these yielded about a thousand pounds a year. For each of the sisters, Shaftesbury agreed to set aside several thousand pounds as a dowry.[7] By 1703, as a result of these financial burdens Shaftesbury owed £7,000 to the Duke of Marlborough and, at least, an additional £2,000 for the dowry of one of his sisters.

As a lord of the manor Shaftesbury has a host of varying responsibilities. He can act as a landlord or dispense charity or arbitrate disputes or make judgments which have the force of law without ever telling us what role he is playing, simply because he does not himself sense any sharply defined difference. In these as in other matters he is simply holding court. We do have an autograph record of his judgments for 1700 and 1701. Most of the notes in the book relate to Shaftesbury's holding court on one estate after another, but there are also sections on "Coppices and Woods," "Household and Family," "Laborers, Hinds, and Parish Affairs," "Husbandry and Country-Business," "Finances," "the Admiralty," and "Parliamentary Interests." On the whole, the notes provide a good picture of farming in Dorset at the time and of Shaftesbury as a landlord. Not only does he record his decisions, he also speculates on them privately, and frequently returns later to add his afterthoughts in the margins.

The role of lord of the manor is itself changing. We have already seen the sort of difficulties he experienced with Cranborne Chase,

7. PRO 30/45/19/2/p. 45.

despite the fact that during his own century there may have been a medieval Chase court presiding over such problems. That the intense emotions, even violence, generated among those who thought they had rights to the Chase go on for over a century after Shaftesbury's era should warn us that this change is taking place slowly. This does not lessen the anguish of the participants, however.

Or consider the patchwork terminology of rents in this changing society. It gets to be a game of tabulating them: in addition to just plain rent, there are the fee farm rents, audit, or quit rents, reserved rents, high rents, rack rents, penny rents, and provisional rents. All of these are paid in cash, except the last, which in one case was fourteen capons per annum. Even the stewards cannot distinguish between some of these relics of the past. George Yeo, bailiff of the Shaftesbury estate of Pawlett in Somerset, divides the rent which he collects into rack rents, audit or quit rents, and high rents. When the Dorset steward audits an account of income he divides it into rack rents, fee farm rents, and reserved rents. The usages can and do differ with locality but quit rents and fee farm rents are specific legal terms and not at all interchangeable.

The land Shaftesbury owned was rented on three bases: by copyhold, at rack rent, or by leasehold. The first is the commonest form. The second, which involves only the land around St. Giles's House and the Somerset lands, is more interesting because it raises the question of whether Shaftesbury was aware of the strongly pejorative sense of the term as we use it now. The *Oxford English Dictionary* lists a few uses of the negative sense of the term as early as the sixteenth century; by the mid eighteenth century *rack rent* almost always means extortionate rent. To Shaftesbury rack-renting is a less favorable method of renting than copyhold.

Perhaps a specific example will make this clearer and show the complexity of land transactions on the estate and the motivations involved. In 1701 Shaftesbury decided to go ahead and convert his rack-rented properties in Cranborne to copyhold. There was no absolutely binding custom against doing this with land on his own estate; moreover, he needed the money and, as he remarks, the houses in Cranborne were prone to fire because they were thatched and close together and thus safer for the landlord on copyhold than at rack rent, where the "lease" is renewed annually.[8] He rack-rented a house with eight acres of land to Nat Symms, a butcher, at £8 and 10s. per annum. Tom Clerk offered to purchase this land on copyhold for £65. Symms then offered £56 for the land and £30 for the house, with 2s. rental over a fourteen-year period. Shaftesbury then offered the house alone for £40 with 2s. rental, but Symms came and begged him to make a new offer for both house and land. He pointed out that he moved to Cranborne in order to work for Shaftesbury's grandfather, that he recently had had the land chalked at some expense, and that he was in part responsible for saving Shaftesbury's life when he fell in a stream as a small child. Shaftesbury then offered him the property for three lives, fourteen years, at £105 fine and 6s. rent, probably reserved for the poor box. Symms accepted this price—very close to his first offer—and assigned the lives to two grandchildren and a nephew. At rack rent the property would have yielded £119; as a copyhold it yields £109, including rent, and the copyholder is responsible for the heriot—a fee in lieu of feudal duties, seldom more than a pound or two. The copyhold is an advantage to the tenant, most of all because he has security. It is just as much advantage to Shaftesbury; he has a tenant committed to the property and he has the fine to add to his cash balance. Since he also converted purely rural land in Somerset from rack rent to copyhold, it was clearly preferable to him; just as obviously, to Shaftesbury rack-renting is not a form of extortion, but simply a different, less desirable mode of landholding.[9]

Lease hold is another alternative, especially for specific portions of a manor—or for the almost innumerable odd properties which Shaftesbury owned. The estate included houses and parsonages and their gardens; coppices, chases, and their purlieus; rabbit warrens; land for grazing cattle and sheep—meadows, pasture, downs, and moors; turverys, chalk pits, and lime kilns; hop fields and malt houses; the Black Bull Inn at Cranborne and the market at Shaftesbury; blacksmiths' shops, grist mills, and paper mills; and yet more.

8. He was here anticipating history. According to T. W. W. Smart's *A Chronicle of Cranbourne* (1841), the town did burn down in this fashion in 1748.

9. PRO 30/24/19/2/pp. 28–29, 40–41.

Many of these might be held by copyhold, but when they were held under leasehold the term varied widely from one year to—the longest I have discovered—forty-three years. The estate assessed rack renters for land tax and poor taxes, whereas leaseholders and copyholders paid the taxes directly.

Much of the land Shaftesbury owned naturally had some sort of ecclesiastical background. A number of estates have tithe farms, and in some cases great tithe farms; part of the proceeds once went to the local priest. All of this terminology is archaic, of course, but it would be understandable enough then, since the earlier ownership of land can be characterized by the old saw that if the abbot of Glaston married the abbess of Shaston, they would be the richest couple in England. The parsonages with glebe land which Shaftesbury holds have a different origin. The decline of religion in the recent past, rather than the dissolution of the monasteries, is responsible for the shift from religious to secular uses. All of these properties, whatever their origin, became the daily business of Shaftesbury whenever he lived at St. Giles's House.

Sometimes Shaftesbury helped settle the division between his own land and another's. On October 21, 1700, he met at Toyd Farm beyond the northeast boundary of his estate with Mr. Pitt and Mr. Freke of Shroton, the Damerham tenants, and the Duke of Newcastle's representatives. On most of the boundaries there was little disagreement, but one "was (according to us) a Grave of a *Felo de se* at the parting of the three Lands (Toyd Rockbourn & Damerham) & at the parting of the Countyes; and (according to them) a Hole dug about a hundred yards or more to the Left. The Witnesses for us were Will: Rook for 50 years, Tho: Holloway for 45, Ambrose Triphook for 55, Francis Triphook for 40, Will: Griffin for 44, and all from their own knowledg. for them only one Henery Hill for 11 years only, by Hear-say only."[10] Pitt and Freke must have been overwhelmed by the evidence because they readily agreed to this part of the boundary. In another instance where Pitt was less satisfied Shaftesbury conceded "for peace sake" five or six acres of sheep pasture. "And to settle this for ever hereafter we then dugg holes &

10. PRO 30/24/19/2/pp. 78–79.

staked it out ordering the People by mutual agreement the Thursday following to meet & bring great stones for the Boundary's perpetuity." An early large-scale map of Dorset and Wiltshire shows that the boundary between the counties—for that is what Shaftesbury and his associates are deciding on—must have been the product of innumerable such decisions over the centuries. The following year he complained of "these fantastical piqued & un-mark'd Bounds, very unlike those of a County which when divided on our Downs are continued commonly in great Dikes or other Remarkable Marks & in a tollerable straitness."[11]

When such neighborly agreement was absent Shaftesbury sometimes sought relief from the courts. Fundamentally he was probably as litigious as most Englishmen of the day, but with Marcus Aurelius looking over his shoulder he must often have resisted the impulse. What could be more destructive of peace of mind than an interminable lawsuit in which all too often the attorneys were the true victors. Although we do not have much of his legal correspondence, there are many references in passing to his attorneys.

Consider the matter of Costards Bushes—a wooded area in the purlieu of Cranborne Chase, which may have once included an orchard as the name suggests. We have a draft of a letter from Shaftesbury written on November 14, 1701, to Thomas Freke, the purchaser of the Chase. It and Freke's reply are studies in envenomed politesse. After regretting that Freke's illness has prevented him waiting on him, he says,

> Having this opportunity I cannot but return my most sincere thanks & Gratitude both for the Favours I have receiv'd from you & for those kind Expressions which I have heard from other hands. This sufficiently assures me of your Freindship & such a Freind as you cannot leave anyone a sufferer for his Freindship nor should I mention that small present of the Bushes in the Chase you were pleas'd so kindly to accept, but because of the uncertainty of when I may be so happy as to see you again now I am soon to be called up to Town & thus being so small a thing as may in the midst of others of more moment be forgot. tho I am well assur'd you will never forget.

Freke immediately replies,

11. PRO 30/24/19/2/p. 123.

I have and allways shall acknowledge your Lordships great Favour in letting mee have the Chase, but More particularly in the Present of the Costers Bushes, I assure your Lordship I would not have given that Price if I did not think they have been part of the Purchass at First; so wishing your Lordship all health, and a good Journey to London when you goe I remain your Lordships Most Obedient Humble Servant.[12]

In any case Shaftesbury must have had second thoughts about who owned the Costards Bushes because he went to court over them. In his "Exercises" he symbolizes too much concern with his estate by a small outline of a house or of a tree; contention he seems to symbolize by crossed swords.

There were three ways in which Shaftesbury could increase the productivity of his land: he could improve his own farming, or encourage his tenants to farm better, or he could find better uses for the land. His own farming was on a small scale. It was quite important as an example to his tenants, though, to see that it was done according to the most modern practices. This is one phase of the second Earl's estate which seems to have been well handled, perhaps the only one. As to encouraging his farmers, Shaftesbury could replace the weak ones when the copy was to be renewed, which he did rarely, or through the terms of the new lease or copy he could control the way the land is farmed, which he tried to do in all cases. Naturally it would be a mistake to see Shaftesbury or the average landowner of the time as a farmer solely for profit. Human values are always important to him in negotiating his leases. It cuts both ways, though; if a farmer's production goes up, Shaftesbury expects a higher rent.

Shaftesbury improved land usage by eliminating rabbit warrens, by draining bogs, by enclosing land and burnbaiting it, by setting up water meadows, and by proper management of woodlands and hedges. Wheat, of course, was the chief crop. In one of these years it brought four shillings a bushel, against two for barley and one and six for oats. However, next to certain legumes, wheat was the crop most likely to exhaust the soil. It took a long time to enrich the

12. The Earl of Shaftesbury to Thomas Freke, November 14, 1701, in PRO 30/24/20/39; Thomas Freke to the Earl of Shaftesbury, November 14, 1701, in PRO 30/24/20/40.

soil for it and even then there was, of course, a wide variation in yields. Often a field was better off in some sort of cover on which sheep grazed. Shaftesbury's dealings with Farmer Hiscock are an illustration:

> Note that tho' Farmer Hiscock be a Laboriouse Man, yet but a Sloven as to Husbandry & tho' his ground be but poor (he having no Sheep-down neither) yet he having been ever poor himself & not having the new way of Husbandry, this Farm is much the wors in his Hands. He hardly clovers any: and French-grass he is frighted at because of the Charg of Seed & length of time loosing the first years profitt: and this notwithstanding the plain advantage of it before his Eyes on the 19 acres which having been sown 22 years since was from Land of 8 or 10s an acre (at most) made to be worth 20s for a douzen years, and even at this time he acknowledged worth 15s. Note also that He lets his Clover remain but a year whereas Biggs of Rockborn, Harris of Martin, & others have of late let theirs lye 3 years & so plowing but 3, but half their land in tillage: the rest making good their arable. and thus John Gibbs my Baily on St. Giles who from the way of husbandry us'd even before which was Corn 2 year & rest 1, has brought it to Corn three years and rest 2, if not 3. & thus the sheep & feeding & so the penning & foddering more & the Labour of the Arable Seed &c less & Corn better. This I call the *Bolder Husbandry* newly on foot amongst us & which the older Selfwilled Farmers or Shallow Men that have no Genius or mettle in their way, many of them, will not be brought to. Of this kind I look upon this Hiscock tho' tyed to him as he is an Old Tenant & had my Grandfathers favour, & promise of good usage when brought (tho' then poor) to rent this.[13]

There were other farmers for whom Shaftesbury also made an exception, but generally he preferred those who followed the "bolder husbandry." Those who didn't were victims of the general inertia of farming, of the way things had always been done. There were also complications in the shift from clover to French grass which the new husbandry required. For it, the soil had to be fine and well drained, nor could it be overfed or trampled. As a result, Shaftesbury had to supply the French grass seed to many of his farmers in order to persuade them to use it.

One way to get more arable land, or more pasture to replace land which had been enclosed, was to destroy the rabbit warrens. Of the

13. PRO 30/24/19/2/pp. 48–49.

two that Shaftesbury was negotiating over in 1700, Black Warren, a few miles northwest of St. Giles's House, is the best example because it illustrates the complex way in which things so often unfolded once Shaftesbury began to look into them. One gets the impression that very little indeed had been done with the general estate in the preceding twenty years. Rabbit warrens were still a profitable venture in the seventeenth century, but not always profitable for the landlord who rented the rights to operate them. Shaftesbury knew the value of most of his land—the areas, the nature of the crop, its quality and exact price. Only the warreners could tell, however, just how many rabbits were being harvested from a particular warren. Growing and marketing rabbits was a highly specialized business which neither his father nor Shaftesbury had any relish for. Another problem was that all around the margin of the warren crops are exceedingly vulnerable. Farmer Biggs, who held about five hundred acres of downland next to the warren, found that he could graze only one sheep per acre on the land; with the warren gone he should be able to graze close to two sheep per acre, and damage to his wheat, fencing, and almost anything that grows would be reduced.

Accordingly, in November 1700 Shaftesbury signed an agreement with the various tenants involved and made financial adjustments. Farmer Biggs had to pay £30 more rent and the other tenants a total of £40. He then turned to the warreners. They wanted him to accept four thousand rabbits instead of twice the number, which, if they had 20,000 in all, was his share. Neighbors estimated that the warrens had as many as 26,000 rabbits, but he accepted four thousand, £100 worth. Then he learned that the warreners had paid their debt to Lord Pembroke, though they remained in arrears to him, and he heard further reports that they had been selling either £140 or £180 worth of rabbits a year in Salisbury, though their rent to him was only £65. On December 2 they brought John Wilmot, a Salisbury rabbit dealer, to plead further for them. What Shaftesbury found out got Wilmot in real trouble. "Now I found this [man] to be for himself only, the men being now his Slaves & kept so by engaging them in his Debt & so in his Mercy according to the usuall oppression of that kind in other Trades." Shaftesbury then offered Wilmot the warren for £285 and when refused, "spoke to the men apart, told them of their Task-master & Extortioner: that since they were undone I would do my best for them, take the Warren into my hands (which accordingly I the next day did, by siezing of it for my Debt) and them into my Service, having no other Servants able to do the Work for me & protecting them against their Oppressor during convenient time would pay them well for their pains & send them to shift for themselves, keeping for them what money I should make above my arrears and £50." Shaftesbury then settled for 15d a pair with Godfrey, another rabbit merchant of Salisbury. "But Wilmot in the meantime finding himself detected & defeated in his design, came over & referr'd himself to me bringing Mr Stringer's letter interceeding for him & was glad to give me £300 which was the least I had told him I would take if he refus'd my first order."[14] Stringer, whom we have seen as Shaftesbury's conscience in political matters, must have had considerable influence, even if here it amounted to Shaftesbury's humoring an elderly man who had been his grandfather's secretary and business partner. In any case Wilmot got a poorer bargain than was offered him at first. One wonders what the results might have been had Shaftesbury been firmer with most of the servants, farmers, and tradesmen he dealt with.

Black Warren was for the time left as woods; more important were Shaftesbury's widespread enclosures of downland, his own land in some cases, common land in others. This land was burnbaited after being enclosed, sowed in clover, and eventually in wheat. As we have seen in the years before, Shaftesbury had objected violently to the practice in Cranborne Chase. Where he receives rent for the land as arable, he is now enthusiastic. Almost all of the common land was enclosed at the request of the tenants who had the right to it. They must of course ask his permission in order to burn. In the one instance in which Shaftesbury burned a large area of common downland, he calculated that the other holders would be well compensated, even though their leases enabled him to burn the soil whether they wished it or not. There was a considerable increase in productivity through burnbaiting. At the outside, grassland was worth but a few shillings an acre in rent. Some of the worst wheat land in

14. PRO 30/24/19/2/pp. 33–34, 89, 98–99.

Shaftesbury's hands is worth fifteen shillings, and it can run as high as forty shillings. During most of Shaftesbury's adult lifetime England was at war, and although there were complaints at times about low prices, the general price level must have been high—sufficient reason for him to expand his holdings of arable land.

Another way that Shaftesbury increased his productivity was by expanding his water meadows. As readers of Andrew Marvell know, it was possible to enrich land by completely flooding it for a short period during the year. Shaftesbury set up new meadows throughout his estate and protected those that were already set up:

> I went to the part of Edmundsham-Common where the Water, which has been allow'd mine these 40 years, was bayd up from me by Joseph Gibbs now Mr Willis's Farmer and finding I had right of common & consequently right to the Water & that the ancient Watercours was through my own land now diverted & yet cutt off from me, I caus'd Wheelock to cutt down the new bay & lett the Water into my Meads, telling Josiah Gibbs that if any one were aggriev'd they might right themselves.[15]

As usual when Shaftesbury pressed, nobody knew who had given the orders—neither Josiah Gibbs, Mr. Willis, nor the ultimate rentor Mrs. Hussey, though they did tend to blame each other.

On the first page of Shaftesbury's part of the journal there is this entry: "Found by mySelf (Mr. Bishop being with me) 4 Young Oaks cutt in the Hedgerow on the Right hand of the Lane going from Waddocks to little Heath."[16] And so every few pages we have evidence of Shaftesbury's obsession with wood, though of course if one knows the value of wood in his area, his interest seems less obsessive. There seemed to have been no estate policy with regard to farmers grazing animals in woodland. Shaftesbury cannot find that he is ever paid for this, and even if his own stock grazes the benefits are dubious.

> The greatest profitt John Gibbs spoke of was the hogg[s] [and] Lambs in coppices newly fell'd, saying they would not touch the Wood: but (in answer) the very touch of their wool is poysonouse as well as their bite, and that they never bite is not probable. besides how judg of hoggs or older sheep when seen at a distance or passing by, in any of my

15. PRO 30/24/19/2/p. 106.
16. PRO 30/24/19/2/p. 17.

Coppices by my self or anyone? so that under this pretence all may come in.

Cropping animals are as dangerous as indiscriminate cultivation. Making a reservation for hogs among large trees in the rare good malt year, he resolves "that never more of any sort [of cattle] from first to last ever come within my Coppices & this for the sake too of my Young Timber, and much Fencing & subdivision of Coppices being by this means sav'd."[17]

The greatest damage is from humans, of course, and the six woodmen hired by Shaftesbury seem unable to protect him. He has only one servant who is absolutely incorruptible, his chief steward, John Wheelock, and Wheelock is no farmer. The thievery runs all the way from a farmer helping himself to an occasional limb to carefully planned culture of timber for sale in Poole. His bailiff feared "the name *Pickthank* & was already suspected & hated." And even setting a thief to spy on thieves—one Sheppard "offered himself to be a spye on the other Wood stealers"—was little help.[18] Shaftesbury must have improved his woodland, but with regard to timber it looks as if he was fighting a losing battle. As we shall see, the real problem was that he did not have enough dependable stewards.

Whatever improvements Shaftesbury was able to make in the handling of wood and in his vigorous effort to increase his arable land and to enrich it, he was able to increase the rents by 5 or 10 percent during the short period of time covered by his diary. All of this raises the question as to how Shaftesbury was regarded by his tenants. Was he seen as the Lord Bountiful he often thought himself to be? Was he an easy mark or was he too harsh with his tenants? On the whole Shaftesbury's major tenants, rich and poor, are a hardy, self-sufficient lot, though the innumerable renters of houses and small lots are notably more subservient. Shaftesbury's ideal, the farmer who was an exceptionally "good husband," proud of his work but genuinely respectful of the Earl's own merits, hardly existed in any simple manner. There was always some complication, yet he seems

17. PRO 30/24/19/2/pp. 115, 37.
18. PRO 30/24/19/2/pp. 108–109.

to have expected a much simpler situation when he took over in the winter of 1699–1700.

This may explain why, for Shaftesbury, when he first became a landlord, the greatest weakness in a tenant was deceit. There is no other explanation for his attempts to search out the ultimate motives of those who rented from him. It took him almost two years to realize that there were no black or white situations, that the bulk of them were gray. Ultimately he came to value good husbandry and a fair return for himself far more than purity of motives. From good farmers he would accept some sort of truce on stealing soil or timber or whatever abuse was being performed. In the brief period covered by the diary only one tenant, Farmer Bagus, became completely intolerable and apparently was eased out when his lease was up.

The sums involved in the copies Shaftesbury had to renew or transfer are quite large, even by modern standards. Shaftesbury's protracted dealings with Frank Fry for Bridmore Farm can serve as an example. Here he settled the fine for thirteen years at £2,600, £2,000 to be paid by Lady Day and the other £600 by Michaelmas. This transaction fell through but it is the only major one that did during the period of the diary. Sometimes he had to wait for his bargain to be accepted; at other times he made last-minute concessions, often after the agreement was signed. Whatever his tenants' private thoughts about him, Shaftesbury was not a harsh landlord.

Nor can it be said that Shaftesbury was a hard master to his servants. Under Wheelock was the home steward and receiver, who supervised the stewards of the various manors and received money due the landlord. Finally there was the bailiff. The rest of the local servants were all associated with the manors of St. Giles's or All Saints, beginning with the court steward, the housekeeper, house clerk, head butler, head woodsman—all the way down through some twenty-five servants—to the boy in the kitchen and the poultry maid.

Wheelock had started as a link boy for John Locke. In 1675 he went to work for Stringer, the first Earl's steward. He continued to work for the Countess Dowager and came along with her estate to Ashley in 1693. He was at St. Giles's House in 1696, though Williams' official departure was not until the following April. Shaftesbury was fortunate to have him, because his comment that Wheelock was the only major servant whom he could trust is, alas, too true.

We have a large number of Wheelock's letters, especially when his master was abroad, and they all show a remarkable mixture of tact, unwearying patience, complete respect, and appropriate humility, yet nothing really servile. After Shaftesbury tells him that his sister Frances has defied him, Wheelock, knowing how sensitive his master is to gossip about the family, writes, "I am heartly sorrie. . . . that any of your ffamily soe neare, & Deare to you; And have been so tenderly used by you; should proceed in any matters with out you thorrough approbation and consent. I never heard anything of it but from your Lordship besides what Mr Hooper was pleas'd to intimate to me some time agoe as a thing he thought might goe on and hop'd you would be reconcil'd to it, to which (coming from him) I could make no replye." [19]

Shaftesbury's notes are full of worries about the motives and misdeeds of his various servants, perhaps because he had trained himself to candor in his conversations with himself. There is never the slightest doubt about Wheelock among these notes, and Shaftesbury paid him well for the heavy responsibilities he carried. Something is missing in the relationship, though. So far as Shaftesbury knew, Wheelock was the perfect servant he hoped to find everywhere on his estate, the epitome of dependability, and yet he hardly ever acknowledges this in his letters. Once when Wheelock senses the possibility that Shaftesbury mistrusts him, he asks point-blank. All that Shaftesbury, abroad, is able to reply is, naturally, I trust you; this is proved by all the responsibilities you carry for me.

Business affairs often required Wheelock to be away from the estate, and if the Earl were absent, as he often was, the full responsibility fell upon the house steward, Henry Dalicourt, a former servant of both the first Earl and the Countess Dowager. Dalicourt had experienced some sort of fall from grace in the past and Shaftesbury had little faith that anyone who worked so closely with the infamous Williams was fit to be trusted; accordingly when he returned to

19. John Wheelock to the Earl of Shaftesbury, February 17, 1704, in PRO 30/24/20/85.

St. Giles's House in the summer of 1700 he hired a new woodman from the estate, whose principal function was in fact to spy upon the estate; he was, as Shaftesbury put it, "an Explorer."

It is best to let Shaftesbury explain his reasons from the section in his journals, under the rubric *Arcanum OEconomicum*:

> I thus engaged Bishop as an *Explorer* & spake to him thus & with these Instructions 'That being confederated against by Tenants, Servants & all, as he saw, & having none to confide in but himself; and as to affaires abroad & in the country (Gentlemen, as Mr Okenden &c; plotting against me or over-reaching in any lay'd design of Parliamentary or Parish-affaires or Estates or Bounds &c;) having not the way of conversing with them & being on the square, drinking in their Companyes, & entering into their Caballs, by which other Gentlemen (as Mr. Banks, Trenchard & other young men as they) could hold up with them, have intelligence & guard themselves & often even take advantages, instead of being passive & always suffering. That therefore I recomended to him *Intelligence*, & would begrudg no money bestow'd as an angel, or Guinea, (when deserv'd) at a time: telling him that he should take all Care to avoid the Odiouse Name of Spye, & beware of bragging (his Cheif Fault) of his intelligence. Observing allways to Chuse for his Instruments the shrew'd & close sort, never the Weak or Open, tho ever so honest. for the former Whatever Knaves possibly they might be (which was of no danger here, since there was no trust repos'd) yet would they not betray *themselves*: the name of *Spye* being so injuriouse to them. and thus He & I being true to ourselves, & never betraying our Informers, we should have Informers enow without any known one, neither in Land nor Woods nor Housing nor Domestick nor Country-affair could I be besett, what News there was, or what design or Plott stirring, I should be the first that knew of it, & could warn others instead of needing to be warn'd myself: And thus too, at length, when it was perciev'd that I knew every thing & by more ways than one; everything would be told me, because despair'd of being kept secret; and the invidiouse Character taken off from him; He eas'd and myself highly serv'd.'[20]

This is a most interesting document. It reveals a great deal of ingenuity on one hand, yet on the other hand it is naïve. Much depends on Bishop, his trustworthiness and his astuteness as a judge of character. James was a local man and thus familiar with the country and

20. PRO 30/24/19/2/pp. 100–101.

its people. Master Freke had recommended him as *"faithful, able &*
stout," and Thomas Freke of Hannington agreed. He had been in service to Master Freke but left him to marry what turned out to be an
ill wife who abused him with a man having "a Crooked body & like
her self," so that he turned to service again. Bishop gave Shaftesbury
a great deal of trustworthy information about farming and provided
him with much intelligence of the kind he desired. We soon find
him riding about with Shaftesbury and assuming some of Dalicourt's functions, though he remains head gamekeeper. Unfortunately he did not wholly live up to Master Freke's recommendation.

More interesting is the light which the paper throws on Shaftesbury's sense of being abused. He is too intensely concerned with his
servants' attitude toward him. When Dalicourt does not mend as
well as he expects, he remarks, "But Parliamentary & Pool affair allowing more Liberty, the Cause perhaps of this, taking off the awe &
late impression which I must therefore renew." Again, typical is his
reaction when a servant, Thomas Read, who had been very useful to
him in protecting deer, sends word that he is leaving Shaftesbury's
service. The Earl goes directly to the kitchen, where Read tells him
that he pays low wages. He had not heard this before and offers to
pay more, but suspects that something else is wrong. Sunday he
finds it is, when Read's name is read in the banns at church. Read
could marry whom he wished, but since marriage would affect his
status as a servant, his master needed to know. Shaftesbury concludes, "Having thus us'd me & as I said before the servants *turn'd
me off, no[t] I him*, I have no more to say to him nor am oblig'd to
him any more." Something is missing in this picture, however cred-
itable it may be to Shaftesbury.[21]

As I have suggested, when Shaftesbury succeeded to the title, he
saw his role as bringing order to an estate which had been disorderly
for almost twenty years. He concludes the first of his several letters
on the household: "Let me have your Best assistance: that I may
hope at last to see good order in a Family, where for so many years
past there has been so little known & this You will find, in the End,

21. PRO 30/24/19/2/pp. 67, 152.

well proves as much your own Good as it will to my satisfaction and content."[22] This impulse to rationalize the management of his estate was furthered by his own highly systematic tendencies, so that his original letter of a little over three pages had grown by 1707 into a 150-page essay on the management of his estate.

The essay has many interesting provisions—the home steward is to keep cash on hand to pay all bills, and anyone who withholds a bill for over forty shillings for six months will lose the custom of the family—but our chief concerns are the many provisions for servants, and we can look only at two or three of these. With regard to illness, Shaftesbury says, "When ever any of the Servants are Sick at anytime, I would have the Doctor sent for, & all care taken of them at my expense, if they are sickly by their own fault & an ill course of life, I shall part with them at last if they do not amend, but if it be their ill fortune only to prove sickly, they need not fear being turned away, as usuall, on that account."[23]

The rules are strict enough. Gifts are always to be conveyed to his neighbors by "the least considerable hand," a boy not in livery, never by anyone involved in their production, so as to avoid a return offer. He will "maintain Peace and Christianity," and if a servant is assaulted he can preserve his life or person but any further action is to be left to the Earl. The regulations on drunkenness and misbehavior are rigorous. Yet throughout it all runs the same sort of paternalistic assurance that is involved in the care of the sick. Every servant who had charge of anything was to carry a copy of the following memorandum:

> That my Lord never do or will allow anything to be done in the way of your Buissnes but by your own hand nor will make any alteration, or give any Order, or Direction in the concerns under your charge without first informing You. and by this means you shall never be impos'd upon or disturb'd by any pretence of contrary Orders allways depending on it that till you hear other wise from my Lord himself he is fully satisfyed with your Behaviour and the Methods you take. And on this account;

22. The Earl of Shaftesbury to Henry Dalicourt, Chelsea, February 7, 1700, in letter inserted in Family Book, PRO 30/24/22/3.
23. *Ibid.*

when in my Lord's absence the Auditor or Head-Servant gives orders that occasion any Doubt, my Lord is to be apply'd to, by Letter: otherwise the Auditor's Advice & Directions are to be follow'd.[24]

Vails and perquisites were a problem for Shaftesbury's servants. In most families these amounted to perhaps 20 to 40 percent of a servant's income, even where guests could be expected for only half of the year. At St. Giles's House there was more to contend with than the usual oscillation between London and the country. Shaftesbury's brother and sisters were never in residence for long and they soon became only occasional visitors. Anthony was, in effect, the family, and at home his health forced him at certain times to live quite privately with very few visitors. Furthermore, it irked him to have his servants dependent upon others. In 1704, then, he simply abolished all vails and perquisites and raised the salaries of all of his staff. The servants were strictly enjoined to refuse all gifts—even so small as a pair of gloves. Some servants who were not eligible also had their salaries substantially raised, too, perhaps as a precautionary measure. Of course this was not all of their income; everyone from Mr. Powell, the court steward, on up received fees and special privileges. Often they were given opportunities to invest in property.

I suppose that if one had to characterize Shaftesbury's treatment of his servants it could be described in his own language about poachers, "threaten high but prosecute seldom." There are several cases where people were fined for dishonesty, but a lot depended on Shaftesbury's judgment of the motive of the sinner and he seemed always able to hope for some improvement in these. Certainly, Dalicourt is an example. Three years after Shaftesbury took over he still lacked zeal and was lazy with his accounts; moreover, after promising to marry Mrs. Skinner, who was in a servant-and-friend relationship to Shaftesbury's sisters, he compromised another woman whom he was forced to marry. Yet Shaftesbury on leaving for Holland offered him fifty pounds and a horse and enjoined him "that he should be regular in his accounts, that he mind all my other instructions and Cheifly what I here tell him of his serving me with better heartiness that has appear'd of late remembering that I will not bear a luke

24. PRO 30/24/22/3/p. 38.

warme service from any but least of all from him."[25] And no doubt he continued to enjoin him until Dalicourt died a few years later, yet for the most part Shaftesbury's methods, with some silent thanks to Wheelock, seem to have worked. He was better served than many of his more demanding peers.

With regard to that group of people most dependent upon Shaftesbury's goodwill—the hundreds of cottagers and their families throughout his estates—he seems to have felt an obligation of charity toward all of them who were needy and deserving. This seems to hold at even the most distant estates. At Beebe in Leicestershire he "Allow'd the 2 old Women Lunaticks . . . 40s. a year from this year forward, instead of 20s. which they had formerly from Matchet in Victualls allow'd them but of which they complain'd as not receiving it."[26]

But Shaftesbury's strongest obligation is to those in his home parishes, St. Giles's and All Hallows. These people are, as he frequently calls them, his family; those who live beyond these bounds are called externs. Here he can make substantial concessions in rent where necessary or make small gifts: "I forbid Vertue the Dairy-Maid selling any more Milk to the Parish-people, but to keep an exact account of it & give it to the poor I nam'd & cheifly for the Children of Green's Family, the Children kept by the Parish."[27] No doubt Shaftesbury records these benefactions with some pleasure, but the real reason for writing them down is that they must be a matter of record—especially where he decides to reduce rent temporarily.

Those who are elderly, widowed, orphaned, or ill and at the same time alone are assisted through the poor rates. Shaftesbury's great grandfather had built a handsome row of almshouses, still standing, which we find him assigning parishioners to—though the demand far exceeded the supply. He is usually willing to help the able-bodied, providing their poverty is not the result of laziness, and he likes to help out young men just beginning as farmers on his estate. He gives Farmer Gerrard some land which he could have gotten £5

25. The Earl of Shaftesbury to Henry Dalicourt and other servants, January 9, 1703, in PRO 30/24/20/67.
26. PRO 30/24/19/2/p. 113.
27. PRO 30/24/19/2/p. 96.

rent on and notes: "This kindness to him first for his Meritt as an industriouse honest young Fellow (of 26 years old) & one I hope to raise: next, as trusting to me in the Bargain . . . and relying on my being a kind & nor a hard Landlord as represented to him & which I hope I have made good."[28] It is too bad that more of Shaftesbury's tenants did not know how responsive he was to trust.

When he first succeeded to the title, Shaftesbury, sounding very much like the author of the first issue of the *Inquiry*,

> propos'd a workhouse that the Children of Idle Familyes might work with those of the more industriouse, having a Matron over them, & I delivering them Materialls, & buying again of them when wrought, in case of Wool & Flax dealers refus'd, or slacken'd sometimes, either through deadness of Trade or as imposing on the people & beating down the price of their Labour. Thus also those of one hand or leg only Lame & on such pretence throwing themselves whole on the Parish, by this means made to half (or more) keep them selves, & driven from such excuses & desire of such occasions through Laziness [and] Vagabonds reduc'd (there being Hemp to beat & other such Work) and the Children (girls especially, now wholly idle) taught industry & Arts, the Parish multiplyed, theiving & Vice suppress'd & Order Establish'd.[29]

One wonders how many parishioners were careless of their limbs, confident that if anything happened the parish would take care of them. In any case, Shaftesbury gave up this notion two years later.

If nothing else, the passage about the workhouse does reveal that Shaftesbury's chief concern is the children on his estates. There is for example the case of the Compton child:

> From Mr Horsey [the parish priest] (last night) & from Bishop & old George Osborne (who wept in telling it to me) that Compton & his Wife barborously treated & starv'd the poor Girl, their own Grand-Child, lately in their keeping of which he had admonish'd them but they revil'd him. Upon this I sent for the Girl & putt her into Betty Hobs's hands. Memorandum that there is 20 & odd pounds of her Fathers in Oliver Compton's hand.

Finally, another relative steps forward:

28. PRO 30/24/19/2/p. 121.
29. PRO 30/24/19/2/p. 82.

Elias Gibbs, Brother to the Lewd Woman of our Parish Rachel Compton: came to me about his Sister and the Children: offer'd what was fair
& charitable particularly to take care of the Elder girl which was legitimate, by breeding her (teaching her Work, knitting button-making, &c)
& putting in her Life in one of his Livings (viz Winterbourn's of £8 per
annum as he assur'd me) I therefore joyn'd in Charity with him on condition his taking the Girl immediately and that I would allow him to
putt her Life in reversion after his own for 2 years purchase instead of
4: being £16 & for 2 years purchase for the 3d life (Harry Green of Win-
bourn) being in all £32. I promising to take old Comptons £20 as part.
so as to take of himself but £12 & (abating the £2) consented to take but
£10: since done in Charity. I promised him also an Elm for reparation.[30]

When the mother returns, Shaftesbury declares "that she should
be us'd with the greatest severity if she refus'd to go to Carolina as
propos'd I offering . . . to pay £5 for her passage." This was in January
1701. When Shaftesbury returned the following summer he found
that her departure had been entrusted to one John Jolliff by Horsey
and the others, despite the fact that they all had given Jolliff a very
bad character. Instead of conveying her to Bristol, "he spent the Parishes & my money . . . & let the woman go: pretending he had ship'd
her . . . this appearing fully before me . . . when I examind him now
on my Return to St. Giles's."[31] What happened to Jolliff or Rachel we
do not know, because the rest of the story is lost.

Shaftesbury was especially proud of the school he set up for the
children of the parish in the chapel of the almshouse during his first
autumn as an earl. His sister Frances reminds him of her maid's
mother, Gammer Betty Sanders, whom he himself remembered
from years past "was very deserving, taught the Children well" reading, writing, simple sums, and taught the girls also to spin, do nee-
dlework, and knit. Gradually Shaftesbury took over the responsibility for paying the way of all the poor children of the parish through
his school.

Shaftesbury's conviction that the very first years are all important
probably comes from his own education as supervised by John Locke,
and especially from his experience with his spoiled brother John.

30. PRO 30/24/19/2/pp. 96, 63.
31. PRO 30/24/19/2/p. 110.

Richard Hiscock was "bred wild & Barbarous & far off from neigh-borhood," which explains why he is growing up badly. He will pro-vide for Thomas Burbage, Jr., abroad because he is the son of two old servants, but will not take him into the family and regrets that he has agreed to pay for his education. He is an only child and very much spoiled by his mother. Finally he threatens to send him off to sea "least they corrupt the rest or grow to be fixt Parishoners & con-tinue the same Race." All the Coneys, he admits, are worthless and best got out of the parish whenever the occasion permits. On the other hand, if a child can be gotten to early enough, if he can be trained and taught honesty and industry, the chances are that *physis* will predominate over *nomos* and the child will grow up to have made the best of whatever nature allotted to him. Young boys he will arrange to have sent to school in the village, so that they learn a trade. Two young men he put through Oxford.

Another responsibility Shaftesbury formally assumed was for his immediate family, although it had been his informally since his re-turn from the grand tour. Anthony's relations with his brother Mau-rice seem easy and warm during the late 1690s and the beginning two or three years of the new century. Few letters between the broth-ers have survived for the 1690s; the most interesting one was writ-ten in 1697. Maurice had ridden from St. Giles's House on a several-days trip to Pawlett in Somersetshire and on his return made a report to Lord Ashley, who had inherited the Somerset manor as part of a bequest from the Dowager Countess. "Its a country not at all to my relish. There is above two thousand acres of ground lying together without hedge or other enclosure than Ditches, bounded all on one side by Bridgewater Channell where the sea is continually working either upwards or downwards." All of the tenants are upset by one Jones, who charges Yeo, the baily, Powell, Dalicourt, and John Gibbs with bribery. Turning to family matters, Maurice remarks that the second Earl treats his wife like a child, that only he and Dalicourt have any notion of how much money he has, and that although he talks often about making some provision for the sisters' marriages, nothing is done and they are unprovided for. Dorothy, now about eighteen, neither distinguishes herself handsomely nor acts "so becomingly as I imagined she might have done."[32] Dullness is her problem and, since Maurice remarks that his own dullness is probably the cause, he probably means inertness or possibly melancholy. There is one highly amusing letter from him where he describes his first political journey into western Wiltshire in mock heroic terms of warfare. On the whole, however, his letters are sober and often unhappy. The self-deprecation is typical of his early letters. Yet, unlike those of his sisters, Maurice's letters always reveal a strongly individual personality; the roots of his ultimate lack of complaisance toward his brother are already perceptible.

Maurice was popular enough to be chosen to stand for two constituencies in the second election of 1701, and Edward Hooper, by now Dorothy's husband, writes to Shaftesbury to explain why he prefers him to stand as a county delegate for Wilts rather than for Melcomb Regis and Weymouth, which he had formerly represented:

> My Lord, I wou'd feign have this undertaking carryed on for severall reasons. Mr Ashley do not express any liking att all for this Country nor takes so much delight in his own as I cou'd wish; he heartily embraced this offer, and if baulked, I fear will not be agreeable att all. If we persist and gain our point, which is not much to be doubted, Twill be the only means to enduce him to spend some time here and bring him in love by degrees with his own Estate, to plant, to enclose, to improve, and to make him a very Active, Chearfull man, and to wean his thoughts from those things etc. which make him otherwise.[33]

Eventually Maurice was to be reconciled to life in Purton, but most of this period he seems to have lived in London with his sisters Gertrude and Elizabeth.

Shaftesbury had four sisters. His earliest letters from them are those of Frances and these are full of woe. She, her unmarried sisters, and Maurice are visiting the Manners family at Haddon Hall in the summer of 1700. Frances is awed by the wealth she sees around her and feels like the poor visiting relation. Could Anthony send the coach back again right away? The Countess and her daughter-in-law keep repeating pointedly that they intend to visit London in August.

32. Maurice Ashley to Anthony, Lord Ashley [1697], in PRO 30/24/21/239.
33. Edward Hooper to the Earl of Shaftesbury, Purton, Wilts., November 14, 1701, in PRO 30/24/22/1/46.

The Earl of Rutland is kind enough, but he took no notice of the fact that he is sister Gertrude's godfather when she asked his blessing. Furthermore, they see no one but the young children. By August she is frantic. There is to be a great horse race next week and she feels that everyone looks at them wondering when they will move out to make more room for the new guests. Shaftesbury did then send the coach.

One is impressed with how difficult it was for Shaftesbury to marry off his sisters properly, even with their dowries, which were generous in terms of the family's wealth. These seem to have come to five thousand pounds or so, though the data is conflicting. We have already seen one of Dorothy's painful misadventures. From the letters we have, it is clear that this must have been repeated for at least two of her sisters. Either Shaftesbury did not provide enough or the man turned out to be worth less than he said or, in one case, death intervened to remove the prospective bridegroom.

Bating the special problems of women involved, there is little most contemporary readers should find fault with in the system of negotiations first and romance later. It is too easy to project our own standards onto their society. All the more because there are resemblances. Among the actors in this story we have enough examples which might well seem to come from our day. Upper-class people easily enough fell into the lower-class habit of becoming pregnant before marriage, as did Lady Carey Peterborough (d. 1709). There are elopements such as that of Lady Anne Manners (b. 1655), though she was provident enough to choose a Whig politician. And some of our characters apparently lived in sin.

At the same time the health of the economy was based on well-managed property, and the purpose of marriage was to maintain the integrity of property and develop kinship relations to protect it further. Under this social system primogeniture was necessary. Gavelkind, or distribution of property equally among heirs, did exist in some parts of England, but widespread use of it would have required a different social system. The English had discovered they could actually destroy the stability of Irish society by forcing gavelkind on them, by enforcing again what had been an old tradition.

Even if we grant that some shifting of property was desirable, it is difficult to realize today how difficult it was to maintain a family line with the mortality rate then. When Mayfair marriages without parental consent began to threaten the system, it was necessary to pass the Marriage Act of 1752 which made unarranged and impromptu marriages more difficult. Indeed, though he had made his three marriages with kinship in mind, the first Earl of Shaftesbury told his grandson that kinship was less important than a strong line. He said one should marry into a strong stock where the family is well thought of locally. Families like the Manners or the Ashley Coopers which have persisted into this time of better health are the exception rather than the rule. Other lines used various pretenses such as having the husband take the name of a female heir to maintain the estate, or they simply died out.

Dorothy married Edward Hooper of Boveridge, near St. Giles's House, and Hurn Court, Hants, in the summer of 1700. Shaftesbury at first had some doubts because Hooper's income was only £1,000 a year, but he had to admit that he had adequate lands in his two estates, which had recently been combined after the death of the last member of the Boveridge branch of his line. Hooper seems to have been all that Shaftesbury could have wished for in a brother-in-law: his letters show him to be a person of sound common sense, and he loved the country where his roots were. Shaftesbury always refers to him as his brother Hooper, and one senses that the word carries more than its conventional meaning.

During this period it is Elizabeth who is most remote from him. The fact that she was so fond of London could account for this, but there is no reason to doubt the intensity of Shaftesbury's affection for his youngest sister, Gertrude (1685–1703), who also lived there—"my second hopes" he calls her. Perhaps he felt she would turn out differently from her older sisters, who were at a more susceptible age when the split occurred in the family. None of the girls had a very stable childhood. Gertrude, for instance, could not have known her father when he wasn't a wholly reclusive invalid. Her mother ran off to Haddon Hall when she was a small child, to return when Gertrude was twelve, and died the year after. After her father's death, the year following, she lived at St. Giles's House but eventually spent much of the year in London. It was there that Gertrude contracted smallpox and died in November 1703, aged seventeen.

Sir John Cropley and Thomas Micklethwayte were closer to Shaftesbury than any members of his family, but there is little information on them for the first years of the century. The three friends were so much together they had little need of letters. Cropley was eight years older than Shaftesbury. John's father was knighted and his grandfather created a baronet shortly after the Restoration. His father died before John was two years old, so that on his grandfather's death in 1676 he succeeded to the baronetcy and to a fortune, to which his grandmother and probably his mother contributed much. The grandfather was admitted to Gray's Inn in 1629 and his son attended Queen's College, Oxford; Sir John's own education was as informal as Shaftesbury's, though it must have been good. It is likely that they met after Shaftesbury left Winchester in 1683.

Thomas Micklethwayte, on the other hand, was seven years younger than Shaftesbury. He was a Yorkshireman from the manor of Swine a few miles north of Kingston upon Hull. Swine seems to have been purchased by the great grandfather of Thomas, who was a physician. His own father was an attorney, but for reasons we do not know he seems to have turned against his sons. When we first hear of Thomas in 1701, he is not long out of Cambridge, where so many Yorkshire Micklethwaytes attended, and he is looking for a job in London.[34]

Shaftesbury tried his best to get both Thomas Micklethwayte and his brother Joseph (ca. 1680–1734), two years younger, solidly established. Joseph proved less of a challenge. He was sent off to Rotterdam, where Furly supervised his education. He eventually became man of business to Shaftesbury's friend James Stanhope (1672–1721). Thomas Micklethwayte was another matter. In a letter to Lord Spen-

---

34. Like Shaftesbury, Cropley in the 1690s also lived in Red Lion Square. Indeed, a rate book in the Guildhall shows him paying rates on two properties there. A decade later Thomas Micklethwayte is listed as a resident of Devonshire Street which leads into the square. When Micklethwayte died he was buried from the parish church there, St. Andrew's, Holborn.

cer written in the fall of 1701, before the election, Shaftesbury begs him to intervene with his father Lord Sunderland and with Henry Guy (1631–1710), a treasury official, to find Micklethwayte a job.[35] After Shaftesbury's success in the election which followed, he felt sure that Micklethwayte would get it. He was fond of looking back on the occasion in the years which followed. He did not wish the secretaryship of state which he was offered by the King. For his services to the Crown he wanted but one thing, a small job for Micklethwayte. This hope evaporated with the King's death in the following March. The vindication he found in the events of the winter of 1701 was shortly replaced by the intense bitterness of Queen Anne toward him. Thereafter Lord Somers could usually rouse Shaftesbury's patriotism so that he would rally behind the party when the occasion demanded it, but it is doubtful that Shaftesbury ever acted again without the memory of his betrayal. He must have gradually realized that the Whigs were no longer Commonwealthmen and that with a number of the Commonwealthmen's goals achieved, a general movement back to the ideals which had motivated them was unlikely.

As I have noted, there are almost no letters of interest between Sir John Cropley and Shaftesbury in the early part of the decade. What letters of Cropley's we do have seem written in another day, for they are stripped of all politesse. Sometimes they contain a date or an address; almost none have any opening salutation. Cropley can show intense concern, usually about Shaftesbury's health, but there is nowhere any pretense. Sometimes he ends with a "yrs.," sometimes not. Only one letter is signed and this with a pseudonym, Arsamnes. Reading a Cropley letter reveals how much one depends upon how an author handles the inevitable mechanics of letter writing as a revelation of his character. There are so many things the two do not have to say to each other, that we would have to have ten times the number of letters we have to judge Cropley's character. They were together too much, they knew each other too well, anyway; and fi-

35. The third Earl of Shaftesbury to Lord Spencer, November 13, 1701, in PRO 30/24/20/38.

nally, in some of the more personal letters, there is an almost automatic instinct not to reveal what is being talked about, not to repeat anything the receiver already knows.

One document does give some real insight into the life at this time of Shaftesbury, Cropley, and Micklethwayte—his brothers, as he calls them. This is a ten-thousand-word narrative, "The Adept Ladys or The Angelick Sect. Being the Matters of fact of certain Adventures Spiritual, Philosophical, Political, and Gallant. In a letter to a Brother," which is dated January 19, 1701/02. There are two copies in different hands among the Shaftesbury Papers.[36] Copy B is a fair copy of A with occasional revisions. Both are by amanuenses. There seems little doubt that the author was Shaftesbury. The work is dated from Chelsea, where Shaftesbury was at the time; both Cropley as Arsamnes and Thomas Micklethwayte appear in the text; the author's late actions for the public were noted by the King; the Quaker heroine claims that she can cure the author's lungs; and finally, the fourth Earl ascribes the book to Shaftesbury and quotes from it in his sketch of his father's life.[37]

There is no way now of telling who the brother was to whom the book was addressed. The fourth Earl assumed that "brother" meant Maurice, but in the first place it is addressed to *a brother* not *my brother*—the word is used in the same sense as *sister* is among the adepts with whom the essay deals. Maurice and Anthony were as close at this time as they ever were, but their correspondence suggests that there always was a certain distance between them despite their common intellectual interests. Nor does it seem possible—despite the reference to Thomas as the "Head of our Family"—that it could be addressed to Joseph Micklethwayte, who is not an intimate of the group.

"The Adept Ladys" begins with a visit to the author by his old friends Chrysogenes and Chrysogenis, along with a Quaker lady. The visitors act very mysteriously, and it is not until they are convinced that the author is suitably pure in heart that they are willing to reveal to him that the Quaker lady is head of an Angelic sect, and

36. Both designated PRO 30/24/46A/81.
37. Rand, (ed.), *The Life, Unpublished Letters, and Philosophical Regimen*, xvi–xxvii.

that all of her bodily excretions turn to gold. He is nauseated when asked to examine this gold, but decides to tease his guests in order to find out more about these marvels, whereupon he learns that the Quaker lady is full of political intelligence communicated to her from the King and various European heads of state.

The author wants to know whether or not the rest of the family of Chrysogenes have been affected by the prophetess, so he visits them and finds, alas, that they are all under her spell. Here he learns of new marvels: she has spiritual visitors at night; she imitates the miracles of Christ; he finds that the person to whom his book is addressed is a convert; and he meets again their son, whom they often have called Sabatius because of his natural passion for magic. When things have become altogether unbelievable, "the fresh and bloomy Arsamnes" appears, drives off the spirits, and carries him home to Chelsea, to the brother, and to a sleepless night haunted by demons.

The next morning they get up and go to Holy Communion. This passage was cited by the fourth Earl, though he did leave out the opening sentence in which it is said they went because it was "now in a manner our Duty, at least for Examples Sake on the Account of our Stations in Parlement." If one reads between the lines, this is a fair description of Shaftesbury's mature faith. His is a church "where a good and Virtuouse Life, with a hearty Endeavour of services to ones Country, and to mankind, joyn'd with a religiouse Performance of all sacred Dutyes, and a Conformity with the establish'd Rites, was enough to answer the highest Character of Religion."[38] This part of the work then ends with a prolonged rhapsody against enthusiasm.

The gallant part of the adventures is added in a postscript. It begins with a discussion of a brother who has a "Mercuriall Bride or [who is] embark'd at least in an Amour with one of those chast celestiall Dames." The author then learns that the sectaries are quite licentious, except that in them is a sign of generosity and greater nobleness of nature. He himself falls in love with a sectary, but he withdraws in horror when he discovers what her wealth consists of and that her virtue is a pretense.

"The Adept Ladys" is a hasty jeu d'esprit and not a very witty one.

---

38. PRO 30/24/46A/81/A version/pp. 37, 38.

From a purely biographical point of view, however, the epigrams and poems which follow are most interesting. There are three epigrams:

> Medea's Knights the SECRET had
> Of bringing Wealth to Greece:
> Our Modern Iasons are not said
> To bring but yeild a FLEECE.

Two poems in tetrameter and pentameter couplets, both of them scatological, follow, and last is "The Golden Lovers. A Ballad, Being a Dialogue Between Mick of the North, & Nan of the Town." The refrain runs, "I have Lov'd thee for all Thou'rt a Drab and a Blouze: / But who can Endure a Chimicall Spouze?"[39]

We know that Mick is Thomas Micklethwayte and almost as certainly we know that Nan is likely to be Anne or Nancy Ewer, sister to Jane Ewer, who was to become Shaftesbury's wife eight years later. Anne is a shadow figure. After a brief reference to her alchemical pursuits in the "Adepts," she next appears in charge of the infant fourth Earl when his parents go to Italy in 1711; she is referred to in late letters and in papers relating to the settlement of the third Earl's estate. Although Jane's name alone appears in the genealogical charts of the Ewer family, it is there because she became Countess of Shaftesbury. Jane refers to "my sister Nanny," and Anne's name does appear in some papers with that of the heir to the Ewer estates, Henry. The most surprising reference to Anne I have run across is the last. When Sir John Cropley died shortly after the third Earl of Shaftesbury, he left his "great estate" to Thomas Micklethwayte, who had the previous year, 1712, succeeded to Swine. At his death in 1718 Thomas, M.P. for Arundel, Lord Commissioner of the Treasury, and Under-Lieutenant-General of the Ordnance, left his wealth to Joseph. Because he died a viscount in the Irish nobility, Joseph's will is conveniently available. It was probated in March 1734 by the principal beneficiary, Anne Ewer, spinster. After writing for a while on a biography such as this one, one begins to wish for less and less evidence, but it would have been good to know more about Nan of the town and her relationship to the Micklethwaytes.[40]

39. PRO 30/24/46A/81/A version/pp. 53, 56–57.
40. This branch of the Ewer line died out when the last male, Anthony Ewer, had

It is hard to tell how much Anthony saw of John Locke after returning from his visit to Holland in 1698–1699. Actually, there was little opportunity. For most of 1699 he was at St. Giles's House, and Locke was in London very little during the winter when Shaftesbury took his seat in the House of Lords. In May Locke resigned from the Board of Trade and settled permanently with the Mashams at Oates in western Essex about twenty miles from London, where he had spent much of the decade before. After 1700 Locke was very rarely in London, and from my evidence Shaftesbury made only one visit to Oates after 1700, at Easter in 1701.

It is not surprising that at this time most of Shaftesbury's friends beyond his immediate circle were also friends of Locke, though it had been several years since they had been close and almost twenty since he had been under Locke's tutelage. For instance, Shaftesbury's most notable neighbor, Thomas Herbert, eighth Earl of Pembroke, had been a friend of Locke's for twenty-five years. Shaftesbury spoke of him as "such a great and valuable man and so Friendly to my Self and Family." Shaftesbury is precise. Herbert was great because he had an old title and the wealth and influence to grace it; he was valuable because he performed public services for the Crown, sometimes arduously, during the reigns of five kings. He is of interest to us because despite his eminence he was unable to prevent Shaftesbury's being thrown out of his admiralty office.

Shaftesbury was vice Admiral of Dorset for only two and a half years. The title should be explained. The vice Admirals of the Coast, as they were called, were chosen from the coastal counties in order to administer naval matters in cases where either poor communication or urgency made it impossible for London to handle them. The office, regularized under Henry VIII, goes back to the Middle Ages. Ultimately the vice Admiral was to defend the kingdom; in actuality he watched over Crown revenues, suppressed piracy and wrecking and so forth. Stricter legislation, the decline of piracy, and the growth of the navy led to a decline of the office. By the time of Shaftesbury's brief career as vice Admiral, his chief duties were to enforce embar-

---

no sons. His heiress Elizabeth, who married Sir Francis Wood, ancestor of the Earl of Halifax, in 1779, inherited Swine, but it went to the fifth Earl of Shaftesbury on her death.

goes and impress seamen, though there may have been other tasks. The office became largely honorary in the eighteenth century and was discontinued in the middle of the nineteenth century. Affidavits show that the average profits of the office ran to about fifty pounds per year during the seventeenth century. It was the honor which attracted, and the office was generally considered a lifetime post.

A brother of Shaftesbury's great-great-great grandfather had held the title for over thirty years. The first Earl had been vice Admiral, and then, without any break in the troubled 1680s, the office was passed along to the second Earl, but Shaftesbury was evicted from the office in June 1702, and apparently did not get it back. His son theorized that the vice-Admiralty was the only office that Anne's ministers could throw him out of in retaliation for his political activities. Pembroke himself stepped aside at the same time so that Prince George could become Lord High Admiral. His influence in naval affairs continued—he was again Admiral in 1708—but he was not strong enough to get Shaftesbury's post back again.[41]

In the case of another of Locke's friends, this one eccentric to say the least, Charles Mordaunt, third Earl of Peterborough (1658–1735), most of the letters that survive are more or less after the fact. Ashley was very close to his eldest son John, Lord Mordaunt from 1697, who was, as Shaftesbury later put it, his "good Friend & Pupill." Our only record of this early friendship is a letter from Mordaunt in 1699 begging forty pounds to pay for books which he is certain his father will not allow, and a second letter eleven days later thanking Ashley for the money. The letter reveals what for his time of life is a typical discontent with his parents, only for John it was to persist. His father, Lord Peterborough, had a real flair and was at times very courageous, yet he was almost incredibly imprudent. One can be kind, as one writer was, and call him brilliant but erratic—most modern writers term him mercurial—but Sir George Clark describes him as a muddle-headed busybody and braggart. Peterborough went over to the Tories, and John Mordaunt, an M.P. as a minor, followed his lead and voted for the impeachment of Lord

41. All of the information here concerning the office comes from R. G. Marsden's articles, especially "The Vice-Admirals of the Coast" in *English Historical Review*, XXII (1907), 468–77 and XXIII (1908), 736–57.

Somers. This does not seem to have bothered Shaftesbury for long, perhaps because he had the satisfaction of seeing the Tories turn on Peterborough. Late in 1702 he remarked to Furly, "My Lord is now come back to his Originall Friends & Principle: & those Sores are all heal'd up, but how it may stand between my selfe & him I know not as to *his* Part. for great Men are not so forgiving as we that are of a lower Genius, and meeker Spirits." [42]

Locke was involved in still another friendship of Shaftesbury's, that with Thomas Stringer, the first Earl's secretary, and Stringer's wife, Jane. Relations between this couple and Locke were breaking down when Shaftesbury returned from his grand tour, chiefly because of an argument over the ownership of the portrait which is reproduced in the first edition of Locke's *Essay*. Locke thought he owned it and the Stringers thought they did. There may have been other reasons too, for Locke, writing from France in 1686, calls Jane Stringer, or Susan as he refers to her, his valentine, yet the following year and the year after he complains to Edward Clarke that the Stringers are neglecting him, and though he was reassured, gradually they disappear from his correspondence.

On Anthony's return in 1689 the Stringers had finally settled in a fine house converted from a priory, Ivy Church near Alderbury in Wiltshire. A simple farmhouse built on the ruins of Ivy Church is all that remains now, but one can still look westward down the hill and over the meadow to Salisbury, its spire and the river. The Countess Dowager had rooms there and the house provided a convenient refuge for Ashley on his visits to St. Giles. Stringer had been lame for a long time, and in March 1702 a surgeon wrote to Shaftesbury that he had found it necessary the day before to amputate Stringer's leg. The patient presented his services in the letter; two months later he was dead. One could point to a number of reasons why Shaftesbury was fond of him, I suppose, but that he remained an ardent Commonwealthman, loyal to the first Earl's memory for twenty years after his death, was sufficient.

The letters of his imprudent but kind wife are puzzling. If she does

---

42. The Earl of Shaftesbury to Benjamin Furly, November [3?], 1702, in PRO 30/24/20/66.

not want one to find out what she is talking about, if she adopts the obscure style of the day, no amount of writing will reveal who, or even what she is writing about—her effusiveness seems to make it worse. On the other hand, when she is lucid Jane can blurt out things which few of Shaftesbury's correspondents would reveal. Jane is one of the first of the Shaftesbury adulators. Before his death he was to establish an astounding reputation for rectitude, the reasons for which are not altogether clear biographically—probably because the reputation was spread by word of mouth and thus eludes us. Jane, who had no reason to court his favor, wrote him, probably after he became an earl, cautioning him to watch over his health,

> after having seen you; that are Great; in the midst of a plentifull for-
> tune; so very Industrious; watchfull; & exactly regular; & carefull in
> all your affairs as plainly appears in all your actions. . . . I hope in god; I
> shall never have cause to shed half so many tears of sorrow for you; as I
> have of Joyfull ones to see you so good. . . . Thus you may see my Lord;
> amongst us fraile mortalls; your greatness is absolutely necessary (in
> our Bishops words) to make you a bright shining light to us all.[43]

One would like to have the remarks of Bishop Burnet. Jane remarried and was still writing lucidly at eighty-eight.

John Toland is another friend whom Shaftesbury may have met through Locke or his circle. Certainly the collaboration of the two men extended beyond *The Danger of Mercenary Parliaments* and the *Paradoxes of State*. For instance, what work is Toland referring to when he writes Shaftesbury from Amsterdam, July 19, 1701, "And now that I had leisure enough to think of it, you may depend on me [to] write that piece which you and I talkt of the last time we went from Chelsea to London"?[44] *Paradoxes of State*, which is based on King William's speech to Parliament, can hardly be referred to here. Secrecy is so much a part of the relationship between the two men that we will never know how closely they worked on pamphlets either anonymous or ascribed to Toland, unless some notable evidence is discovered.

I have found only two letters of Toland to Shaftesbury that were

43. Jane Stringer to the Earl of Shaftesbury, n.d., in PRO 30/24/45/iv/78.
44. John Toland to the Earl of Shaftesbury, July 19, 1701, in PRO 30/24/20/28.

actually signed, and on one of these the signature has been almost scored out by Shaftesbury. Usually, Toland will suggest near the end of the letter that no signature is necessary. Once he signs himself, "you know who." Typical of the air of secrecy is the sentence with which he ends the last letter to Shaftesbury that I can find—October 22, 1705—"I lodg at Mr. Ridley's in de lay Haye's street; It has a Door into the Park, by which any man may come to me incognito"—though there is little chance that by this time any of Shaftesbury's servants, much less their master, ever slunk through the park to the door.[45]

Shaftesbury is well aware of the embarrassment Toland can cause. In the summer of 1701 he wrote to Furly about Toland's relations with Lord Macclesfield (1659–1701), envoy to Hanover, "I am sorry but not surpriz'd that he should not take his measures more justly so as not to offend or Disoblige My Lord Macclesfield in his present Character & Circumstances. I begg you to acquitt me to my Lord with all honour & respect as you have opportunity either by Word or Letter."[46] Shaftesbury had his own reasons for allowing this relationship to go on for a while longer.

Shaftesbury also was busy with politics during the three years after he became an earl. How does this fact fit in with his Stoical meditations, where he continually deplores his political activity and the type of human situations it involves? As we have seen in his meditations, the intensity of his distaste for an action is often directly proportional to the ability of an action to preoccupy him and all of his energies. As a result, frequently the meditations better reflect what he does well or naturally rather than what he dislikes doing.

The meditations are not only a counterbalance, they also provide him with a rationalization for doing what he presumably is rebelling against.

> If these Things sink away in thy Memory; & the Impressions of those other prevail; if thou canst not be present at once with these things & with those, if it remains then, either that thou shouldst wholly retire;

45. John Toland to the Earl of Shaftesbury, October 22, 1705, in PRO 30/24/20/105.
46. The Earl of Shaftesbury to Benjamin Furly, July 21, 1701, in PRO 30/24/20/29.

or in the phraze of a piouse Writer *be present, as not present; act, as tho' not acting; use, as tho, not using;* but as concern'd about another USE: the Attention being still elsewhere & to other things: firmly fix'd, never suspended, never interrupted by any Attention to ought else. And if other Matters cannot be carried on upon these terms; if this lower degree of Attention will not serve for outward things; if on this account there be less Ability, less Dexterity, less Management . . . Be it so. (Ex., 164–65)

We cannot be sure how much his mind remained fixed on the other use; we can be sure that he was a very able practical politician when he wanted to be. He lacked the deviousness of his grandfather, yet the evidence suggests that he was able to don a mask and do all that it required of him quite convincingly. In a sense his views made him an idealized version of the first Earl. He not only subscribed to his grandfather's credo but had the additional burden of proving him right, very much after the fact.

There are two sides to Shaftesbury's activities, theoretical and practical. Since theory is usually simpler than practice, and in this case more evident, it will be better to look at it first. Even in the 1690s Ashley had been something of an anachronism. He called himself a member of the Country party, a Roman Commonwealthman. If Parliament is to fulfill its role, it must remain on a country base, representative of those who pay taxes, and it must be free of royal interference. The title of a pamphlet from Shaftesbury's collection, published in 1698, makes it clear enough how the franchise is to be reformed, "A scheme of the proportions of the several counties in England paid to the land tax in 1693, and to the subsidies in 1697, compared with the number of members they send to Parliament." No more Old Sarums, in other words. Royal interference is to be blocked by excluding all office holders from Parliament by legislation.

Shaftesbury has been commonly regarded as a monarchist, probably because it is difficult to find any openly antimonarchial sentiments in his writings.[47] Recently, however, there has been an effort

47. For this and for a good account of Shaftesbury's politics, see Robbins, *The Eighteenth-Century Commonwealthman.*

to stress his collaboration with John Toland and his possible sponsorship of a number of republican works published in the late 1690s.[48] Some of the evidence depends on the words of Toland, who, whatever his solid abilities as a writer, is about as trustworthy as Baron Munchausen and less discreet. There is no confirming evidence among Shaftesbury's fairly elaborate financial papers, but neither is there any record of some other monies we definitely know he did spend. He does brag of his associations with "free writers," as he calls them, and he was remarkably successful in concealing an association with Toland, Parson Stephens, and others. It would also follow the thinking of his grandfather were Shaftesbury to feel just as happy under some sort of parliamentary government with a restricted franchise, an aristocracy, and a king—but only for the sort of royal stability he felt Englishmen needed.

Shaftesbury feared the Crown; he feared the cross even more. This was the reason he said that he was more or less born a member of the Country party and then chose to be a Whig. It might seem, with the gradual shift going on in party allegiances during his lifetime—especially with the movement of the Tories toward being the Country party—that he had a choice. Actually so intense was his fear of the dominance of the Church that there was no choice. Toryism he equated with extreme Anglicanism and an extreme Anglican could just as easily be a Catholic—this explains his intense interest in what was going on in Hanover.

This also was the reason he backed King William so strongly in the year or two before the latter's death. The new Grand Alliance between England, the Holy Roman Empire, and Holland was signed in late August of 1701, and about two weeks later, upon the death of James II, Louis recognized his son as King of England. As Shaftesbury pointed out a few months later in *Paradoxes of State*, it was a time when Englishmen had a choice of being pro-English or pro-French. His letters during 1700 to 1703 are full of fears that Europe is drawing closer to "the monarchy of one," the dominance of Europe

48. See, for example, Blair Worden, "Edmund Ludlow: The Puritan and the Whig," *Times Literary Supplement*, January 7, 1977, pp. 15–16, and his lengthy introduction to a book he edited, Edmund Ludlow, *A Voyce from the Watch Tower* (1978).

by a single Catholic monarch, rather than the balance of power between France and the Empire, which Shaftesbury believed the Protestant states could bring about.

The terms *Whig* and *Tory* are basically religious for him, then.
The parties, too, seem to have followed this low- and high-church
pattern in their voting. On secular bills the parties were much less
consistent. In his excellent *British Politics in the Age of Anne*,
Geoffrey Holmes sums up the evidence.[49] There are seven division
lists surviving, or eight, if the list on the repeal of the place clause in
the Act of Settlement is included, and six of these are Commons
lists. Commons voted consistently two out of three times, the
House of Lords—with only two lists—only every other time. A list
of electors for the town of Shaftesbury among the Earl's papers may
accurately represent the state of the parties there. The writer does
not know how the electors voted with respect to Sir John Cropley,
but he tries to guess. Most electors are marked either T or W, but
there are also TT, WW, and TW, and about 15 percent are marked
"Doubtful." Certainly, these categories grew more rigid as Anne's
reign progressed.

The flexibility with which Shaftesbury applied his theories—his
support of William when he thought Protestantism was threatened,
for example—makes it dangerous to generalize, but J. H. Plumb is
certainly right in calling Shaftesbury's views as old-fashioned almost as Sir Roger de Coverley's.[50] When he says this Professor
Plumb is thinking of an aristocrat, however unfashionably, continuing support of the independence of the legislature, a battle which the
Earl himself finally comes to believe has been won, no matter how
much vigilance might be necessary. The fear which never goes away
while he yet lives springs from that persistent linking of Toryism
with Catholicism, which may seem rather irrational today. To argue
his point of view, though, the danger of a Jacobite rebellion remained, and only we know for sure that it was never to succeed. And
Shaftesbury had enough power in Wiltshire, Dorset, and Hampshire

49. Geoffrey Holmes, *British Politics in the Age of Anne* (1967), 39.
50. J. H. Plumb, *The Growth of Political Stability in England, 1675–1725* (1973),
138n.

for his activities to earn the real enmity of Anne and her ministers—perhaps they feared the specter of his grandfather.

This brings us to the practical side of Shaftesbury's activities. During the period with which we are concerned, three Parliaments sat, the fifth and sixth of William's reign, elected in January 1701 and December of the same year, and the first of Anne's, elected in July 1702. We cannot be sure of how active Shaftesbury was in the first of these. In September 1700 he seemed sure of dissolution and promised Thomas Freke of Shroton he would do what he could, despite his new rank. But in October he was sure that a new election would be postponed until forced by the Triennial Act at the end of 1701.

This he thinks will be an advantage, first because Parliament before it was prorogued had made headway in restricting the powers of the Court, in keeping the Excise men out of Parliament, for instance. Second, because the Tories, who have only come into power recently, will have an opportunity to show their hand. Meanwhile the Whigs, who have been shamefully complaisant toward the King, will have a better chance to assess their position and see the folly of their behavior. Nonetheless, Shaftesbury assures Furly that he will remain busy. And it is good that he did, because on December 10 William dissolved the Parliament, which had been prorogued the previous April.

Shaftesbury's attitude toward the first Parliament of 1701 is illuminating. The new Parliament sat on February 6 and it was not until March 4 that Shaftesbury began to suspect that it was Tory in sentiment. Indeed, as late as February 18 he was certain that the majority was Whig, because Parliament had wished to act more strongly against France than did the King's ministers. Yet, as Shaftesbury's household book for this year shows, he entertained this session some of the most powerful men in the country, to say nothing of the host of other observers he had in the House of Commons. Nor was this supporter of lost causes at all obtuse in his perceptions. The point is that the terms *Whig* and *Tory* do not altogether have the meaning that they were shortly to acquire. Whether a member is one or the other can only be determined by his average voting record, not the other way around.

At the end of the session in June, Shaftesbury summarizes his views of it. Members of Parliament are seriously at fault for dragging their feet in the struggle against France, and Commons was venal in the impeachment of the Whig ministers. On the other hand, some positive things have been done. The Bill of Succession, for instance, has been passed, and the £100,000 taken away from the King has been restored to him. It is the King who most disappointed Shaftesbury. First he gave up his friends and, finally, his cause. If the King would only have faith in Parliament, they would respond very strongly, giving him as much as he could ask for in the struggle against France.

As early as May of 1701 Shaftesbury was hoping for the dissolution of a Parliament which he felt was chosen when the nation was still in the dark—the more, as he said later, because "our Adversarys have, after 12 years mistake, learnt their right Game. they act the Commonwealths-men & herd with us." And although Parliament was not dissolved until November 11, Shaftesbury was already busy lining up votes in July. There are a large number of letters among the Shaftesbury papers relating to the election, but it is likely that these represent only the tip of the iceberg. Typical is the correspondence with Sir George Hungerford of Cadnam in northern Wiltshire, who had been Knight of the Shire for at least three terms of Parliament and frequently voted with the Tories. On the twenty-eighth of November, 1701, he tells Maurice that he has received a very obliging and friendly letter from Shaftesbury and his reply is "that I doe decline standing for a Knight of our Shire, and the rather that I may be the better inabled to promote your interest towards you being one." Five days later Hungerford writes to supporter Mr. Hall:

> After I parted from you at Salisbury, I lay that night at Amsbury where I got such a paine in my left shoulder, I was not able to move my left arme, or turne in my bed, I am indisposed still, soe for that and for some other reasons I have thought fitt to desist standing for the county, and you may be pleased to acquaint my friends, Mr Thorpe, and others, that I am making all the interest I can for Mr. Ashley.[51]

51. The Earl of Shaftesbury to Benjamin Furly, August 26 [1701], in PRO 30/24/20/31; Sir George Hungerford to Maurice Ashley, November 28, 1701, in PRO 30/24/20/43; Sir George Hungerford to Mr. Hall, December 3, 1701, in PRO 30/24/20/45.

Whatever happened nationally, the election was an overwhelming success for Shaftesbury. On December 13, 1701, Nathaniel Pope, an elector of Shaftesbury, begins an effusive letter to him: "The glorious Successes that your Lordships most Pious and Indefatigable Endeavours for the good of this Kingdom in particular and all Europe in generall in this Iminent Conjuncture has been bless'd with, and the Joy that I have conceived for them, Enforces this presumption (for which I humbly beg your Lordships pardon) heartily to Congratulate your Lordship on the Same." He goes on to thank Shaftesbury for letting him and other friends of the town "be partly Instrumentall in so brave a Cause as that of giving a Check to the Jacobiticall ffrenzie that has soe long Raign'd uncontroul'd in this County."[52]

Shaftesbury gives a clear picture of his role in the elections in a letter to Furly sent on the twenty-ninth of December:

> I had the strongest Obligation on Earth upon me to act with vigour as I have done since the Opportunity the King has most happily given us & it has pleas'd Providence to bless me with great Success. for having my Province (& that a very hard one) in two Counteys long in the hands of the most inveterate of the Advers Party, I notwithstanding carryed all that I attempted in both. in one of them (viz: Wilts) which my Brother & his Friend represent instead of 2 inveterate Toryes wee have there mended the Elections by 8, which is a difference of 16 in parliament. and in Dorsetshire (my own County) we have gain'd also considerable: My Freind Mr Trenchard being in the Room of a Constant ill Vote for the County: & my Freind Sir John Cropley being also brought in by me at the Place of my Name Shaftesbury, which was ever intirely in their hands since my Grandfather's death, but which I have now intirely recover'd and made Zealouse. and as a Token that the King himself is right as we would wish, he yesterday gave me most *hearty Thanks for my Zeal & Good Services* on this Occasion, and this before much Company.[53]

Although it is not possible to confirm completely the results of the election from the returns finally published in 1878, because we do not know the party of all those chosen, there was a very heavy turn-over of M.P.'s in Wiltshire.

52. Nathaniel Pope to the Earl of Shaftesbury, December 13, 1701, in PRO 30/24/45/i/84.
53. The Earl of Shaftesbury to Benjamin Furly, December 29, 1701, in PRO 30/24/20/49.

Shaftesbury's daybook, in which he records among other things payments to servants in houses he visited, shows him to have been remarkably active during the months before the election. He had energy, then. He had rank, and the power it gave him he wielded with subtlety—and if that would not work, shamelessly. For him all enmities were temporarily suspended, so long as the individual could help. He went deeply into debt. The Duke of Marlborough's loan to him later of seven thousand pounds must have been used to help repay the debt. His name still had some of its old magic in the southwest among those who were anti-jacobitical, and, above all, the King's purpose and his, he felt, perfectly coincided. He was courted in almost every election thereafter, but such a combination was not to occur again.

According to the fourth Earl's biography, the King offered Shaftesbury the post of secretary of state, which he refused. Later he said himself:

> My Zeal for the Revolution & the late King's Cause made me active for the support of that Government & for the Establishment of the Protestant Succession: and it was my good Fortune to have my Services well thought of by the King, & acknowledg'd by him with great Favour. I had the Honour of many Offers from him: but thinking I could best serve Him & my Country in a disinterested Station, I resolv'd absolutely against taking any Employment at Court. The only favour I ever ask'd of the King was a small Office for a Friend of mine who had been assistant to me in serving him. He kindly granted it: But I lost the benefit of his Promise by the greatest of Losses that happen'd soon afterwards in his Death.[54]

This is a fair statement of the situation. He was to wait a long while for the small favor.

We have a letter from Maurice when he was actively campaigning in the next election in the late spring of 1702, but although Shaftesbury was again busy politically at this time, there is much less evidence of it. Even Furly is warned that the Earl cannot speak freely to him. The discretion was necessary enough, for according to Shaftesbury the Tories attempted to take action against him in the House of Commons for his open interference in the previous election. The

---

54. Memorandum [?] by Lord Shaftesbury, July 9, 1703, in PRO 30/24/20/73.

Court was in a difficult position. It could only revenge itself to the extent that Shaftesbury was obligated to it and he was little indebted to the Court. It could and did refuse to act on Micklethwaite's appointment. As we have seen, it had already taken his vice Admiralty away, on account of his political activity in the second election of 1701. The Earl's covert activities, with Cropley as his agent, probably went on for years and account for Queen Anne's settled animosity toward him. As we will see, proof of these activities is hard to come by.

≫VI≪

The Years
of Retreat
1703–1707

In November of 1702 Shaftesbury wrote to Furly saying that from public affairs he was "much withdrawn & must be more so, not only because of this season in which it is not so proper for such as I am to act; but in truth because My Efforts in time of Extreamity, for this last year or two, have been so much beyond my Strength in every respect, that not only for my Mind's sake (which is not a little, to one that loves Retirement as I do) but for my Health's sake & on the Account of my private Circumstances I am oblig'd to give myself a Recess."[1] The following month he shut down St. Giles's House, reducing the staff to the minimum needed for maintenance, and moved to Chelsea, where despite his health he took his seat in the House of Lords.

There are few letters either to Shaftesbury or from him during the following winter and spring.[2] During this time his thoughts were focused on one idea: to go to Rotterdam. But, as he tells Furly on June 11, 1703, "it is the most publick place & common Landing & passage of the English, so it will be the hardest for me to be private, without great care. . . . I . . . am now as bad again as when I retir'd for respite & recover'd my self by my last Retreat in Holland." He for some reason cannot use stoves, so that his chamber must be small, "to be well warm'd in the Winter by the fire only." He goes on to say that he may come to Furly's "house where I may sometime meet a

1. The Earl of Shaftesbury to Benjamin Furly [November 1702], in PRO 30/24/20/66.
2. Possibly the eye troubles he complains of in April account for this; more likely the vagaries of preservation are responsible. Were it not for the letters kept in Rotterdam by Furly's descendants, we would have almost nothing from the period.

Friend: but except your self & family will entrust no person to come to my own Lodging."[3]

A fortnight later he continues, "I must be more troublesome in this Concern of my Privacy than I was last time, by so much the more as I have made my self more known in the World & have acted a more Publick Part which will place a great many Eyes upon me that will seek for Mistery where there is none & think my Retirement rather a Pretext than a Reality"—as some are now representing it. "I am now only thinking of a safe & good Convoy: fearing nothing so much as falling alive into French hands: therefore should lay hold of any Vessel of Warr English or Dutch, where I was sure at least of making good Resistance."[4]

Obviously many eyes would be watching a person of Shaftesbury's rank, the more so because his disaffection with the Whigs was known, he had some sway among the younger lords, and he retained his influence in the Commons. That he wrote Furly with more than a trace of the paranoia which came upon him when he was under pressure is obvious from his fears about the French. When eight years later he was forced to throw himself on their mercies, he was overwhelmed by their attentions. He refused their offer to reside in Montpellier; he accepted, bemusedly, an escort of horsemen across southern France. To the French his nobility was more important than who his grandfather was, but Shaftesbury never was able to forget the 1680s and he may have seen the same forces at work in England and France in 1703.

Lord Nottingham (1647–1730) signed the pass to go to Holland on August 5, 1703, and on August 13 os Shaftesbury wrote to Wheelock that he had come safely to Rotterdam. He arrived in Holland in a bad humor, though his sickness may have colored his mood. A typical letter to Wheelock opens, "I thought you had not been in the World 'twas so long since I heard from you." He then goes on to lecture his steward on the necessity of identifying each letter and finally turns to a lecture on thrift—which is in a sense a lecture to himself.

3. The Earl of Shaftesbury to Benjamin Furly, June 11, 1703, in PRO 30/24/20/71.
4. The Earl of Shaftesbury to Benjamin Furly, June 25, 1703, in PRO 30/24/20/72.

By contrast, Wheelock's letters are warm when it is appropriate but always models of propriety and sincere complaisance. Furthermore Wheelock is very busy. The estate is now understaffed because shutting down St. Giles's House the previous December had little bearing on the farms, which continue to need constant, paternal attention. They had taken several months of Shaftesbury's time from each of three years. One senses too, reading Wheelock's account of his troubles, that the tenants realize all too well that the landlord is away.

Good stewards were hard to find and Wheelock must have known that he was more valuable to Shaftesbury than Shaftesbury was to him. On the other hand he has been in the family for nearly thirty years, so that he takes the only tack available:

> If I have acted contrary to your Lordship's Interest or the Interest of the ffamily I am heartily sorry for it. Hard ffate has always attended me but now more than ever if this be soe. Look which way I will I find enmity in all here. Mr. Dalicourt by having spoken ffreely to him for his negligence in your affaires. John Gibbs by not speaking to him much about affaires, for he that stands corrected may hope for ffriendship. Mr. Bishop . . . for Lessening the Number of his Doggs and intermedling with his affairs as he calls it. The Workmen Curse me for Lessening their pay and work and turning them of. The Country for my speaking sharpe in not making heartily welcome as they say. Your ffriends, ffamily and tradesmen's because its thought I am heaping up Wealth. But I can bear all this with ease since I know my Innocence in the Latter and have gain'd the other in aiming at your Service, but if after all these I have gain'd your Lordship too, I have Lived to Good end.[5]

One hopes that Shaftesbury noted the lack of grammatical logic and, another sign of excitement, the number of double f's. Wheelock had once been taught to write this way, but times changed and so did Wheelock.

Most of the news Shaftesbury received from home this winter was bad. His favorite sister Gertrude died of smallpox in November 1703. On the twenty-seventh of that month a severe storm had lifted sheets of lead from the roof of St. Giles's House and blown down walls and uprooted trees to the cost of at least five hundred pounds.

5. John Wheelock to the Earl of Shaftesbury, January 8, 1704, in PRO 30/24/45/i/126–27.

Sister Dorothy, of a "tender constitution," is approaching confinement; in every letter Shaftesbury expresses his concern about her.

Shaftesbury was quite serious about the need for thrift. There is no way of telling how much he has spent on his estate during the first three years. However, he does speak of the pains to which he has gone to make it pleasant—one index which survives is the number of family portraits, and most of them must have been done from 1700 to 1703. Fixing up the estate, allotting portions for his sisters, and financing elections have cost him at least nine thousand pounds, and he still has one portion to pay, Elizabeth's. Shaftesbury gives his solution to the problem several times:

> I shall keep in my Compass of about £200 for the year that I stay here & if this dos not do, it shall be yet less & the Time longer. for I will never return to be as I was of late *richly poor*. that is to say to live with the part of a rich Man, a Family & House such as I have & yet in Debt & unable to do any Charity or bestow money in any degree. If I find my House at St. Giles & Rank greater than I can sustain with my Estate. I'll rather give up my Family and sell all. So that I may have something to do good with.[6]

The astounding thing is that the plan worked. Not counting the £130 at least that he gave away, Shaftesbury did manage to live on £200 for the year. Even with Sir John's assurances, Shaftesbury is unwilling to believe Wheelock's statement that the short-term debt has been paid off in the spring, with £2,000 left over for Shaftesbury to do what he wants with. By the fall of 1704, when he returned, the surplus had doubled.

The need for thrift was, in part at least, only a pretense for the Earl's cutting off his annual payment to Toland, whose ties with him had been growing weaker year by year. In the autumn of 1703 Toland begged 200 guilders of Shaftesbury, who then wrote to Wheelock, "So now this shall end & indeed it is time; not only because of my private affaires that require Retrenchment of things of this kind, but because of the Person, whose prophane & loose Ways over-ballance all the Good (I think) that either he has done or can do, unless he

---

6. The Earl of Shaftesbury to John Wheelock, Rotterdam, November 6, 1703 NS, in PRO 30/24/20/78. By *family* Shaftesbury means his servants and dependents.

reforms much more. But for poor Stephens, when New Years day comes I would have you send him his Ten Guineas & be exact to the Day."[7]

Among other bad news from home this winter was the marriage of his sister Frances without his full consent. We do not know whether there had been proposals for her before; it seems likely there must have been. In any case she was still unmarried at twenty-six. She then fell in love with an M.P. from Great Bedwin in Wiltshire, Francis Stonehouse. Shaftesbury took an immediate dislike to the notion of Stonehouse as a brother-in-law. Possibly he had Tory leanings. He has been pronounced both a Tory and a Whig, so that we really do not know the answer, though Shaftesbury surely would have. It could be that the two fell in love before any arrangements were made, which would reverse the normal order of things among their class.

It must have been Frances who involved their bishop, Gilbert Burnet, in the matter of her marriage. In a reply to him, Shaftesbury reluctantly consents: "I shall be no way a hinderance to the Match, tho for reasons I would by no means give your Lordship the trouble of hearing, I can never be for it, or in the least concerned in it." He has arranged by act of Parliament for his sisters' dowries and Frances is of age. Anything additional he can do will be done for those sisters who dispose of themselves according to his wishes.[8] The Stonehouses sought to mollify him when he returned from Rotterdam the following summer and seem to have succeeded in some degree.

We might expect to find the key to what Shaftesbury and Furly talked about during the visit in the letters which they wrote before it. However, we get only part of the story. Shaftesbury's letters are intended to explain the intricacies of politics in the English Court and Parliament to Furly and to other merchants of Rotterdam. Furly in turn serves as a reliable source of foreign news, everything from court gossip to military and moral actions. Since Furly was not required to explain the complexities of Dutch government, his must

7. The Earl of Shaftesbury to John Wheelock, n.d., in PRO 30/24/20/80.
8. The Earl of Shaftesbury to Bishop Gilbert Burnet, February 5, 1704 NS, in PRO 30/24/22/4/p. 3.

have been an easier task than Shaftesbury's. How, for instance, was a Commonwealthman to explain the workings of the Whig and Tory parties in 1701 and 1702? Shaftesbury had to criticize bitterly his old friend and correspondent William Hysterman of Amsterdam for siding with the Tories when they rallied round the flag, after Louis XIV proclaimed James III king of England in 1701. "But I allways hop'd that the Holland Whigg-Party & Friends of Liberty (such as Mr Hysterman & his Friends) better knew or at least in time would come better to know their Friends here & who they were that on the one side only could support & on the other side could never but supplant this our present Government." Later in the year he is still intensely suspicious, but all there is to do is wait: "The People have now an Opinion that these Men & this very Ministry will serve their turn & carry on things abroad for their own honour & pursue the Warr vigorously. . . . even You abroad are willing to think well of our Ministry. the Experiment must be tryed. it may be dangerouse: but it must be tryed. if they shew themselves soon (by their Violence in any kind) we shall soon be rid of them."[9]

There was little said about the war, which must have been a chief topic of conversation in Rotterdam. The Dutch were generally proponents of free trade; the mercantilist English had every reason to suppress trade with the war going on. For much of the war there was trade between Holland and France, and, just as important, the correspondence with France which enabled Amsterdam's financial centers to function without hindrance continued too. There were some efforts to suppress both the trade and correspondence, but as the war progressed the English came around to the Dutch view. The two men may have found it advantageous to avoid the topic in their letters. The only document we have on the topic is a letter remonstrating against trade with the French, signed by ninety-five Rotterdam merchants—including John van Twedde, Shaftesbury's friend, who must have supplied it. The reasoning is not Shaftesburian but very practical: the Swedes and Danes will largely profit; the French will

9. The Earl of Shaftesbury to Benjamin Furly, January 6, 1702, in PRO 30/24/20/52; August 10, 1702, in PRO 30/24/20/65.

also profit; Dutch brewing and distilling will suffer; and because of the embargo, local merchants who had anticipated it are already overstocked with imported goods.[10]

The only other topics besides English politics and Continental affairs discussed in the letters of this period are protégés and children. For instance we can follow Henry Wilkinson's career from servanthood, through being bonded to Furly, with Shaftesbury's support, for six years to learn the trade, and finally setting up in business. This adventure came to an ambiguous conclusion, but Wilkinson's beautifully clear letters are a blessing, since they provide a constant check on the letters of Furly. It is ironic that Shaftesbury's most voluminous correspondent should also be his most illegible one. It is comforting to know that Locke also had trouble reading Furly's hand.

Despite Shaftesbury's resolutions in 1698, it appears from his correspondence that he then met a large number of people during the visit to Rotterdam. This time he kept his resolution so thoroughly that Le Clerc imagined him depressed: "Mylord de Shaftesbury est toujours à Rotterdam, où il ne voit presque personne. J'ai peur que ce Seigneur n'ait eu quelque chagrin, et qu'il ne donne dans la mélancholie. Ce seroit un très grand dommage."[11] If we leave Paul Crell out of consideration, Pierre Bayle would seem to be correct when he wrote to Locke that Shaftesbury saw only the Furlys and himself.

We do not have any record of what Bayle and Shaftesbury talked about, and there are few letters.[12] The friendship was a natural one for Shaftesbury and no doubt he would have been happy to help him financially had Bayle's fierce pride not prevented it. He did work out an elaborate plan with Desmaizeaux whereby he donated books and

10. Public letter from Rotterdam merchants, June 8, 1704, in PRO 30/24/45/i/135–36.

11. "Lord Shaftesbury is still at Rotterdam, where he sees almost no one. I am afraid that my Lord has experienced some grief which makes him melancholy. That would be a very great shame." Jean Le Clerc to John Locke, Amsterdam, June 24, 1704 NS, in *Lettres inédites de Le Clerc à Locke*, ed. Gabriel Bonno (Berkeley, 1959), 130.

12. Seven of Bayle's letters to Shaftesbury have been found, all of them copies, and none of Shaftesbury's to him. Bayle's letters are attractively full of literary affairs and gossip, but it is obvious from his letters to Shaftesbury that they were not regular correspondents. They did continually exchange compliments in the correspondence of Furly, Wilkinson, and others.

Bayle in turn gave his old books away. He also managed to give Bayle a watch. Elisabeth Labrousse, who knows more about Bayle than anyone else, tells me that she does not think he would have accepted a gift from anyone else, and she feels that Bayle's reverence for the nobility, oddly enough, explains part of his enthusiasm for Shaftesbury. Just before Bayle's death, the Earl was able to do him one final favor. Some one of Bayle's many enemies had convinced Lord Sunderland that he was dealing with the French, and Shaftesbury disabused him.

After Bayle's death in 1706 Shaftesbury described with great precision just what he had gained from the conversations in Rotterdam. The letter is to Jacques Basnage (1653–1723), a Huguenot minister in Rotterdam and a friend of Bayle:

> I know very well that it is in Religion and Philosophy as in most things; that different opinions usually create not only dislike but Animosity and Hatred. It was far otherwise between Monsieur Bayle & my Self, for whilst we agreed in Fundamentall Rules of morall Practice & believ'd our Selves true to these, the continuall differences in Opinions and the constant disputes that were between us, serv'd to improve our Friendship. I had the Happiness to see that they lost me nothing of *his*: and I know my own encreasing every Day, as my Advantages encreas'd by his improving Conversation. I may well say *improving* in every respect, even as to Principles in which the Enemys of Monsieur Bayle wou'd least of all allow him the Character of a *Promoter*. But if to be confirm'd in any good Principle be by Debate & Argument after thorow scrutiny to re-admit what was first implanted by prevention; I may then say, in truth, that whatever is most vallewable to me of this kind has been owing in great measure to this our Friend whom the World call'd *Scepticall*. Whatever Opinion of mine stood not the Test of his piercing Reason, I learnt by degrees either to discard as frivilouse, or not to rely on, with that Boldness as before: but That which bore the Tryall I priz'd as purest Gold. and if that Philosophy whatever it be, which keeping in Bounds of Decency, examines things after this manner, be esteem'd injuriouse to Religion or Mankind, & be accordingly Banish'd the World, I can foresee nothing but Darkness & Ignorance that must follow.[13]

13. The Earl of Shaftesbury to Jacques Basnage, January 21, 1707, in PRO 30/24/22/4/pp. 32–33. Some students of Bayle make the addressee to be Henri Basnage de Beauval (1656–1710), editor of the *Histoire des ouvrages des savants*, brother of Jacques; but Elisabeth Labrousse is certainly correct in her *Inventaire critique de la*

Paul Crell must have spent a good bit of time with the Earl in Amsterdam. How Shaftesbury was able to predict that this young Pole who apparently did not understand a word of English would turn out to be a good secretary is hard to say. Shaftesbury knew that his own eyes would never be the same again, but surely an Englishman might have served the purpose with less trouble. In any case it is difficult to argue with successful predictions. Before Shaftesbury left Holland he had committed himself to sending Crell to Leiden for a year of study with Thomas Crenius (1648–1728) and Jacob Gronovius (1645–1716). Shaftesbury had managed to live in Holland for nearly a year at £200; he granted Crell £500 for the expenses of his year in Leiden.

Part of Crell's attraction for Shaftesbury, his dedication to the classics, can be seen in Arent Furly's description of a visit to Crell in Leiden:

> Its a pleasure to see how every corner of his room is fill'd with renown'd Greeks & Romans; I was scarce an half an hour with him, but I imagin'd myself at Athens in the midst of a learned croud; O divine rapture! but alas of too short a duration; for no sooner was I struck with admiration & reverence for their Great Wisdom & Virtues, but I perceived them to be of another & More noble Generation, than that of My contemporarys, to whom I returned with shame & confusion.

Arent Furly is also an intellectual protégé of Shaftesbury's and he well knows what his master wants to hear. Arent's father makes it clearer why Shaftesbury's odd choice turned out to be a proper one. To Benjamin, Crell is "an industrious, indefatigable, ingenious, Learned, young man, of a [sweetest] disposition, great Sobriety & Singular Modesty."[14]

The Earl had for some time kept in touch with what was going on in the court at Hanover, through Furly's letters, among others. He continued to do so in Holland by means of a long correspondence begun by the British emissary there, Sir Rowland Gwin (1659–

---

correspondence de Pierre Bayle (Paris, 1961), 324, that it is directed to Jacques. The addressee is obviously a clergyman.

14. Arent Furly to the Earl of Shaftesbury, October 10, 1704 NS, in PRO 30/24/45/i/154–55; Benjamin Furly to the Earl of Shaftesbury, August 10, 1705 NS, in PRO 30/24/45/ii/70.

1722). They had known each other before, probably in France during 1686 and 1687, though Shaftesbury's remark is maddeningly ambiguous. Speaking of the post of Hanover, he says, "I am necessitated to think you of any English man the most fitted; being consciouse as I have been, of the Services you did at a former Court (our then presumptive successor's) where I first Knew you and where, as a Omen of my being forever a bad Courtier I made choise of you (an English man and Whigg) instead of any other to present me."[15]

The correspondence started nonetheless on a rather cool but polite note. In this same letter, Shaftesbury remarks that

> if those persons of your Court are such as you describe, there are yett Treasures of Happiness in store for England and the World. I can rely on your Judgment sooner then on most Persons living; but cannot help in my self a naturall Diffidence of Courts, after having been deceiv'd so much in one I so early lov'd, and had such thoughts of, as to believe it no less then impossible to have seen it sacrifize its best Friends & lay it self att last so low, by such repeated acts, and by loosing even that degree of Faith & Gratitude which attends common Policy & Interest. Every thing in Nature seems to demonstrate this Truth, that Things are to be maintained & advanc'd by the Principles on which they were founded. But Courts are Super-natural things, & subservient to none of these rules. All is miraculouse there, and out of the order of Common human Policy.

Nowhere is there a clearer statement of how bitter Shaftesbury was over his betrayal by King William, though this must also reflect his attitude toward Queen Anne and his personal problems at the time, especially with Lady Frances.

Later in the spring, Shaftesbury receives through Gwin greetings from the Electress of Hanover and a letter from the Queen of Prussia inviting him to visit her. I suppose that if Shaftesbury were to visit any court, he might have accepted this invitation, but in addition to the fact that his distaste for courts in general has recently been sharpened, he is genuinely committed to retirement and this makes it doubly unwelcome. He knows very well that this is in part due to a busybody acquaintance, Harry Davenant—perhaps a relation of

15. The Earl of Shaftesbury to Sir Rowland Gwin, January 23, 1704 NS, in PRO 30/24/22/4/pp. 1–2.

the political writer Charles Davenant—and he tells him off rather bluntly, in about as strong a letter of reproach as Shaftesbury was likely to write to anyone he wished to remain friendly with. The reply is late: "I confess there may have been a little more perhaps in my silence this time than usuall. . . . Onely that You are a little too kind to me, talk too much of me by a great deal, & to too great People. . . . For your own Creditt's Sake, since you have drawn so much honour upon me, pray see to bring me off the best you can."[16] In the typically flowery letter to Gwin he is filled with gratitude: "The undeserv'd Regard which the Electrice is pleas'd to express for me with the notice taken of me by the Queen of Prussia, & the Letter from her which you have communicated to me, is so great an Honour that I cannot pretend to make any Return my Self," and, in short, there is too little time before his return to England for him to make the visits, which is a polite lie to cover the fact that he has no desire to make them.[17]

No letters to the Earl from Sir John Cropley or his other friends in England were saved. We have only Wheelock's—preserved because they deal with estate matters; yet it is clear from them that by the spring of 1704 Shaftesbury was pressed to come home by all hands. Wheelock becomes almost poetic on the topic at times: "I wish to god your Lordship was at this your most delightsome seate. Where the softness of the morning and evening Aire and the pleasant views of the place would be the best Balme to your Eyes and Lungs and the rideing to see your Estate and the thoughts for Improvements would infallibly divert those Rheumes, so that wee should not doubt to see your Lordship restor'd to your perfect health and vigor."[18]

In midsummer of 1704 Shaftesbury decided that both he and his pocketbook were in good enough shape that he could return to England. What happened was a disaster. The port where one left as a passenger for England was The Brill, on an island about twenty miles southwest of Rotterdam. Now the old port is largely cut off by

16. The Earl of Shaftesbury to Harry Davenant, April 19, 1704 NS, in PRO 30/24/22/4/pp. 5–6.
17. The Earl of Shaftesbury to Sir Rowland Gwin, April 19, 1704 NS, in PRO 30/24/22/4/p. 7.
18. John Wheelock to the Earl of Shaftesbury, St. Giles's House, July 29, 1704, in PRO 30/24/45/i/137.

shifting of the coastline. Here great fleets would gather, in war or peace, to await a fair wind. One traveler in 1674 estimated three hundred sails in his flotilla. When the word was given, all of the ships would set forth at their various speeds for England. The trip home in the narrow quarters of his ship was nearly fatal for Shaftesbury, though. Because of the war it was necessary for the ships to travel with an escort. The commanders must have decided that the wind was fair at The Brill, but no sooner were they well at sea than it shifted and the whole fleet was driven north to the coast of Zeeland. When nearly a month after he first boarded the yacht Shaftesbury came ashore at Alborough in Suffolk, all of the good done by breathing the air of Rotterdam for almost a year was wiped away, and he was seriously ill.

The following twelve months were a period of illness for Shaftesbury, and perhaps this is the best place to say what we can about his health generally, at this great distance in time. By the end of September 1704 he was feeling better again and according to his journal he arrived at St. Giles's House on October 8 from Little Chelsea. Later that month he suffered a relapse and, according to a letter which Wheelock sent to Rotterdam, he was in serious condition. The payments to Drs. Christopher Pitt and John Sagittary of Blandford are frequent during November. One of the two letters we have, definitely written during the last months of the year, is a fragment of a deathbed message written to an unknown correspondent, which is critical of Locke's views and takes an understandably idealistic attitude toward his own career. He kept to bed in January and February of 1705, but on a fine day went forth and suffered a third relapse. It was not until the middle of August that he was well enough to venture back to Little Chelsea, where he stayed for almost three months. After a brief appearance in the House of Lords he returned to St. Giles's House on November 15. By the end of 1705 he had been home sixteen months and only four of them had been spent at Chelsea. It was this pattern of movement between Dorset and London he was to follow—when he was wise—during his last few years in England.

Dr. John Pau must have seen Shaftesbury during his severe illness of August of 1704. In any case after Shaftesbury's relapse in the spring of 1705 he asked for a full report on the state of his health and so we have a several-page report by Dr. Pitt. Pitt, like most of his colleagues, was a humoral physician, so that his description of the roots of Shaftesbury's illness, a "Scorbuticall Disorder from a too Acid Dyserasy of his Lordships blood"—a scurvy-like disease caused by an acid distemper of his blood—is of little help, but the symptoms that lead Pitt to this conclusion can tell us something. In the first place, asthma had been long known and it has rather distinctive symptoms; there is little doubt that Shaftesbury was severely asthmatic by 1705. Sometimes he could only breathe while sitting up. He also suffered from a tertian ague, a fever on alternate days, associated with the most violent sweats, and he was afflicted with an eye ailment which was worsened by his illness. Doctor Pitt prescribed cinchona bark, quinine, for the fever and a mild purgative for the sweats. Happily there is no account in the statement of his being bled—a perfectly sound procedure according to humoral theory— though Shaftesbury had had himself bled the previous August.[19]

While asthma is easy to diagnose, tuberculosis is not. Asthma is incredibly painful, but with a sensible regimen of the sort that Shaftesbury followed it should not drastically shorten life. When he died at forty-two in Italy an autopsy had to be performed because only the body and the heart were to be sent back to Dorsetshire. The lungs were found perfectly collapsed against the ribs. It is possible that the fevers he suffered from were tubercular—the violent sweats would reinforce this, but I admit this is conjecture.

Shaftesbury's own memory of his earlier life is not reliable enough to be of much assistance in diagnosis. The way he remembered it, he first fell ill after serving in the House of Commons for two or three years in the 1690s. Actually his childhood had not been especially healthy. Margaret Shaftesbury writes to Locke in 1682, "Dalli had before sent us word, he had, had, aswell'd face, which I apprihened he ought to be otherwise treated for, then is usuall in such complaints, he haveing binn all this yeare subject to a sharpe humer, that

19. The report is designated PRO 30/24/20/100.

has griped him many times."[20] It is not possible to tell what is meant here by a humor, but the following month Jane Stringer thanks Locke for the good news of her "little boys health." Lady Margaret may well have meant fevers because she uses that term in describing to his mother a similar attack four years later. Shaftesbury may have forgotten these earlier illnesses, or, more likely, he simply put them out of his mind as we are all inclined to do with unpleasant circumstances.

The real question is whether the state of medical art was such that there may have been a possibility his early death from respiratory disease might have been avoided. To this question the answer is yes. Despite the humoral theory, much medicine was then empirical, that is, based on repeated observation of cause and effect. The connections between avoidance of tuberculosis and fresh air, good nutrition, and a regular life were well known. They have had to be relearned in our own time. In 1694 Richard Morton (1637–1698) speaks in his *Phthisilogia: Or a Treatise of Consumtions* specifically of "Asthmatical Consumption." "A thin and open Air is more necessary in the cure of this Consumption, than in any others. Neither indeed can this Kind of Consumptive Persons live long, with the use of the most generous Medecines, in a foggy or smoaky air."[21]

Shaftesbury always feared falling into a consumption, just as the asthmatic Locke did. The principal danger was of course London itself. In non-plague years, tuberculosis apparently caused 20 percent of the deaths during the post-Restoration period. This was still another reason for Locke's traveling to Montpellier and Rotterdam. In England he finally decided to live at Oates in the home of the Mashams, and if he was always under pressure to return to London, there were friends like William Popple who tried to persuade him to stay away.

Shaftesbury seemed unable to heed his own warnings, so that he had to fall into a serious illness before he did anything about it. His friends and family were too well aware of this. Maurice told him

20. The Dowager Countess of Shaftesbury to John Locke, December 27, 1682, in de Beer, II, 565.
21. Richard Morton, *Phthisilogia: Or a Treatise of Consumtions* (1694), 214.

bluntly late in 1704: "It still seems to me very strange that you allow your Illness constantly to be returning by neglects or Omissions or faults of your own. It were no difficult matter I shou'd think after such & so long an Illness to resolve not to under-doe in necessary Caution. The trouble you make your Self & voluntaryly take upon you in your Health is what may not be unjustly assignd as partly the Cause of your general, Ill health & its strange therefore that so great a Necessity does not prevaile with you to think of a remission."[22]

There are almost too many reasons for this behavior in a man who was always capable of great self-discipline: self-deception in the early stages, his desire to serve his country, his desire to be with his friends when they could not come to St. Giles's, and for his last years, that peculiar fatalism—a desire to take each day as it came—which was grounded on too many brushes with death, and on his Stoicism growing in potency year by year. Even in 1705 he wrote about his health to Furly, "This I can assure you, that if I thought it of no use to the Publick I shou'd not be at the pains I am at of preserving it, for I was never very fond of life at any time: much less of preserving a Weak & sickly one, as mine perhaps for the future may prove."[23]

When Shaftesbury returned from Rotterdam, he found Locke seriously ill. Maurice Cranston says the Earl visited Locke at Oates, which I have not been able to confirm independently.[24] Shaftesbury did not arrive from Holland until August 27. He does write to Locke on September 7 saying that when he is perfectly recovered from his weakness his first thought will be to see Locke, whose illness he has heard of. There is a possibility he may have seen him between his own initial sickness and the relapse which followed. Locke died October 28, 1704.

The radical split between his own ideas and those of Locke must

22. Maurice Ashley to the Earl of Shaftesbury, December 8, 1704, in PRO 30/24/22/1/45.

23. The Earl of Shaftesbury to Benjamin Furly, February 24, 1705, in PRO 30/24/20/94.

24. Maurice Cranston, *John Locke* (1957), 472–73. He no longer has his notes.

have caused Shaftesbury a great deal of anguish. Here was a man who helped to choose his mother to marry his father, who cared for his mother in her pregnancy, who supervised his education, who had identical political sentiments when Commonwealthmen were becoming scarcer daily, who introduced him to some of his best friends, and, above all, who was advisor to his grandfather and seems to have kept the faith as well as he could under difficult conditions. No doubt Shaftesbury meant it when he called Locke his friend and foster father, "to whom, next my immediate parents as I must own the greatest Obligation, so I have ever preserv'd the highest gratitude and Duty."[25]

Shaftesbury, so far as I know, never during his lifetime publicly attacked Locke. After Locke's death, however, he had no such compunctions about assailing him privately. In December 1704, when he thought his own death was near, he thus wrote a friend about Locke's dying letter to Anthony Collins (1676–1729): "The piece of a Letter which you sent Savours of the good Christian. it putts me in mind of one of those dying Speeches which come out under the Title of a Christian Warning-piece. I shou'd never have guess'd it to have been of a dying Philosopher." He then begins on a counter-charge.

> As for *good wishes* You have abundance, tho' without Complments. For *Loving Me*, or *my Memory* be that hereafter as it may prove best for You or as You can bear it. *The use* I wou'd have you make of it, is, that our Life (thank Heaven) has been a *Scene of Friendship* of *long* duration, with *much* and *solid Satisfaction*, founded in the Consciouseness of doing Good for Goods sake, without any further Regards. . . . Thus runs my charge to You: something different (as You see) from the admir'd one, given by our deceas'd Acquaintance.

The letter ends, "I have never yet serv'd God or Man but as I lov'd and lik'd: having been true to my own and Family Motto which is LOVE, SERVE."[26]

His strongest condemnation of Locke was not printed until three years after Shaftesbury's death. Though it is part of material which we must read with the qualification that it was intended for a young

---

25. The Earl of Shaftesbury to Jean Le Clerc, February 8, 1705, in PRO 30/24/22/2.
26. The Earl of Shaftesbury to a Friend, December 2, 1704, in PRO 30/24/22/2.

man entering the clergy, this could have affected only the intensity
with which Shaftesbury spoke. The thought must remain the same:

> *Innate* is a word he poorly plays upon. The right word, though less us'd,
> is *connatural*. For what has *Birth*, or the *Progress of the* FOETUS *out of
> the Womb*, to do in this Case? The question is not about the *Time* the
> Ideas enter'd, or the *Moment* that one Body came out of the other: but
> whether the Constitution of Man be such, that being adult & grown
> up, at such or such a time, sooner or later (no matter when), the Idea &
> Sence of *Order, Administration,* & *a God*, will not infallibly, inevita-
> bly, necessarily spring up in him. . . . Thus *Virtue*, according to Mr.
> Lock, has no other Measure Law or Rule, than *Fashion* & *Custome*.
> Morality Justice Equity, depend only on *Law Will* and God indeed is a
> perfect *free Agent* in his sense; that is, *free to any thing* however ill. for
> if he wills it, it will be made Good; Virtue may be Vice, & Vice Vertue
> in its turn, if he pleases. Thus neither *Right* or *Wrong, Virtue* or *Vice*,
> are any thing in themselves; nor is there any trace or Idea of em *natu-
> rally imprinted* on human Minds.[27]

Until the day of Shaftesbury's death, his attitude toward Locke remained a classic example of real ambiguity: reverence for the man
and all that he had done for him; detestation of Locke's ideas and
their implications for society.

It might seem that Shaftesbury had enough to do preserving his
health this winter, but there were a number of other matters to be
taken care of; first, something he had not heard for quite a while—a
cry for help from the Whigs. Elections were likely in the spring and
Lord Somers wrote to him apparently late in December 1704:

> I am going to take so great a liberty that I could not reasonably hope for
> pardon if it proceeded from my self. But I only write the Desires of
> many of your Lordship's humble servants who intend not to give over
> Soliciting your Lordship to lay your commands on Mr. Ashley to be a
> Candidate for Wiltshire at the next Election. The D. of Somerset D. of
> Bolton Lord Kingston & Lord Wharton have met with several Gentle-
> men of the Country who are in Town, & they all agree that there is a
> fair prospect of successe, & bid mee assure your Lordship of their best
> endeavours & that they cannot think of any body else to joyn with

27. The Earl of Shaftesbury to Michael Ainsworth, June 3, 1709, in PRO 30/24/
20/143; compare Shaftesbury, *Several Letters Written by a Noble Lord to a Young
Man at the University* (1716), 38–44.

Mr. Ash, whose son has bin pressing Mr. Ashley in the most earnest manner from his Father to stand with him, but as yet he is not to be prevail'd upon.

Somers got a cool reply:

> I know the difficulty there is in engageing a Man of strict Honesty in a Kind of Ambitiouse Service of the Publick, where Courtship and Application is become a necessary part. and I have felt the weight of this 'ere now in my Brother's Case, when with so much difficulty I prevail'd with him to Act the Candidates Part for the Publick at a time when I my Self was in a Condition to Act in it. But being unable to show him the Example, I am the more necessitated to leave him to his free Choice, & perfect Liberty as I have long promis'd him.[28]

This answer merely reflects what he had bitterly decided on in Rotterdam, the year before.

Of course he did not tell Somers the real reasons for his reluctance, but he was more candid to Awnsham Churchill, the publisher. After assuring Churchill of his support at Dorchester, he says,

> 'tis what I am unable to do the Publick any Service in, by my Brother's having (as I heard) declin'd Standing in a more important place, & my Brother Hooper's being so much discourag'd by his former Repulse and the Severe opposition & usuage He mett with from the Whigg Interest at that time. nor were we more fortunate in the Service of the same Interest this last Election for our Country, the Person whom we then strove to serve having disclaim'd us. . . . there is little Creditt gott by serving a Court at the best: but it is hard Service indeed to make Interest for a Court that is so generously dispos'd as to give its Interest to its Enemies with priviledge of making themselves the Country-party by opposition.[29]

He seems to have had enough of the Apostate Whigs.

Somehow by the time May 1705 and the elections came around, this situation had changed and we can only guess at the reasons. Certainly Maurice was resolute enough in December. We do not have Shaftesbury's letter to him giving him his freedom, but we do have

---

28. Lord Somers to the Earl of Shaftesbury [December 1704], in PRO 30/24/20/87; the Earl of Shaftesbury to Lord Somers, December 25, 1704 (dated as 1704/5), in PRO 30/24/22/2.

29. The Earl of Shaftesbury to Awnsham Churchill, January 29, 1705, in PRO 30/24/22/2.

Maurice's sour reply to it, in which we can see clearly the beginnings of an estrangement between the brothers. Among other things Maurice says, "As to the Liberty you grant me, as I think Necessity gives me my discharge, so cannot I but thank you for subscribing to it, tho to your Cost; as you seem to intimate it to be; That end of the Choice which I take in this circumstance I doe not see what it can cost you; But had I taken the Other it coud not be but upon the terms of Its costing you Considerably. . . . There is a Right no One can Buy; & upon intense consideration I think you have not bought all my priviledges."[30] This attitude seems unlikely to have changed, so that it is likely Shaftesbury's own resentment against the party softened and he applied further pressure on Maurice.

Moreover, the Whigs tried deceit. Late in January Shaftesbury received a letter from a Mr. Burgess—probably Daniel Burgess (d. 1747)—telling him that "A Great man, in high place near the Queen, has heard that your Lordship did restrain Mr. Ashly from putting up for it."[31] Shaftesbury wrote back immediately, but already Sir John Cropley had told Burgess, and he in turn had assured the great man, the Duke of Somerset, and Lord Somers that the report was untrue.

Then, too, would Shaftesbury have preferred to see a Tory victory? This is what political acquaintances asked him, knowing that whatever he thought of the Whigs, he was opposed still more to the Tory policies with regard to the Church and to France. The Whigs certainly moved away from Shaftesbury's position, rather than he from theirs, but this did not leave him any more comfortable, for he was a political leader in what had become a splinter group. Inevitably he had been forced to fluctuate before, and as the election grew closer, perhaps he wavered this time.[32] There is also some indication that he grew happier with Parliament's performance in January and February. In any case, Maurice stood and on May 13 Shaftesbury gave money to the ringers to help celebrate his election. Sir John was

---

30. Maurice Ashley to the Earl of Shaftesbury, December 8, 1704, in PRO 30/24/22/1/45.
31. [Daniel?] Burgess to the Earl of Shaftesbury, January 20, 1705, in PRO 30/24/20/89.
32. See, for example, Hill, *The Growth of Parliamentary Parties*, 89.

chosen for Shaftesbury, having first gotten the Earl to promise that he would be wholly uninvolved.

The ailing Shaftesbury was called on in January 1705 to perform still another service. Le Clerc wrote from Amsterdam that he intended to publish a brief life of Locke in the April issue of his *Bibliothèque Choisie*. He had written to Lady Masham, yet she could tell only of the last years of Locke's life, and he needed to know more about Locke's relations with the first Earl. Especially, he would be interested in knowing more about the background of the first Earl's famous *delenda est Carthago* speech, raising money for war against the Dutch in 1673. The whole essay would seem affected if this matter were not discussed. Our interest in the episode is that it gives us some insight into Shaftesbury's attitude toward his grandfather, a subject which prudence had taught him to avoid, no matter how strongly he might feel. Shaftesbury wrote immediately telling Le Clerc that he had been ill and that it would take a little time for him to gather information on Locke from townspeople and others, but he will do as he can. He goes on to say he has also written to Peter King, Locke's heir, and remarks that what he is "most concerned for is the vindication of that Relations Memory which is so Kindly joyn'd by You . . . with that of our common Friend."[33] King was very busy in the courts so that by the time he brought the transcriptions of Locke material to Salisbury in March, and his man brought it on to St. Giles's, it was too late for it to be included in Le Clerc's account. The latter, worried about an April publication date, took an almost nagging tone in his letter of February 27, and Shaftesbury decided to go ahead with his own account of Locke's early life and mail it off.

Shaftesbury said that the first Earl spoke "the Kings sense, as the Kings Mouth" when he delivered that fateful speech. Locke had seen the first version of the speech that the first Earl wrote, but then the cabinet so changed it that, when Shaftesbury had to deliver it, he had Locke standing by him with a written copy to prompt him should he fail in his delivery. The third Earl feels that his grandfather's behavior at this time is best explained as an attempt to woo the King away from the Duke of York, who was actually conducting the campaign

33. The Earl of Shaftesbury to Jean Le Clerc, January 13, 1705, in PRO 30/24/22/2.

against Holland. The first Earl broke all off when he discovered the King was a papist, "For my Grand Fathers Aversion & irreconcileable hatred to Popery, was (as Phanaticisme) confess'd by his greatest Enemys to be his Master-Passion nor was it ever said that the King left him: but he the King. for nothing was omitted afterwards by that Prince to regain Him; nor nothing to destroy him when that was found impossible." As an intense lover of Holland and its blessed freedom, the third Earl will admit this incident was "the one and only thing which I repine at in his whole Life."[34] We shall see other regrets later, but essentially this remained Shaftesbury's position until his death.

When Le Clerc's essay of nearly seventy pages appeared, Le Clerc was glad to hear that Shaftesbury was pleased. Among other favorable things, he had said of the first Earl of Shaftesbury:

> C'etoit un Seigneur qui avoit une vivacité & une pénétration d'esprit tout a fait extraordinaires, un jugement solide & exact, une mémoire excellente, des sentimens nobles & génereux, & avec tout cela un temperament gai & enjoüé, qu'el conserva même dans les tems, auxquel il eut de facheuses affairs. Il avait beaucoup lû, mais il avoit encore plus d'usage du mondes.[35]

Shaftesbury's account of how the speech took the form it did was given in full. In a letter, describing how well the essay was received in Holland, Le Clerc goes on to say,

> J'ai peur que le mémoire de Mr *Locke* ne fasse un effet tout contraire en Angleterre, & que a la ne m'áttire des querrelles de la part de vos *Jacobites*. On m'a assuré qu'on a entrepris de le critiquer, & à cette occasion L'éloge de Mr. *Locke*, & se cela est, il faudra que j'essuye patiemment des injustis, car je n'attends pas à outre chose.[36]

34. The Earl of Shaftesbury to Jean Le Clerc, February 8, 1705, in PRO 30/24/22/2.
35. "He was a gentleman who had a vivacity and a sagacity of wit altogether extraordinary, a judgment solid and exact, an excellent memory, emotions noble and generous, and with all that, a temperament gay and sprightly, which he maintained all of the time, even when things went badly. He had read much, but he understood even better the ways of the world." *Bibliothèque Choisie*, ed. Jean Le Clerc, VI (1705), 353–54.
36. "I fear that the memoir of Mr. Locke has had a contrary effect in England and that it has drawn me into quarrels with your Jacobites. I am confident that it is their business to find fault and on this occasion with the elegy to Mr. Locke, and if that is the case, it is necessary that I bear patiently the injustices, for I did not expect any-

—which must pretty well describe Shaftesbury's own feelings on the matter.

The correspondence with Sir Rowland Gwin continued in a desultory fashion through 1705, though a number of letters are missing. In one melancholy letter Gwin gives a detailed account of the death of the Queen of Prussia, who had come to Hanover in high spirits to attend a carnival in the company of her beloved Sophie, the Electress, where she took a great cold and suddenly died. Had her physicians taken his advice and let a large amount of blood she might have been saved, he remarks. A placeman who had not been able to get into the House of Commons again—which explains his position as advisor to the court at Hanover—Gwin wonders whether Shaftesbury can find him a safe Whig seat in the West. One can imagine how Shaftesbury responded to this last suggestion. He did deplore the death of "that wonderfull princess," all the more sadly because he once knew her and she had never forgotten him.[37]

When Shaftesbury had "got up March hill" as he put it, his health began to improve and his daybook reflects more activities. Late in March he must have gone several times to Boveridge, an easy ride of seven or eight miles, to see his favorite sister Dorothy, who was expecting a child. When the niece was born on April first he rewarded the Hoopers' bailiff who brought the news and also sent a guinea off to Doctor Pitt who had visited Dorothy. He also took up bowling this spring, a fact that shows up in the daybook. Perhaps it was changing fashion that caused private bowling greens to die out after the Revolution. But in any case keeping up a proper green requires a good bit of sophisticated maintenance and even for a person of Shaftesbury's rank it may not have paid to keep a green up unless it were used constantly, which would not have been the case at his house. So the shilling or two Shaftesbury paid out for himself, his Sister Betty, Mr. Coke, Sir B., and others this spring may have sup-

---

thing else." Jean Le Clerc to the Earl of Shaftesbury, September 17, 1705 NS, in PRO 30/24/20/104.

37. Sir Rowland Gwin to the Earl of Shaftesbury, Hanover, February 6, 1705 NS, in PRO 30/24/45/i/179–80; the Earl of Shaftesbury to Sir Rowland Gwin, February 24, 1705, in PRO 30/24/22/5.

ported a public green, attached to a tavern as they commonly were, perhaps the Bull in Wimborne St. Giles, which he leased out.

The changing situation in public affairs obviously cheered Shaftesbury during 1705. His optimism was never suppressed for too long, but the contrast between his attitude in February 1704 and that a year later is startling. Abroad it is not merely the victory at Blenheim and the capture of Gibraltar, with their promise for the coming year, but the whole tenor of his foreign correspondence, which assures him that the world is further away now from the universal monarchy which he feared so much.

With regard to the situation at home, Shaftesbury remained a Roman republican until his death. We do not know how much he was committed to the new Whigs at this point; there never was to be any absolute commitment. It is more likely that the optimism which appears in his letters to Furly during the spring of 1705 reflects the coming into power of men and groups he can trust, or trust more, to carry out the policies he favors. Only three letters survive which have any bearing on the actual elections that took place in May; one of these, written from Leiden by Crell at the beginning of July, quotes Shaftesbury as saying he had been very active politically. It is hard to know which he needed most, but apparently he found both the strength and the spirit.

St. Giles's House was less isolated than many, yet it could not have been a pleasant place in which to lie ill of a winter, especially if one's best friends were all active in parliamentary affairs three days' ride away. The session was over by the middle of March in 1705 and Shaftesbury's life was soon cheered by Thomas Micklethwayte, and Sir John Cropley could not have been far behind him. As we have seen, Betty was there at least by June to remain until August and Maurice must have been there in May. Not only this, but Shaftesbury began to ride out a little further than Boveridge. Late in May he visited Lord Arundel (1633–1712), a papist, at Breadmore in Hampshire, which is about twice as far; on the first of June he went still further to Shaftesbury; and on the fifteenth of June he may have gone still farther when he visited Lord James Russell (ca. 1650–1712), fifth son of the Duke of Bedford.

It is possible that Shaftesbury overdid his social activities, because he had another relapse in July. By the next month he felt well enough to go to Chelsea and arrived there on the twenty-second of August. One of the many reasons which drew Shaftesbury to London at this time was to meet Crell on his trip from Leiden. It was an interesting experiment and one that Shaftesbury knew his friends were unlikely to approve. He writes, probably to Cropley, "that (You alone excepted) I have not One [friend] but wou'd be apt make sport with the odd Associate I have made up with."

Shaftesbury is most anxious that Crell sail in a good convoy, with a Spanish or French pass for him, "he being a Polander & Neuter," and, with a touch of his old fears, he hopes that Crell will appear to be a young man seeking his fortune in England who knows of no one beyond those to whom his letters are directed, least of all the Earl of Shaftesbury. Furly and Wilkinson took good care of Crell. Harry chose one of Furly's ships, the *Susanna*, which had an "armall defence of 4 guns & sailes under Convoy of 6 men [of] war," captained by a personal friend, John Howlatson, who "does assure me he'l take care for him & when it pleaseth God that they are safe arrived he'l himself conduct him to your Lordship att Chelsey & he'l provide all necessaries for him." There need be no fear of duty on his books since he has letters from the rectors of Leiden. The Deity was pleased sooner than he often was, and after lying windbound for two or three weeks—part of which Crell spent in a room at The Brill so that his studies could go on uninterrupted—the fleet found a fair wind, and on September 4 Shaftesbury wrote to Furly that Crell was with him. When Shaftesbury went back to St. Giles's House, Crell went on to Cambridge where he seems to have learned English very rapidly, indeed. Crell's own almost weekly letters written in Latin, the only language he and Shaftesbury shared fluency in, are so full of the Ancients that there is room for little else, alas.

This year John Toland went to work for Harley, and, as F. H. Heinemann points out, Shaftesbury seems to have broken off relations completely. As Toland boasted to Shaftesbury, "what My Lord Sommer's Ministry wou'd not give me, and what I wou'd not ask of My Lord Nottingham's Ministry, the present Ministry unsought has offer'd, and I am willing to accept."[38] Shaftesbury must have been gratified to learn later, in October 1705, that Toland had given up coffee houses, but what did he think of the pamphlet supporting Harley's ministry, *The Memorial of the State of England*, which accompanied the note he received? Since the author was not known immediately, it is ironic that Toland would admit the authorship to the now distant Shaftesbury, who certainly preferred a braggart Whig to a soberly retired Tory. It was an act of extreme imprudence or simple bravado, maybe both.

John Locke had learned to his sorrow about Toland in 1696, when arguments from his Essay appeared in *Christianity Not Mysterious* and he had to defend himself against Stillingfleet. Locke remarked that "if vanity increases with age, I always fear whither it will lead a man." Toland was a braggart; he used men's names without their permission; he was rude to Shaftesbury, and perhaps to other nobles, since he betrayed even the trust of royalty. Molyneux said he habitually chose the wrong argument for the wrong place. Yet he must have been a brilliant talker and his talk must have revealed a highly intelligent and agile mind. Even when Toland was thirty-two, William Hysterman had hopes that something could be done: "I took the freedom to give him severall salutory Instructions for his conduct . . . . for he promises much, if bound to Human prudence."

Toland had other attractions for Shaftesbury. First, he was a skilled writer on political subjects and, oddly, no matter how much he may have betrayed others, he did not betray Shaftesbury alive—barring publication of the *Inquiry*, which did not perhaps too much bother its author. Again, until Toland went over to Harley he had been for as long as Shaftesbury had known him a solid Commonwealthman, the editor of Harrington and the biographer of Milton. Finally, the author of *Christianity Not Mysterious* was a freethinker par excellence. That his rationalism was entirely different from Shaftesbury's has little bearing on the matter; it is the free thought which is significant. The least charitable explanation of why Benjamin Furly and Shaftesbury's final friend at Naples, Don Giuseppe Valetta

38. John Toland to the Earl of Shaftesbury [1705], in PRO 30/24/21/237; F. H. Heinemann, "John Toland and the Age of Enlightenment," *Review of English Studies*, XX (1944), 125–46.

(1636–1714), welcomed freethinkers and built huge collections of free thought, is that the opposition against any sort of freethinking was so strong that anyone against the establishment was welcome. More charitably it is possible to see in these men a genuine relish for diversity of thought, in some ways the most remarkable form of tolerance. So it was in some degree with Bayle, with whom Shaftesbury confessed he hardly shared a view in common. When Toland finally went over to Harley, he must have pulled out the last prop from under a structure whose very standing was a matter of compromise. No doubt Shaftesbury communicated with him after 1705, but no letters have yet turned up.[39]

That fall Shaftesbury again intervened in the affairs of Lord Peterborough's family in an attempt to prevent John, Lord Mordaunt, from leaving his father's house. John joined the army as a captain in 1703 and as a lieutenant colonel of the Grenadier Guards was a leader of the attack on Schellenburg in July 1704, and was wounded at Blenheim the next month. Apparently Lady Peterborough had in her care Lady Frances Pawlett (ca. 1684–1715), daughter of the second Duke of Bolton (1661–1722), and John fell in love with her. The Duke refused dowry, perhaps because of the duplicity involved and

---

39. Toland finally has an excellent bibliographer in Giancarlo Carabelli, the author of *Tolandiana: Materiali bibliografici per lo studio dell'opera e della fortuna di John Toland (1670–1722)*, published in Florence, 1975, with later revisions. He is now at work on a biography.

Some light is thrown on Harley's career by J. A. Downie in his *Robert Harley and the Press* (Cambridge, 1979), but the author pursues his thesis so avidly that the first part of his book—where, indeed, he has less to go on—provides a fascinating display of the creative historical imagination at work. Space allows the citation only of the simplest of many examples: Downie's ascription of *The Danger of Mercenary Parliaments* to Ashley and his assertion that Toland merely saw it through the press. I had assumed that in this case, as on other occasions, Ashley merely outlined the essay and left the actual writing and publication to Toland.

As we have seen, Ashley, in fact, became ill in the spring of 1698, and this illness, and his disgust, drove him to Rotterdam in July so that he could not stand for Commons that fall. Downie's conclusions are made more plausible by his killing off the second Earl more than a year ahead of time (p. 22): Now a nobleman, Ashley cannot stand for Commons (p. 34) and becomes available in London to write the pamphlet (which Downie assumes came out in the fall). The truth of these matters was known in Shaftesbury's day, and whatever was later forgotten was recalled a century ago when Thomas Fowler studied the Shaftesbury manuscripts and published his *Shaftesbury and Hutcheson* (1882). That Downie takes such freedom with solidly established facts should be sufficient warning against any blanket acceptance of his elaborate structure of suppositions.

certainly because he thought his daughter had been betrayed into an unequal match. Lady Carey Peterborough thought Frances had neither looks, sense, nor—above all—money. Peterborough was not wealthy, not does it seem likely that Bolton was as rich as a duke ought to be. One recalls that Sarah Churchill tried to prevent her husband from accepting the title duke of Marlborough until they were prosperous enough. Lady Peterborough's letter to Shaftesbury contains the first account he must have seen of Peterborough's moment of triumph, riding through his troops—who had mistakenly been ordered to retreat—leaping off his horse, drawing his sword and tossing the scabbard away, then rushing up the hill with his troops now at his heels to take the outworks of the fort at Monjuich. To persuade Shaftesbury to intervene with John, and perhaps with Bolton, about the marriage, Lady Peterborough invokes the spirit of Locke and the memories of happier days when Shaftesbury frequently came to see them at Parson's Green in Fulham. Shaftesbury replies that he is deeply sympathetic with her problem and regrets that illness disables him from doing much to help; he then stoutly defends John as a loyal son. He may have brought ruin on himself by disobliging a father "whose Severity he has so much Reason to fear," but she has a different role as a mother. Considering the services of Peterborough and his two sons, this is a public matter. Which brings him to Queen Anne, an excellent sovereign, "the best of Wifes and best (tho' most unfortunate of) Mothers. Her hand alone can heal so sad a Wound as this." Especially, Shaftesbury continues, if her great opposite, "the most detestable of Princes," reconciles the breaches of those who serve him.[40] Lady Masham (1658–1708) writes to Shaftesbury in a similar vein this year, but typically she is so auricular that without his replies no one is likely to find the precise details of what she is asking his advice on.

In November another letter from Gwin arrives, assuring Shaftesbury that the high respect of the Electress for him continues. Twice

40. The Earl of Shaftesbury to Lady Peterborough, draft misdated June 1704, in PRO 30/24/22/5. Her letter to him is dated September 6 [1705], in PRO 30/24/21/233. Obviously the *Complete Peerage* is wrong in saying the marriage of John and Frances was in 1707. Their son, later the fourth Earl of Peterborough, was born in 1708, a year before his father's death from smallpox.

in the letter he says that the Electress and her son and his family are utterly devoted to the Queen, which makes it all the more the pity that "some People have had the folly and impudence to persuade her Royall Highness to tell her friends, that she will not come over, if she is invited." Coming to England is precisely what Gwin thinks she ought to do in order to forestall a Jacobite attempt on the throne should Anne die.[41] For a diplomat, Gwin has the reputation of being too much a gossip, but the remark is interesting because it precedes the ill-fated Tory motion in the House of Lords actually to invite Sophia, her son, and grandson. In Hanover, at least, the subject of such an invitation must have been on everyone's mind for some time. The Regency Bill finally passed by this same Parliament must have brought a degree of calm to both royal households.

The last letter we have from the stay at Chelsea went to Lord Somers along with a copy of *The Sociable Enthusiast*. As one might expect, the letter is too archly coy; Somers surely knows who the author of the book is. Shaftesbury's reticence is largely due to the philosophical subject matter. For this reason if publicly dedicated to Somers it would be "a coarser Present" than *A Tale of a Tub* was. Shaftesbury discusses at length why men of affairs can no longer afford to be thought of as philosophers. "There was once a time when States Men and such as govern'd in the Senate & in the Field thought it no disgrace to 'em to give many Spare-Hours to Philosophy." It is gallantry and superstition, those fruits of the middle ages, that have changed all of this. "Knight-Errantry made the fair Sex the Rule of Every thing." " 'Tis a Lottery-Chance what Lady disposes of Our Interest, or what Priest takes last possession of our Soul." Shaftesbury cites a number of current examples known to Somers and him, then crosses them out and retreats to the age of Charles II, when the gallants also scoffed at common religion and "the Monarch himself too, at the Bottom as great a Cully in this kind as he was in another." "The Whore & Confessor clos'd the Scene." "Christianity is super-naturall Religion: & Gallantry is super-naturall Love." He then becomes bitterly ironic on the contrast between the

41. Sir Rowland Gwin to the Earl of Shaftesbury, November 10, 1705 NS, in PRO 30/24/45/iii/125–26.

Ancients and the Moderns and finishes by lecturing to Somers on the true role of a statesman.[42] The letter reveals the growth of Shaftesbury's philosophic certainty; it shows that he is thinking, as always, of where his grandfather failed; and, further, it makes one marvel at the difference in tone between this private dedication and his later public dedications to Somers. Would that we could more often see what is really on the author's mind on such occasions.

We have so few letters from this period in 1705 that it is difficult to speak about Shaftesbury's health in Chelsea. He did write to Harry Wilkinson on the ninth of September saying that his health was good, and Harry wrote to him on the tenth of November NS saying he had heard he is well, so that everything went well up to the early part of October. I suspect that the smoke was light enough not to bother him in Chelsea, despite the prevailing winds, but when he started to come up to London for the opening of Parliament he began to suffer again as he had in 1704. Or perhaps he was merely waiting to take the oaths, which he did on the ninth of November. By the fifteenth he was back at St. Giles's.

There are only two letters of any moment in December. The first is an amusing one to the Lord Keeper, Sir William Cowper (d. 1723), in which Shaftesbury attempts, successfully, I hope, to get his brother-in-law Hooper out of being sheriff of Wiltshire and a Tory-leaning gentleman into that post, very expensive in all counties. There is only one major piece of correspondence in December, and it is the most vexing and troublesome letter among all the thousands of pages of the Shaftesbury correspondence. It once seemed so difficult to handle that I wondered what to do with it.[43] It is obvious from Benjamin Rand's excisions from the "Exercises" that he had seen the letter and, knowing of Shaftesbury's reluctance to marry, assumed he was a homosexual and decided to conceal what he felt was the evidence.

In the first place, despite the emotional warmth of this letter, we will see that there underlies it a strain of intellectual idealism,

42. The Earl of Shaftesbury to Lord Somers, October 20, 1705, in PRO 30/24/22/4/pp. 13–20.

43. When the late Professor George Sherburn, who had seen more personal letters of the era than most scholars, read it, he admitted that he had never seen anything even resembling it.

which becomes manifest only when Shaftesbury speaks of abiding the choice of whomever he loves, even the meanest servant. Although we may pay lip service to the ideal, it has pretty largely gone out of our culture since the eighteenth century. Thus seventeenth-century essays on heroic friendship and even Jonson's ode on Carey and Morrison fall upon ears which are in part tone deaf to the implications. And how many of our age read Lovelace's "The Grasshopper" without ever fully realizing that he is giving friendship as high a place as honor among his intellectual ideals? And even here we would have to grasp that honor is itself an intellectual ideal rather than a blind commitment. The precise meaning of the language must escape us because we cannot turn back the clock. To us, love, like the gallantry which Shaftesbury deplores, is almost wholly emotional.

Furthermore, what Shaftesbury saved is just part of a letter beginning in the middle of a thought with a line of asterisks to replace what went before; it is written by an amanuensis, and is preserved very much as were his comments on Locke's dying letter to Collins, as an example of thought and style well worth saving. Almost all the letters of which he had copies made during this period were of this sort or they deal with politics or international affairs. Across the top is a note in his own hand, obviously made later, because he crossed out one date and put in another: "Coppy of mine to Br: writt Jany: 22d. 1704/5 Coppyed & Sent Decr 24 1705."

The fragment was very consciously preserved, then. What are the possibilities of Shaftesbury's preserving it if he thought it contained compromising material? Absolutely nil. Especially among the nobility, private and public lives are completely separate. Haley's monumental account of the *public* life of the first Earl is largely that. Were anyone to attempt a private life, there would be little direct evidence for it. At best it would consist of accounts like Dorothy Shaftesbury's of his kindness and charm; at worst it would be anecdotes supposed to reveal character, or simply gossip. What precisely was the childhood illness from which the second Earl suffered? Despite the fact that he was for a while a member of the House of Commons and many contemporaries must have known, we do not. A biographer of the third Earl is more fortunate, but in spite of all of Cropley's letters, we shall never know anything of the texture of the life led by him, Micklethwayte, and Shaftesbury. Almost all the material on Shaftesbury's relations with his sisters has been learned by indirection and through circumstantial evidence. That Shaftesbury would cherish a letter that consciously revealed him as a homosexual is inconceivable.

The letter is too long to quote in full, but the gist of it is easily conveyed by passages. "Know then that the first & only cause of my Engagements with that Youth, was his previouse Acquaintance with You & my other Friends, and in particular the Love he show'd for You & the Pretences he made to your Friendship." Actually Shaftesbury at first disliked Bawble and did not take any pains to conceal it. But the youth continued to ingratiate himself, and Shaftesbury's friends, including his correspondent, supported his effort. But it was not so easy for Shaftesbury to make friends now—after his trip to Holland in 1698–1699—and he persisted cool, for years, despite continual ingratiation by Bawble and the persistence of his comrades.

> Thus it went on. At length, Time Custome, Familiar Appelations, Names, Manners, with a hundred little things (such is Human-Nature) began to work on Me; & joyning with what I have allready told You, taught him to take possession of my Heart. *The Bawble* gain'd. I play'd too; aukward as I was, & grown grave. With Play came in Things Seriouse. Then Vows, Professions, Services, endearing Actions; till my easy Breast quite open'd, & I receiv'd him in, after the long Resistance I had made. This is my Story. Thus I lov'd. too easily Perhaps & to my Cost; as I now find. but not so easily can I *unlove*. I never yett Lov'd any Soul in any degree that I could afterwards cease to love, or love but in a Less. This is true; even to the meanest Servant, such as in my Youth found Means to steal on my Affections. & more so, since Age of discretion has given Me Choice. In Friendship I must abide the Choice. Friends I have thus taken, are with Me *for better for wors*. . . . I may loose Friends but they can never loose me.[44]

What piece of folly the youth had committed that lost him the friendship of Shaftesbury's friends is not revealed. Obviously it took some time for Shaftesbury to reveal that he loved Bawble nonetheless.

Christmas at St. Giles's must have been quiet in 1705. Normally

---

44. The Earl of Shaftesbury to a Brother, January 22, 1705, in PRO 30/24/20/110.

one can depend on New Year's exchanges of letters with friends and family for news of Shaftesbury. If there were any of these, they have not survived; there is nothing more than a record of gifts to servants. One note suggests that Micklethwayte was there and it seems likely that Cropley was too. It is possible that there was less celebration than usual because of Shaftesbury's health. He reports the end of this bout of illness in a letter to Wilkinson at the end of January; all he needs of him is spa water, which Henry sent over in heroic quantities during the spring.

One sign that by January of 1706 Shaftesbury is feeling better is his renewed interest in Anglo-Dutch affairs. His Rotterdam friend John van Twedde had written him late in November explaining that although the Dutch Whigs represented commercial interests who stand to profit immediately from a peace, profits were not the real root of their desire to end the war. What the Dutch Whigs really feared was that if they did not get out of the war now they would end up ruled by a stadtholder, governor, or captain general. All that was really necessary was a clear statement from Queen Anne that she would not permit an infraction of Dutch liberty. Then she could count on substantial support from responsible elements among the Dutch Whigs for continuing the war.[45]

Shaftesbury begins his reply with an apology for not writing sooner; he has replied in the sense that he has been acting on van Twedde's letter. He feels the real issue is liberty, and "I had rather see Liberty lost here than there. since here it may be recoverable but there never." The English can interfere against a foreign yoke in Holland; against a domestic one he hopes they will never be tried. "You may deliver us best not we You." The English cannot, it seems, exist without a prince and "Princes are not Hero's in this kind. . . . But when Holland is subjected. . . . Liberty looses its Sanctuary: the Cause of Soverains sounds instantly in a louder Manner through the world." He acknowledges that there are many special interests being served in England, but so long as they have a Whig ministry there is no real danger to liberty there or in Holland, and no minister dare

45. John Van Twedde to the Earl of Shaftesbury, November 24, 1705 NS, in PRO 30/24/45/ii/128–29.

meddle in this for fear of being detected. There is far too much mur-muring and suspicion on both sides and, granted, too many private ambitions are being satisfied. Yet if you wish to discover a "con-ceal'd Tory, Jacobite or Papist. speak but of the Dutch." Part of the trouble is that King William, the founder of the present liberty, con-ducted his own foreign policy and the Whigs who were introduced to international affairs knew only his own party in Holland. This situa-tion persists to some degree, admittedly, and must be fought, but the insinuation that Whigs recognize no other sort of commonwealth than their own is utterly false. What must be done is to work to edu-cate the honest party on both sides of the Channel; "'tis said that a Disease is half cur'd when known. . . . if in time I discover any thing worse than I now suspect You shall not fail to hear of it." Shaftes-bury concludes that they must return to the fight against France, which aspires to universal monarchy.[46] There is no way of telling how effective Shaftesbury was in communicating views like that of van Twedde to the ministry. Obviously the more powerful the Junto and its supporters are—now they were on the rise again—the better Shaftesbury will be heard. Somers held his proxy, and Sir William Cowper, later Lord Cowper, and the third Earl of Sunderland were his friends.

Parliamentary concerns absorbed Shaftesbury's attentions in Feb-ruary, specifically the self-denying clauses to be added to the Re-gency Bill. There was already a provision that no holder of a govern-mental office should sit in Commons after the House of Hanover came to the throne. A Tory measure to make this binding in the im-mediate future failed; then a more restricted measure proposed by a small group of Whigs passed in Commons but lost in the Lords, and finally a compromise was worked out. It is clear from a letter of Cropley's to Shaftesbury that at least some parts of the Whig mea-sure had been developed by the third Earl beforehand.

The two letters by Cropley to Shaftesbury at this time give one a look at a strange world behind the House of Commons, so strange that if there were anything of the braggart in their author, one would

46. The Earl of Shaftesbury to John Van Twedde, January 17, 1706, in PRO 30/24/22/2.

be inclined to disbelieve part of it. Some of it is believable enough. We learn, for one thing, why sessions of Commons are such a strenuous experience for Cropley, yet he is so seldom seen. Invisibility is the price of being Shaftesbury's agent in Commons, and he seems to prefer working behind the scenes to any other role. The squadron, as he calls it, of which he is part consists of about thirty members, which seems a reasonable figure. No doubt their support is valuable in a House where the margins were never very wide; their real power comes when they perceive an issue on which they seem committed to vote with the Tories. They may have been called the whimsical Whigs but the force behind them is exactly the opposite, principles. It had been so from Shaftesbury's very first speech in Commons on the Trial for Treasons Bill, and he stuck with it on the Standing Army measure, the Triennial Bill, and so forth. No matter which party is in charge, too strong a central government is dangerous to liberty, Shaftesbury feels. It is easy to believe Cropley when he says that the "Ld Keeper all most cry'd to me to prevail with me to quit the clause as fatal to their being."[47]

At first it might seem surprising that Cropley is so delighted with the results; the Court he feels simply gave away too much of what Shaftesbury had hoped for in the original clause. Cropley voted against the new clause merely to maintain a consistent pose, and because he did not want to be detected as an accomplice to a bargain. James Stanhope, who along with Sir Richard Onslow (1654–1717), was a principal speaker for the bill, seems to agree: "The concessions made by the Lords are something, but I must own I doe not understand their management for they have granted too much or too little . . . had they taken our clause and given it with good grace it might have secured the administration under the reign from any thing of that kind whereas they have now made a substantial precedent to alter even in this reign, and I do not wonder Mr H &c. take it as they doe."[48] Stanhope had to leave before the debate was finished.

47. Sir John Cropley to the Earl of Shaftesbury [1706], in PRO 30/24/20/114. Cowper was Lord Keeper.

48. General James Stanhope to [?], Plymouth, February 24, 1706, in PRO 30/24/20/113. Probably to Cropley; none of his letters among these papers are directed to the Earl. Mr. H., of course, is Harley.

On his way to Plymouth to join the fleet, he stopped at St. Giles's House to visit Shaftesbury.[49]

It is when Cropley gloats that he strains credibility. He makes several remarks like this, for instance: "The self denying act we have obtain'd . . . was chiefly owing to me and the extorting it was as their blood" and "Old Madam I hear says if she had a 100 votes she would give them all just to keep me out of Parliament." There is no doubt whom he intends as Old Madam; though the Queen was not old, physically, she must have seemed so. Cropley always insists to Shaftesbury that he has given the impression that he is acting only on his own motives and principles; he would not be able to fool the ministry, however. If his estimate is at all true, it explains that the anger of Anne and her ministers was not merely based on the Shaftesbury name and her resentment over what happened in 1702, but that she had good reason for making him wait for five years—and until he had too many sympathizers in the ministry—to any longer refuse him the little favor of a job for Thomas Micklethwayte.

As soon as he heard what had happened to the whimsical clause, and probably before he found out that Cropley felt he had really won, Shaftesbury wrote a consoling letter, which remains interesting for the insight it gives into the motives of one who was so often politically, as in other ways, out of step with the times. In the first place, he says, nothing gives greater satisfaction than acting on principles, whatever the outcome. Secondly,

> There's nothing that in the growth of Liberty I dread so much as a Surfeitt. nothing so dangerous as being fed too high. Our Court-Patriotts that have fedd us hitherto with so niggardly a hand have been better Nurses of us than they imagine. . . . And there may be a plain Reason why such as You and I shou'd appear for every right thing yet there is many a One which whilst we Countenance and promote we may tremble for. Did I not tremble think You for the Treason Bill when there were such Plotts within and for the disbanding the Army when there

49. The fact that Stanhope was appointed an executor of Shaftesbury's estate is usually laid to a friendship that began with his reading *Characteristicks* while a prisoner of the Spanish. This of course is wrong. One can understand why Shaftesbury might destroy Stanhope's letters; yet among the Stanhope papers now at the Kent Archives Office there are no letters from Shaftesbury to Stanhope and a copy of only one sent in the opposite direction.

was such force abroad? what think you of . . . the Quallification Bill. Think You that even at this Hour I shou'd not tremble if such a Bill were like to pass? but the time will come when the Self Deniall Bill shall be full and Perfect & th[u]s afterwards crown all and rivett our Constitution.

I talk (You see) in a high prophetick Strain & methinks you may take it as truely Prophetick, since treated as I am and treated as I and my Family have been & still are, I shou'd naturally be the last to think well of this Generation: but I have as full Faith in this as any prophesying Christian of the Conversion of the Jews: with this difference that I actually see the work advancing and a considerable Progress allready made.[50]

For the next two or three months Shaftesbury seems to have been largely concerned with the affairs of his family. Obviously he was delighted to have the Hoopers living so close to him. Near the end of January he buys a copy of Ogilby's *Fables* "for my nephew Ned Hooper," and he also paid two pounds and thirteen shillings for a scarlet cloak for him. There is another entry in the daybook in April: "To my sister Hooper's maids when the children went hence, Betty Osborne a broadpiece Jane 1 guinea Sarah 1/2 guinea." Note that it is the children who went home, though considering the Hoopers' way of living and the age of the children doubtless Dorothy was there to go, too. The sums are substantial enough to indicate a fairly long visit to the home of a secluded thirty-five-year-old bachelor. St. Giles's must have seemed a little smaller with them there.

Shaftesbury's attitude towards his sister Frances seems to have softened in the two years since she married against his wishes. Stonehouse wrote him in the middle of February that she had miscarried, and the day he received the news Shaftesbury replied in a sternly homiletic tone. Apparently they yet had no children but there had been other miscarriages:

> I am obliged to you for yours and heartily bless God for my Sister's Escape (as you well observe) *for this time.* I doubt not therefore but Experience and the Advice of Physitians and Able People in so known a Case will guide you and her to the only Means of Saving her Life against *the next Time* which is, that it may be at a greater Distance;

50. The Earl of Shaftesbury to Sir John Cropley, February 18, 1706, in PRO 30/24/22/2.

that Nature and Remedyes may doe their part during a Respite. . . . Besides I know I speake this to a Person of more Experience and Years than myselfe. . . . Nor is my sister so much a Girle. You must forgive my Gravity and (perhaps) Over Seriousness. Every one is in some Measure excusable by their Character.[51]

Whether Frances immediately became pregnant again despite Shaftesbury's warning we do not know, but she was dead some six months later. The evidence for this is positive enough; surprisingly, though, it consists only of a single letter to Shaftesbury from Will Stone, a soldier with Marlborough, dated only October 13, full of military details about the campaign of 1706 and concluding with condolences on the death of Lady Frances. Shaftesbury never refers to her again in the materials we have and it is possible that Frances was rather like his brother John must have been, such an object of remorse that he preferred not to talk about her.

As usual, the servants were troublesome this spring. His woodman and sometime spy James Bishop must have naturally enough aroused considerable resentment among the others on the staff. Bishop was accused of defaulting on a loan of two hundred pounds and putting some of Shaftesbury's money in his own pocket. He apparently was taken off the hook on the first charge by a deposition from the lender, and although Wheelock's audit of Bishop's accounts seems to show he had been claiming money that he was not entitled to, it is typical that we find him still on the payroll the next year and in trouble again. It is something of a wonder that Shaftesbury, who could handle people above the rank of servants with such finesse, should fail so often with the servants themselves.

There is little record of Shaftesbury's activities for the balance of the spring. Except for the soreness of his eyes, he apparently kept well by sticking to his regimen. He was busy about the estate and also busy filing legal briefs. Matthew Tindal (1657–1733) was sent seven broadpieces for his *Rights of the Christian Church Asserted Against the Romish and All Other Priests*, and the news of the con-

51. The Earl of Shaftesbury to Francis Stonehouse, M.P., February 16, 1706, in PRO 30/24/22/1/44.

quest of Madrid was properly celebrated when the word reached St. Giles's on April 29. The Earl visited Salisbury, his sister Dorothy's at Boveridge, Thomas Freke at Shroton, and Lord James Russell at Ferne.

On the twelfth of June Shaftesbury left St. Giles's House for Chelsea. Obviously he had his reasons for leaving Dorset at the finest time of year to go to Chelsea out of season. The pattern he had previously set up usually brought him to Chelsea just as the smoke was daily becoming more and more unbearable, especially when the wind was from the northeast. It now became a question of finding how to spend enough time near London, and with a minimum of discomfort, so that he could set his financial affairs on a solid footing, satisfy his desire to be part of the greater world, and enjoy the privileges and responsibilities of his rank.

During the spring of 1706 Shaftesbury somehow became involved with a scurrilous publication against the government, *A Letter to the Author of the Memorial of the State of England* (1705), written by his old friend the Reverend William Stephens. The timing was unfortunate because the ministry was becoming increasingly Whig in complexion. The incident began in 1705 with the publication of a high-flying Tory assault on the state of the Church in general and the failings of Lord Marlborough, among others, in particular: *The Memorial of the Church of England*, ascribed to James Drake (1667– 1707) and H. Paley. According to Coxe, the printer was convicted but then fled. Early in September, Toland, now in Harley's pay, began writing his *Memorial of the State of England* in reply and was able to send Shaftesbury a copy. There seems little doubt that Harley was behind the pamphlet. Toland wrote to Shaftesbury, "I shall onely tell your Lordship, that it is really your fault, if this book be not so good as you wou'd have it, since my Design of seeing you some weeks ago was to advise about it. However it has given full Satisfaction to him that encourag'd the work."[52] Beyond the tone, at once pious and sycophantic, there is little Shaftesbury might complain of in an essay devoted to praising religious toleration and occa-

52. John Toland to the Earl of Shaftesbury, October 1705, in PRO 30/24/20/105.

sional conformity. At the end, though, after defending Godolphin and Marlborough and his Duchess, Toland turns to fulsome praise of Harley, who was not attacked in the first memorial.

It is hard to see just why Stephens decided to reply to Toland, but if he was paid, we do not know who did it. Surely, Shaftesbury had nothing to do with the tract, because in defending the ministry of the 1690s Stephens takes positions which the Country Whigs strongly opposed. For instance, the essay favors the standing army. Stephens not very artfully assumes the role of a defender of the present administration, who is too easily bowled over by the opposition. Why did Marlborough retreat from the Moselle and permit the French to ravage the territory abandoned? Why did he not push across the Ische toward Brussels? The letter from the Dutch general Slangenberg tells the real story; Marlborough kept the allies in the dark and had no real intention of attacking. Stephens then turned his attention to Queen Anne and to Harley, who certainly should not have been left out of the first memorial, a person determined "to frustrate the good affects of our late happy Revolution, a Man who had deserted and betray'd all Parties."[53] Only Peterborough, who needs help to consolidate his Spanish victories, is praised.

The Messengers of the Press ferreted out Stephens' printer and through him, the author, who soon felt the wrath of the ministry. He was summoned to appear the first day of the term of the Queen's Bench and then sent off to await his fate on the last day of the term. He writes to Shaftesbury about this when he thanks him for his annual gift. "Mr. Harley generously told me that he from his heart forgave me what was sayd of him in the book. 'Twas Toland's abominable flattery of him in the State memoriall which led me to publish all the scandall I had heard of Him."[54] On the last day of the session

53. William Stephens, *A Letter to the Author of the Memorial of the State of England* (1705), 29. Downie in his *Robert Harley*, 91–92, assembles evidence to prove that Charles Davenant's suspicion that Thomas Rawlins had his share in the pamphlet was in fact the truth—that he wrote it. Davenant actually describes the essay as written by "Trenchard, Rawlins and his republican club." This could well be an example of the sort of sponsorship common to the day, but if Stephens knew someone else actually wrote the pamphlet why did he not mention the fact to Shaftesbury and perhaps save the annual pension he was receiving from him?

54. William Stephens to the Earl of Shaftesbury, January 26, 1706, in PRO 30/24/20/111.

he was convicted and sentenced to a fine of a hundred marks and, much worse, to stand twice in the pillory, a risky business. To complicate matters Shaftesbury's name somehow was associated with the pamphlet; perhaps it was discovered that Stephens once wrote for him and still received a pension; perhaps it was simply malice. The Duchess of Marlborough intervened with the Queen, after receiving a letter from Stephens saying that if he stood in the pillory it would kill his wife and asking what then would happen to his six children. The Duke was satisfied with the outcome. Shaftesbury, on the other hand, was rightfully exasperated. He had tolerated the knavery of Toland too long; the persistent foolishness of Stephens was still more unbearable:

> Your going so contrary to any Notions you had drawn from my *Conversations* wou'd have given Me no disturbance: But since you had so wholly forgott Me in your Work, you shou'd have remembered Me at least in your Recantation, and shou'd not have given the World to judg that it was from the Conversation of your Friends without Distinction, that you receiv'd such Impressions as those. As for the great Lord, I never had any Obligation to him, though I have done him Justice often. . . . Butt as for the Commoner he is my old Friend and in Young Days was my Guide and Leader in Publick Affairs nor have I ever broke Friendship with him. The different judgments in Publick affairs has long broke all Correspondence between us. . . . with my good wishes only, I bid you Farewell [55]

The letter to Stephens is the only one remaining for July; indeed, there is a gap all the way into September. His son mentions that Shaftesbury saw Mr. Vernon and Mr. Lyddal often, crossing the river sometimes to see them.[56] Also during this visit to Chelsea the oddly rounded hand of Paul Crell, now writing in English, appears among Shaftesbury's correspondence. Shaftesbury did manage to spend more time in London under his new scheme. Late in September, however, he ventured from Chelsea into town to see some friends and came down with a violent fit of coughing. It continued after his

---

55. The Earl of Shaftesbury to William Stephens, July 17, 1706, in PRO 30/24/22/2.
56. Probably James Vernon (1646–1727), M.P., Secretary of State, 1698–1702, Teller of the Exchequer, 1702–1710. Liddell must be the one suggested as sponsor for Wilkinson by Shaftesbury in December 1706; see PRO 30/23/45/ii/60.

return home and he fled to lodgings in Hampstead, where he still coughed. Finally, he went a little further out in Hampstead to the manor house at North Hall, where he could breathe freely and enjoyed what he described as a "short but very advantageouse Retirement."[57]

Shaftesbury wrote some interesting letters during this period. We have only his last two letters on the subject of Horace to Pierre Coste. This discussion actually began in the year before, when Coste spent the summer at St. Giles's House.[58] It was, as Shaftesbury says, when they were riding at St. Giles's that he assigned further study of Horace to Coste. It is a pleasant thought, the Earl taking his exercise, as he did whenever the weather permitted, and the Huguenot minister riding through the incredible greenness of the Dorset summer, talking of Horace.

The relationship between the two men is complex. We have already seen that Shaftesbury had persuaded Arent Furly to give his fragmentary copy of *The Sociable Enthusiast* to Coste in order to get his reaction, yet on the subject of Horace, Shaftesbury sounds like a pedagogue. It is a matter, I guess, of who knows what. Certainly Coste is more than a tutor of French, an amanuensis, and translator. He was widely and thoroughly educated, an author in his own right, and apparently longed for a Walloon congregation of his own, at a time when there were far too many displaced ministers of his faith. Besides a common love of the Ancients, an honest and open candor bound the two men, as Shaftesbury expressed to him: "I am not afraid to use the simplicity, which you and I are admirers of, and which I may reckon upon as the chief Tye of our Acquaintance and Friendship. I am confident I may well call it the beginning and foundation. . . . For there is nothing constant but what is simple. All other Relishes are changeable as they are complexe and variouse. . . : It becomes us therefore to hold our simplicity, as what we think the

---

57. This may have been the manor then owned by the third Earl of Gainsborough (1684–1714). His wife was Shaftesbury's first cousin and her daughter, Susanna (d. 1758), married the fourth Earl of Shaftesbury. Anthony was to return there, later.

58. Shaftesbury paid the expenses of Coste's trip to his next job as tutor to the son of Edward Clarke at Chipley, Somerset.

only Integrity."[59] Anyone who has thought much about why friend-ship declines or persists could agree with this.

These last two letters of Shaftesbury's tend to overlap, and per-haps we would have to see Coste's reply to the first to see why Shaftesbury wrote the second, which he must have been proud of, since three copies have survived. He begins the first by attacking André Dacier (1651–1722) as having the wrong background for judg-ing Horace. How is it possible for someone so immersed in French court life to judge someone who eventually rose above his own court? We need to be aware that Horace's works reflect three differ-ent periods of his life. The first, seen only in retrospect, is his origi-nal *Free Republican State*, when he served under Brutus, and like so many early men of the commonwealth, he was basically a Stoic. If we eliminate the skeptics and new academics, there were only two philosophies then, one civil, social, and theistic, the other, the op-posite. Next Horace was drawn into the second of these philosophies, Epicureanism, the creed of Maecenas. Finally, however, the original philosophy reasserted itself and the mature Horace was born. The real Horace is seen veiled in his fables, where the message is always that Maecenas is the town mouse and Horace, the country one. All of this is elaborately documented with scores of references, where Horace is interpreted with just the right degree of his ever-present worry. We must not, Shaftesbury says, leave Horace "to the learned Art of Criticks whose only Business is to improve Difficultyes & confound the most ordinary & plain Sense of Authors in order to say something extraordinary themselves."

Coste was not thoroughly convinced by these arguments, so that still another letter was necessary, one based on the paradox that we cannot know how good Horace was until we sense how evil he could be. It is interesting in the light of the letter which Rand suppressed because he thought it sure evidence that the Earl had homosexual tendencies, for here Maecenas is attacked as "one of the infamous Creatures for *Effeminacy* in the vilest and most un-manly sense of

59. The Earl of Shaftesbury to Pierre Coste, October 1, 1706, in PRO 30/24/45/iii/43.

that Word." But Horace eventually found that he paid too dearly for imitating the rich. It is again the contrast between the intensely complex mores of a court in contrast to the simple and honest moral code now available to all Englishmen who wish to embrace it. Shaftesbury even offers an English example, which is rare in him: "The witty Lord Rochester [as he is called] came once in a visit to a grave Relation of mine, who hearing of his Debauches, took upon him kindly to reprove him, and advis'd him, tho' but for his Interest sake, in respect of the World, to do otherwise. My Lord, said he [with a great deal of simplicity] if you will believe me, I have no other way of making my Court at White-hall."[60] Though he may have been more proud of his second essay on Horace, the argument seems less convincing than the one he wrote at Chelsea.

As Shaftesbury mentions in his "Exercises," he also wrote his "Pathologia" at North Hall.[61] This essay of around three thousand words is the only longer Latin work of his we have. The rigorously logical structure of the essay is reminiscent of the *Inquiry*; the thought, however, is purely Stoic. The point of his writing it was to prove that Horace was essentially Stoic, which in this context would probably mean that he was a theist, who believed fundamentally that the world is orderly. A page of introduction leads into a huge chart of all the emotions, the perturbations of the soul—present and future— which are juxtaposed to constant states of the soul. Even though he also gives the Greek equivalents, the terms are difficult to render without more reference to Stoic philosophy than is possible here. Thus joy—in a physical sense—and anguish, both present states, and desire and fear, which refer to the future, are contrasted with three constant states: that joy which arises from the love of truth and the highest good, and two states directed to the future, a will toward the highest good, and circumspection. All of these states are in reference to objects outside of us; we also react to our own impressions within. Toward the beautiful and the ugly seen internally these emotions cause *jactantia*—which combines the sense of both agitation and ostentation—and shame; with regard to the future they

---

60. The Earl of Shaftesbury to Pierre Coste, North Hall, November 15, 1706, in PRO 30/24/45/iii/52v–53, 54.
61. PRO 30/24/26/7/1.

result in affectation—the desire to be thought well of, and shame. The three parallel good states are magnanimity and, with respect to the future, philosophic ardor or will to the beautiful, and modesty. After half a page of commentary on these emotions, Shaftesbury turns to the inherently evil emotions: pride, envy, ambition, and malice.

The application of this psychology to Horace is full of citations to the Ancients and to modern Horatians. His general argument is that Horace, while laughing, gives us a very full picture of the Stoical view of the mind, as in the third satire of his second book. It is all a matter of judging his irony, and his laughter, aright. Of particular interest in view of Shaftesbury's later writing is the long discussion of the nature of laughter with which the treatise ends. Nothing he was to say later on is so precise, for his later prose in English tends to avoid the pedagogic style which is essential here.

Though its Stoicism is rigorous enough, the overall effect of the essay is much more humane than that of the rather mechanical first book of the *Inquiry*. It shows us, too, that the French Prophets provided an occasion for his saying in the *Letter Concerning Enthusiasm* what he would have said sooner or later, if he were to publicly defend the concept of that term he had already developed, but not published, in the *Sociable Enthusiast*. In the *Letter* he assailed a type of zealots, to which he had always objected, making *enthusiasm* in the wrong sense a by-word, yet much of his argument had already been worked out in an entirely different context, as he defended the Roman satirist against Pierre Coste's charge of impiety.

Shaftesbury had settled at North Hall in the hope that he could stay long enough to finish with some business matters and, as had been his custom, at least appear and take his oath when the House of Lords first sat. He seems not to have confined himself to North Hall, because he refers to paying the upkeep for Sir John's coach when his own was not there; it is likely, then, that he ventured into town and suffered for it. Moreover, the opening of Parliament was delayed—it eventually opened on the third of December—and Shaftesbury remarked in November that there was little chance of their accomplishing much before the Christmas recess. He made arrangements for Cropley to deliver his proxy to Lord Somers—as he was forced to do too often in these years—and left North Hall for St. Giles's House, stopping for the night at Bagshot and again at Stockbridge, to arrive there on the twentieth of November.

Shaftesbury spent a good deal of time with Lord Somers while he was in London, so that with all his other sources of information it can have come as no surprise when the Queen acceded to a number of pressures and appointed a member of the Junto, Charles Spencer, Earl of Sunderland, as secretary of state for the South. In any case, four days after the appointment was announced, Shaftesbury—apparently feeling that the millennium had come—wrote letters to Lord Somers, the Duke of Marlborough, and Lord Sunderland. He hates to bother Somers again "but the Changes that are now happen'd and the favourable Aspect of Affairs at Court makes me begg your advice, whether I shou'd not take this Occasion to apply by Letter to My Lord Duke of Marlborough, at least to acknowledge to him the favorable Notice he was pleas'd to take of me when your Lordship mention'd me to him as your Friend & spoke to him of my Affaire."[62] His affair is the appointment of Micklethwayte to an office with the army.

The letter to Somers is simply a cover for the fact that he is writing to Marlborough on the same day. Again he repeats in the letter to the Duke the tale of King William's promise to intervene on behalf of Micklethwayte. But later "others in the same Circumstances had the Benefitt of the King's Promise, by her Majesty's great Goodness. But it was my Misfortune to receive both in this & other respects very distinguishing Marks of her Majesty's Displeasure; tho' consciouse of having otherwise deserv'd."[63] He has not forgotten the loss of the vice Admiralty, though possibly he may have forgotten the threat of action by the House of Commons against him for interfering in their affairs. The letter to Sunderland is in a very effusive vein, congratulating the public on having Sunderland to serve them and asking the minister to present his letter to Marlborough. Just

62. The Earl of Shaftesbury to Lord Somers, St. Giles's House, December 7, 1706, in PRO 30/24/22/4/p. 21. One rough measure of the extent of Whig power in the government is the number of Junto Lords in the ministry. At this time the Junto consisted of the Lords Halifax, Orford, Somers, Sunderland, and Wharton.

63. The Earl of Shaftesbury to the Duke of Marlborough, December 7, 1706, in PRO 30/24/22/4/p. 22.

before Christmas, another member of the Junto, Charles Montagu, Earl of Halifax, offered to support Somers in the request, a fact which in later years delighted Shaftesbury, perhaps because it was unexpected. The appointment of Sunderland caused a general reshuffling of political appointments, high and low, but as Shaftesbury was to realize gradually, Thomas Micklethwayte was not to be included among the new appointments.

Also this December, Shaftesbury said good-bye to Henry Wilkinson, who was now in London. His apprenticeship to Furly has ended on a rather sour note, for from June on Shaftesbury had been receiving notes from Benjamin detailing, though rather cryptically, Wilkinson's failings; the fact that Furly's business was poor because of the war could not have helped much either. Next to Cropley and Micklethwayte, Furly was certainly Shaftesbury's best friend, yet he had long since learned that Furly was impetuous when it came to benevolence and sometimes in his suspicions, so that he often had to discount Furly's more emotional remarks. Wilkinson's character comes through rather clearly from Shaftesbury's letters, and it would be hard to fault his final judgment of him. "He is indeed but too vain & talkative & pragmatical, tho' with abilities & Talents sufficient if he wou'd well enough employ them."[64] Shaftesbury concludes— though he actually did a good bit more, especially in regard to recommendations—"I have now left him to the Wide world with a small sum & cloaths fitted out to take his Fortune." It is good to know that the last we hear of him Wilkinson is prospering, having returned to Rotterdam and married the wealthy widow of a merchant.

Beyond a series of gifts listed in his daybook there is little evidence left of what Shaftesbury did at Christmas in 1706. There are still those who suffered for their allegiance to Shaftesbury's grandfather. To one of these, a Mr. Sansome, he gives a guinea, and another goes again to Michael Ainswood (Ainsworth), the father of a young man whose education at Oxford he was to sponsor. Shaftesbury must have visited Boveridge, where he gave Lady Dorothy's maid a broadpiece and also gave his little nephew, Neddy, money to

64. The Earl of Shaftesbury to Benjamin Furly, December 2, 1706, in PRO 30/24/21/121.

distribute to the other servants. Among many other gifts there is one to a favorite, Robert Bacon, the town of Shaftesbury's fiddler, which carries a typical notation, "the only honest fellow of them that resisted temptation for his New Years gift."

Lord Somers, in a letter written shortly after New Year's, 1707, seems to assume that Shaftesbury has seen Cropley, so it is possible that both he and Micklethwayte visited St. Giles's House for a short time. Surely the three friends were as close as ever up to Shaftesbury's death, yet while he has more time than he once did, Cropley and Micklethwayte are obviously beginning to feel the pressure of their own affairs. Also the session of Parliament began very late this year and Cropley, as we shall see, had enough to do in London with matters that Shaftesbury had been forced to leave undone when he fled London.

One reason why it was necessary for Shaftesbury to move most carefully in his dealings with the Duke of Marlborough in December 1706 was that he had been trying unsuccessfully to repay him all or part of his note for seven thousand pounds borrowed in 1703. Of course this should have been wholly separate from getting a job for Micklethwayte, but in retrospect it seems likely that the same sort of bias functioned in both instances. Here is an instance where so much testimony has survived that it is not so easy to dogmatize as it might be, had we less.

There are other personal elements involved, too. The Duke's man of business with whom Shaftesbury and Wheelock had to deal was Anthony Guidot. He was in an ill humor due to a fit of stone, and does not seem to have been very trustworthy anyway. An unknown correspondent writes a letter to Shaftesbury justifying Guidot's behavior in this case, yet nonetheless remarks, "to tell your Lordship any thing of G—— Character would be no news, so that the fault you will easily lay at his door, especially he having an eye to part of your estate, paying in your debts a very unacceptable busines to him."[65] The Duke himself, who returned rather dramatically on

65. [?] to the Earl of Shaftesbury, December 1706, in PRO 30/24/20/123. Later the Duke and Duchess were forced to sue Guidot.

November 18, had other things on his mind. Meanwhile, the relationship between the Queen and the Duchess had already deteriorated and the Duchess was often absent from town. Shaftesbury himself was ill and was staying near town solely to settle the debt, so that the burden of interest would be removed from his estate. The business required a neat sense of timing; certain fee farm rents had to be sold on a leasehold, and the Duke paid in such a way as to lose the least interest on the sum involved. It was too much for Shaftesbury.

Much correspondence must have preceded the first letter we have from Shaftesbury to Guidot, a rough draft of which is in the Victoria and Albert Museum, for it is difficult to imagine an earl writing such a pleading letter to a commoner. Though he was never really skillful on intricate property matters when he was well, Shaftesbury's wits were keen enough for him to triumph in most situations in a very competitive world. Of course he did not know how much consumption was then involved with his asthma, nor do we. All he knew was that his diseases could destroy him any winter, and when they descended on him he felt all the insecurity that comes from the fear of not being able to cope. To make things worse, something went wrong with the sale of the fee farm rents, and Wheelock's letters to Shaftesbury during the following two months have that same reassuring, soothing tone we can see in those letters he wrote his disheartened master in 1703 and 1704.

It was Shaftesbury's understanding that the Duke and Duchess had agreed to accept part or all of the sum on the specified date in 1706, probably Michaelmas, September 29, and he felt sure that Guidot had not told his mistress that the money was ready. Guidot claimed to Wheelock that he needed six month's notice or at least that he had to find some assured place to deposit the money. After Shaftesbury had been bedeviled by the problem for several months, it was at the end of January magnanimously resolved by the Duchess, who had originally made the loan on the advice of Godolphin: "But it is all past now & all I can doe is to assure your Lordship I am very sorry for any inconvenience that has happened to you, & that I will order Mr. Coggs to receive the whole mortgage or any part of it, just as it happens most easy to you at this time, which may be paid him in money, or like as you please."[66]

Shaftesbury seems to have recovered rapidly from the fit of asthma he had suffered from in November and December of 1706. He was specifically forbidden to go abroad when ill, but by mid January we find him staying with his sister Dorothy at Hurn Court, Hampshire, about five miles northwest of Bournemouth. Edward Hooper had inherited this estate when a relative, Sir Edward Hooper (b. 1662?), died without heirs. A few days later, Shaftesbury visits a near neighbor, Humphry Sturt (d. 1740) at Harton. By the end of January his fevers had returned, but by the middle of February he is off on another excursion where he visits the handsome home of General Erle at Charborough Park, near Wimborne Minster. The General was off, probably attending Parliament at this time of year; Lady Erle and their son-in-law Sir Edward Farnley (d. 1728) were home. Three days after this Shaftesbury stayed for a while at the home of another political associate, Lord James Russell, whose house may have been near Kingston Russell, about twenty miles west of Charborough Park.

Domestic concerns preoccupied the Earl this winter. Wheelock writes to him in January quaintly putting it that two gentlemen wish to be allied to him, which means that they both wish to marry his sister Elizabeth. Shaftesbury had complained earlier that Elizabeth was never taught to care for him. He goes on to say to Wheelock, in a letter from Holland, that she despises "me and mine, St. Giles and all else, when made the finest for her sake & to please & winn her & her sisters." Which means, in short, that of his sisters she was the one who most persistently stayed in London, which he regarded as the ruination of women, as did his father. She continued to live with Maurice after Shaftesbury returned, but they begin to correspond and their ties grow progressively stronger. Looking at her letters it is hard to imagine that she was ever defiant; indeed, her

66. The Duchess of Marlborough to the Earl of Shaftesbury, St. James's, January 28, 1707, in V. and A., Forster MS 48. E. 23, No. 178. The tale of how a number of manuscripts from St. Giles's House mysteriously appeared in the collection of John Forster is an interesting study in Victorian scholarly ethics. It can be followed in the Broadlands MSS. at the Historical Manuscripts Commission.

complaisance is so strong in them that there is little room for anything else. Here is a typical opening sentence, probably written in the spring of 1706:

> Since you are so obligen Dear Brother to think on so insignificant a thing as I, by letting Me have the favour and happiness of your kind letters which is of the greatest satisfaction imaginable, and that you so kindly tell Me that you can Make My Dull nonsense in some Manour agreeable to you, I'm suer I have incouragement enough to proceed in it, with wishes that twas possible, for me to Make anything I write really entertaining.[67]

She was now twenty-five and these are the first proposals that we have any record of, except that Wheelock does mention that one of them had applied before and was approved. The successful applicant was a widower, James Harris (1674–1731), who had been married to an heir of Lord Somers and lived not too far away in the Cathedral Close at Salisbury. Wheelock stopped there to tell him that three thousand pounds of the dowry were ready when he wanted them. They were married on the twentieth of April, probably at Hurn Court. A formal visit to the newlyweds at home had to await Shaftesbury's return to St. Giles's House in the autumn; he arrived bringing a set of plate worth a hundred pounds.

Because it might reveal something of Shaftesbury's character, one would like more details about the problems of Katherine Ashe. There is a letter from her to Shaftesbury written in March 1707, which manages to detail all sorts of perils in the style of Lady Masham or Mrs. Stringer, so that one has not the slightest idea of what she is talking about—simply, she has lost a child which she can no longer mourn, she has been in great peril, and she will now depend on her brother's advice and Shaftesbury's protection. The note is signed "your Lordships most dutifull daughter." After the death of Cropley's father, his mother had married again; this is her daughter by the second marriage and it is likely Cropley is the brother referred to. Shaftesbury also endorsed the letter "my daughter," and it seems likely that she, rather than one of her children, is his goddaughter, though we cannot be sure; especially since she married Sir James

---

67. Lady Elizabeth Ashley to the Earl of Shaftesbury, n.d., in PRO 30/24/22/1/1.

Ashe, later M.P. for Downton and Sherell of Wiltshire, in 1698, which would create a problem as to when Shaftesbury became her godfather. We do not know the details of her sorrows—which become common gossip in London—except that Ashe, whom she was to leave in August, must have been the cause of most of them. Shaftesbury, who rarely had occasion to buy presents for women, sent her a muff as a gift on the first of May, 1707. Cropley later remarks that she is a great favorite of William Lowndes (1652–1724), Secretary to the Treasury, and says if Lowndes—whose spouse had just presented him with twins—needed a wife and child and she a husband, he could make a match. She died of St. Anthony's fire in 1717.

The variety of Shaftesbury's activities this spring gives us a good sampling of daily life at St. Giles's House at the time. First, there are letters to Joseph Micklethwayte, who is readying himself for serving as Stanhope's secretary in Spain. This sort of correspondence, which Shaftesbury is involved in almost every year after 1700, is remarkably pious; indeed, it sounds rather pompous to our ears, though it was precisely what was expected of him in his day. In most cases, as with Ainsworth and Henry Wilkinson, for instance, it is difficult to imagine Shaftesbury talking any differently, but in the case of Arent Furly, we get a chance to see Shaftesbury shifting personae as one might the gears of a car. Not long after he became well acquainted with him, Arent somehow came across a defective copy of *The Sociable Enthusiast*, which Shaftesbury wishes to find its way into the hands of Coste. Shaftesbury treats Arent as a co-conspirator, addressing him as a fellow intellectual. But the moment Arent, through Shaftesbury's intervention, goes to work for Lord Peterborough and faces a world of temptations, he becomes the subject of homilies, as if the first personality had never existed.

And there were always the servants to worry about. Henry Dalicourt, the home steward, was in failing health, but according to Shaftesbury's usual policies he is kept on instead of being retired, thus depriving "a failed gentleman" of a good post, as a friend put it. One can see how dependent Shaftesbury had become on all sorts of help with his bad health and the peculiar schedule it forced on him. Sir John developed a severe cold in January and later had a fit of the stone, so that when Shaftesbury needed another officer to supervise his timber, Thomas Micklethwayte had to take over the hiring. The whole process illustrates the difficulty of hiring good servants, since the position was regarded as one of great trust, especially by Shaftesbury, who worried continually about his trees. Micklethwayte worked all the way from the end of January until the middle of May in order to hire Richard Parry for the job. He finally got him—after he proved not to be a papist and his health improved— but the quest was wearying. Near the end Micklethwayte resolved not to come to St. Giles's House until the steward was hired.

Shaftesbury was also involved with his ornamental plantings. There remains from April 1707, in the hand of an amanuensis but with emendations in Shaftesbury's hand, an elaborate set of plans covering the house, the terrace, from the grotto upward behind the bowling green, the lower canal, the old wilderness, the river walk and further, all of them accompanied by philosophical justifications for the changes. Shaftesbury acknowledges that some of his transplantings are the result of his correspondence with a parson named Eyre who lives close to Rockstead, nearby.

He also writes to Mr. Eyre about husbandry, especially as it is discussed in the various manuscript essays of Mr. Lisle of Wiltshire.[68] Shaftesbury found these papers fascinating. He had been growing sick of the large farm left in his hands "till reviv'd & spirited by what I have read," and he offers to go and see Mr. Lisle in Wiltshire or perhaps he will even be so fortunate as to have Lisle visit him. No one could doubt after reading these letters that the secret of much of Shaftesbury's charm lay in his modesty, even though it did not serve him well in politics. He returns one set of Lisle's papers in May; another, brought by Eyre in the autumn where he himself is mentioned personally, Shaftesbury sends back in December and also offers almost shyly a roughly two-thousand-word essay on manure. It begins by demonstrating the superiority of ox dung to cow dung, then turns to the superiority of that from wild animals to domestic; he next contrasts manure from hermaphrodites and perfect creatures, and finally he demonstrates philosophically why the weather fold—cow

68. This is likely to be Edward Lisle (1666?–1722), author of *Observations in Husbandry* (1757).

manure—is inferior to the ewe fold. He ends by revealing how much he has changed from the Shaftesbury of a decade before, though his audience must be taken into account:

> Mean while I have this inexpressible Satisfaction in these sort of specu- lations; that with their help in this Country-Retirement I can converse more intimately with Nature; view the greatness of her Design and Ex- ecution, & in the simplicity and Uniformity of her operations descry that sovefaign hand that guides & governs all, with infinite Wisdom and Bounty: so that a student of this sort can never fail not only to be- lieve; but to be (if I may say so) ever consciouse of a God, & wittness to his Divine Economy: which is the excellent Use Mr. Lisle makes of this study, & is beyond the other advantages he has deservingly reap'd from it.[69]

Along with these other interests, there was also county politics. In nonelection years, as we have seen, Shaftesbury did little more than keep his fences mended locally. We do not know why Shaftesbury, at the end of the spring in 1707, expected a parliamentary election to be held for Poole. He was not alone in this thought, because Sir John wrote him that the Duke of Newcastle was going to ask him to sup- port a candidate for Poole. It had been Shaftesbury's own seat in the House; Maurice, his grandfather, and in earlier days other Coopers and Ashleys had represented it. In any case, late in April Shaftesbury received a letter from the mayor of Poole, countersigned by a num- ber of burgesses, asking him if he would support his brother-in-law Edward Hooper as representative for Poole, where the right of elec- tion was held by the mayor, aldermen, and burgesses, within and without the town.[70] His reply was cautious, but soon things were un- der way. The burgesses were dissatisfied with their present represen- tatives, Samuel Weston and Sir William Phippard (d. 1723), a mari- ner, and it would be good if Mr. Hooper could come to Poole as soon as convenient. The reluctant Hooper had stood before there and withdrawn, yet he had worked hard for the Country Whigs in Dorset

---

69. The Earl of Shaftesbury to Mr. Eyre, December 17, 1707, in PRO 30/24/22/4/ pp. 55–56.
70. George Lewen and others to the Earl of Shaftesbury, June 23, 1707, in PRO 30/24/45/iii/76–78.

in earlier elections, and his two long letters on his candidacy show that he handled the burgesses very professionally and even planned to stand for burgess in his own town, Christchurch. As we shall see, Hooper failed in the actual election almost a year later.

The session of Parliament was over on the twenty-fourth of April and Sir John stayed on in London into May but then went to St. Giles's. Micklethwayte's last letter on the Parry business was written on the third of May, so he must have arrived in Dorset about the same time. Either when they arrived or shortly later Shaftesbury had a recurrence of fever. Doctor Pitt made at least three visits, his last time because of Sir John's "earnest entreaty," and Mr. Horleck, the apothecary, also visited the house; yet by June the second Shaftesbury was off to Chelsea.

Even before he left for town Shaftesbury was growing impatient with the way in which Somers and Sunderland were handling the matter of finding a post for Thomas Micklethwayte, something which all had assumed to be settled the previous December. In July he writes a surprisingly blunt letter to Lord Sunderland:

> The Prejudice I know to be only against my Self; nor shou'd I have won-der'd at it hither to, as Party-Matters have influenc'd. But at present it must be easy for your Lordship to remove a Court-Prejudice against a Whigg-Friend. and I can assure your Lordship that it would be as easy for that Friend to bear the Prejudices of a Court, had he not such a Friend there as your Self. 'tis your being there has forc'd him to ask, & now forces him to insist. . . . In another Ministry I bore this easily: If I bear it ill in yours, you will not (I hope) be Surpriz'd.[71]

Elsewhere in the letter he points out that the source of his problems is his ardent Whiggery, and there may be a vague hint that he will withdraw his support of the ministry. In reply, Sunderland protests that his friendship for Shaftesbury is as strong as ever, and his sense of indebtedness too; that he personally knows Micklethwayte's worth, but that "things at Court are far from being upon the foot that all honest men wish." He is confident that if they stick to their princi-ples, they will prevail. Shaftesbury's reply to this is purely politesse.

Sir John had had a long interview with Lord Somers in May on the

71. The Earl of Shaftesbury to the Earl of Sunderland, July 22, 1707, in PRO 30/24/22/4/pp. 41–42.

same subject, and his conclusions seem valid enough. Somers seemed ashamed of the way Shaftesbury had been treated, but underneath this Cropley feels that Somers and Sunderland intend that Shaftesbury should bear the Court's ill usage still longer. Despite Somers' bending over backward to ingratiate himself, he wants to stay out of Godolphin's way. In short, he wants Godolphin to court him, instead of the opposite. Cropley's reply was that Shaftesbury did not need to be assured of Somers' friendship; merely asking the favor was proof that he knew he had the friendship. Neither of Micklethwayte's friends knew which way to turn and thus they remained in suspense.

Shaftesbury sent a manuscript copy of *A Letter Concerning Enthusiasm* to Lord Somers in September, and it seems likely that writing it occupied some of his time at Chelsea. Shortly after the end of the month he hastily packed up and, spending a day at Sir John's estate in Beachworth, Surrey, moved to Dorset, where he arrived on the eighth of October. It was almost as if he knew ahead what he later found to be true, that the east wind was to blow steadily across Chelsea for most of October carrying the smoke of the city with it.

Not while Shaftesbury was at Chelsea, nor for a long time before at St. Giles's House, had his brother visited him. Even when one makes allowances for Maurice's retiring nature, this shows how cool was the truce between them. In October the truce turned into open hostility. The trouble probably had its roots in a strange letter which his steward had sent Shaftesbury in January, very unlike Wheelock's usual, pragmatic correspondence. He recalls his prayer the night before about the first Earl: "I earnestly pray'd *Heaven* that if it was consistant with the Beatitude of *all things* that I might heare the Charge of that Bright Angell against me and that I might take his Directions for my Acting better for the good of those Noble Soules deliverd through his Loyns for the Bennefit of Suceeding Ages." What he sees in his dream is a recollection of the old Earl talking to Anthony as a child, telling him that he could arrange a marriage now which would add two or three thousand a year to Anthony's estate, plus twenty for himself in ready cash, but he wants to leave the choice to Anthony, if he will only remember that honor and riches may be obtained many ways but there is no substitute for a wife from a worthy and honest family, beloved in their country, who have gained and maintained their estates by honest means and have brought up their family healthy and well-bred.[72] This letter turned out to be strangely prophetic, but its immediate effect was to set Shaftesbury thinking about the continuance of his line.

In October Maurice wrote him a letter about Carolina and about the Ely lease. According to Maurice, he and John Archdale had not been successful in blocking the efforts of Lord Granville (1665–1707) to meddle harmfully in the affairs of the province, so that now things had gone far enough that the Proprietors as a group were likely to be sued by the populace, and the only solution he can see is to make the profitless colony over to the Queen for whatever she desires to give for it. The answer Maurice wanted was largely a matter of common sense and did not require the special knowledge of Carolina which his brother lacked, but Shaftesbury merely told him he was prudent enough and would take the right action.

On the matter of the Ely rents, Shaftesbury's reply looks offhand but in reality is not. There are two documents involved here, one the actual leases and second the legal statement of his intent with regard to the income from them. Earlier he must have told Maurice that he thought that he had already had a statement of intent assigning the income to him. Now that he has returned to St. Giles's House, Maurice wants him to look around to see if he can find the assignment.[73] Shaftesbury's reply must have been maddening to Maurice. He says that he can find no old papers on the lease in the house; fortunately, though, just before the Bishop of Ely's death he was able to get a new lease for him. Thus the only danger Maurice need feel is from Shaftesbury himself and there is nothing to fear from that quarter. Actually, of course, this was the quarter from which Maurice had the most to fear. There exists an early memo by Shaftesbury to himself saying he has assigned the income to Maurice, irrevocably one assumes, as were the dowries to his sisters, yet as we have seen he has used the income from the lease to pressure Maurice into standing for

72. John Wheelock to the Earl of Shaftesbury, January 25, 1707, in PRO 30/24/20/128.

73. The relevant papers are PRO 30/24/22/1/pp. 34–40 and 30/24/22/4/pp. 46–47.

Parliament. Maurice's reply is sarcastic. If he is to have the income from the Ely rents only at his brother's pleasure, at least this is nothing new. One phrase in Shaftesbury's reply makes his whole intention clear, as he intended it to: "If I do it, it must be *Willfully*: & that I hope can never be a fear with You, nor worth my giving my self any trouble with Lawyers: which however I should be glad of, in a certain Family-case, when ever you shou'd give the occasion." In other words he has no intention of making the assignment unless Maurice marries, to give some prospect of carrying on the line. Maurice certainly saw the implication of the letter, and the fact that he takes no note of it in two later replies is some sign that this was not the first time the subject was brought up. His tone in replying is one of resignation. It is ironic that he waited until after Shaftesbury's marriage before he married Katherine Popple (d. 1721), for he must have known her for some time.[74] It is possible that Maurice had become entirely too reclusive to carry on the family traditions, and Shaftesbury thus found it necessary to go back on his agreement in order to prod him. Whatever his reasons, the whole affair makes Shaftesbury look like an Indian giver.

The six years of waiting had seemed so long that Shaftesbury must have looked back on December 1707 as the month in which the millennium came. The small favor he asked, a post for Micklethwayte, was granted. Although he had striven for this so long, there is some question whether attaining it or the freedom he now felt was most important to him. When the ministry sought to chastise him in 1702 there was no way to get at him and it had to resort to the silly pretense of taking away his vice Admiralty, which had remained in the family for three generations through all adversities. Shaftesbury was willing enough to enjoy all the prerogatives of his rank, but he knew, as only a Stoic can know, how obligations can make one a slave to fortune and the whims of mankind. He was never again to incur a strong obligation which he could not repay from his own resources, his friendship, or wealth.

74. She was Andrew Marvell's (1621–1678) grand-niece.

It seemed almost like serendipity; however, Shaftesbury and Cropley had seen enough of politics to suspect it was not, even if they
were never able to figure out all the reasons behind what happened.
A full year after Shaftesbury had been assured by Somers and Sunderland that the matter was settled—though of course it was not—
Cropley was talking idly with Shaftesbury's old political advisor,
Robert Molesworth, and mentioned the difficulty they were having
getting a post for Micklethwayte. The old apostate had now turned
Court Whig, and there is no record of any communication between
him and Shaftesbury for at least seven years, so that Cropley was
startled to hear Molesworth say that he would see Godolphin that
very day about the matter. The Lord Chancellor immediately asked
the Duke whether he had at one time requested the post for Micklethwayte of him, and when Marlborough said he had done so, Godolphin sent Molesworth to tell Cropley that it was settled. A day later,
at a meeting to confirm the decision, Godolphin was so candid and
warm in his professions of friendship for Shaftesbury that he dis-
armed even the cynical and jaded Cropley, and on the fifteenth the
Earl wrote his letter of thanks to the Lord Chancellor.

Cropley was probably correct in his guess as to why the ministry
changed their mind about Shaftesbury's request; they had decided to
gain as much credit as they could with the uncommitted Whigs.
This is confirmed by Molesworth's continual depreciation to Sir
John of the Junto and Kit-Cat Club Whigs, as so flexible in principles
that they could not be depended on to run the country. There is also
the peculiar twist which the matter of Parson Stephens took. When
Shaftesbury privately repudiated him, he did so in part because Stephens had failed to apologize to him in his public repudiation of his
pamphlet replying to Toland. Yet, according to Godolphin, when it
came to saving Stephens from the pillory, Shaftesbury's name was
spuriously put forward as a petitioner; thus the ministry in sparing
him thought it was doing the Earl a favor.

It is not so easy to figure out why Sunderland and Somers could
not follow through on their promise of December 1706, or why, if
they were not absolutely certain, they made the promise in the first
place. This may only be the measure of the Junto Whigs' hopes, at

first, and their growing disappointment as 1707 went on.[75] Perhaps, as Cropley suggested, Somers wanted Godolphin to come to him. Perhaps, too, there was hidden animosity against Shaftesbury himself; his hand in managing the Self-Denying Bill may have become clear to them. Whatever the reason the decline of their favor with Shaftesbury is clearly measured in Cropley's attitude. In December 1707 he is offended when Molesworth makes a joke about the way in which he could do in a day or two what Lord Sunderland could not do in a year. At this time, Cropley thinks that Shaftesbury should write to Somers and Sunderland. Four months later when Micklethwayte takes the post, he tells Shaftesbury not to bother writing, he will see that they get what little thanks are due them.

According to Shaftesbury's daybook, he must have fallen ill during November, but in December there is only a guinea paid for medical care, and that to Doctor Pitt on a chance visit. It was just as well, because he had more guests than usual this Christmas season. In addition to Cropley, there was a Mrs. Williams, who must have been a friend of Cropley's because she arrived with his sisters and his step brother Edmund Bowyer. One gathers from their impatience to get there that this was an occasion for them; it must have seemed so also to the reclusive Shaftesbury, for he had to hire extra servants and he is still giving gratuities to the servants at the end of February "for doing well when the company was here."

There were the usual Christmas gifts to servants, which Shaftesbury, when the occasion warranted it, preferred to give in broad pieces, or even scepters—worth twenty-six shillings—rather than the usual guineas. He also endowed the school in Shaftesbury with an annual gift of thirty pounds and began this December his modest allowance to support Michael Ainsworth at Oxford. Shaftesbury's well-known letters to him—which were returned to the family and then went to the Record Office—are models for the pious and avuncular tone which he adopted, quite properly, in addressing Wilkinson, Arent Furly, and Joseph Micklethwayte. So long as they are read with this specific persona always in mind, they reveal a good deal about Shaftesbury.

75. See William L. Sachse, *Lord Somers: A Political Portrait* (Manchester, 1975), 252–68.

The World
Beckons Again
1708–1710

From a biographer's point of view 1708 is a strange year for Shaftesbury. There is more ample correspondence than for many earlier
years, but it is so centered on politics and, later, marriage that we
almost completely miss his daily existence. This situation is further
complicated by the fact that he leaves St. Giles's House late in the
spring and because of a very severe winter is forced to remain near
London, at Beachworth, until the beginning of February 1709. Not
only does he keep fewer copies of his own letters sent from Chelsea
and still fewer of letters received; the daybook for Chelsea—the one
which the fourth Earl had when he wrote his life of his father—has
disappeared.

Sir John Cropley's letters to Shaftesbury, which begin on New
Year's Day, are more detailed than ever before, and well they might
be; never had he such a tumultuous domestic political situation to
report on, and to this must be added the Pretender's tragi-comic attempt in late February to invade Scotland, which became a major
issue in the election, however doomed it may have been from the
outset. It is unlikely that anyone will ever lay bare all the levels of
intrigue which were involved in domestic politics that winter, but at
least by watching Cropley at work in the House of Commons we can
determine Shaftesbury's own role in what went on there. Queen
Anne and her ministers certainly regarded Cropley as a puppet whose
strings were controlled by the Earl.

He begins with a note of caution. Shaftesbury should do nothing
at all which will endanger his health or his purse. Furthermore, this
is one of those times when political inaction, real or apparent, is the
best course. The ministry "trimming and being (in a new way between the 2 old partys) . . . have room enough to be easy under the

burden of elections." The last ministry laid great stress on the management of every election; this ministry does little except "in a few particular places . . . tis so gently done & unseen & so as really to signifye very little." "Receive Micks favour & return at its coming handsome acknowledgements." "It is good though that you intend to be at St. Giles's the week before elections, for if you ever completely retire from elections don't admit it. The only problem is your brother's 'violence' to the court on your being oblig'd & consider'd. his behaviour I know will be outrageous. he shall loos his aim and not in the least hurt where he will intend it." "I hear . . . he determines not to stand at Weymouth. I can plainly tel my Lord Treasurer his ill behavior to you . . . since he boasts of it."[1]

When Cropley refers to the present ministry, he means the current policies of Lord Treasurer Godolphin and Marlborough, because beyond putting Sunderland in over a year before, there had been little change in the ministry's composition. With the Lords Wharton (1648–1715) and Somers still excluded from office, the ministry was trying to steer between the two parties, and Cropley's advice on moderation seems sound. No doubt too his fear that the idealistic Shaftesbury will let his passions run too high for this particular situation is well based.

The portrayal of Maurice as openly opposed to his brother's interest and having some influence at Court is rather surprising. Unlike Cropley, who spent every moment he could spare from parliamentary activities at his estate at Beachworth in Surrey or in Dorset, Maurice is a true Londoner, but we have no way of knowing who his associates were. This may be a new development because for the first time Cropley seems to rejoice that Maurice does not intend to stand again for Parliament. There will be more on this subject later.

Not long after writing this letter Cropley went to St. Giles's House, but leaving Micklethwayte behind there when he returned abruptly to London, he was on the scene to report the fall of Robert Harley, whom he had reported as skating on thin ice in his previous letter. Cropley's account of this affair is reinforced by a similar version given him by Stanhope and reported to Shaftesbury in March. And it

1. Sir John Cropley to the Earl of Shaftesbury, January 1708, in PRO 30/24/21/144.

was used by Geoffrey Holmes and W. A. Speck, who have made a fine attempt to reconstruct the motives behind and the precise order of events in Harley's attempt to woo the Tories, and his failure.[2]

Another matter which has interested scholars is the arrangement the Earl was to make with Cropley's rather extreme opponent at Shaftesbury, Edward Nicholas (1662?–1726). Two seats were available for the town. W. A. Speck, who comments on the rarity of such reciprocal arrangements as were made there, suggests that this one had become traditional, but offers no evidence beyond that for 1708.[3] It is possible that Speck is right, but it is also possible that the "safety" of the seat is being confused with a previous arrangement being made for it. Shaftesbury hated to lose; in fact, this is one of the very few elections since 1695 in which either he or one of his candidates failed to be elected to a seat after standing for it. Normally he would canvass the electors, informally, of course, and determine whether safety could be guaranteed through his influence. If it could, he would jump in with both feet to assure the seat was safe; if it could not, he normally would not permit his candidates to stand.

The degree of Shaftesbury's collaboration with the Tories in 1708 is clear from Cropley's comments about Shaftesbury's Tory friend, Francis Gwin. "I had a message today from F. Guin desiring to give me by word of mouth the firm determination to doe to the utmost in their power to oblige & honour you. he hopes that if they support all they can your Interest or at least no way disturb it you will give them quiet in Wilts."[4]

The coming spring election was all settled in Westminster, Shaftesbury thought, through elaborate and secret negotiations with Tory and Whig leaders, long before anyone mounted the hustings. For Shaftesbury there was the advantage with respect to his health; indeed, it seems unlikely that Cropley would have stood had not some such arrangement been worked out. Cropley returned to Westminster at the end of January with complete directions as to how it was to

2. Geoffrey Holmes and W. A. Speck, "The Fall of Harley in 1708 Reconsidered," *English Historical Review,* LXXX (1965), 673–93.

3. W. A. Speck, *Tory and Whig: The Struggle in the Constituencies, 1701–1715* (1970), 58.

4. Sir John Cropley to the Earl of Shaftesbury [February 1708], in PRO 30/24/ 21/150.

be handled. A Mr. Cole was to be the intermediary to William Et-tricke, Tory M.P. for Christchurch. Shortly after Cropley saw Cole, Nicholas himself appeared full of praise for the Earl. Of course Crop-ley was not willing to let it go at that; a formal meeting was arranged in the company of the son of the first "pine" lord, probably Henry Hyde (1672–1753), later fourth Earl of Clarendon: "This gentleman met me with my Brother Nicholas, who in an agony told me he, be-fore the gentleman, that he there engaged his honour . . . that he pro-test'd he had not one friend or vote in Shaftesbury but he would faithfully endeavour should be devoted to you. that on his honour he would doe no one act the most simple of its kind without your con-sent & approbation." After many more protestations Cropley re-plied, "It depend'd on himself. that the contest could be singly for me no longer and if at worst you [Shaftesbury] need'd either strength from Court Juncta or City, each would be at hand to give it."[5] Thus the rather cynical agreement was concluded, though the participants had overlooked one possible hitch.

Cropley's reference to a Tory nobleman as a "pine" lord is drawn from a six-page allegory Shaftesbury had written, probably earlier this same winter, "The Fable of the Oaks, the Pines, and the Pinas-ters." When Diana sets up her government on a principal island in the Aegean, a dispute arises among her supporters: the Oaks, who despise enclosure and love openness, and are supported by the hama-dryads, and the Pines—supported by fauns, satyrs, and foreign deities —who are easy of cultivation, who belong in palaces, and thrive on enclosure. Indeed, the hamadryads point out that the satyrs need the dense shade to cover their activities and that they love mystery and dark policy so much they may learn to worship them. Diana loves fresh air, lives in open fields, and maintains the rights and liberties of forests and mountains, which she guards; yet she cannot make up her mind and leaves matters to the oracle of Delphi, who is more decisive than usual. The oracle observes that on the whole the Pines are much affected by the myths of the golden age and long for it in a way which should deter any deity dependent on Jove rather than Sat-urn. Some of the goodliest Pines could be separated to stand as an

5. *Ibid.*

example of upright growth; this, though, would require more love than Diana's ministering nymphs could supply. Diana must then choose the well-rooted and secure Oaks, for the worst thing of all is inaction. But she is repelled by their knottiness and roughness, and when first the Pines and then the Oaks withdraw from her grove, she decides to cultivate the scrubby growth that remains, the Pinasters. These do very well when the weather is good, but when it turns severe, and they do not have the protection of the other trees, they are despoiled, which the Pines view with pleasure, the Oaks, with pity. Such is Shaftesbury's commentary on the effort of Queen Anne, Marlborough, and Godolphin to set up a government independent of the strong factions of either party, even though he realized that by accepting favors, he was becoming a supporter of the Pinasters.

Cropley had been insisting that the ministry's attempt was likely to succeed; in his reply to the letters of February the Earl persists, however: "You wonder at me perhaps for being so stubborn in my Judgment; especially now I have Stanhope's Judgment (which of all in the world I most esteem) against me. But I still stick to my Fable, and laugh at the poor weak Oaks who blame the great Ones for their Sturdiness. . . . But far be it from us too to enter into the repining measures of the softer and more plyant Oaks. We may ply or comply on account of our private Obligations to the Nymphs, & our *no Obligations* to the great Oaks." But if a letter comes saying he is supported by the great Oaks, "then good by Nymphs! & all my Obligations to them!"[6]

Consider the election to be held at Shaftesbury in April. Cropley's victory will be celebrated as if there were a contest, though actually there is none because an agreement had been worked out with the Tories in February. And this agreement was easier to come to because Shaftesbury is now obligated to Godolphin. On still another level of motivation, he will throw the Lord Treasurer over in a minute if a real crisis arises. Somers may perhaps know this; it is more likely, though, that the Junto has by now written off Shaftesbury's support, though the ministry obviously needs it.

6. The Earl of Shaftesbury to Sir John Cropley [February or March, 1708], in PRO 30/24/22/4/pp. 65–66. The fable is designated as PRO 30/24/22/7/pp. 91–96.

One other subject which Cropley brings up, and which is important only because Shaftesbury in his reply so well demonstrates the intensity of his idealism, is the attempt to introduce voting by ballot into the House of Commons. This was experimented on in a disputed election case at Ashburton and proved, as Holmes puts it, not only long-winded but a physical endurance test, since no one was allowed to move for any reason while the balls were being dropped by the voters into the balloting box. The idea failed but was to be revived twice later.[7] Cropley remarks, "This affair you must know was begun in jest. It was intended to be defeat'd in the difficulty of making a standing order for a future Parliament."

Whatever the original sponsors thought of the measure, Shaftesbury took it quite seriously as a further blow to control of voting by the Court and he was disappointed at its failure. The method of voting was Venetian, which must have suggested his line of argument, that England must take chances, precisely because it is not Venice.

> I don't at all wonder Stanhope is startled: & so am I too. But without startling and trembling I had never seen Trienniall-Bill, Treason-Bill, Disbanding-Bill nor any other great Thing. . . . We may be truly said *to work out our Salvation in fear & trembling*. Venice & such standing Governments that are founded for Eternity, [are] secure from all Evills from *within*. . . . But for us Gentlemen of yesterday, who till the Revolution never enjoy'd any thing like Liberty, and who now we have it must owe it more to the weakness of our Crown'd-Heads, than to any Pollicy or Vertue of our People or their Form of Government; I must begg Pardon if I act a little according to my Hott-spurr Inclination, and run willingly into a thousand dangers, walk near Precipices, and *drive* (as they say) *to an Inch* in order to gett but an Inch or two upon the Court, and advance in any Commonwealth Project.[8]

His brother seems to have gone his own way this spring. Although Cropley several times predicts that Maurice will not stand, he finally does and is chosen. Nowhere is there any sign that he was coerced; indeed, it seems likely that he chose to stand because he did not want to lose the prestige after serving so long. Many of these problems would be cleared up if we could unravel the story of Grub

7. See Holmes, *British Politics,* 145–46.
8. The Earl of Shaftesbury to Sir John Cropley [February or March, 1708], in PRO 30/24/22/4/pp. 66–67.

Hall, which Cropley refers to all spring. Maurice is an inhabitant of the hall, and all the other members, with the exception of Pelora, follow his attitudes: mistrust of Shaftesbury, suspicion of his relationship to Godolphin, and disappointment when Micklethwayte is awarded his post. They are also anxious to see Hooper chosen for Poole. Other unidentified inhabitants are Don Juan and presumably his spouse. There is one very amusing dialogue where Sir John is forced to defend the electoral arrangements at Shaftesbury against Don Juan, who does at least have probity, Cropley admits. The final rather gross scene where Cropley, anticipating "the Mob," comes to tell them of Micklethwayte's success is highly amusing.

Maurice cannot be Don Juan; he had known Katherine Popple for a long time but did not marry her until 1709 or 1710. Furthermore Shaftesbury made a cryptic note in a memorandum book in 1712: "A set of Char . . . for Lucilla (for Pelora)." The problem is fascinating, but as with many others relating to Shaftesbury, posterity will have to unravel them if it seems worth the effort.

As for Micklethwayte, he had to wait for his post, but considering the sort of problems Godolphin was facing, not very long. In February, Molesworth told Cropley that Godolphin intended the stamp or salt office for Micklethwayte and that he was delaying because the salt office, which was worth £200 more, would not be ready for a short time. Meanwhile, with a governmental crisis going on, Cropley began to worry about the behavior of some of Micklethwayte's London associates, so that he wrote the Earl: "I should be very glad if you would keep Mick one week longer with you after your receiving this on some pretence or other with out naming my desiring it, for some of his particular friends are so warme on this late scene that has past. I would fain have them a little cool & matters settle before he comes amongst them."[9]

While the crisis was on, Shaftesbury was willing to be patient about Micklethwayte's job, but in March his patience began to wear thin, so that he sent a note, now lost, to Godolphin. Whatever he said in it produced results, for the Lord Treasurer immediately set an

9. Sir John Cropley to the Earl of Shaftesbury, February 7, 1708, in PRO 30/24/21/146.

appointment with Cropley. He has an office, the Treasurer of Trans-ports, where he has experienced great abuse and needs an absolutely honest man. The office involves the war and will be over when there is peace, but if Micklethwayte will take it he will never lack a job so long as Godolphin is in office. Furthermore he offers to provide jobs for mayors, aldermen, and other of Shaftesbury's friends. Cropley ac-cepted the offer and later he himself received an offer of a job paying £1,000. He felt friendship was more important than money, and re-plied "that he [Godolphin] was the only minister I would ever apply to for favour of that kind. At present I thought I could best serve him & the publick being free." To Shaftesbury he remarked of Mickle-thwayte's appointment, "I can with Holy Christ now say you have made my future burdens easy & my Yoke light, you may lay all you please now upon me." "My gratitude to you must not be in words, as you don't care for them, I thinke them needless too." [10]

Cropley did his best this spring to calm Shaftesbury's political passions and his constant fear that someone was conspiring against him. He had succeeded fairly well until late in April when, a few days after he had written the good news about Micklethwayte, he received a frantic note:

> I have nothing to say but *come away instantly,* and sorry I am that I have been so lull'd asleep, Mr. Cornish coming down at last. No visit or advance or shew of Peace or Countenance from Gentry or a Soul of Mr. Nicholas' Party, and besides this one Mr. Tench an East-India Mar-chant (as reported) having sett up & spent money last Saturday & walk'd the Town which is in an uproar.

Shaftesbury goes on to say that he has sent to Boveridge for Hooper to come to walk the town for Cropley. [11]

Shaftesbury had known that Cornish, a placeman, might stand as early as December, but there seemed little to worry about so long as he remained in London, especially since Cornish had to resign his place or find someone to stand in for him. Apparently he intention-

10. Sir John Cropley to the Earl of Shaftesbury, April 15, 1708, in PRO 30/24/21/153.

11. The Earl of Shaftesbury to Sir John Cropley, April 26, 1708, in PRO 30/24/21/156.

ally deceived Cropley about his movements and obtained permission of Lord Sunderland, who supposedly did not expect him to act without first consulting Shaftesbury. Thus he threatened the well-made arrangements, whether he won out over Cropley or defeated the Tory, Nicholas. Cornish was soon enough convinced of the futility of his effort when he made his formal appearance on the scene and spoke with the electors. Nothing could better illustrate the sort of compartmentalized habit of thought so characteristic of Shaftesbury than the letter he wrote to Lord Somers, who received it between two kind letters from the Earl dealing with his book on *Enthusiasm*. Of Cornish he says,

> For till the Gentleman, who declar'd himself sent down by my Lord Sunderland, had met his Friends, and found the settled Bent of the Town, I had no mark or Testimony of his coming any otherwise than as an Enemy. Yet the Event has now made it appear that a common Civility (if it cou'd have been aforded me) wou'd have absolutely secur'd that Gentleman's Election, and sav'd me the officiouse Civilitys of a Contrary Party. But it is my misfortune to receive so little of this kind from my own Party, that I cannot so much as obtain a handle or Opportunity to joyn my Interest with theirs.[12]

All of this is true enough, except that it is unlikely that Shaftesbury knew until spring that Nicholas was so weak that Cornish could have unseated him without affecting the vote for Cropley.

Much of this first letter deals with Poole and the fate of Hooper, who had been first in the field by almost a year. This election was not settled by the time the first was written, but nine days later when he wrote the second, George Lewen, the mayor, had with the backing of the Duke of Bolton defeated Hooper. The following year he vigorously repelled an attempt of Lewen's to be friendly again in a letter complaining of the fall of Newfoundland to the French. In a bitter and whimsical letter he tells Lewen that it is disloyal people like him who have weakened the influence of this colony so important to the port of Poole and thereby lost it. Of course Shaftesbury

12. The Earl of Shaftesbury to Sir John Cropley, May 13, 1708, in PRO 30/24/22/4/ pp. 81–82.

never lost his keen interest in politics, but this was his last active venture into it.

Obviously much of Shaftesbury's correspondence with the Furlys in 1708 is lost; enough remains to show that the friendship continued with its usual warmth. During the spring Shaftesbury supports the suit of Benjohan (1681–1728) for a daughter of a Mr. Wright, who was probably Furly's banker in London. Shaftesbury does not think he has done much, but when the marriage is all arranged, Benjohan is thankful to him. And Benjamin is delighted with his daughter-in-law.

In July, speaking of the advice he formerly gave to various citizens of Rotterdam, Shaftesbury writes to Furly, "I have none that seek my Opinion—and so I am free of the Burden of justifying Courtiers & Great Men, which to such a one as I am, is a hard Task at best; since great Men will have great Faults, and when their Politicks are good their Moralls will be ill and their Lives give Scandall to such a For-mall Liver as I am."[13] One wonders whether he is thinking back to his experiences of the spring.

He did have great hopes of finding leadership and private virtue combined in Stanhope, whom Arent Furly writes to him about in the fall.[14] Arent, left behind in Barcelona because of illness, describes the preparations for the attack on Fort Mahan, its success, and the death of the general's brother during the battle. Benjamin ends the year with a long plea for Shaftesbury's intervention in an idealistic cause and also informs Shaftesbury that, finally, at the age of seventy-two, he has bought a home of his own in Rotterdam.

Shaftesbury also kept up his correspondence with Coste during 1708, but only a single letter, from July, has survived. Coste must have visited St. Giles's House this year, for he repeats a long quota-

13. The Earl of Shaftesbury to Benjamin Furly, Chelsea, July 22, 1708, in PRO 30/24/22/4/p. 89.
14. There are among the Shaftesbury Papers in the Public Record Office a vast number of rather precise letters, and even councils of war, reflecting Furly's service in Spain with Peterborough and Stanhope. I have said little about these because they do nothing toward illuminating Shaftesbury's character.

tion from a manuscript of *A Letter Concerning Enthusiasm* which he had seen at Wimborne—though why he repeats it is something of a mystery. It is several hundred words long and does not exactly follow the printed text which was published later in the month. Of course none of the manuscript versions survive, so that there is no way of checking it against them. In the letter he does describe the regimen by which Shaftesbury survived his long stay in the London area this year. Zephyr, the west wind, has blown so long that he believes Shaftesbury is losing his fear of the north-east wind: "J'espere qu'il soufflera assez long temps pour vous faire passer agreablement quelques Mois à Chelsea. Mais s'il en arrive autrement, je ne vous plaindrá pas tant que vous lever à Beachworth, conversant tantôt avec les vivans, & tantôt avec les Morts, tous gens d'élite, qui chacun ont les charmes particuliers. Pour moi, je suis uniquement reduit à la conversation des Morts."[15]

Shaftesbury had long given up hope that Maurice would marry, and this fall he set about finding a wife for himself, more or less under protest. Wheelock's strangely prophetic appeal to him in 1707 was the first of many, and he could no longer deny their logic. It is almost impossible to define what *family*, ideally persisting in a transitory world, meant to Shaftesbury. Some of it we can see, though: not just carrying on as he did in a principled and disinterested manner his grandfather's political traditions; also honoring the complex of family relationships he had woven, which we can see an amusing side of in his attempt to fill his home with tangible symbols of these relationships, badgering the aging Duke of Rutland to sit for a portrait and finally settling for a copy of an earlier painting. It was the powerful sense of a very old name, of land long held, and, just as important, his extended family centered on St. Giles's House and spreading over thousands of acres in a complex relationship of de-

15. "I hope that it will blow long enough for you to pass some agreeable months at Chelsea. But if it does happen otherwise, I should be pleased if you moved to Beachworth, conversing on the one hand with the living, on the other hand with the Dead, the best types of two peoples, each of which has its particular charms. As for me, I am reduced solely to conversations with the Dead." Pierre Coste to the Earl of Shaftesbury, July 3, 1708, in PRO 30/24/45/iii/140. Presumably Coste was still at the home of the Clarkes at Chipley Park, Somerset.

pendency and responsibility. The son of an only son, Shaftesbury would have all the share of immortality he expected if these could be preserved for the benefit of the locality, the county, and the nation.

On the other hand, as a suitor he had several disadvantages. First was his health. He was more and more living from day to day. Although he claimed that all would be well if he could stay at St. Giles's House, we know well enough how he suffered if he stepped out of his regimen. He was no bargain even as a country gentleman. Then, there was his manner. No matter how much he charmed Lady Wentworth, one could only get so close to a person who led his life in so many separate compartments, without running into a wall. Furthermore, he had been a recluse for six years, though he now admits he cannot study so relentlessly as he used to and perhaps is a better suitor because he has had to learn more trivial ways of filling his time—he has now learned to play cards. Though too honest, he is a good enough courtier; the question is whether his skill will still function, whether he will retain his aplomb, when he applies these skills not to another nobleman or a fellow politician but to a lady he seeks for a wife.

Finally there is the matter of what Shaftesbury expects in a wife. He talks some at times of the wildness of his youth, but except for an obvious fondness for the bluestocking Lady Masham, which Locke shared, there is in no letter an expression of affection for any woman outside of his family. His life had become increasingly centered on men. He can see a successful marriage in the Hoopers, but on Dorothy's part this is due to her sweet disposition, her training, and the fact that she had little to do with the town.

Moreover, the sort of solidity of character yet joined with innocence and modesty, along with a sufficiency of well-grounded education, is easier to find as one goes down the social scale; at his level they are quite rare. Thus he tells Furly in November, "My only Brother (who might with better success perhaps try his Fortune this way in a lower Rank of Gentry) refuses to think of Marriage & leaves the heavy part upon me; which I only call *heavy* on account that there are so few of my own Degree, or of those Circumstances that

can justify my Marriage, who have any sort of Education that promises Good."[16]

It was a Sunday, the nineteenth of September, that Shaftesbury
first saw Lady Anne Vaughan. Her father had a house in Chelsea, and
Shaftesbury had heard many wonderful things about her character
and education. One glimpse of her person was enough; this was the
woman he wanted to marry. As Lady Mary Montagu (1689–1762)
rather waspishly said, she was "educated in solitude with some
choice books, by a saint-like governess: crammed with virtue and
good qualities." Her father, Lord Carbery (1640–1713), on the other
hand, had been a "conspicuous profligate" even in the court of
Charles II; "worse than Sir Charles Sedley" was the way that Pepys
described him. He had become a strong Whig and had been a member of one of John Locke's clubs, which is where Shaftesbury most
likely met him first. Having repaired the family fortunes while governor of Jamaica in the late 1670s, he determined to keep what he
had gotten, to the extent that it seems likely that he had no intention of marrying his daughter off and losing money thereby. Shaftesbury knew his miserly nature and seems to have eventually sensed
the truth of the matter, as we shall see, but it took him too long to
do so.

Because Lady Anne was so rich and so piously dutiful she presented a very peculiar problem. Naturally he would have to proceed
through the father—in fact he seems to have wished to do this before seeing any more of the daughter—yet if she were so dutiful and
he did succeed with the father she might marry him without ever
being convinced that he was not after her money. The procedure
then was first to assure her somehow, then see the father, and lastly
court the lady.

Unfortunately, when Shaftesbury began upon this involved
courtship in September 1708, the east and northeast winds began to
blow across Chelsea and he was forced to retire to Sir John Cropley's
estate at Beachworth, twenty-odd miles to the south of London, near

16. The Earl of Shaftesbury to Benjamin Furly, November 3, 1708, in PRO 30/
24/21/161.

Reigate.[17] This geographical barrier was but the first of many impediments that arose to block the scrupulous and hapless suitor. The whole business would take on an air of comedy, were it not for his ardor, unbelievable to anyone who was not accustomed to looking behind his usually calm mask. Thus when he first tells Robert Molesworth of finding this paragon and deciding only she would do, he says, "I have on a sudden such an Affair thrown a-cross me, that I am confident I have zeal enough rais'd in me, to hinder you from doubting whether I sincerely intend what I profess. There is a Lady— who is in every respect that very person, I had ever fram'd a picture of from my imagination."[18] Molesworth, who was to become Shaftesbury's confidant and perforce his negotiating delegate, had most likely been chosen because he had a cousin who could assure Lady Anne that the Earl's intent was honest before he began in earnest on the father. The cousin was the remarkable, though fated in her marriage choices, Rachel, Lady Russell.

Yet Molesworth was certain that if Shaftesbury proceeded as he intended he would be accused of approaching the daughter first— about the last thing he would wish to be accused of. He should begin at "the right end," as Molesworth called it and the cousin should intervene later. On October 11, then, Shaftesbury wrote from Beachworth to Lord Carbery describing his circumstances and offering himself as a husband for Anne. It would have been easy for Carbery to refuse Shaftesbury on account of his health; instead he seems to have answered evasively, though appearing kindly. Looking at Lord Carbery's friends and the positions he held, such as the presidency of the Royal Society, it is hard to believe that he had not a good side, but if so it died with him. Hardly anyone from the peerage during the time has left such a poor reputation. One can only conclude that he answered Shaftesbury in the same way he had answered others before him and others who came later, because he delighted in toying with suitors. It must be admitted that in most cases there was a certain rough justice in doing just what he did.

17. Beachworth, the house he lived in this winter, may still exist, but there is nothing in the standard histories of Surrey to lead one to it.
18. The Earl of Shaftesbury to Robert Molesworth, September 30, 1708, in *Letters . . . to Robert Molesworth,* 3.

Late in October Shaftesbury did manage to get to Chelsea and again found Carbery friendly but still evasive. After a few days the northeast winds intruded and he had to flee back to Beachworth. This happened again in November and then he decided he would be unable to go to Chelsea again this winter. All the while he worried about Lord Carbery. Does he think I want his money? Is he worried about my health? Does he think I am too diffident about his wealth? Then he begins to worry about Anne. Would she prefer some one more sprightly? Does she want someone younger? From letter to letter his ego is pumped or deflated according to the status of his hopes. He is delighted to hear that Anne during a previous transaction had bemoaned the possibility of greatness without virtue. Surely this is the one noblewoman in all of England for him, absolutely destined for him.

One senses reading these letters to Molesworth what has happened to Shaftesbury during the past few years. From the very first he had proclaimed the supremacy of principle over party; there never was any doubt about his political morality. Yet we know from his "Exercises" that his rigid personal morality was something to be concealed. The worst a political idealist can be called is a fool, but there is something unbearable in a man who is too demonstrative about his personal morals. These are very candid letters, indeed; and he allows his personal morality to surface. At times he actually becomes what a later generation of Englishmen, reviewing his life, came to look at him as, the truly moral nobleman.

Enter a new villain to thwart the course of ideal love, the weather, the worst winter in human memory. Even in October, Shaftesbury sensed that the winter was coming on fiercely, as he put it, and this must be the reason he was more rarely in Chelsea than usual, though he felt he had a better reason than ever to be there. He put off his return to St. Giles's and then put it off again, waiting for the weather to clear, but it did not. All over Europe rivers froze; pack ice was seen floating in the English Channel. Beachworth lies in the valley of the river Mole, and at one point in January Shaftesbury remarks that it is completely impossible for even a horse to move; his letters can only be carried out of the valley by foot messengers. Meanwhile Molesworth had come down from Yorkshire to London and, as Shaftesbury's deputy, paid an official visit to the Vaughans at Chelsea, though the weather was so bad that Shaftesbury wondered whether this last short trip was feasible. By the time he heard of this visit he was back at St. Giles's House, where he finally arrived on the fifth of February. Molesworth promised a second visit and Shaftesbury was so encouraged by the results of the first mission that he writes he will come to Chelsea immediately if the second goes well, though everything at St. Giles's House is confused by the weather and by the death of his home steward Dalicourt, whose papers are all out of order.

By April 15 the weather had cleared enough for travel, and with high hopes Shaftesbury left St. Giles's House for Chelsea. Again, the fates intervened. He writes to Molesworth, "But not a Star, but has been my enemy. I had hardly got over the unnatural winter, but with all the zeal imaginable I dispatch'd my affairs, and came up from the West, thinking to surprise you by a visit. The hurry I came away in, and the fatigue of more than ordinary business, I was forc'd to dispatch that very morning I set out, join'd with the ill weather which return'd again upon my Journy, threw me into one of my ill fits of the *Asthma* and almost kill'd me on the road. After a few weeks I got this over, and my hopes reviv'd."[19] Finally, then, on June 15, 1709, he got to see Lord Carbery again, who was "as civil and obliging as ever." "But I found he was deaf on this ear. . . . I see there is no hope left for me. . . . I am afraid he thinks but the worse of me, for pretending to value his Daughter as I do: and for protesting, that I would be glad to take her without a farthing, present or future; and yet settle all I have, as I have offer'd him." "There is no help for this, when men are too crafty to see plain; and too interested, to see their real Friends and Interest."[20] All one can say about Shaftesbury's zeal was that it was more inspired by reason than is usually the case. Perhaps Lord Carbery might have given in if Shaftesbury had ever been able to communicate with him; as things turned out, one is glad that he didn't.

19. The Earl of Shaftesbury to Robert Molesworth, Beachworth, June 3, 1709, *ibid.*, 36.
20. The Earl of Shaftesbury to Robert Molesworth, Chelsea, June 15, 1709, *ibid.*, 37–38.

Apparently Lord Carbery never did consent to his daughter's marrying. Anne waited but a few months after his death early in 1713 to marry the grandest, in terms of title at least, of her suitors, Lord Charles Pawlet (1685–1754), heir to Shaftesbury's old enemy the Duke of Bolton. It was a marriage based wholly on money and in even fewer months Pawlet made this absolutely clear. As Lady Mary Montagu says rather delicately, "My Lord made her an early confession of his aversion." He finally settled down with Lavinia Fenton (1708–1766), Polly Peacham of *The Beggar's Opera*, who was his mistress for twenty-three years. To prove his love, though—and emphasize his detestation of the paragon—he offered a preferment to whatever clergyman would be ready to marry them after news of Anne's death arrived. Joseph Warton (1722–1800), the bishop-to-be, took him up on this and traveled with them on the Continent in 1751. One is happy to report that he left a little too soon.

It remains only to comment on Shaftesbury's political activity in the latter part of 1708. As the time grew near for him to present himself at Court, his attitude grew more favorable toward the ministry, and, as we have seen, he had a further falling out with the Junto, so that he began to look forward with more pleasure to the whole prospect and is flattered that his views are taken seriously. Unfortunately this was not the year and he was able to appear only few times in the summer and perhaps once in the fall. Looking back to his first visit to Godolphin, he remarks, "The little time I have had since with him, I employ'd the best I cou'd, in such advices and such offers of service as became me."[21]

Actually when the rest of the Junto came in during December 1708 Shaftesbury was pleased. He was especially happy about the closeness of Somers to Godolphin, and Lord Wharton he considered true steel, though to Molesworth he disapproved of his private morals in a way he might not have five to ten years before. The proof of the new ministry's integrity is that they accepted his Tory friend and neighbor, Lord Pembroke, as head of the Admiralty, though they might have preferred some lesser Whig. In all, he felt that the world

21. The Earl of Shaftesbury to Robert Molesworth, Beachworth, January 6, 1709, *ibid.*, 19.

was coming around to his way of thinking, though he had also learned something about his own species of idealist:

> The rugged paths we walk through, give us a rugged pace; and the idle supine illiterate creatures of a Court-education, have a thousand advantages above us: and can easier borrow from our character than we from theirs; tho' of right there shou'd be nothing fair and handsome, in which we shou'd come behind 'em. And it ought to be a shame, that a mere Courtier shou'd, for his Interest-sake, be more assiduous and better behav'd in every respect; than the man who makes court for his Country.[22]

As one might expect, very little of Shaftesbury's correspondence has survived for the early winter of 1708–1709, when he was frozen in at Beachworth. The only things of interest are his letters to Furly on the subject of the latter's irrepressible altruism in a case of civil injustice in Amsterdam. The victim, an attorney, paid £400 on behalf of an East Indian merchant, who had amassed his wealth after leaving as a poor soldier, and the money was to repay the widow of a man from whom he had borrowed while he still lived in Holland. Since the money was to go to orphans if there were no heir, the attorney tried to get a full copy of the will to make sure the widow was the heir, but had to be satisfied with an extract which seemed to prove her rights. Only years later when he was ordered to pay another £150 did he learn that she was only the heir so long as she did not marry again. She had remarried before the original repayment, so that the attorney sued the lady for £400. Apparently she was a widow of much influence, for the alderman, the sheriff, and even the church which had custody of the orphans all turned against him. The attorney lost the suit, the sheriff won a criminal libel suit against him, and, the last we hear of him, he was sentenced to twenty-five years in an insane asylum—all of which is described in lurid detail.

In reply to an urgent request that he intervene, Shaftesbury replies that he no longer has the influence in Holland he once had. Furthermore, he says, "I am one who out of Love to Common-Weal and the

---

22. The Earl of Shaftesbury to Robert Molesworth, Beachworth, January 6, 1709, *ibid.*, 20.

Interest & Reputation of free Governments (besides my particular Affection for that Mother-Nation of Liberty) wou'd do all I cou'd to hide & conceal these Blemishes & cover the Nakedness of our Dear Parent."[23] These anomalies arise because, in a democratic state, authority must be deputed to men, who are after all human. How much worse it would be in a monarchy where the whole citizenry is constantly under threat. Again, in appealing to the public, the attorney is practicing sedition, which may be justified against an absolutist state but is most dangerous to a republican government.

Both old friends shortly realized that they had gone too far, too hastily. Furly apologized for seeking Shaftesbury's aid. He had been to The Hague and realized that he would have to leave the poor gentleman's fate to Providence. Shaftesbury admitted he had been too hot against sedition. Perhaps he remembered that the Queen thought he had supported sedition at home. His only concern was for Furly's health:

> Tis your self I am concern'd for, & griev'd to hear how you have expos'd your self for this Gentleman's sake. I hope that what you have remaining of Health & Strength, you will manage better for the future. As for my own State of Health tis so very indifferent & I have again pass'd another so sad a Winter; that I speak feelingly. What I have remaining of Life, I will employ the best I can. But the less I have; the better I ought to manage it. And this is my Duty as it is yours.[24]

The spirit of malignity which had grown up between Anthony and Maurice during the eighteen months since the younger brother had absolutely refused to marry seems to have weakened somewhat after the Earl decided to do his best to carry on the title himself. Maurice is both pleased and surprised at the outcome of the two brothers' melancholy task of settling the estate of their old Huguenot physician, Lewis Pau, in March 1709. Dr. Pau had served Locke once, and when they were in London, he treated both brothers, as he had the tutor of whom they both were fond, Daniel Denoune.

The two brothers were executors of the estate and Coste helped Maurice to catalog the library. Pau in his will revealed that his son

---

23. The Earl of Shaftesbury to Benjamin Furly, January 13, 1709, in PRO 30/24/21/168.
24. The Earl of Shaftesbury to Benjamin Furly [1709], in PRO 30/24/21/167.

had been born before he married his wife Lucretia; perhaps it was necessary to admit this in order to protect the trust he left for the child. None of Shaftesbury's several letters have been found; Maurice makes it clear in his weighty prose, though, that his brother speaks of him warmly:

> I cannot omit the adding my own [thanks] for your approbation of my endeavours to execute the desires & dying requests of an Old Acquaintance whose conversation and Skill in his profession, I cannot but think have been an entertainment & advantage both to you & me. My thanks are the more owing because you are pleas'd to refer the beginning of the friendship you shew'd him, to his entertaining you with an account of me & to the recommendation of One who lov'd me.[25]

Late in March of 1709 Shaftesbury commented in a letter to Joseph Micklethwayte, "I have no time to write to your Brother this post: the good weather being come at last has for this day or two set me at liberty to take the Air & I have been very buisy with my Workmen & affaires." This sums up the two months from mid February to mid April. As we have seen, Shaftesbury had a mixture of good, bad, and indifferent servants—not the sort of household to which one returns, two months late, with pleasant expectations. Furthermore the incredibly severe winter must have left its traces everywhere, though with regard to crops England was better off than the Continent.

As to the affairs which busied him, and which, he thinks, were in part responsible for his own illness later, the letters offer us a sample. To William Bowles, Jr., of Shaftesbury, whose only distinction seems to be that he is an ancestor of the poet of that name, he writes a very bitter letter about the son of John Gatehouse who has been sent off as a soldier undeservingly:

> I have heitherto no way shewn my self an Enemy to you or your Family. And Mr. Nicholas well knows the Fairness of my proceedings. If Friendly measures are to be broaken I must acquaint others with it and determin my self accordingly. in the mean while I must desire to know upon what foot I stand, that I may either acquit you of the trouble of

25. Maurice Ashley to the Earl of Shaftesbury, March 24, 1709, in PRO 30/24/22/1/12.

any future correspondence, or shew my self as I am inclined to be, Sir, your humble servant.[26]

Bowles, who was likely to be older than Shaftesbury, is obviously a Tory, but of course he cannot afford to receive from the principal nobleman of the town a letter wherein all the polite phrasings of the day are meticulously inverted against him and his.

Or, for another example, consider the Costards Bushes, which once again troubled the peace of his tree-loving soul, as they had almost every year since he became an earl, and before that. This time he replies to Cropley, who had told him that he heard expostulations against Shaftesbury's own harvest of timber, which Shaftesbury feels have provoked open cutting by his opponents:

> Whatever others doe, [I] will my self be strict in my word, that let officers do what they will, I will do nothing against Mr. Freke on that account, till I have sent and writ to let him know, and to hear directly whether it be by his orders or no, that any trees at Costars are cutt down: for tho' all were to be cutt down at once, I would suffer it rather than stirr till I had acquir'd his answer, and bin assur'd of his setting me at Liberty from my word.[27]

These two letters do illustrate a change which has gradually become obvious in Shaftesbury's reactions to trouble in his later years. He is on the whole less litigious, less prone to look for trouble. On the other hand, when he is absolutely sure he is in the right, he comes out with it, bluntly, and whether his antagonist is Bowles or Lord Somers, it makes no difference. Some of this may be simply the result of a naturally candid man maturing. It is also true that he feels now less conspired against, or, better, being both courted and obviously respected for his moral strictness, he has a sense of power which can counter any conspiracy against him.

As he tells us in his diary, Shaftesbury left St. Giles's House for Chelsea on April 5, and he must have been full of hope that Molesworth had persuaded Lord Carbery to change his mind. He had no

26. The Earl of Shaftesbury to William Bowles, Jr., April 3, 1709, in PRO 30/24/22/4/p. 107.

27. The Earl of Shaftesbury to Sir John Cropley, April 2, 1709, in PRO 30/24/22/4/p. 106.

chance to find out right away how Molesworth had succeeded, for he no sooner reached Chelsea than asthma settled in on his weakened body and he was forced to flee to the fresher air of Beachworth. The first letter we have from Chelsea this spring was written to Furly near the end of May, enclosing a letter to introduce his old friend to Lord Townshend, who was ambassador plenipotentiary to Holland at the time. He admits that he is weak, and a few days later in June he is back at Beachworth, the letter to Carbery still unwritten. Perhaps he wanted to make sure that he could follow up the letter personally, though he also must have feared writing it too.

It was from Beachworth that he sent a copy to Lord Somers of his newly published *Sensus Communis: An Essay on the Freedom of Wit and Humour* along with a very strange letter of dedication, if it could be called that; for none of his books was publicly dedicated to Somers, though two of them were directed to him as letters to an anonymous lord. This letter was strange because only on the surface was it the typical effusion on Somers' virtues; most of it was a long, complex, and very sour irony on the official reaction to his *Letter Concerning Enthusiasm*. There had been only a trace of this in his more conventional letter that went along with *The Moralists* the previous December. Perhaps now it was becoming clear to Shaftesbury just how bitter the response of popular writers and clerics was. Whatever his impulse, the irony is so complex and intricate that it is often ineffective. One can no longer clearly orient appearance and reality, so that the satire loses some of its force. The letter is worth glancing at, though, because it is a candid expression of his ideas to another nobleman. Most scholars in discussing Shaftesbury's ideas at this time turn to the conveniently printed letters to Michael Ainsworth. As we have seen, these letters are in a sense candid, but they spring from another persona and their often pious tones conceal the sort of thoughts and convictions we see here. Speaking of his writing the *Essay*, Shaftesbury says that "all his Aim is, in plain sense to recommend *plain Honesty* which in the Bussle Made about Religion is fairly dropt. The Defenders of Religion as well as its Opposers are contented to make nothing of a Meer Name of Virtue. The Priest (as a Trader) makes a bargain of it, or Lottery-Adventure with a sure Return of a Million per Cent and more, if you have the Luck to hear good Councell and chuse the right Fund. The Atheist (a cautious Dealer) supposes it a Game of Interest; a Play for Fame or Fortune. Neither of the two comprehend that Honest Motto *prodesse quam conspici.*"[28]

The last three and one half pages of the letter are an expansion on the theme that, "as the Case of our Salvation is stated to us," Somers is sure to go to Hell, while a country curate who has saved a soul or two will enjoy the pleasures of Heaven:

> For the *Children of Light* have a Magnanimouse Contempt of this *earthly Jerusalem*, and pray daily for its Distruction, and for the coming of that Kingdom which shall put an end to all *Fleshly Power and Worldly Gloryes*. But for us *Worldlings* who are given to think so gloriously of our Country and the Prosperity of our Nation, and Brethren *after the Flesh*, tis in reality, my Lord, a great Happiness for us, And very much our Interest that your soul should be in no better a way than it is. We cannot however be but sorry that It should fare the worse hereafter in an other world, for having taken so much Care of us and our affaires in this.

Perhaps the bitterest lines in this speculation on Somers' coming damnation are in the passage where he turns to the war and suggests that so far as he is concerned there is little to choose between the priests of his eternal enemy, France, and those of the Church of England: "What souls your Lordship may have help'd to save for Eternity God Knows. 'Tis certain, many Sinners have bin sent, without Confession or Absolution, into an other world, dureing this Bloody Warr; which 'tis confess'd may be too justly lay'd at your Doore. And if wee allow Salvation in the Romish Church, tis in vain to plead for your Lordship that by this warr alone we have bin saved from Persecution and Dragooning." English writers did not ever benefit directly, as the Continentals did, from Shaftesbury's aesthetic theories, but long after his ethics had been corrupted and degenerated into a fad and he himself became regarded as a trivial writer, his countrymen never forgot that in attacking the Cevennois he had made ridicule the test of truth and thereby seemed to threaten the faith of many Englishmen.

28. The Earl of Shaftesbury to Lord Somers, May 2, 1709, in PRO 30/24/22/4/ pp. 111–14. Probably, "To do good for the sake of doing good."

We do not know when it came into Shaftesbury's mind that he should follow the advice of his grandfather and marry a woman who was simply of good family rather than his impossible paragon, one who, instead of possessing an education which must have made her a species of moral bluestocking, was simply well-bred, a lady who offered neither Anne's beauty nor wealth. His thoughts on the matter he outlined to Molesworth on the nineteenth of July. This he did after he had made up his mind whom he was going to marry, though he did say to Molesworth:

> What a Weakness then . . . wou'd it be thought in me, to marry with Little or no Fortune, and not into the highest degree of Quality neither? Will it be enough, that I take a Breeder out of a good Family, with a right Education, befitting a mere Wife, and with no advantages but simple Innocence, Modesty, and the plain Qualities of a good Mother, and a good Nurse? . . . Can you and my other Friends, who press me to this, bear me out in it? . . . The Experiment, however, shall be made, if I live out the Summer.[29]

From other letters, it is obvious that he is asking Molesworth, "Since you have been pressing me to marry, can you stand behind me in this sort of marriage?" She is to be like the wife in Horace's second epode, which he cites, chiefly married for her chastity and, in the older sense of the word, her virtue.

This is a Stoic choice and not only does he not care how many realize this, he is prepared to revel in their mingled discomfort and scorn. All those who misunderstood his courtship of Lady Anne will see their error, and at the same time he is turning his back on his class and their motives for marriage: the frank pursuit of fortune, the desire for power and security that is satisfied by having the right relations, and a wife preferably beautiful but if not, at the least fashionable. The secrecy with which he is going to proceed will first ensure that no one interferes; secondly, it will ensure the maximum theatrical impact when the marriage occurs.

Ten days before his letter to Molesworth Shaftesbury had written to Wheelock that he is now engaged in earnest.

29. The Earl of Shaftesbury to Robert Molesworth, Beachworth, July 19, 1709, in PRO 30/24/22/4/pp. 128–29.

She is well born on both sides Father's and Mother's, and in both senses of a good Family, and of worthy, virtuouse and good Parent's, right to the Publick, related to me, and long acquainted. But as particular Friends as they are, I have not seen any of 'em this 8. or 9. Year since my Health chang'd, and I retir'd from Town and Business. . . .

I know more of them, as to their Characters, than I ever can expect to know of any Woman while I live. They are a healthy sound Breed, and the Youngest (they tell me) is the strongest Constitution of all, well proportion'd, and of good Make. No Beauty—— More I know not as to her Person: for I shall not see her my self, till I have determin'd all else.[30]

Shaftesbury had decided on Jane (1689?–1751), the youngest daughter of a country gentleman, Thomas Ewer of Bushy Hall, Hertfordshire. I have suggested that one of Shaftesbury's links to the family was her sister Nan, the heroine of the poem "The Golden Lovers."

We have seen several occasions where Shaftesbury lost the coolness with which he tried to look upon life, so that it comes as no surprise that he lost it again as he approached the borders of this strange new world. Shaftesbury's letters grow progressively more frantic, all the more so because, despite his very good health during the period, he kept falling further and further behind the schedule he had laid out for himself.

One problem was getting all the legal matters settled. Because he was rather self-consciously marrying without money, there were few papers to be signed, simply a jointure of six hundred pounds and a few other papers, including some changes in his will. Shaftesbury's habit of retaining the best possible professional assistance worked against him now, because Robert Eyre (1666–1735), later Lord Chief Justice, could not be found, no matter how hard Wheelock sought him. Finally, Shaftesbury gave up and again pressed Samuel Mead into service.

When the papers were arranged and signed, he saw his bride to be, and one of the challenges he had set himself was resolved most pleasantly. He had decided to marry without regard to money, and if all he heard regarding Jane Ewer were true, he was also marrying

30. The Earl of Shaftesbury to John Wheelock, July 9, 1709, in PRO 30/24/22/4/ p. 130.

without regard to beauty. This may be why he referred to her as a breeder in his letter to Molesworth; the word had been in good usage during Shakespeare's day, but was approaching the point where it was derogatory when applied to humans. It was pure serendipity to discover, then, that she was not homely, though he retains some suspicions about his own judgment in deciding otherwise. On the eighth of August he writes to Wheelock from Windsor, where he had gone to see Godolphin.

> But I can now tell you (which I cou'd not before) that I have seen the Young Lady and I protest I think she is injur'd in having been represented to me as *no Beauty* for so I writ you word before I had seen her. Whether I am partial I can't say positively. for when one comes, as I did, to the sight of one whom one had chosen by Character & had determin'd to be one's Wife; one may be allow'd to be a little byass'd in judgment as to the person & appearance of the Lady. one may be suppos'd to see with other Eyes than ordinary and 'tis fitt it shou'd be so. Therefore with these *other Eyes* of mine, let me tell you I think I was wrong when I said from common Report, that she was *no Beauty*. For I think her a *very great Beauty*.[31]

This change of life also offers an opportunity for retrenchment. We have no way of knowing whether a change was necessary or not. He had been living on a reduced scale since his return from Holland, most of the improvements at Wimborne St. Giles having been made before he left. He now plans to sell the Chelsea house, transfer the library there to St. Giles's House, and choose some place near London where there is better air. The Chelsea house may have been large enough for his new situation, but by now he had established that at no time of the year could he be sure of breathing there. His case is so much like Locke's that one wonders whether, if he had had the good sense to spend long periods at some place so remote as Oates, he might not have lived his life out normally. On the other hand, Locke was not a political idealist, nor did he have a Stoic attitude toward his own survival.

He also wants to retrench at St. Giles's House and bitterly re-

---

31. The Earl of Shaftesbury to John Wheelock, August 8, 1709, in PRO 30/24/21/177.

proaches Wheelock, who seemed to have been expecting money to be added to the estate by the marriage.

> Pray mark all my Steps & see on what Rule and principle I proceed. *Debt* you know I cannot, nor will bear. Fortune I now expect not by a Wife. I have purchas'd Pentridge. I have a Sister's portion unpaid. I have Bond and Book Debts besides. And do you think I will have double Houskeeping & an Estate in Hand?—No—I have my Stock to part with. the Time is good for it. 'Twill yield me a price, & My Old Servants & Lazy Parish-Drones & Hangers on must look out for themselves. My Baylif must have due notice from you. My Under Baylif & Granary-Man must go to his Estate. Brewers, Bakers &c. must be retrench'd. No more Stewards to succeed Dalicourt, & You alone by Parry under you, must do with what is left.[32]

As usual in such families, it is Wheelock, the steward, who does the dirty work. And as to the stringencies Shaftesbury is carrying out, his estate is not large for his rank, but most of his peers would be lucky if theirs were as well managed, despite the shortcomings. On the other hand, who can say what might have happened had he not become hypersensitive about poverty every few years?

The house where Shaftesbury planned to move was Little Doods in Reigate, which was owned by Nathaniel Owen, a Quaker.[33] Shaftesbury knew the air to be good, since Beachworth was so close, and it must have been comforting to know that Sir John Cropley was nearby. Somers was lord of the manor at Reigate, though he did not live there. Little Doods still stands, on land once monastic, and because it is such a compact structure, one can get the feel of how it must have appeared to Shaftesbury then. The wall in front, which once had a gate where pilgrims on the way to Canterbury were fed, stands right on the street. Across a shallow courtyard the house rises, heavily gabled with steep, tiled roofs. It looks to have been built in the middle or early part of the seventeenth century. Although most of it is now obscured by vegetation, the house is framed in wood, with the bulk of the surface covered in what appears to be plaster, gray in tint. The facade is obtrusive and pushes at you, be-

32. The Earl of Shaftesbury to John Wheelock, July 22, 1709, in PRO 30/24/21/174.
33. Wilfrid Hooper, *Reigate: Its Story Through the Ages* (Guildford, 1945), 151.

cause from the long gable roof two gables thrust forward, and between them, covering the front door, a porte-cochere sticks out even further than the gables, modeled after them but only one story high, rather than two. A third story peers out, set well up in the main gable. The fine doubled bay windows, which look out at you, are the best feature of the facade. No one of the four sets is exactly like another, yet this hardly disturbs the vigorous symmetry of those gables. The tall windows do not prepare one for the fact that the ceilings inside are relatively low for the area of the rooms. It does not pay to theorize about interiors at this distance in time. One hopes that the ornately splendid central staircase and the fine decorations carved in the wood trim were there in Shaftesbury's day. From the abundance of windows in the back one looks out on a garden several times the size of the court in front of the house.

The fashionable world knew that Shaftesbury's Chelsea house was for sale. This he had no objection to, since it would make a buyer easier to find, but he was most anxious that they learn nothing whatsoever about his other plans. First, there is Reigate to take care of. He is sure that something can be worked out about the two housekeepers he is to have there, Belle Skinner, who had moved to St. Giles's House some time before, and Mrs. Herbert from Chelsea. But how is he to keep the world, neighbors and tradesmen, away from his door? The thing to do is to move in gradually. He tells Wheelock, "Now if I come & pass but a night or two there & am off & on, for a week or two before your Return from St. Giles's, the Stare will be over & I shall less disoblige Mr. Thurland & the forward Neighbourhood of such a tattling, gossiping Place, in refusing to receive company at the very first. They will be us'd to my retirement afterwards & when the Wonderment is over, they will not rail at me for Pride or Humour in refusing Visitants."[34]

Even Shaftesbury's brother apparently did not know of his approaching marriage. Wheelock is told to "take notice, & set down the time it [a letter to Maurice] was deliver'd. for I design to give time for answer (from my brother I mean) before I conclude the

34. The Earl of Shaftesbury to John Wheelock, Beachworth, Tuesday Night, in PRO 30/24/21/176. Edward Thurland was a member of a prominent local family. Owen had purchased Little Doods from him.

Buisness intirely." But sending the letter is obviously a formality, for his brother has little opportunity to refuse. It is to be "left about 7 or 8 a Clock *at his Lodging*, whether he be there or no." The messenger is not to inquire as to where his brother is but is to proceed directly to Lord Godolphin with a similar message for him. Lady Rachel Russell was also to receive a letter that day.[35] His friends are to have short notice too. Again to Wheelock he says,

> And in reality shou'd I not find you (as I do the rest of my Friends & well wishers) heartily delighted & rejoyced with this prospect I have given, it will be very surprizing to me. . . . I shall distinguish Affections towards me at this time by the Tokens of this kind (whether of Joy or Heavyness) better than by any thing else that has happened, or can ever happen in my Life. Those who have been ungratefull, Unworthy & treacherouse Friends will be thunderstruck with this account when they hear what they so little expected; believing all my Talks of Marriage to be only threats or boasts: and that if any thing tempted me it wou'd not be so much my Family's preservation & Concern of Children, as Riches, Interest, or at least Witt, Beauty or some of those tempting objects which they thought I was by my retirement, safe from.[36]

It must be a great thing at one stroke to separate the sheep from the goats among your friends, but as most of us would, Shaftesbury approaches the moment with mixed feelings.

As the happy day approaches, Shaftesbury's letters grow more and more repetitive and yet harder to understand. Since he is to marry out of church and canonical hours, Wheelock must pick up his license from the archbishop, "or his next underling (I know not what his title is)." He also worries Wheelock continually about the ring, and one can sense how proud he is already of Jane. "I fear you have forgot the Gold Ring. Pray get a handsome plain one immediately of this size (which I here enclose) or rather a little bigger, because of allowance for growing plump, since at present they [her fingers] are lean tho' large & strong as you have seen."[37]

35. The Earl of Shaftesbury to John Wheelock, Thursday Morn., in PRO 30/24/21/178. The letters referred to are dated August 24.
36. The Earl of Shaftesbury to John Wheelock, Windsor, August 8, 1709, in PRO 30/24/21/177.
37. The Earl of Shaftesbury to John Wheelock, August 25, 1709, in PRO 30/24/21/178.

Four days after this on August 29 Shaftesbury was married at Beachworth to Jane Ewer. His friends, most of whom must have feared for the success of his first choice, were delighted. Lady Wentworth probably reflects the opinion of the fashionable world: "Lady Shaftesbury is . . . . a pryvit Gentlewoman of noe great famely, her name is youer or such a kynd of name. Ther is a mother and another sister, but he has carred her without soe much as one sarvent of hers with her to a hous he has at Rygate, whear he had provyded a good discreet wayting woman for her of Bell Skinners' recommending. Bell Skinner is with them as a companyon; al this is under the Rose, I beg."[38] Shaftesbury could not have cared what they thought or felt that he should conceal, so long as they left him alone. A few days before the marriage he gave his own opinion to Wheelock: "There is nothing on Earth wanting to me: & I have fulfilled in all respects the Injunctions of my Grandfather & have taken care of his honour & Name & Posterity, after that the ill usage & Ingratitude of others had made me despair, & apprehend nothing remaining but Ignominy."[39]

By moving too rapidly into the house at Reigate, Shaftesbury caught a severe cold but by the end of September had so completely recovered that to Cropley he appeared better than he had for many years, so well that Sir John hoped the public too would have good signs of it. He seems to wish that Shaftesbury would be able to take some more conspicuous role in the ministry of Godolphin, who in a reply to a letter thanking him for his congratulations on the marriage had pressed Shaftesbury to visit the Court again and kiss the Queen's hand. Enough was known of his sort of illness at the time that the vanity of any hope that Shaftesbury could become really active and continue to live should have been obvious even to Sir John. Shaftesbury himself, living in his day-to-day pattern, certainly did not share these illusions.

One of the last letters of congratulations came from General Stanhope in Spain, who had been in an attack on Cadiz, which to his dis-

38. Lady Wentworth to Lord Raby, December 9, 1709 in Cartwright (ed.), *Wentworth Papers*, 98–99.

39. The Earl of Shaftesbury to John Wheelock, August 25, 1709, in PRO 30/24/21/178.

appointment came to no conclusion. I have remarked elsewhere that their friendship had begun several years before, though this in itself does not account for his being appointed a trustee of Shaftesbury's estates when they had spent so little time together. How did he become the sort of friend whom the Earl would trust with this responsibility? To Shaftesbury, Stanhope was a man who, in Marvell's words, both knew and acted, one of the few people who had a solid grasp of Shaftesbury's ideas and was at the same time an active person who could put them into effect. As Shaftesbury points out, this is an ancient habit fallen wholly out of fashion. There was a time when military commanders not only carried the philosophers' works as Stanhope does but the philosophers themselves, "if they could tempt them abroad." Some of Stanhope's weaknesses as a military commander must have been apparent at the time—his impatience of bureaucratic complexity which led him to rashness; others, such as the strategic weakness of his whole campaign in Spain, are better seen by hindsight. On the other hand, Stanhope's firmness, his courage, his genuine warmth and affability, and his Stoicism in the loss of his brothers were clearly evident then. In any case, Shaftesbury regarded the whole Spanish expedition as a too convenient form of exile for Stanhope, long before he was captured and the Tories made it one in reality by not seeking his release. Shaftesbury saw politics as Stanhope's true vocation.

All this explains why Stanhope is one of the few persons who received philosophical letters from Shaftesbury. In a letter thanking him for the congratulations, for instance, Shaftesbury gives his final views on Locke. There is no doubt about his deep personal affection for Locke and his sense of indebtedness. Philosophically, Locke is at once an ally and an enemy. He destroys scholasticism effectively, for "he is of admirable Use against the Rubbish of the Schools, in which most of us have been bred up." But instead of looking back as Shaftesbury does at the glories of ancient thought thus revealed, Locke creates new patterns of thought, on morally insecure foundations, because he is in truth still fighting the schoolmen. "*A ghost indeed!* Since 'tis not in reality the Stagirite himself nor original Perapatetick Hypothesis, but the poor secondary tradatitiouse System of modern and barbarouse Schoolmen which is the subject of their continual Triumph."[40]

Almost all of the rest of Shaftesbury's correspondence for 1709 involves his marriage. There are few exceptions. Robert Molesworth writes a long letter in November which begins with more congratulations, then he applauds his own role at some length, and finally gets down to business, which is to persuade Shaftesbury, whose health has now improved, that he should pay court at St. James's twice a week. Not that he wishes Shaftesbury to risk asthma; even if he should get as far as Lambeth and sense a shift in the wind, he should turn back to Reigate. It is too bad that we do not have the reply to this. The following month there are two letters in Latin— almost undecipherable—from de Wit which deal with the intricacy of Dutch politics. The letter which must have delighted him the most was from Le Clerc in Amsterdam sending a copy of his edition of Menander, dedicated to Shaftesbury. This was the greatest tribute a proponent of the Ancients could receive and Shaftesbury waited a long time. As early as 1689 he had received a note from Padua telling him that a scholar named Patin would be happy to dedicate his book on ancient marbles to him and there is a manuscript among the Shaftesbury Papers which looks like part of the book, yet the copy of the book I have examined has no dedication to Shaftesbury. Then, too, he had hoped that Gronovius would dedicate his *Epictetus* to him, and he probably would have, had he not already decided on the Grand Duke of Tuscany. Obviously a scholar of the stature of Gronovius did not have to peddle his dedications, and certainly Shaftesbury would have been hesitant to suggest himself. Le Clerc was no Gronovius, as Shaftesbury knew, but he felt the dedication of the Menander was well worth the two hundred pounds he sent him.

We have very little information about Lord Shaftesbury's life in 1710, very much less than for any year since he became an earl, and it contrasts strongly with the last two years of his life for which we could, if we wished, put together a week-by-week account. Lady

40. The Earl of Shaftesbury to General James Stanhope, November 7, 1709, in PRO 30/24/22/7/pp. 9–13.

Wentworth's reaction to his marriage is about typical of what he must have imagined the fashionable world would be saying behind his back, and the thought must have reinforced his determination to live in great privacy in order to regain his health, to withdraw still further from a world into which he had barely emerged for seven years. He also needed quiet because he was pouring much of the energy he had available into writing. *An Essay on the Freedom of Wit and Humour* appeared in June of 1709. Between this date and the end of March 1711, when the volumes of his works began to appear, it seems likely that he wrote most of *Soliloquy*, about 200 pages long, and all of the *Miscellaneous Reflections*, say 350 more, then put all of his books into *Characteristicks*, three volumes meticulously edited with elaborate footnotes and an index, and including a revised version of his *Inquiry*. All of this may explain why Shaftesbury wrote so few letters, or, rather, wrote so few that he needed rough drafts for or kept copies of, but it does not account for the absence of letters written to him. These must have been lost; it seems unlikely he would have discarded all of them.

There are only two letters in his copybooks for the first five months of 1710. The first is a letter of recommendation for Mr. Lisle of Weymouth to Lord Godolphin.[41] The only interesting point here is that Shaftesbury remarks that this is the first favor he has asked since Thomas Micklethwayte's appointment in 1708; Godolphin must have wished he had more such friends. The other letter is a rather ironic note to Thomas Walker, the genealogist, correcting some copy for a genealogical text he proposed. He finishes, "Your Book must needs have been incorrect since in two or three places I have corrected my own Name, which you will see right spelt; as I subscribe Your humble Servant, Shaftesbury."[42]

There is one other item from the period among the papers: a detailed account of the discussions on March 16, 1710, in the House of Lords on the case of Henry Sacheverell. As his note to Godolphin suggests, Shaftesbury had little to do with politics in 1709. Even if

41. If Godolphin is being asked to help town officials, as he promised to, this is probably George Lisle who was mayor of Weymouth in 1696 and again in 1708.
42. The Earl of Shaftesbury to Thomas Walker, Reigate, April 23, 1710, in PRO 30/24/22/7/p. 15.

there had been occasion he would hardly have had time—frozen in at Beachworth, then to remote Dorsetshire, and finally back to London, again, to be immersed in property transactions and his marriage. In 1710, though, no one with Shaftesbury's interests could ignore politics.

With the appointment of Lord Orford (1653–1727) as First Lord of the Admiralty in November 1709, all of the Junto but Lord Halifax were in the government. The price they paid for this was excessive, though. Every concession Queen Anne was forced to make strengthened her determination to do something drastic in order to rid herself of the Junto's tyranny, and Harley was standing beside her in the background. She did need Marlborough. On the other hand, though the Queen turned her back on his wife, the Duchess was not willing to let her forget her presence. Moreover, the country was weary of war and Louis had sought peace for two years and was willing to settle to England's advantage but for certain provisions for Spain which the Whigs insisted upon. So when Henry Sacheverell (1674?–1724) preached a Guy Fawkes Day sermon, later widely reprinted, favoring nonresistance and condemning toleration and occasional conformity, and Godolphin and the Junto decided to punish him, not in the courts as Somers suggested, but by impeaching him in the House of Commons, the priest became a martyr and a popular hero. The mechanism that would destroy the ministry was set in motion.

Barely twenty years had passed since the Revolution and a Jacobitical priest now rises to advocate a state of mind which would have made it impossible, and he is listened to widely. One principle Shaftesbury never wavered on was the superiority of the claims of a freely chosen House of Commons and the House of Lords in any struggle for power with either the Crown or the clergy. On the other hand, this does not mean listening to the mob, and it is most ironic when professors of conformity to authority seek to use the mob to destroy a government, as he feels the Tories had done in April. The people as a whole deserve only praise for their restraint.

And such is the Disposition of those pretended loyal men . . . who but a month ago were raising Sedition & appealing to the People whom in their hearts they abhorr. But Thanks be to God the sound part of our

People were far from being mov'd. They bore the insolence of the Conspirators & suffer'd many days the Insults of a lewd, jacobitical & popish Rabble, of which not one is like to be punish'd by the Government. They cou'd have easily . . . righted themselves & defended their Houses & the Persons of their Friends: but so noble a Testimony have those call'd Whiggs given of their regard to Magistracy, that when unprotected & expos'd, they wou'd do nothing in their own defense.[43]

As he tells Le Clerc on July 19, he is forced to leave Reigate immediately for St. Giles's House because of the ferment that has been raised in Dorsetshire as elsewhere by the Sacheverell affair. We don't know when he finally returned to Reigate, but he probably took with him his wife, who had not been pregnant long. Shortly after he arrived in Dorset he received a letter from Sir John telling him that the dissolution of the present Parliament is inevitable. This Shaftesbury feels will be dreadful for Europe and must in part be due to the conniving of France. "Wo be to the Instruments they have employ'd for this purpose; and double Wo to those Apostate Brittishmen, who have push'd this affair so far, that if they do not at once carry all for France, and the St. Germain Family, are for ever undone." On the other hand, the Revolution is probably safe. "I value not what Parliament there is: We can have none that will undo what the Last has done and pronounc'd in the cause of Liberty and the Revolution. All they can do is to strike at some particular Men."[44] Commonwealthmen such as he and Cropley are right in feeling ambivalently toward the Whig politicos. If they can extricate themselves, fine. If not, we should remember the dastardly things they have done to us. "They made Us suffer sufficiently. 'Tis their Turn to feel: Let em not murmer."

Only one letter of Cropley's from this series remains. The chief interest to us is that it shows how anxious Harley was to court Shaftesbury, but it begins with a strange remark about the coolness of Lord Somers: "I take it for granted he will lay down but I take it as much for granted he is & has acted so coldly that he has some views

43. Lord Shaftesbury to Benjamin Furly, May 22, 1710, in PRO 30/24/21/183.
44. The Earl of Shaftesbury to Sir John Cropley, July 24, 1710, in PRO 30/24/22/7/ pp. 20–21.

of his own." This sounds very much as if Cropley suspects Somers of dealing with Harley and the Queen.[45] When asked by Harley to set a time for a meeting between them, Cropley replied he would do so whenever it was at Harley's leisure, and then Cropley says, "I was answer'd it must be my time & that if I knock'd him up at 12 at night I might freely doe it. however I staid 'til I had a time set which was yesterday morning. I found him all alone, his business was to desire me to acquaint you that nobody on earth honour'd you more than he did & to acquaint you allso that if you had any commands for him it would be the greatest pleasure in the world to him."[46] After a number more of such flowery pronouncements, Harley assured Cropley that the war would be carried on until a good peace was made. Cropley tells Shaftesbury that he knows this advance will be received by him with finesse, neither too enthusiastically nor in any way that Harley could feel slighted.

In the reply Sir John received one can see again how the two men differed, Cropley, the practical politician, continually smoothing over the rough edges of the blunt discourse of the political idealist, Shaftesbury:

> I am very sensibly oblig'd by the Compliments and Civilitys express'd to You, in my behalf, by Mr H—— on his coming in. He dos me no more than Justice in depending on my Esteem and Friendship. . . . 'Tis what our Family-acquaintance, our common Education, and my Entrance into publick Affaires with him, and Long Union, cou'd not butt preserve inviolable. . . . As for the Little Interest or Influence I have in my Country or, wherever besides in the World, he may command it, when I see by Efects which way his Councills steer. The Measure of my Regard towards Ministers is from their Measures towards France. We shall soon see what our new Ministry will prove, in this respect.[47]

Aware that Sir John will try to phrase this more gracefully, he warns him, "And this I enjoyn You to tell him Frankly, else he shall hear from me himself in as plain Terms or plainer." There is some evidence that Harley intended to persist in courting Shaftesbury. On

---

45. Somers' biographer William L. Sachse seems to think so. See *Lord Somers*, 290–92.

46. Sir John Cropley to the Earl of Shaftesbury, n.d., in PRO 30/24/21/165.

47. The Earl of Shaftesbury to Sir John Cropley, August 19, 1710, in PRO 30/24/22/7/p. 31.

August 11, Charlwood Lawton (1660–1721), a Tory politician, writes to Harley from some place in Worcestershire, "I go tomorrow from hence and shall be next week at my Lord Shaftesbury's at St. Giles in Dorsetshire for a few days."[48]

In May of this year Michael Ainsworth finished college and Shaftesbury sent him off to his old friend Gilbert Burnet for ordination. He tells the Bishop almost all of the story of the ten-year education of the boy, bringing him up from very humble beginnings to his present status, all except the long series of letters of moral instruction he wrote him. Michael's education may not, in modern terms, have been expensive, but considering how often Shaftesbury felt pinched, it was remarkable that he never hesitated, and he showed this sort of loyalty in all of his philanthropies. The time and money, the concern, he devoted to Michael are representative of the best in Shaftesbury's benevolence; there was no political advantage or literary patronage involved, hardly the remotest possibility that Michael would attract the public's attention.

About the same time on May 26 he sent *Soliloquy* to Lord Somers with a very odd letter, even stranger than the one which had accompanied the *Essay* in 1709. After referring to a "late Combustion in the literate World," which I cannot identify unless it means that Shaftesbury's authorship of the *Letter* was somehow revealed to the reading public, he spends most of the remainder of the letter chiding the man, Somers' friend, who had threatened to publish the *Letter Concerning Enthusiasm* as a work of Jonathan Swift. Then he gives assurances to Somers that he now intends to be very discreet. Nowhere are there any periods of fulsome praise such as one might at least expect to hear an echo of, even in a private letter. Somers, as usual, remained the first one to see the work Shaftesbury had written.

There is very little other literary correspondence this year. Shaftesbury knew that Coste was translating the third part of the *Memoirs of Sir William Temple*, which had been published the year before by Jonathan Swift, because he sends him a long list of corrections relat-

48. Charlwood Lawton to Robert Harley, August 11, 1710, in Historical Manuscripts Commission's *Portland MSS.*, IV, 571.

ing to his grandfather, which he hopes will be included in the new edition of the whole work. This apparently was an *embarras de richesse* to Coste; he replies that his editor is pressing him for corrections and additions and that in any case there is not the occasion for inserting much of this, as Le Clerc had in his essay on Locke. In any case, he will do what he can.

There is also a long letter to Le Clerc in which Shaftesbury tries to console him for the attacks made by Richard Bentley (1662–1742) on his fragments of Menander. Upon seeing the Menander, Bentley sat down and was able to make *ex tempore* corrections to over three hundred passages. He then mailed the manuscript to the archenemy of Le Clerc, Peter Burman (1668–1741) in Utrecht, who published it that year with his own introduction. Bentley had used a pseudonym but Burman recognized his handwriting. Obviously Le Clerc was not qualified to edit Menander, but why Bentley would attack violently a man with whom he had once had a long period of friendship is something of a problem. The struggle attracted wide attention. Le Clerc was as much a dictator in his own field as Bentley was in classical studies, and Annie Barnes surveys most of the theories of what lay behind the animosity in her biography of Le Clerc.[49] Shaftesbury, whose admiration for Bentley's scholarship was only equaled by his discontent over the man's lack of good sense, was able to give Le Clerc the clue as to how he would be able to retaliate. Bentley had been circulating in London extracts from his *Horace*, which Shaftesbury remarked "will be the most elaborate Monster that the Learn'd world ever saw produc'd."[50] This was an exaggeration, yet there were enough weaknesses apparent when it came out the next year that Le Clerc had his revenge.

In July, Shaftesbury made a will. There had been an older one, to which he added codicils when he was married the year before; this one, however, is to reflect in proper form the changes which have taken place in his family and probably alters the trusteeship. The will itself is straightforward enough, as such things go, and it in-

49. Annie Barnes, *Jean Le Clerc et la république des lettres* (Paris, 1938), 215–24.
50. The Earl of Shaftesbury to Jean Le Clerc, July 19, 1710, in PRO 30/24/22/7/ pp. 16–19.

volves sufficient contingencies to make sure the property remains in the family: first, possible heirs male and female of the Earl are taken up, dowers specified and so forth. It then treats the heirs of Maurice. Failing succession here, the will turns to Dorothy and her family, where the eldest son, at that moment his darling nephew Ned, would inherit the estate if on reaching majority he were willing to take the name of Ashley. The children of Elizabeth, Lady Harris, are next in line.

The only surprise comes in a letter Shaftesbury wrote to Sir Samuel Eyre, his solicitor, about the will. Most of the letter is in the contingent mode, and there is little reference to things as they are. All is to be arranged so that the minimal conflict with the laws and Chancery results. When he does shift and refers not to what is possible but to what is, he says, "But as to what Objection may be made concerning my Brother's Marriage to a second Wife of a better Extract, and Fortune, in case he has no issue male by this present one." And later when he is speaking of the education of Maurice's hypothetical son by his present wife and the dangers of providing for his education he makes the comment, "For if I cannot take him from the hands of such a Mother, Family & Generation of sordid, base, enthusiastick and wicked People, I shall be the more sorry for having contributed anything to his Education and had rather he should be comitted meerly to Providence."[51]

The stone in Purton church states that Katherine Popple married Maurice in 1713, and it is clearly in error. She lost her father in 1708 and though it is painful to learn what Shaftesbury really thought of the Popples, no doubt they are the ones referred to. Since he complained bitterly before his own marriage the previous August of Maurice's refusing to marry, his brother must have married Katherine in the ten months between Shaftesbury's marriage and the writing of this letter on the third of July, 1710. In these days before the Marriage Act was passed it was possible for the plighting of a troth to constitute a marriage, and Thomas Micklethwayte may have en-

51. The Earl of Shaftesbury to Sir Samuel Eyre, July 3, 1710, in PRO 30/24/22/4/ pp. 157-59.

tered into such an arrangement with Anne Ewer, but Maurice had no reason for attempting to conceal, however briefly, the nature of his relationship with Katherine; nor would there be any legal advantage. Nothing he could do further would be likely to arouse any more wrath than Shaftesbury had already felt for him at times. A letter we have already looked at, to Sir John on August 19, closes Shaftesbury's copybook for 1710. No letters of the period directed to him seem to have survived.

❧VIII❦

The Patterns of
Shaftesbury's Later Thought
1704–1713

Before considering Shaftesbury's *Philosophical Rhapsody* it would be well to see where it lies among his more serious studies. His earliest printed philosophical work is his preface to the *Select Sermons* of Benjamin Whichcote published in 1698. He must have begun this after Thomas Firmin's death the previous year. In 1699 *An Inquiry Concerning Virtue or Merit* was published by Toland, but as we have seen there is evidence that Shaftesbury began working on it and probably completed it long before he wrote the preface to Whichcote. Still another reason for assuming that the *Inquiry* is early is that by the time *The Sociable Enthusiast* was printed his fundamental attitude toward humanity seems to have changed markedly. The same bitter judgments of humanity we find in *Inquiry I* are typical of his letters from the early 1690s—those on Carolina, for example. But a decade later, the edge has gone from his bitterness, even though he may have no better practical hopes for the human race. He has grown up, he has gone through a period of self-examination in Holland, and, despite his illness and his complaints, these are better times for him. We must also, I suppose, give some credit to the idealism of Plato, whose influence is obvious by 1700.

He began to write his "Exercises" between the time of his arrival in Holland and his return in April or May of 1699. Surely the next "philosophical" work was "The Adept Ladys," which is dated January 19, 1702. It is not yet published. Following this is *The Sociable Enthusiast*, which was printed privately in 1703 or 1704, for a very limited distribution. S. F. Whitaker in a fine article, perhaps too modest in its conclusions, established that Arent Furly had found an imperfect copy of the *Enthusiast* in Rotterdam and then described it

313

in a letter of September 6, 1704 NS.[1] This contradicts Shaftesbury's own statement about the book to Lord Somers in a letter dated October 20, 1705, that "No body has sett Eyes on it, nor shall, besides yourself."[2] Whitaker also remarks that the book appears to be of English rather than the finer Dutch workmanship, which could push the date of its printing back to 1703. The two copies in the Record Office are, so far as I know, all that survive, Arent's having disappeared and that of Lord Somers probably burned up in that infamous fire that destroyed his library.

The Sociable Enthusiast is in the form of a dialogue, which oddly enough is stripped of much of its drama by being recited in the past tense. There are three major figures: Palemon, a young man of high rank and character, who knows all about the nature of plants and animals but has little fondness for mankind. He is an engaged person and a rationalist, yet scrupulous in matters of religion. Then there is Philocles the quondam skeptic, who carries the burden of the argumentation. He knows nothing, believes all. Finally, there is Theocles, the mild enthusiast with no trace of bigotry, all understanding and forbearance. He loves the muses and they love him. Theocles bears Shaftesbury's message, but we must heed his prefatory note, that "as for the Characters, & Incidents; they are neither wholly feign'd nor wholly true."

Palemon begs Philocles to recount what they had talked about the day before, which he does and then looks back earlier to two days spent in discussion with Theocles. The sequence of tenses becomes mixed up—even Shaftesbury shows some confusion in his emendations—so that it is difficult to tell whether he recounts all three days to Palemon in one day or two. Palemon, already a convert, must in the twice-told dialogue, first appear a skeptic, only revealing the full extent of his own change in attitude at the end of the essay. Obviously, I am not the first to note how muddled the book is; in his *Miscellaneous Reflections* Shaftesbury admits its weaknesses as a dialogue and yet defends them. First, in a very long paragraph he

1. S. F. Whitaker, "The First Edition of Shaftesbury's *Moralists*," *The Library*, 5th series, VII (1952), 235–41.
2. The Earl of Shaftesbury to Lord Somers, October 20, 1705, in PRO 30/45/22/4/p. 13.

proves, by recasting it, that he could have told the story straightforwardly, but he related the story as a philosophical adventure or rhapsody to avoid giving the impression that a dialogue was involved. After all a writer must create some impression of verisimilitude and he was "put to a hard shift, to contrive how or with what probability he might introduce Men of any Note or Fashion, reasoning expressly and purposely . . . for two or three hours together, on mere PHILOSOPHY and MORALS" (Char., III, 287). These subjects are now relegated to the school, the university, and pulpit. In any case the mode is now altogether unfashionable. In the *Miscellaneous Reflections* he also speaks of "the direct way of DIALOGUE; which at present lies so low, and is us'd only now and then, in our Party-Pamphlets, or newfashion'd *theological Essays*," which is a glance at the replies in dialogue to his *Letter Concerning Enthusiasm*. It is hard to know how to take all of this, for, as the preliminary notes to Shaftesbury's *Second Characters* prove, his miscellaneous style involves one of the most complex personas of the day. He laughs at others continually, loud and very softly, but often he is the butt of his own humor.

Days one and two of *The Sociable Enthusiast: A Philosophical Adventure, Written to Palemon* are largely concerned with repeating, adding to, and rarely, modifying what has already been said in *Inquiry I*. Indeed, the book is cited and Theocles, especially, defends "our friend" against his opponents. Only one printed response to *Inquiry I* has been found so far, but enough copies of the treatise must have been distributed to cause a good deal of comment, if Shaftesbury's defense is any measure.[3]

Some of the differences between the *Inquiry* and the *Enthusiast* are due to a sagacious change in the nature of the persona he offers us. Consider the attitude toward a future state. In the *Enthusiast* a strong conviction of reward and punishment is necessary until man can be led up to affection and a disinterested love of God. The existence of a future state he proves quite traditionally by the imperfections of this world, which seldom rewards virtue. And he asks in a Miltonic vein, how would there be merit in the world without the

---

3. See A. O. Aldridge, "Shaftesbury's Earliest Critic," *Modern Philology*, XXIV (1946), 10–22.

sort of trial which an imperfect world provides? Philocles is even willing to accept miracles so long as they happened in olden times and are received from the best authorities. Neither Catholic saints nor those other saints of the seventeenth century need apply, though. Any reader of the "Exercises" knows that Shaftesbury's personal belief in these propositions is weak. But the therapeutic "Exercises" should also teach us that how a man acts is far more important than the real truth of what he believes. Contemporary Americans are especially suspicious of this theory of truth; Shaftesbury as a moralist never had any hesitations, which is one of many reasons why he is opposed to systems. Shaftesbury's moral comments, indeed his very attitudes, when he talks to servants, to farmers, or when he writes to Wilkinson, Ainsworth, or even Arent Furly are irreproachably pious in the most conventional sense.

When his ultimate purposes are metaphysical rather than moral, Shaftesbury usually speaks with a different sort of conviction:

> For as the Branch is united, and is all one with the Tree, so is the Tree with the Earth, Air, and Water, which feed it, and as much as the fertile Mold is fitted to the Tree, as much as the strong and upright Trunk of the Oak or Elm is fitted to the twining and clinging Branches of the Vine or Ivy; so much are the Leaves, the Seeds, and Fruits of these Trees fitted to the various Animals; and they again to one another, and to the Elements in which they live, and to which they are in a manner join'd, as either by Wings for the Air, Fins for the Waters, Feet for the Earth, and other things of a like nature. (SE, 91–92)[4]

Theocles is speaking, but all of the three speakers are what now would be called ecologically sound. Philocles asks Palemon, who knows much about natural history, whether the unity of visible nature does not imply a continuous design. When Palemon admits this truth, Philocles then asks whether this does not imply a universal mind which alone can view the whole universal system at once and see it reconciled of inconsistencies.

It is because Palemon sees nature as a whole that he is distressed by natural evil when it occurs. Philocles has an explanation for him new to Shaftesbury's published work. Natural evil is caused by con-

4. The last five words are explained in the 1709 edition, "inward Parts of a more curiouse nature."

flict of systems. One system is "o'erpowr'd by a superiour Rival, and by another Nature's justly conquering Force" (SE, 29). Prodigies are merely another reflection of the order persisting in the great chain of being, which is universally recognized as just in its workings. "Every corruptible and mortal Nature by its Mortality and Corruption yields only to some better, and all in common to that best and highest Nature, which is incorruptible and immortal" (SE, 29–30).

In addition to loving nature, Palemon loves individuals; but he hates mankind for their corruption. This is perhaps the weakest phase of *The Sociable Enthusiast*, for the treatise is in a sense too cosmic in its point of view to devote much time to the problem. Perhaps the best exchange takes place between Philocles and Theocles on the subject of friendship, private and public. Philocles admits that he never found it unpleasing to serve a friend. He also admits that gratitude and bounty are among the chief acts of friendship. Theocles then asks him whether weaknesses discovered in the giver should diminish gratitude in the receiver. No, Philocles replies, it makes it more satisfying because the weaknesses can be borne as failings in a friend. Theocles gets him to concede that bounty is owed to relations whether or not they are deserving. And with this he asks:

> Consider then what it was you said, when you objected against the Love of *Mankind* because of Human Frailty; and seem'd to scorn the *Publick*, because of its Misfortunes. Where can we with Pleasure exert Friendship, if not here? To what shou'd we be true and grateful in the World, if not to Mankind and that Society to which we owe so much? What are the Faults or Blemishes that can excuse such an Omission or that in a grateful Mind can ever lessen the Satisfaction of making a grateful kind Return? (SE, 45)

The appeal becomes even stronger when we recognize the strength the bonds of natural affection have for Shaftesbury, and his conviction that weak man is safe only in a strong society.

Most of what is new in *The Sociable Enthusiast* is focused in the third book where Philocles is by the rhapsodic utterances of Theocles solidly convinced of the truth of what he says. During the last thirty years or so a considerable disagreement has arisen over what Shaftesbury intended, especially when the *Enthusiast* in its successive forms is contrasted with the *Inquiry*. No two interpreters of Shaftesbury are ever likely to agree in full—he has too many roots in the past and augured too much for the future. Yet a good many of these disagreements are resolved when Shaftesbury is looked at broadly, and readers admit, as his critics sometimes fail to, that he shares the eclecticism of his day. In a world where the whole intellectual milieu was in upheaval, Shaftesbury chose a novel means to preserve his inheritance. Those who followed him, however, Continental aestheticians or English moralists or still others, picked and chose as they wished. Of course, they chose differently. Most disastrously for an understanding of what Shaftesbury attempted to do, certain phases of his thought were generally ignored by all who borrowed from him.

For the first time in *The Sociable Enthusiast* he publicly revealed how strong the appeal of the past was for him. In later editions this was toned down, so that the truth that he would have preferred to have been born a pagan was somewhat obscured. Publicly he admired Roman republicanism; philosophically he is a follower of Marcus Aurelius, Epictetus, and Xenophon; in art, the choice of Hercules was his ideal subject. Study of the Ancients is the privilege of the few but they are brothers in this regardless of rank. One of Shaftesbury's most meticulously revised letters is the one that he wrote to Pierre Coste, Locke's amanuensis, on the subject of Horace. His classical correspondents range from General Stanhope and the great Dutch scholar Gronovius, whose *Epictetus* he had hoped to have dedicated to him, to Stanhope's man of business, Arent Furly, and his own librarian Paul Crell. As Theocles remarks to Philocles in a passage on retirement, which was tactfully altered before the work was reprinted as *The Moralists*, Horace and Virgil, however different, "both join'd, to love Retirement; and for the sake of such a Life as you call contemplative, they were willing to sacrifice the highest Advantages, Pleasures, and Favour of a Court, more agreeable and polite than any that has since been known" (SE, 38).

Nor is there any question about the Platonic influence in *The Sociable Enthusiast* and elsewhere among Shaftesbury's works. Take his attitude toward science, for instance. Shaftesbury is quite willing to use the discoveries of contemporary science, but only to the point where one grasps the variety and splendor of the world and at the same time understands its underlying coherence and harmony: "But 'tis in vain for us to search the Mass it self of *Matter*: seeking to know its Nature. . . . If knowing only some of the Rules of *Motion*, we seek to trace it further, 'tis in vain we follow it into the Bodys it has reach'd. . . . In vain we try to fathom the Abyss of *Space*" (SE, 159–60). And with a glance at Locke: "In vain we labour to understand that Principle of *Sense* and *Thought*, which seeming in us to depend so much on Motion, yet differs so much from it, and from Matter it self. . . . And thus are we made sensible that the Nature of all the Beings in this Universe is *Incomprehensible* . . . attended nevertheless with such Assurance of their Existence, as is beyond the Report of these our Senses. . . . By which we may learn that the Assurance we have of the Existence of these Beings . . . comes from Thee, the God of Truth" (SE, 160–61). Nature has a greater lesson to teach.

More specifically it is clear that much of the Platonism in *The Sociable Enthusiast* follows the general pattern of the Cambridge School. Ernst Cassirer long ago cited direct parallels between John Smith's *Select Discourses* and the thought in *The Moralists*. The Cambridge men represent what was an extreme case of a growing tendency among broad churchmen, a tendency which can only be understood in relation to the growth of atomism and the stress among some writers on the sanctions of reward and punishment. Shaftesbury and the Platonists look on the Deity in an optimistic, Arminian way as a God who consults his own goodness in giving laws, a God who is served best by disinterested love, rather than slavishly by men who see God reflected in their own cramped and peevish minds, a God whose mind is paralleled by the best qualities which an ideal human mind could achieve in theory.

As we noted before, he is distinguished from the Platonists by the absence of references to Christ, and he is also much less dogmatic than these churchmen in his attitude toward innatism. He moved from a precisely Lockean definition of moral sense in the *Inquiry* to something more broadly based, what is best defined as a temper— "all that flows from your good Understanding, Sense, Knowledg and Will; all that is engender'd in your Heart . . . and all that derives it self from your Parent-*Mind*" (SE, 210). "If you dislike the word *Innate*, let us change it, if you will, for INSTINCT; and call Instinct, that which Nature teaches, exclusive of Art, Culture or Discipline" (SE, 212).

Obviously it is a reasonable approach for a Platonist to focus on the central role of an inward colloquy, involving a tension between actuality and the ideal. We know how poorly Shaftesbury thinks of his own conduct from the "Exercises," and the same book illustrates one phase of the dialectic in action. Does this mean that, as some suggest, we must then abandon the notion that the moral sense was first defined by Shaftesbury in purely Lockean terms? Are the Platonic dialectic and the Lockean epistemology compatible for Shaftesbury? Both Robert Marsh in his excellent *Four Dialectical Theories of Poetry* and Stanley Green in *Shaftesbury's Philosophy of Religion and Ethics* attack E. L. Tuveson's *Imagination as a Means of Grace* for its decription of the Lockean origins of moral sense, and presumably they would also object to my similar description in "Shaftesbury's Moral Sense," were they aware of it.[5] All we can conclude is that Shaftesbury did not see any incompatibility, since in 1711 he described the moral sense in terms which will seem Lockean enough to anyone well acquainted with Locke's works and with

5. Robert Marsh, *Four Dialectical Theories of Poetry: An Aspect of English Neo-classical Criticism* (Chicago, 1965); Stanley Green, *Shaftesbury's Philosophy of Religion and Ethics: A Study in Enthusiasm* (Athens, Ohio, 1967); Ernest L. Tuveson, *The Imagination as a Means of Grace: Locke and the Aesthetics of Romanticism* (Berkeley, 1960); Robert Voitle, "Shaftesbury's Moral Sense," *Studies in Philology*, LII (1955), 17–38.

Some of the problems in accepting Professor Tuveson's thesis may arise from the eccentricity of his footnotes. As I have pointed out, Ashley first defined the "moral sense" in his 1699 edition of the *Inquiry* and later he added the aesthetic analogy when he hastily revised the work for the first edition of *Characteristicks* in 1711. On page 53 Tuveson cites the passage defining the moral sense using the words of page 27 of the 1699 edition, but he says he found them in *Characteristicks* (1711), where they are phrased differently—see II, 28 of this edition. He then cites the passage on the aesthetic analogy from the 1732 edition. This edition is identical here to the final edition of 1714, but there is a very similar passage on II, 28 of the 1711 edition which he does not tell us about. Despite the fact that he cites from it twice, there is no mention of the 1699 edition in Tuveson's book, so that one is left to infer that Shaftesbury made all these changes between 1711 and 1714. There is no doubt of the authenticity of the date of the first edition—which is held by the British Library and elsewhere—because we have a letter from Stringer in 1699 specifically referring to it. Professor Caroline Robbins has provided me with a poem which William Popple wrote on the occasion of its publication. The poem is dated 1699 in a contemporary hand.

Locke's arguments in letters to Lord Ashley in the 1690s. And the Earl coupled it with an analogy which is dialectic in impulse and Platonic in spirit.

In regard to his Platonic impulses, Shaftesbury did not sit down one sunny afternoon and begin *Characteristicks*. It is instead a pastiche, the product of over twenty years of thought by a mind which was agile, receptive, and very fruitful. Ideally, had not illness, his family and personal affairs, his changing tastes and a very short life been involved, he might have made it more of a piece. Yet one does not know whether it would ever have become more than a miscellany. Shaftesbury when young was a systematizer; when older, he said the final word on systems.

Shaftesburian "enthusiasm," which is fed by the imagination, also reflects his Platonism. The ultimate purposes of the rhapsodic meditation on nature seem to be moral, though it signalizes a revolution in aesthetic thought. Book Three of the dialogue tells the story of the conversion of Philocles to the belief of Theocles by alternating rational and rhapsodic and imaginative utterances. In the rational sections Philocles provides a counterpoint; in the rhapsodic section he largely listens to Theocles. Both reason and rhapsody are necessary to convince him. Obviously the protracted raptures of Theocles are in a sense cognitive. From these utterances Philocles may learn nothing more than he has already learned rationally, but the inspired meditations fix in his mind permanently that the cosmos is unified and is presided over by a benevolent spirit.

What Susie I. Tucker describes in her book which she calls an extended footnote to the *O.E.D.* definition of *enthusiasm* tends to confirm this. The word, which had been a technical religious term in the seventeenth century, either negative or positive or both, expanded broadly and rapidly as the seventeenth became the eighteenth century, and by 1750 it involves philosophy, writing and the various arts, and even love.[6] When Philocles is satisfied to be called a *new enthusiast* Theocles replies,

[I] am content you shou'd call this Love of ours *Enthusiasm*; allowing it the Privilege of its Fellow Passions. For is there a fair and plausible

6. Susie I. Tucker, *Enthusiasm: A Study in Semantic Change* (Cambridge, 1972).

Enthusiasm, a reasonable Extasy and Transport allow'd to other Subjects, such as Architecture, Painting, Musick; and shall it be exploded *here*? Are there Senses by which all those other Graces and Perfections are perceiv'd? and none by which to comprehend this higher Perfection and Grace? Is it so preposterous to bring that Enthusiasm hither, and transfer it from those *secondary* Objects, to this *Original* and *Comprehensive One*? . . . But it is not instantly we acquire this Sense by which these Beautys are discoverable. Labour and Pains are requir'd, and Time to cultivate a natural Genius, ever so apt or forward. . . . Is Study, Science, and Learning necessary to understand all Beautys else? and for *the Sovereign Beauty* is there no Skill or Science requir'd? (SE, 199–201)

Thus it is only by hard training, by strict reasoning, and by enraptured fancy—creative imagination—that there is any hope of the individual glimpsing the ideal. Shaftesbury turns to the very old tradition of inspiration in art to resolve his metaphysical problems. Ultimately his suggestions were to have far more impact on art than on metaphysics.

For England, these changes by which mankind gets back some of the qualities stripped from reason by English empiricism are well discussed by Professor Tuveson in his *Imagination as a Means of Grace*. There is of course no way of precisely determining where these ideas began. As R. L. Brett remarks, before beginning a chapter on Shaftesbury's effect on later thought, "The tracing of so-called literary influences is a dangerous and generally a profitless pursuit. The influence of one writer upon another is rarely a direct and simple matter, for writers, like other men, live amid a complicated field of forces, personal, social and intellectual, and their work is generally the product of all of these."[7] The roots of Shaftesbury's thought are old, as are those of Locke, but it is ironic that only fourteen years after the publication of the *Essay* Locke's own disciple should be laying the basis for the refutation of the book's main presumption.

A number of ideas which appear later in Shaftesbury's works are adumbrated in *The Sociable Enthusiast* and most of these can be passed over until they are developed more fully. One, however, is stated so clearly that it will pay to look at it now: "Therefore the

---

7. R. L. Brett, *The Third Earl of Shaftesbury: A Study in Eighteenth-Century Literary Theory* (1951), 186.

Beautifying, not the Beautify'd, is really Beautiful" (SE, 204). It is statements such as this that really explain why so many more books on Shaftesbury have been written by Continentals than by Englishmen. And the full explanation still eludes those who think in moral terms. Even so shrewd an observer of broad currents of thought as Charles Verecker may know but seems unwilling to venture: "During the last two and a half centuries, Shaftesbury, not unlike Byron, has enjoyed a more exalted reputation on the Continent than at home. It is not easy to explain this addiction, but at the time no doubt his championing of universalist optimism met with approval wherever Leibnizian influences penetrated."[8] Verecker shortly turns, quite properly, to Hutcheson, a more systematic moralist. It may well be that empiricism is to blame for the fact that a century later, notions such as these had to be imported back to England from Continental writers who had first learned them from Shaftesbury's *Characteristicks*.

This particular passage from the *Enthusiast* comes when Theocles, borrowing from Plotinus, is using an artistic analogy to explain the nature of the first order of beauty, forming forms, the minds of men themselves. Divine inspiration had always been an element in aesthetic theory, but the theory usually focused, as in Aristotle, either on the artifact or on the effect upon the audience. The ultimate result of statements such as this was to turn attention to the artist and thus supply a basis for Romantic critical theory. For Shaftesbury's own purposes, he had found what seemed to him a far more effective way of bridging the gap between the actual and the ideal than the concept he had once based on Lockean epistemology, yet he remained until the end a moralist.

Although Shaftesbury's notebooks show that he was busy during the interval, it is at least four years after the printing of *The Sociable Enthusiast* that another philosophical work of his appears. Happily, the mysteries which surround the original publications of *An Inquiry* and *The Moralists* are absent in the case of his *Letter Concern-*

8. Charles Verecker, *Eighteenth-Century Optimism: A Study of the Interrelations of Moral and Social Theory in English and French Thought Between 1689 and 1785* (Liverpool, 1967), 57. See especially the last chapter of Ernst Cassirer's *The Platonic Renaissance in England*, trans. James P. Pettegrove (Austin, Tex., 1953).

ing Enthusiasm (1708). He sent Lord Somers a holograph copy in another's hand in September 1707. The following March, Shaftesbury discovered that a friend of Somers to whom it had been lent had given it to a "worthy Character of good Estate, great Reading & wonderfull Curiosity in the search of Books & Authors." This reader had passed it around to various members of his club, one of whom made a copy and intended to have it published as by the author of *A Tale of a Tub*, to whom all ascribed it. Shaftesbury then wrote to Somers begging him to burn or conceal his copy of the *Letter*, and his letter gives us a candid glance at the motives behind his writing the essay. In the first place, though he may not have intended it to be published, he does not fear acknowledging it or dedicating it to Somers. His own reputation, as he said the following July, "he values not: For be it treated as it will; It can neither hurt nor benefitt the Publick, whose service he is so unfitt for." He made only one change for publication: in the manuscript he said that if an old prelate can believe in fairies, a heathen poet should be able to believe in the muses. It seems very likely that the old prelate, referred to in correspondence as a bishop now active in the Whig cause, is Edward Fowler (1632–1714). Later in the year when Shaftesbury's edition was published to forestall the one to be published by the club member, the old prelate was apparently protected by changing "you know" into "you once knew" in the printed version.[9] Despite the uproar caused by the publication, only stylistic changes were made in two later editions. He was willing to expand and explain his theory elsewhere, but Shaftesbury had made his statement and he was willing to stick by it.

The clamor over the French Prophets which gave Shaftesbury the opportunity to write his *Letter* has been well described.[10] The Camisards were a group of Huguenots that grew up in the Cevennes after the revocation of the Edict of Nantes in 1685. They were ruthlessly repressed, but instead of fleeing fought back vigorously in an exceed-

9. The Earl of Shaftesbury to Lord Somers, March, 1708, in PRO 30/24/22/4/pp. 67–70; to the same, July 12, 1708, in PRO 30/24/22/4/pp. 86–87; *Lettre sur l'enthousiasme* appeared in the same year at The Hague.

10. James Sutherland, *Background for Queen Anne* (1937); Ronald A. Knox, *Enthusiasm: A Chapter in the History of Religion with Specific Reference to the XVII and XVIII Centuries* (1950), Chap. 15; and, better balanced, Grean, *Shaftesbury's Philosophy*, Chap. 2.

ingly bloody campaign. According to Ronald Knox, they had English support; this must have been nominal, however. What the English may have welcomed in France was soon found to be unwelcome at home, when several Prophets emigrated to England in the winter of 1706. Their prophecies delivered in every possible antic manner—from trances, in languages unknown to the speaker, with all sorts of bodily contortions, even walking on hands—soon found them converts and sympathizers. The Huguenots disowned the Prophets and three preachers were pilloried, but naturally they thrived on repression. At the same time a rather astonishingly large literary effort was mounted against them and it succeeded very rapidly only because the Prophets themselves made its success inevitable. As one essayist remarked, they had to be fools rather than knaves, because no knave would ever date his prophecies so exactly. April 29, 1708, was the date when London would be destroyed by divine fire. This was not critical, however, since other dates had also been chosen. However, May 25 of the same year did prove fatal. The Prophets agreed that then, six months after his burial, Dr. Thomas Emes would arise from the grave. The Train Bands were called out to control any mass hysteria which might arise. This all too precise timing explains why the publisher of the *Letter* says in the original preface of 1708 that he would have published the essay the summer before, had he been able to find a copy. Tardy pens and tardy publishers account for what came out later; such wellings forth are not stopped off all at once. After May of 1708 only the diehards among the Prophets remained and they were no longer infectious.

In his *Letter* Shaftesbury argues that the melancholy Prophets and other fanatics should be laughed at, not punished. Only ridicule will provide the test whether their gravity is true or false. False gravity is contagious and if we rely on the magistrate to counter it, it may well grow worse. "It was the Wisdom of some wise Nations, to let people be Fools as much as they pleas'd, and never to punish seriously what deserv'd only to be laugh'd at." Nor need we fear mixing raillery and religion. Indeed, good religion requires good humor, which is the best preventative of enthusiasm and atheism. So long as we use good manners we never fear good humor. Too often we look to God only when we are in trouble and the God we envision is often the reflection of our own emotional turbulence. God is either good or he does not exist; this presumption is prior to both revelation and reason. First we must find out according to the cool principles of reason what is the life of a good man, and then live it. One may become a fair judge of music without being a musician, but only a good man can know the good God. Man, of course, has a natural inclination to enthusiasm, and it is our task to distinguish the ordinary species from divine enthusiasm or inspiration. The latter moves the right sort of heroes, statesmen, poets, orators, musicians, and, even, philosophers. An irrational impulse is just only when a good man can examine its roots in a rational manner and find them sound. As if to emphasize the point, Shaftesbury refers to himself in the final paragraph as "your Enthusiastick Friend." What began as an attack on false enthusiasm ends up as a treatise on telling the false from the true species.

Ronald Knox calls the *Letter Concerning Enthusiasm* "the only considerable literary work to which the Camisard agitation gave rise," and I suppose he is correct. Writers were, at least, debating its merits for decades after the rest of the anti-Camisard literature was forgotten and the French Prophets themselves had slipped from human memory. No doubt almost all of what Shaftesbury said in the *Letter* was coffeehouse conversation in certain groups in London, yet one is reminded of a story which has become attached to the first Earl of Shaftesbury. When asked by a lady about his religious persuasion, he replied, "the religion of all wise men." And asked further what that was, he responded, "wise men never tell." By speaking out in deistic tones, Shaftesbury joined the Enlightenment, described by Peter Gay in his brilliant essay as "a single army with a single banner, with a large central corps, a right and left wing, daring scouts, and lame stragglers." It was a philosophic family, drawn together by, among other things, "the demands of political strategy" and "the hostility of church and state."[11]

Although it was not ascribed to him immediately, the *Letter* is the first of Shaftesbury's works to attract much attention. The preface to

11. Knox, *Enthusiasm*, 368; Peter Gay, *The Enlightenment: An Interpretation* (2 vols.; New York, 1966–69), I, 7–8.

Whichcote was done in a very arch manner, in a place where most would expect broad churchmanship, and the underlying cynicism must have been missed. Although it has been pointed out that the early version of the *Inquiry* was responded to, it does not seem to have made much of a splash. Whether or not we believe Shaftesbury destroyed copies, the 1699 *Inquiry* is a very scarce book, and, as I have pointed out, we have records of only three or four copies of *The Sociable Enthusiast*, which was printed but not published in 1703 or 1704.

Shaftesbury certainly knew what to expect when he published his *Letter Concerning Enthusiasm*. The Church realized it was under attack not merely from the traditional forces of innovation but also by Deists and those whose doctrines smacked of absolute infidelity. If the Deists and atheists felt freer after 1688, there was also a vast army of defenders on the other side ready to rush hastily into print.[12] I have read three of the immediate replies to the *Letter Concerning Enthusiasm*. Edward Fowler, the Latitudinarian bishop of Gloucester, is the most brilliant, though his shotgun response lacks definition.[13]

The issues are better defined in *Remarks upon the Letter Concerning Enthusiasm. In a Letter to a Gentleman* (1708). In the first place the author objects bitterly to the mixing of ridicule and religion. Some bounds are necessary on religious speculation or perfect infidelity will result. Secondly he protests that Shaftesbury's definition of God, partly from the Cambridge Platonists, partly Stoic, does not go far enough. To goodness must be added wisdom, righteousness, and purity. He must legislate against immorality, else how pure? He must enforce penalties, how else wise? He must discriminate, how else righteous? God is not the supreme manager but the supreme governor. Similarly he objects to Shaftesbury's definition of goodness as love of the public, study of the good, and promoting the interest of the world—is there no mention of righteousness and ho-

12. John Redwood's *Reason, Ridicule and Religion: The Age of Enlightenment in England, 1660–1750* (1976) gives some idea of the number of issues involved and the ferocity of the struggle.

13. Bishop Edward Fowler, *Reflections upon a Letter Concerning Enthusiasm, To my Lord XXXX. In another Letter to a Lord* (1709). See also *Bart'lemy Fair: Or An Enquiry After Wit* (1709) by Mary Astell. And also *Remarks upon the Letter Concerning Enthusiasm. In a Letter to a Gentleman* (1708).

liness here? Finally, all through his *Letter* Shaftesbury, ever the philosophe, had made slyly disparaging comparisons, and some not so sly, of the Ancients with the Moderns. According to his cyclic concept of history the world began to decline in the first centuries after Christ and is now rising slightly, a concept which puts most Christian history in the dark and superstitious ages. Thus the author of the *Remarks* fails to believe the story of the old prelate believing in fairies, which Shaftesbury had told to make the classical poets' faith in the muses more acceptable, and he bitterly rejected the identification of the fathers of the Church with the enthusiastic French Prophets.

Despite Shaftesbury's disclaimer about his reputation, he was sensitive on one point: he wanted to establish a reputation for personal integrity to counterbalance that acquired by his grandfather, whose ideas for England were as completely embraced as his character was deplored. It does seem likely from the evidence that the superficially optimistic, and more trivial, phase of his thought did, by forty or fifty years after his death, triumph over what he said in the *Letter*, but why did he expose his ideas on Christ and the Church in a public controversy when he could have implied these things elsewhere, politely, with a fraction of the risk to his reputation for piety? Granted, he did not expect it to be published at first; on the other hand, his only compunctions involved the comment on Fowler. I think that the answer is that, though the essay seems slight, it definitely exposes fresh ideas which are important to the development of Shaftesbury's thought as a whole.

Although ridicule had always been used in the way he used it, who in the modern world had spelled out so clearly its function in distinguishing false from true gravity? Although scholars have not found them, no doubt Shaftesbury has predecessors. But Shaftesbury got the credit. Ridicule and raillery are entirely too perjorative to convey his meaning, as he soon realized, and afterward he stresses the state of mind, good humor, which he also had clearly defined in the *Letter*, though too far on to do him much good, even if most of his audience had been disposed to understand him.

This brings me to the second major idea he brings forth: the distinction between false and true enthusiasm. Within a year or so *The*

Moralists is to be actually published for the first time and dedicated to Lord Somers. Unless his readers clearly have this distinction in mind they will not be able to understand what he will be saying in that book. In his time the word *enthusiasm* had a universally negative ring to it in philosophy or religion. Only in aesthetics was it acceptable and there in a very limited sense.[14] What better occasion for him to distinguish between the two meanings than during the furor over the French Prophets?

Shaftesbury's success always depended on finding an adequate reply to Locke's epistemology and his first version of the "moral sense" was cast in Lockean terms. From the "Exercises" we find that his own thinking on enthusiasm was shifting over in the period from 1698 to 1700. He defines very precisely what it means to be in this sense rational, what the mind must be stripped of. On his second journey to Holland in 1698 he says, "If the Writer of *the Table* describ'd, after such a manner, *Imposture* & her Cup; if the Draught was such in those days; what is it now? and how deeply have *We* drunk?" "Consider the Age: vulgar Religion: how thou hast been bred: and what impressions yet remaining of that sordid, shamefull, Nauseouse Idea of Deity." But when these impressions are purged, "then it is that thou mayst soundly, un-affectedly, & safely sing those Hymns to God which the Divine Man mentions" (Ex., 102, 100).[15]

Two years later, January 20, 1700, though not yet pure, he is willing to proclaim himself an enthusiast in a way which renders all other sorts of enthusiasm analogous but far subordinate. After describing love of the artificer as enthusiasm, he writes,

> Happy Me, if I can grow in this sort of Enthusiasme, so as to loose all those Enthusiasms of every other kind, and be whole towards *this*. Shall others willingly be accounted Enthusiastick, & even affect this sort of Passion as Virtuoso's, Men of Witt, Pleasure, Politeness, each in their severall ways, & for their severall Objects (a Song, a Picture, a Pile of Stones, a Human Body, a Shape, a Face:) and shall thou be concern'd at being found Enthusiastick upon another Subject, so far excelling in itself, & which is Originall to all the rest?" (Ex., 153)

14. See again Tucker's admirable *Enthusiasm*.
15. The *Tabula Cebetis* is referred to and the divine man is Epictetus.

329

Only a rational man contemplating a rational God can be genuinely enthusiastic. He feels that he has found the answer already to what Locke had to say about enthusiasm in the fourth edition of the *Essay*: "And what readier way can there be to run ourselves into the most extravagant errors and miscarriages, than thus to set up fancy for our supreme and sole guide, and to believe any proposition to be true, any action to be right, only because we believe it to be so."[16] The *Letter* prepares the way for *The Moralists*.

Sensus Communis: An Essay on the Freedom of Wit and Humour (1709) defends Shaftesbury's *Letter Concerning Enthusiasm*, while at the same time more cautiously restates what he said in that essay, and it also gives a definition of what he means by *common sense*, which is almost but not quite another subject.[17] The trouble with his defending the *Letter* was that he was not willing to admit that the also anonymous *Sensus Communis* was by the same author. Yet he took no real pains to conceal the fact. For instance, he says, "I have known some of those grave Gentlemen [to?] undertake to correct an Author for defending the Use of Raillery, who at the same time have upon every turn made use of that Weapon, tho they were naturally so very aukard at it" (Char., I, 65). The three immediate responses to the *Letter* which I have seen all used raillery to attack the railer, though only Bishop Fowler really is awkward, largely because he uses too much of it. Even the subtitle of *Sensus Communis* seems to be a response to the critics of the *Letter Concerning Enthusiasm*.

More important than Shaftesbury's defense of his *Letter* is his clarification of what he meant by *ridicule* in that essay. Considering the circumstances of its publication, there was plentiful opportunity for misunderstanding; Lord Somers is hardly typical of its eventual audience. Shaftesbury sent a copy of *Sensus Communis* to Somers but, as he explained in the very bitter letter which accompanied it, he did not dedicate it to him, because he did not want him to be publicly linked with a supposed enemy of the Church. The book is di-

---

16. Locke, *Essay*, II, 437.

17. *Essai sur l'usage de la raillerie et l'enjouement dans les conversations qui roulent sur les matieres les plus importantes*, signed S.C.S.V., appeared in The Hague in 1710, translated by J. van Effen. The next year Shaftesbury used illustrative citations from it in the second English edition of *Sensus Communis*.

rected to a friend who with Shaftesbury has recently spent an evening with a group of skeptical gentlemen. The conversation ranges widely and by the time it is finished, every issue, large and small, has been reduced to stuff and nonsense. The friend is puzzled by this and *Sensus Communis* is Shaftesbury's explanation.

First he rejects the punning, metaphysical humor of an earlier day in favor of the easy, light, yet functional humor of his own time, a humor which is consistent with the free dialectic now preferred over the heavy rhetoric of the past. Of course, with regard to this sort of wit, he is speaking of private discussion among friends. Those met accidentally should not be forced to listen to what is unpleasant to them, and only those of slavish principles would attempt to impose their principles on the vulgar. In contrast to this sort of open discussion, it is partial skepticism which is to be feared. The real knave attacks nothing overtly; these men laugh at themselves as heartily as at others: "Let the *solemn* Reprovers of Vice proceed in the manner most sutable to their Genius and Character. I am ready to congratulate with 'em on the Success of their Labours, in that authoritative way which is allow'd 'em. I know not, in the mean while, why others may not be allow'd to *ridicule* Folly, and recommend Wisdom and Virtue (if possibly they can) in a way of Pleasantry and Mirth" (Char., I, 134). The others are "those to whom a natural good Genius, or the Force of a good Education, has given a *Sense* of what is *naturally graceful and becoming*." Ridicule is not so significant as the good-humored mood from which it must spring if it is to be functional. As A. O. Aldridge pointed out in one of his earliest articles, it is the demeanor of the discussion which will determine whether ridicule is allied with reason.[18] And it is clear from these quotations that the ridiculers must be balanced and well disposed; in short, they must be essentially moral men.

Shaftesbury's conversationalists so ridicule almost everything that they are unable even to agree on a meaning for *common sense*, to which they constantly appeal in positive tones. He himself follows the most ingenious commentators on the Latin satirical poets who define the term "by a *Greek* Derivation, to signify *Sense* of the

18. A. O. Aldridge, "Shaftesbury and the Test of Truth," *PMLA*, LX (1945), 129–56.

Publick Weal, and of the *Common Interest;* Love of the *Community* or *Society,* Natural Affection, Humanity, Obligingness, or that sort of *Civility* which rises from a just *Sense* of the *common Rights* of Mankind, and the *natural Equality* there is amongst those of same Species" (Char., I, 104). These "social feelings or *Sense of Partnership* with Human Kind" are the final version of Shaftesbury's moral sense and in this popular context are preferred to *koinonia* in the footnotes.[19]

How different is this from the Lockean definition which he framed, probably a decade and half before? In the first place, *sense* is everywhere equated to *passion* or *affection* in the text, so that there is no difference in this aspect of moral sense.[20] Secondly, in the final pages of *Sensus Communis,* Shaftesbury proceeds up the ladder from the commoner pleasures to the highest: "Nothing affects the Heart like that which is purely from *it-self,* and of its *own nature;* such as the *Beauty of Sentiments; the Grace* of Actions; *the Turn of Characters* and *the Proportions and Features of a human* Mind" (Char., I, 135–36). The artists who portray these "carry a double Portion of this charm about 'em." In other words, they reveal the highest truth and they do so altruistically. "For Who of them composes for *himself?*" Underneath all this verbiage the moral sense remains essentially the same, an affection towards an affection.

In no other work of Shaftesbury's are there more references to Hobbes than in *Sensus Communis.* How is it possible, he asks, to agree to a contract in a state of nature where there are no norms to enforce it? If indeed mankind did come to an agreement, moral standards must have preceded the agreement. Again, he feels that the modern Epicurean has misread his master, for Epicurus by the very fact of banishing concern for relatives and countrymen acknowledged the force of social affections, whereas the Hobbist acts as if such affections are nonexistent. This leads to discussion of the herding instinct, which is true self-interest. "A Life without *natural Affection, Friendship,* or *Sociableness,* wou'd be found a wretched one, were it to be try'd. 'Tis as these Feelings and Affections are in-

---

19. *Final* because this was his last full definition.
20. For a discussion of the meaning of the term in the two versions of the *Inquiry,* see my "Shaftesbury's Moral Sense."

trinsecally valuable and worthy, that Self-Interest is to be rated and esteem'd" (Char., I, 121). Faction is merely a perversion of the confederate faculty, yet confederation can only go so far, which is a chief reason for the establishment of colonies.

The whole discussion must be seen in terms of the audience of these three popular essays, and Shaftesbury's concept of them. Most of them would be as unlikely to respond to an argument based on the larger community of mankind and the universal good as they would to his abstract description of the moral sense in the *Inquiry*. These are matters which in *Characteristicks* he will confine to the more serious second volume. Here he reduces the social organism to a scale which will have meaning for his prospective readers.

Soliloquy, or Advice to an Author (1710) is in many ways Shaftesbury's most engaging work. His miscellaneous and familiar style is fully developed in it. According to a copy of the 1711 edition revised by Shaftesbury as copy for the 1714 edition of *Characteristicks*, most of the essays must have been read aloud, or he simply has a good ear, because he is much concerned with the sound of his phrases—jingling words and strings of monosyllabic words are expunged, for example. Almost every page of the third and final edition of *Soliloquy* involves some change. Most of them, however, are merely mechanical or involve altering sounds. The sentence units remain the same, though much shorter than in the earlier writings, and there are fewer antitheses. They flow together well yet can be very pointed when he wishes. Many of the things one would have liked to have said are said here in this essay. The relaxed miscellaneous style is a help with this, because some of his best sentences are what a comedian would now call "throwaways"—as, for instance, "the most ingenious way of becoming foolish, is *by a System*."

Nowhere in Shaftesbury's works does he refer so often to the superiority of the Ancients over the Moderns. In one respect he is simply more confident and outspoken. At the same time he took precautions; the response to his *Letter Concerning Enthusiasm* had taught him how dangerous it is to mix philosophy and religion together. At one point he defends Christianity against tellers of traveler's tales, such as Locke: "Tho *Christian* Miracles may not so well satisfy em;

333

they dwell with the highest contentment on the Prodigys of *Moorish* and *Pagan* Countrys" (Char. I, 456).[21] Most of the time he insists that his topic is generically separate from the divine, and that it would be presumptuous for him even to speak of religious matters. "It becomes not those who are un-inspir'd from Heaven, and un-commission'd from Earth, to search with Curiosity into the Original of those Holy Rites and Records, *by Law establish'd.*" As to drawing from the Bible, Milton was an exception because of the mythological flexibility of his characters; normally "the Manners, Actions and Characters of *Sacred Writ*, are in no-wise the proper Subject of other authors than Divines themselves." However, "tho the Explanations of such deep Mysterys, and religious Dutys, be allotted as the peculiar Province of *the Sacred Order*; 'tis presum'd, nevertheless, that it may be lawful for other *Authors* to retain their antient Privilege of instructing Mankind, in a way of Pleasure, and Entertainment. *Poets* may be allow'd their Fictions, and *Philosophers* their Systems" (Char., I, 358, 361).[22]

Most of what Shaftesbury has to say in *Soliloquy* on the Ancients and Moderns is based directly on a cyclic but rather supple theory of history best developed in the *Miscellaneous Reflections*. The most powerful stimulus to achievement in human affairs and in the arts is freedom. The word does not refer to a specific political system, though some are certainly preferable to others. Its real measure is the diversity of opinion on all subjects and the degree to which that diversity is tolerated. Life under a benevolent despot may be free, and so may life in a nation where slaves are held, though Shaftesbury disapproves of the practice. Looking back, then, Greece "that sole polite, most civiliz'd, and accomplish'd Nation" stood first among free nations.

> For tho compos'd of different Nations, distinct in Laws and Government, divided by Seas and Continents, dispers'd in distant Islands: yet being originally of the same Extract, united by one single Language, and animated by that social, publick and *free* Spirit. . . . Thus *Greece*,

21. See also I, 350–53.
22. The passage is bitterly satirical, but he means what he says about laws governing religion; this is the justification for the religious system which he feels that men most need.

tho she *exported* Arts to other Nations, had properly for her own share no *Import* of the kind. The utmost which could be nam'd, wou'd amount to no more than raw *Materials*, of a rude and barborous form. And thus the Nation was evidently *Original* in Art; and with them every noble Study and Science was . . . *self-form'd*. (Char., III, 138–40)

Next came Rome, borrowing from Greece and gradually polishing her own arts and sciences until they reach a high degree of finish in the final days of the Republic. The Empire put the fate of the nation too much in the hands of a single man. As the reigns of the Antonines proved, freedom could exist, but almost inevitably the Roman state descended into tyranny.

With the coming of Christianity, the Empire went on, and political tyranny, too. A new impediment to freedom was the insistence on intellectual conformity, and gradually all of western Europe descended into the Gothic age. Liberty began to revive during the Renaissance, and, speaking of England, Shaftesbury says, "We are now in an Age when *Liberty* is once again in its Ascendant. And we are our-selves the happy Nation, who not only enjoy it at home, but by our Greatness and Power give Life and Vigour to it abroad. . . . 'Tis with us at present, as with the *Roman* People in those early Days, when they wanted only repose from Arms to apply themselves to the Improvement of Arts and Studys" (Char., I, 222–23). Shaftesbury is optimistic about England's progress, but there is no certainty that it will continue. The Glorious Revolution assured for the time freedom from political tyranny, and he is well aware of the state of intellectual freedom in his time. He expects to acknowledge formally his authorship of the *Letter Concerning Enthusiasm*, with no fears of the magistrate enforcing conformity. He is sure, too, that literature is moving toward the simple after all the quibbles and puns of the past age, and the poets of the seventeenth century are to be congratulated for throwing off rhyme. Even in Greece the degree of freedom varied. On the other hand, England is still at war with an absolutist monarch and the continual growth of ceremony runs counter to simplicity.

One characteristic which separates the ancient author from the modern is the natural tendency of the ancient to colloquize. After citing the desire of Persius to carry into the temple "a mind pure in

its inner depths," Shaftesbury remarks, "This was, among the Antients, that celebrated *Delphick* Inscription, RECOGNIZE YOUR-SELF:
which was as much as to say, *Divide your-self*, or *Be* TWO. For if
the Division were rightly made, all *within* wou'd of course, they
thought, be rightly understood, and prudently manag'd. Such Confidence they had in this Home-*Dialect* of SOLILOQUY" (Char., I, 170).
Later on he is more specific:

> When by a certain powerful Figure of inward Rhetorick, the Mind
> *apostrophizes* its OWN FANCYS, raises 'em to their proper *Shapes* and
> *Personages*, and addresses 'em familiarly, without the least Ceremony
> or Respect. By this means it will soon happen, that TWO form'd *Partys*
> will erect themselves *within*. For the Imaginations or Fancys being
> thus roundly treated, are forc'd to declare themselves, and take Party.
> Those on the side of the elder Brother APPETITE, are strangely sub-
> tle and insinuating. . . . till being confronted with their Fellows of a
> plainer Language and Expression, they are forc'd to quit their myste-
> rious Manner, and discover themselves *Sophisters* and *Imposters*, who
> have not the least to do with the Party of REASON and *good Sense*.
> (Char., I, 188)

This is, of course, precisely the method which Shaftesbury himself
had been using in his private "Exercises." As he says, the idea is ancient, but why, if it worked for him, did he wait twelve years to refer
to it in one of his final essays? The reason is, I suspect, that he identifies the method of inner colloquy with his own intensely Stoic discipline, which he was so successful in concealing from his contemporaries. After his usual fashion he thinks in terms of personae, and
the Stoic persona is almost the furthest removed from those he is
addressing in his relaxed and miscellaneous manner. At least four
different moral personae are addressed by Shaftesbury; first the average man with whom he deals in his court book, from servant to
small landholder, and sometimes his protégés, Wilkinson and Ainsworth. This person, the unphilosophical man, strongly needs the
discipline of religion "by law established," and Shaftesbury is quite
honest in recommending that its habits must be instilled at an early
age for him to be effective as a moral person and good citizen. Secondly, there is the more fashionable person to whom he gradually
turned his attention in the first and third volumes of *Characteris-*

ticks. Deception is the key to Shaftesbury's method with him; he must be tricked into thinking about serious matters. He may well be conventionally pious, and his faith should not be affronted; nonetheless, he must be weaned away from the belief that God can ever act without full benevolence. Shaftesbury seems to have felt that the more pious this person was, the less sensitive he would be to the protective sarcastic tone he adopted in these essays. The third persona is made up of thoroughgoing classicists, true disciples of the Ancients, those who have learned the lesson of *The Moralists*—Crell and General Stanhope, for example. These are the philosophers, and to them Deity becomes the more remote figure of Shaftesbury's Platonic-Stoic universe. Fourth comes the well-concealed Shaftesbury in his "Exercises." Whereas the third persona is exposed to dialectic truth, truth for this persona is therapeutic truth of the colloquy. A statement may be equally true and equally formative but for the third it is stressed because it is true, for the fourth because it is formative. Of course, the Stoic sage can never really exist. By striving earnestly to be one, by continual exposure to formative truth, the disciple reaches a point where he can let *ataraxia* take care of itself and turn his attention to *koinonia*. The closest analogy I can think of is the meditative mode of religious experience common in the earlier seventeenth century; the parallel is not exact, though.

Obviously certain truths may hold for all these personae. Just as obviously, one must work from one level to another with great care, which is all the more reason for admiring the fine general essays which have been written on Shaftesbury, such as Martin Price's chapter in *To the Palace of Wisdom*.[23] It did not occur to Shaftesbury immediately, then, that the method which he had used in his secret meditations had a broader application. This he developed in *Soliloquy*.

By far the best essay on the inward colloquy is that of Robert Marsh in *Four Dialectical Theories of Poetry*. He tends to use the term more broadly than I do. Some of my reasons for not doing this

23. Martin Price, *To the Palace of Wisdom: Studies in Order and Energy from Dryden to Blake* (Garden City, N.Y., 1964).

have already been stated. Too, if colloquy is absolutely central to Shaftesbury's thought, the rapture of *The Moralists* is devalued, and, more important, making the inward colloquy so important, though it was published last, distorts the situation historically. None of the tremendous epistemological pressures to which Shaftesbury was reacting become evident. The difference is simply a matter of approach. An amusing example of this is Marsh's denial of Tuveson's thesis that Locke's notions of sensation and reflection affected Shaftesbury. Both sides are right. Marsh is a synthesizer and his unhistorical approach is symbolized by his use of the Robertson edition of *Characteristicks*, which eliminates all the emphases which Shaftesbury felt were so important; Tuveson is basically a historian, though I do not agree with all his theses. It may sound heretical, but in the case of someone so complex as Shaftesbury both conflicting writers make valuable contributions to the subject.

The second volume of *Characteristicks* contains Shaftesbury's revision of *An Inquiry* and *The Moralists*; the third volume, his *Miscellaneous Reflections* and in some copies the English version of his *Judgment of Hercules*. The *Miscellaneous Reflections* provide a commentary on the first two volumes, intended to draw the various tracts together. In this they succeed to a great extent—not that Shaftesbury exceeds the norms of his day in deception regarding the true facts of publication. He was forced to admit that the *Inquiry* was published without authorization in 1699. *The Moralists* is listed as being first published in 1709; on the other hand, *The Sociable Enthusiast* never was published in the ordinary sense of the term.

How Shaftesbury felt about his editions is in part explained by the fact that he calls John Darby, his printer and publisher, his amanuensis. It is true that his best statement of this was written when he was piqued by the response to his *Letter*, but he went on using the term until his death. All of Shaftesbury's books starting with the *Inquiry* were circulated in manuscript, as was common then. How is an author to protect himself from the errors inevitable in this process? The answer is quite simple. Have the book printed, supervise the process, and then all of your friends can enjoy accurate copies. If still others want copies, the publisher can provide them. *Soliloquy* was printed for John Morphew, but Darby, publisher of *Characteristicks*, was also its printer. So voluminous were Shaftesbury's instructions to him for every detail including all features of layout and ornamentation for the 1711 and 1714 editions that having separate printers would have introduced many errors. This explains why *Characteristicks* is such a beautiful book at a time when English books were about the ugliest produced anywhere. More important, the arrangements for publication reflect Shaftesbury's notion that the publisher is merely an amanuensis of the author, however much self-deception the idea may involve.

As one might expect, the first miscellanies which comment on Volume I of *Characteristicks* deal with a wide variety of topics. This is in line with the loose and apparently disorganized structure by which Shaftesbury hopes to recommend to fashionable people "MORALS on the same foot, with what in a lower sense is call'd *Manners*; and to advance PHILOSOPHY (as harsh a Subject as it may appear) on the very Foundation of what is call'd *agreeable* and *polite*" (Char., III, 163). Some of the topics, such as his theory of history, we have already considered; others are best passed over because they are not significant enough for the development of his thought. However, the third miscellany deals with *taste* and gives us a chance to see how far Shaftesbury has progressed from the man who in his early twenties wrote *An Inquiry Concerning Virtue*.

Shaftesbury calls the various attributes of mind "faculties," but all his life he was aware that Locke had convincingly reduced them to agencies and had again banished innatism. Although Shaftesbury believed moral ideas connate in man—he may not be born with them but their development, in potential at least, is inevitable—he constantly strove to shore up his epistemology with analogies. As we have seen, the first version of the moral sense, though he did not call it that, was an affection toward an affection, which he sought to validate by paralleling it to the affection one member of a family feels toward another, *natural affection*. It was an attempt to evade Locke in his own terms. Later he added another analogy, that of our reaction to beautiful objects. This made more sense then than it does in the present state of aesthetic theory, because then it was assumed that all beauty arose from numbers and harmony. Shaftesbury was in a sense providing a mathematical assurance of correspondence between individual moral judgments and the good. By 1710, he seems confident that the battle has been won: "Nature will not be mock'd. The Prepossession against her can never be very lasting. Her *Decrees* and *Instincts* are powerful; and her Sentiments *in-bred*. She has a strong Party *abroad*; and as strong a one *within our-selves*" (Char., I, 354).

Though the predisposition toward it is connate, taste itself can only be attained by contact with the world outside. The English, "the latest Barbarous, the last *Civiliz'd* or *Polish'd* People of EUROPE," have a special need of it. As Robert Marsh has remarked, it is very easy to be led into confusion by Shaftesbury's use of abstract terms, but here at least he is as precise as he can be. *Relish, good taste,* and aesthetic *judgment* are all equated, depending on whether he is stressing their affective or evaluative functions. A man can be said to possess good taste when he reacts positively in a more or less automatic fashion to what is good in the arts or in morals, though, of course, developing taste to this level is a laborious process. Taste is in turn based on enthusiasm, which as we have seen is easily led astray. One must continually reexamine the roots of enthusiasm, an affection, to make sure that they are rationally sound. Their rationality depends on how much they are inspired by the order and symmetry to be found both in the arts and, as Shaftesbury believes, in the spectacle of good actions.

His use of the virtuoso as the model of the man of taste is useful both analogically and in pointing to the pitfalls one may fall into. For one thing, Shaftesbury takes an acknowledged relationship between the viewer and the art object and presses it into service morally. There results a hierarchy of virtuosos ranging from the simplest collector of ingenious objects, through the accomplished patron of the arts, to the moral virtuoso: "To *philosophize*, in a just Signification, is but to carry *Good-Breeding* a step higher. For the Accomplishment of Breeding is, To learn whatever is *decent* in Company or *beautiful* in Arts: and the Sum of Philosophy is, To learn what is

just in Society, and *beautiful* in Nature, and the Order of the World"
(Char., III, 161).

With regard to pitfalls, the collector of cockleshells and the vain
devisor of useless systems, Shaftesbury remarks, mockingly, are
akin: "*Creation* it-self can, upon occasion, be exhibited; *Transmu-
tations, Projections,* and other *Philosophical* ARCANA, such as in the
corporeal World can accomplish all things: whilst in the *intellectual,* a set Frame of metaphysical Phrases and Distinctions can serve
to solve whatever Difficultys may be propounded either in *Logick,
Ethicks,* or any *real Science,* of whatever kind" (Char., III, 160). As
with Milton, it is the moral function of an activity which determines its value. The collector whose chief impulse is to collect is as
vain as the philosopher who delights only in systematizing.

It must be clear that Shaftesbury's moral theories could be stated
in purely rational terms. Why did he not do so? Why so much stress
on an affectively based quality such as enthusiasm, no matter how
securely he thinks it rooted in reason? The answer is, I think, tied
up with the restrictions which Locke had put upon reason. Even if
Shaftesbury did not believe that the only function of reason was
ratiocination—that reason had become an agent rather than an intuitive faculty—he needed mental properties which would reach up to
apprehend the Platonic-Stoic cosmos, a vertical, rather than horizontal, Lockean concept of mind:

> Something there will be of Extravagance and Fury, when the Ideas or
> Images receiv'd are too big for the narrow human Vessel to contain. So
> that *Inspiration* may be justly call'd *Divine* ENTHUSIASM: For the Word
> it-self signifies *Divine Presence,* and was made use of by the Philoso-
> pher whom the earliest Christian Fathers call'd *Divine,* to express
> whatever was sublime in human Passions. This was the Spirit he allot-
> ted to *Heroes, Statesmen, Poets, Orators, Musicians,* and even *Phi-
> losophers* themselves. (Char., I, 53–54)

Without this element, Shaftesbury's philosophy would have remained a more or less forgotten species of seventeenth-century Platonism. As it was, the English missed the element of challenge and
reduced much of his thought to its least common denominator,
until by mid-century most of that had become accepted and boring.

Only the Germans seized upon this fruitful notion of the creative imagination, so that it returned to England almost a century later.

II

In his prefatory notes for *Second Characters* Shaftesbury sums up in 1712 what he considered the major change in his thought during the past decade:

> In this View examine & recollect sometimes in seriousness the ["Exercises"] *old* & *new* (with the Chapters of the Divine man etc) particularly what is said in the *old* about the [End]. . . . and in the *new* on . . . [beauty]. Also Sensus Communis . . . Effect of *poetick* (& so *plastick*) Art, viz. and "in vocal Measures of Syllables & Sounds, to express the harmony and numbers of *an inward* kind." And follows next page, viz.: "That what we most admired even in the Turn of outward Features, was but a misterious Expression of Something *inward*" etc. Also a little below again . . . of the same Treatise: "For all Beauty is Truth." . . . with all that follows in that remarkable virtuoso-place of Maxims, which must be in part or whole copied & commented at large in Second Characters, showing the dependency of the *first* on *2d*, i.e. of 'Characteristicks' on this new Treatise, and *vice versa*.[24]

Most of it is here: the shift from the *end* to *beauty* as a goal; the parallel effects of poetic and plastic art, dependent on harmony and numbers, and the further parallel in moral judgments; the identity of beauty and truth; the notion of a readily seen whole. And, finally, that dependence of the *Second Characters* on his earlier works, which he did not live long enough to establish.

Some of these ideas we have seen before. Here, however, they will be seen largely in the artistic framework of the *Second Characters*, which was finished so far as it got in 1712, but not printed until Benjamin Rand's version came out in 1914. We will look first at the "Exercises," that most sensitive indicator of Shaftesbury's state of mind, then at the sorts of changes as *The Sociable Enthusiast* became *The Moralists*, and, finally, at the *Second Characters*.

It is possible to date with some precision the shift from devotion to the end, to the pursuit of beauty. In the passages from the "Exercises" written in Holland in 1698–1699 he dwells often on "The

24. PRO 30/24/27/15/43, r. Greek in translation.

End," yet in the subject index which lumps together with dates all the meditations on specific subjects, we find this is the last such entry—he never returns to the topic in these terms. In London during January of 1700 he exclaims:

> O Soul! think how noble will be thy State, when in the manner that thou art taken with other Beautyes, other Simplicityes & Graces, thou shalt proportionably contemplate & admire that cheif Originall Beauty, & that perfect Simplicity & Grace of which all other is the Shaddow Reflection & Resemblance. How well it will be with Thee, when all those other inferiour secondary Objects are lov'd according to their order, never but *last*; and the First Object, *first* in its due place & rank; anticedently to all; with an Affection above all other Affection besides; and according to just *Natural Affection*, not that which is called so towards a Relation or Friend. . . . Is this *Enthousiasme*? Be it: and so may I be ever an Enthousiast. . . & even affect this sort of Passion as Vertuoso's, Men of Witt, Pleasure, Politeness, each in their severall ways, & for their severall Objects (a Song, a Picture, a Pile of Stones, a Human Body, a Shape, a Face;) and shall thou be concern'd at being found Enthousiastick upon another Subject; so far excelling in it self, & which is Originall to all the rest? (Ex., 152–53)

Thus Shaftesbury makes the natural affection he had described in *Inquiry I* in Lockean terms into something dependent upon inner harmony and numbers and clearly Platonic in basis. Shaftesbury is highly eclectic; he was never a metaphysician and, as we know, he despised comprehensive systems. The shift from Stoicism to a dualistic system occurs naturally in him because he keeps his eye upon the end he wishes to achieve. It is altogether possible that he felt no conflict at all. The Lockean explanation tells how the mind works; the Platonic analogy, why.

When Lord Ashley was preparing the Whichcote sermons for an edition in 1698 he made extensive marginal notes in his own hand. He may well have gotten the idea at this time. But there is no way of telling, since he had long been acquainted with the works of Plato. The question of where Shaftesbury got his Platonism is really no question at all. Here it serves only to underline the point I made about Shaftesbury's remaining primarily a moralist all his life. The table of contents of *Second Characters* confirms this: a short letter dealing wholly with art, an artistic study of his great moral painting, a purely moral treatise, and a treatise intended to link art with morality.

I like to speculate about the four books in Closterman's portrait of Shaftesbury, typically in a toga, which appears in the first volume of the second edition of *Characteristicks*, because I know that its subject, who specified every minute detail of the emblematic engravings in the same edition, had something in mind for each. The upright volume on the right is Xenophon's *Memorabilia* of Socrates, a primarily moral work involving no theory of forms but a notion of beauty like that in Marcus. Underneath it is a volume on which we can read in Greek, PLAT, obviously the ultimate source of his Platonic analogy and ideal of beauty. Next to it a reversed volume of considerable size which should be Arrian's *Discourses* of Epictetus. Clutched to his breast is what ought to be the most important volume in the portrait. Since it is reversed there is no way of determining the exact title of this little book; the title is concealed just as it was in his published works, yet it must be the *Meditations* of Marcus Aurelius.

Turning to the evidence from the "Exercises" for the persistence of his Stoicism, almost every time Shaftesbury begins to recover his health, he renews his Stoic resolutions. Thus in January 1707, after an illness:

> Since recover'd from thy long Distemper, & now likely to live for some time, & as far as a broken Constitution will permitt to be active again in affaires of the Publick & Friends; remembering the first & early Cautions (more necessary & incumbent now, & in this State). *the Laws*, as in Parlement &c: with which thou must now again take up; begin as formerly (for there is need enough after Neglect, & so much Time given to Bodily affaires and Weaknesses) begin as above p. 124. &c: upon *Familiarity, Character* &c: remembering the *natural Secretion.* remembering *Modesty*, the *Decorum*, & the *Deformity* & *Nauseousness* there spoken of (p. 134) as belonging to a certain *Openess* & *Affectation* of *Intimacys*. for now these things are growing again . . . & bring back to the same Follyes & now more than ever inexcusable Manners & Character. (Ex., 369)

Such passages always embarrassed Rand, and some of them were silently revised in his *Philosophical Regimen*. Obviously, he recalled Shaftesbury's habit of surrounding himself with men, his great reluctance to marry, and a letter or two—left out of Rand's edition—and he assumed these passages from the "Exercises" to be positive proof that the secret life which Shaftesbury was steeling himself against was homosexual. I usually juxtapose such passages to others in the "Exercises"—for instance,

> know the Condition & Law, however terrible It appear:
> *To take Pleasure in Nothing.*
> *To do Nothing with Affection.*
> *To promise well of Nothing.*
> *To Engage for Nothing.* (Ex., 177)

One of the most repulsive passages in the "Exercises" is where he compares discussing his personal affairs with others to passing around his phlegm and stools for their examination. He knew too well that moral lessons are easy for any one to learn, and forget. The only hope is to make them so intense and gripping that it is impossible to forget them for a moment, a very old Stoic practice. If the mind is all, the body must be depreciated in the bitterest terms possible.

Although this practice of Stoic renewal persists throughout the "Exercises," the Earl's style changes. The prose becomes more flowing and imaginative, pungent and vigorous. His increasing mastery of Greek shows throughout the text and the headings. The index to the second volume has forty topics; only twelve of them are in English, though often they translate English terms in the original. He also cites more frequently Latin authors, Plato and the Greeks, and now even the Bible.

More remarkable is the change in content, in spirit rather than ideas. Never after 1704 did he go long in good health, but the only despair in the "Exercises" is moral despair. He seems to have learned to live for the day, and progressive bouts of illness add to his courage in facing what he can never escape. Through calm resignation he becomes more genuinely the philosopher he had striven so hard to be earlier. Consider this passage written in 1707:

> The Overthrow of all Character is from an over promising, or desponding View of Affaires administer'd. tho' originally it is from the pride that all ill arises. The first leads to a sort of Undertaking; the other to a Resigning: both equally wrong. Matters having a little succeeded, Self-

Applause arises, and hence Engagements & Forewardness, beyond the Measure and True Tone of Life. On the other side, Matters growing ill, or succeeding a little worse than ordinary, Self-Disparagement arises & thence Aversion to all Buisness. Love of Privacy, and violent Affectation of Retreat & Obscurity. . . . Meer Pusilanimity! as the other was Rashness & meer Madness. (Ex., 386)

This is the history of his own life Shaftesbury is writing, and a little later:

Let Temper, therefore, rather than Principles bear the Charge. Be severe over thy self; but appear so, as little as may be, with safety. . . . a sincere Carriage without Affectation may bear Thee easily through all this. Nor is inward Severity (in the thwarting either of Joy or Greif) so very hard to be hid, if honestly meant. (Ex., 388)

The first passage describes what he was; the second, what he was becoming. Or, again, listen to him speaking in 1706:

Besides many better & weightyer reasons for a Good Man's disregard of Esteem & Fame . . . there is this good warrant on his side; that in reality a true Character was never well relish'd or understood by the Criticks & nice Judges of the world. . . . Soc[rate]s & Dio[gene]s appear'd as Buffoons, and the first a Dangerous one. . . . The People of themselves were well inclin'd towards them. . . . Tis here, as in the Vertuosoworld. The half-witted & half-learned who have only a smattering of the Arts, are pragmaticall, conceited, & only ingeniouse in chusing constantly amiss. . . . They can see nothing naturall in that which is so very near Nature. Yet often a very Child or Peasant shall find Likeness & bear Testimony to Nature, where these pretended Artists are at a stand. (Ex., 192–93)

The real test of a philosopher is, I suppose, his attitude toward death. He had faced it often, so that there is little bravado in this intensely Stoic passage:

To dye any Death is *natural.* for one Door is the same as another. the Natural or *Un-natural* is in the going out: how this is done: with what Mind. for if with a right mind, this is all that the Nature of a Rational Creature requires or needs. . . . *To dye,* when over is to *do Nothing,* when not over it is *to live.* Tis in Life therefore, or no where, that Death is. Tis Death indeed to fear Death. 'Tis Death to live & dream. See that thou dost not truly live this Death: and 'tis no matter what Death thou dyest. (Ex., 224–25)

Shaftesbury probably wrote this in 1703–1704. In the few years left to him death came more frequently into his letters; never does he refer to it with anything but this same cool equanimity.

Obviously, he saw no life after death. This is interesting, because the second volume of the "Exercises" does show a change in his attitude toward the Deity. This we saw in the prayers of *The Sociable Enthusiast*. It may just be that his new Platonic spirit has more reality for him, though Marcus was surely pious enough. In any case his faith is now strong enough that he becomes increasingly impatient with atheism and those who conceal their lack of faith under other names: "What is this *Deisme* they talk of? What difference from meer *Atheisme*? Is it some secret Vertue (like Magick) which they assign to Things? Is it the Plastick Nature? or Epicurus's Atomes?— But Epicurus was more sincere. for his is only a God for the Vulgar *ad Populum Phaleras*. but he pretends not to bring this into Philosophy nor resolve anything in Nature by this, or any such like Principle" (Ex., 249). I think he knew the answer to his question and it may have contributed as much as Toland's other failings to Shaftesbury's growing mistrust of him.

Turning from the changes in Shaftesbury's manuscript diary to those in his published works, the most extensively revised of all, *The Sociable Enthusiast*, would seem a good place to start. The most drastic changes in the content of the book occurred when the Earl revised *The Sociable Enthusiast* for the 1709 edition of the *Moralists*, the last two revisions being largely stylistic. Whole pages are crossed out, the spaces between the lines and the margins are filled, and the blank pages and a separate book are full of additions, with the result that the 1709 version is about 20 percent longer than the original.

The revisions to the 1709 *Moralists* fall into several classes. Much of the added and revised materials merely strengthen and clarify arguments we have already considered in regard to the "Exercises." Other changes reflect matters we have discussed elsewhere. He openly attacks "modern deism." Epicurus was honest by contrast; he set his gods apart and did not paper over his atheism by giving himself a pious-sounding label. In other alterations we find him further down roads we have already seen him set out on. *The Moralists* reveals a keener sense of the complexities of human psychology. In this it anticipates his still more subtle approach in *Second Characters*. He also turns further away from his past idea of the world as a single animate being; there is a more subjective emphasis that what is around us may be a world of dream and shadow, though this has no effect on the Stoic character of his moral system.

Other changes are worth pausing over for a moment. I have remarked that his first references to Platonism seem to have been made about 1700. By the time he published *The Sociable Enthusiast* he was in full pursuit of the parallel between aesthetic and moral experience. So far as I know Shaftesbury had no special musical talents, but naturally he used musical figures in his illustrations—naturally, because music with its connections to harmony and numbers was the art with the closest connection to being something "*in itself*, and in the nature of things." After writing *The Sociable Enthusiast* it must have occurred to him that the application to his own particular interest in visual arts was just as logical, so that in a long addition he speaks of "laying on the colors," "drawing," "moral painting" and refers to "our picture." This tendency even brightens the imagery of his descriptions. In *The Sociable Enthusiast* we have: "The Charms of the then declining Day, the Freshness of the Evening, the beautiful Horizon made by a setting Sun, these were Objects that cou'd make Impression on you" (SE, 7). This becomes in the 1709 *Moralists*: "The Verdure of the Field, the distant Prospects, the gilded Horizon and purple Sky, form'd by a setting Sun, had Charms in abundance, and were able to make Impression on you" (Mor., 12–13). By 1709 the visual analogy had become dominant in Shaftesbury's mind.

Also in startling contrast to the personal dogmatism of the *Inquiry* is Shaftesbury's insistence in *The Moralists* upon withholding judgment. This probably reflects his own experience with the reaction to his *Letter Concerning Enthusiasm*, for he repeatedly insists that his virtuoso enthusiasm should not be confused with the fanatic variety. Actually, among the worst sort of dogmatists he now realizes are the Deists. The world needs to make use of the ways of the Academy: "There is a certain way of Questioning and Doubting, which no-wise sutes the Genius of our Age. Men love to take Party instantly. They can't bear being kept in suspence. The Examination torments 'em. They want to be rid of it, upon the easiest terms" (Mor., 8).

Another change between *The Sociable Enthusiast* and *The Moralists* is a change in Shaftesbury's way of referring to his god. In the first work we have "O mighty *Nature!* Wise in thy Designs, powerful in thy Operations, and bounteous in thy distributions and Providence O Divine and Universal Spirit! or rather thou Divinity it self, Supreme and Sovereign" (SE, 141), which becomes in the second, "O mighty *Nature!* Wise Substitute of Providence, impower'd *Creatress!* Or Thou impowering DEITY, Supreme CREATOR!" (Mor., 158). It is likely that in the *Enthusiast* Shaftesbury did not fully realize all the implications of the new cosmology he was adopting. In a sense, nature is the Stoic's deity, if we take nature to mean the soul of the world, not mere atoms. She is no longer that in the second passage, merely an empowered creatress, and the separation from deity, the mind of the universe, is made unmistakable.

In summary, then, Shaftesbury's final concept of God is a degree more humane than his first. Of course, he had always felt that the sanctions of divine reward and punishment are necessary for most men. It is at a somewhat higher level—the readership of *The Moralists*—that the difference is obvious. Now it is possible to address them more candidly because the languages of Christianity and Platonism are much closer to each other than that of Stoicism is to either. At the highest level, though, his personal religion remains without an afterlife and Christless, just as it had been before. Yet now at least he can allow himself the luxury of prayer.

Shaftesbury was at Naples only a month or so after his arrival in November 1711 before he had another project under way, this despite the fact that he was still at work revising *Characteristicks* for its second edition. The book was to be called *Second Characters, or The Language of Forms* and was to consist of "A Letter Concerning Design," "A Notion of the Historical Draught of Hercules," "An Appendix Concerning the Emblem of Cebes," and "Plasticks, or the Original Progress and Power of Designatory Art." The first two were completed. The "Notion," written in French, was published in Paris that autumn and the "Letter" not until the fifth edition of *Characteristicks* in 1732, though it does appear in some copies of the 1714 edition. There is a translation of the *Tabula Cebetis* among Shaftesbury's papers but no appendix, and the major work, "Plasticks," survives only as a group of disconnected notes. Professor Rand may have regarded himself as a Pygmalion in reconstituting these notes; however, when one compares the results with the original, it has to be confessed that Dr. Frankenstein may have occasionally helped him out.

Rand has a good account of the genesis of the work in his introduction. It was too late to stop Shaftesbury from working on the text and plates for the second edition of *Characteristicks*, but his friends wanted to make sure that he began nothing else until he was able. Shaftesbury writes Thomas Micklethwayte in February 1712, "Sir John writes to my Wife against your putting me upon new projects about *Philol*: He reasons extremely well upon it." But Shaftesbury feels that there is little to fear from what are now only virtuoso studies. He goes on, "I am so vain in the mean while as to believe that if I rub over this remaining Winter-month, and am in for living, once more, so as to pass another Summer (as I now really begin to think I shall) may besides my *Devices* and *Flourish-Works*, make some agreable Advancements in the Virtuoso-kind (whether with relation to Char——cks or not) which may entertain You and my Friends."[25]

What Shaftesbury had in mind was actually as taxing as anything he might have attempted. In both the revised *Inquiry* and *The Moralists* he had compared the moral experience to the aesthetic experience. Now in "Plasticks" he intended to reverse the procedure, to publish a book on art which would have concealed in it a moral message. Shaftesbury had his doubts that *Characteristicks* reached the genteel audience he had in mind for it—"ladies, beaux, courtly gentlemen, the more refined town and country wits, notable talkers." Yet, since it was fashionable, these same people comprehended art, or pretended to comprehend it. Everything in the new work was to

25. The Earl of Shaftesbury to Thomas Micklethwayte, February 2, 1712 NS, in PRO 30/24/23/8/pp. 125 and 127.

emphasize ease. The style was to be miscellaneous; foreign languages were to be confined to the footnotes and English authors cited in the text; and a dictionary was to serve to define terms of art and the like. Meanwhile he intended "to *twist*, as it were, & interweave Morality with Plasticks, that supream Beauty, with this subaltern, those high & severe Maxims, with these curiouse & *severe* also in their kind." Thus, by turning away from Nature and treating second characters far more specifically than he had before, he would introduce his audience insensibly, his word, to the first characters of morality.[26]

The first treatise in the *Second Characters*, the "Letter Concerning Design," is only about ten pages long and there would be little reason to pause over it, did it not contain Shaftesbury's clearest statement of the dependence of the arts on popular freedom. These were dark days for his chosen party, but Shaftesbury feels sure that the succession has been established; indeed, he himself has been in touch with the House of Hanover for over ten years. Most of what his grandfather had struggled for is now accomplished, and when the final treaties are signed England should be able to look forward to a long period of genuine parliamentary monarchy, and with it a gradual raising of the popular taste, progress in the fine arts, and finally real moral progress.

It is true that he has not much to go on yet—chiefly the superiority of the British military, despite all the special training France gives her officers in academies. Even in the arts, though, there is some evidence. Courts corrupt taste and stultify the arts. Charles II looked to France and did little to help English music, but now that popular, rather than princely, genius has turned to Italy, we can see some advancement—a judgment not all of Shaftesbury's contemporaries would agree with. It is true that nothing yet has been done in painting. In architecture too much of the restoration after the fire has been done hastily and under the wrong direction. Two major monuments remain to be built, the Prince's Palaces and the House of Parliament; and would the public now stand to see a Hampton Court built? No, no more than they would tolerate a new cathedral

26. PRO 30/24/27/15/43, r.

which looked like St. Paul's. Shaftesbury looks very sourly on the art of Sir Christopher Wren, with its concessions to the too recent past, its gothicism. In any nation the level of popular taste is inextricably entwined with the form of government.

"A Notion of the Historical Draught or Tablature of the Judgment of Hercules," modeled in some respects after the *Tabula Cebetis*, was sent with the "Letter Concerning Design" to Lord Somers from Naples on March 6, 1712 NS and is far more elaborate than the other treatise. The essay was written in French so that the painter Paolo de Matteis (1662–1728) could follow it. It appeared in the *Journal des Sçavans* for November 1712; a translation of the work by Shaftesbury appeared in 1714 and was appended to the second edition of *Characteristicks*.

The story of the choice of Hercules is recounted by Socrates, following Prodicus, in the second book of Xenophon's *Memorabilia*. Hercules appears standing at a crossroad, pondering which way to take. On the severe road to one side stands Virtue; on the soft and easy path, Pleasure awaits him. The two argue their cases at some length, and as the tale ends Hercules is about to decide. Important for Shaftesbury's discussion of the painting is the fact that Prodicus says almost nothing about the background against which the discussion takes place. Shaftesbury wants his painting to be a tablature: "*a Single Piece*, comprehended in one *View*, and form'd according to *one single* Intelligence, Meaning or Design; which constitutes a *real* WHOLE, by a mutual and necessary Relation of its Parts, the same as Members in a natural body." Obviously some sort of background will have to be drawn in, but it must remain subordinate so that the "*seeming Truth* (which is the *real Truth* of Art) may with the highest advantage be supported and advanc'd" (Char., III, 348 and 349).

The essay is full of common-sense suggestions for handling the three figures in the painting—most of these ideas chosen by systematically considering the possible alternatives. Sometimes the choice of handling is very clear. For instance, what should the time scheme of the picture be, presuming as Shaftesbury does that it must for verisimilitude reflect a particular moment? Are they accosting him, beginning their discussion; is he torn with passion trying to make up his mind; or, assuming the painter can extrapolate, has he already made up his mind? Obviously the greatest emotion, therefore the most powerful, is centered at the moment of judgment, which Shaftesbury calls the vital moment. This the painter must render, although it is perhaps the most difficult of the four to represent. Since Virtue is speaking last, Hercules must be silent so as not to interrupt the sublimity of her speech. Most historical painters have too many people talking anyway, and, furthermore, he must be in a position to turn down the easy path or up the difficult road. For a skillful artist the mixed emotions in his face during this scene should be no real problem; "the Artist has power to leave still in his Subject the Tracks or Footsteps of its Predecessor: so as to let us behold not only a rising Passion together with a declining one; what is more, a strong and determinate Passion, with its contrary already discharg'd and banish'd," as when we see traces of tears on the face of someone transported by joy to find suddenly a loved one not dead after all.

Virtue offers more choices of handling than Hercules. Obviously, in her peroration, she should be standing up, just as Pleasure should be seductively reclining. What should she be doing with her hands, though? Shaftesbury finally decides that her free hand should be pointing up the hill which she is persuading Hercules to climb. The other hand, grasping the magisterial sword or Parazonium, should be toward Pleasure, the fingers slightly spread in a gesture of rejection. There is considerable precedent for a serene visage for Virtue, but Shaftesbury has little trouble in proving that a mood of "enthusiastic agitation" will be more effective simply because it will express the real situation with more accuracy.

Verisimilitude and unity of action are the key to the background and ornamentation. Shaftesbury is well aware of the mixed allegorical-historical paintings then so common, especially in his youth. Thus, although the painting is an allegory, no irrelevant "*Machine-Work* or *Divinitys* in the Sky" are necessary here. Nor at the opposite pole should there be anything of the "emblematical or enigmatick kind," such as the complex designs just completed by Shaftesbury for the second edition of *Characteristicks*. Hercules is identified by his lion skin and club; near Virtue lying casually on the ground are her helmet and a bit, symbolizing forbearance and en-

durance; near Pleasure are some wrought dishes and "certain Drap-
erys thrown carelessly on the ground, and hung upon a neighbouring
Tree, forming a kind of Bower and Couch," which with her "Image
of the effeminate, indolent, and amorous Passions" will identify her
sufficiently. These are but a few of the details over which Shaftesbury deliberates. He feels that everything should be handled with
such a simplicity, that if one came upon the scene at a turning of the
road, it would be immediately obvious what was going on and one
could turn directly to consider the more profound implications of
the struggle rending the breast of Hercules.

Shaftesbury got no further than making notes for the last part of *Second Characters.* Professor Benjamin Rand must have devoted a lot of
time and energy to his editing of this part, called "Plasticks," under
conditions which three-quarters of a century later are still far from
ideal.[27] Any new edition of the work will surely have to follow something like his arrangement. Besides the credit due him for going
about a necessary job with much vigor, there is little else to say
positively, for the lapse of time does not account for the eccentrici-
ties of his work, to say nothing of its carelessness. I suppose that the
worst thing Rand does, or fails to do, is to give his reader any idea of
what the manuscript looks like, beyond suggesting that Shaftesbury
might not have printed the prefatory memoranda. It is a book of over
a hundred pages, arranged like a chaotic version of the "Exercises,"
the difference being that form suits content in the latter, and once
the form has been figured out, the content can be reordered systematically, which is not true of "Plasticks." Too much of the text consists of memoranda by the author to himself, footnotes upon footnotes, all of which Rand prints, separating "text" from notes in an
arbitrary way.

So far as I can determine the transcription is better than that in
the *Philosophical Regimen.* This, however, is faint praise; almost
every page contains a blunder. Sometimes Rand is especially vexing.
How one who knows Shaftesbury's hand so well as Rand does would

27. The MS. of this section of the projected work is written in a separate, green
vellum-bound book, PRO 30/24/27/15.

read M^cC for M^rL is hard to understand, but thus a whole series of notes referring to John Locke become nonsense. "Plasticks" contains enough new material that it was worth editing no matter how badly, and by an odd chance, many of the memoranda which Rand sought to elevate into text give us a rare chance to see the way Shaftesbury's mind works when he writes.

Almost every detail in "Plasticks" can be accounted for in terms of Shaftesbury's theory of history; he is looking backward to an era which at best we can only approximate and never excel. Since, barring politics, he is regarded as a pioneer of new ideas, this is very paradoxical, though were we as wrapped up in the struggle of the Ancients and the Moderns as his contemporaries were, we could see better where he stands. It is also true that by looking backward he reapplies old ideas, in Plato, for example, which in future times were again to become indispensable in human thought. Last, despite his hindsight, Shaftesbury is very much the creature of his own day. All he can do in many cases is adapt old ideas to modern instances, and he does so with a peculiar acuteness for man's shifting concept of himself, because he sees psychology as wholly moral.

Even the title "Plasticks, an Epistolary Excursion in the Original Progress and Power of Designatory Art" is puzzling. It is true that Shaftesbury inserts in a footnote at the beginning of the book an elaborate chart, where we learn that first characters are words, verbal shorthand and various ciphers; second characters refer to some branch of either sculpture or painting, plastical or graphical; and third characters are emblematic, true or false, which mediate between the two. They are third because they are last historically. He calls the work "Plasticks," because he subsumes both plastical and graphical under that name. Actually none of this means much unless we look at it morally. Second characters are forms, whereas the first are forming forms—they have the potentiality of shaping behavior. *Characteristicks* deals with the first, and this treatise on designatory art, with the second. The progress of both characters is inseparably tied to the level a society reaches, and this level is as closely bound to the degree of freedom the society enjoys.

Shaftesbury's approach, typical for his day, is as historical as that of his archenemy Hobbes. As republican Greece represented the apogee of human liberty, it also produced man's greatest literature and his greatest art. With the decline of political freedom in Greece came the age of the philosophers and a decline in art—despite the dependence on Plato, Socrates is Shaftesbury's favorite Greek philosopher. Rome enjoyed two periods of freedom, during the republic and under the Antonines. Shaftesbury's republicanism notwithstanding, it is not the form of government but—if any one thing—how freely men may express themselves which is the best index of freedom. The growth of the Roman church was a disaster for freedom because it combined the repressive forces of religion and government. Freedom again arose in the Italian city-states. It was assured, because no matter how repressive a specific government might become, the individual could hope to move to another city. The art of Italy is proof of its freedom; northern Europe is too Gothic, too primitive still; France is highly polished yet suffers under political repression—a low culture and a bad culture. As we saw in "A Letter Concerning Design," Shaftesbury feels that England is on an ascending curve of freedom. Why won't it keep going on up? In part, I suppose, because his faith in a particular theory of history is really based on admiration for the past.

The success of any society in achieving the sort of freedom that Shaftesbury hopes for depends in large part on the common opinion which man has of his own nature in that society. He says his last words on Locke here, and it pays to attend him, because his words are prophetic. Those disciples of Descartes who made animals into machines are bad enough; still worse are those who ridicule instinct and innate ideas simply because these notions were misapplied by other modern philosophers, as they were by Plato. Of course what saves man, and animals, from the conclusions of these philosophers is that the sovereign plastic nature sets boundaries to the wantonness and bestiality of corrupt men; else men and animals would soon descend to levels beyond what could be imagined by the crudest ryparographer—the painter of grotesque forms. Sooner or later, "the Breed when mix'd & blended, in time & after several consequent generations, display's & opens it self, & the orders return to their first natural secretions, purity & simplicity of Form." Locke made the word *instinct* so unfashionable that "it was safer for a

Gentleman who was a Lover of Sports to say seriously upon the subject of his Chase, that his Dogg *Joler* or *Tomboy reason'd*, or *meditated* than that he had *natural Sagacity* or *Instinct.*"[28]

It is not until Shaftesbury turns specifically to art and the subject of taste that we see the full force of his argument, why the human spirit, given the proper conditions, continually reasserts itself in generation after generation of men. Pedantry or bad taste in painters results from bad prints or sculpture or drawing without masters, from haste, from the artist's temptation to prostitute himself, from the want of proper nude models beyond harlots and porters, and, finally, from the tendency toward affectation or too self-conscious style. The gentleman critic's taste fails because he makes himself a party, espouses a manner, because he becomes too fond of one master and because he falls in with painters and becomes subject to their flattery. Were men more instinctual some of these weaknesses might be less obvious. Instinct is dominant in animals; man has less of it because he also has reason which enables him to reach above instinct. In him the criterion of the beautiful, as the good, is ultimately taste—a word, alas, that no longer has the element of strength which Shaftesbury saw in it. Taste, as we have seen, is a joint activity of reason and imaginative enthusiasm.

For the artist or any creative worker, the secret lies in the proper control of phantasies, fleeting forms, perceived between sleeping and waking: "From these fleeting Forms (call 'em the *Effluvia* of *Epicurus* or the *Ideas* of Plato) the Proficient collects still, joyns, disjoyns, compares, adds, subtracts, modifies, tempers, allays fear of wildness. . . . *These* drive away, beat down: *Those* mark, note, remember, raise, re-pass. So Raphael. So Guido." And later in a passage which might serve as a motto for the whole of "Plasticks": "Tis not the *je ne scay quoy* to which Idiots & the ignorant of Art would reduce everything. Tis not the δοκει [what attracts]: the *I like* & *you like*. But *why do I like*? And if not with reason & Truth I will refuse to like, dislike my Fancy, condemn the *Form*, search it, discover its *Deformity* & reject it."[29] Truth seems to be the fruit of careful, steady, thoughtful, and, above all, patient observation of the world.

28. PRO 30/24/27/15/9, v. and SC, 106.
29. PRO 30/24/27/15/9, r. and 12, r. and SC, 143–44.

Following Rand's method, based on Shaftesbury's index to "Plasticks," there follows a section on discouragements in art. Chief among these is the complete absence of any opportunity to see the naked body in the way ancient artists did. Modern man does not care for his body as the Ancients did, and too often he dresses it in fashions which can only distort it. And it is sad to consider that so much of the impulse for art has come from the popish priesthood; not only was Raphael (1485–1520) demeaned by having to draw cartoons for tapestry and make altar pieces as commanded, he and other artists were given Christ as a figure to draw: "Chief support of painting what?—X'!—wretched Model! Barbarian. No Form, no grace of shoulders, breast. . . . no *Demarche*, Air, Majesty, Grandeur, a lean uncomely Proportion & Species, a mere Jew or Hebrew (originally an ugly scabby people) both Shape & Phyz: with half beard, peaked not one nor t' other. Lank clinging Hair, sniveling Face, hypocritical canting countenance & at best Melancholly Mad & enthusiastical in the common & lower way."[30] One can imagine the results of the publication in his day of this part of what Rand calls text. The absence of Christ from his writings was clear, he knew, to all, but blasphemy was not his style.

The other chief discouragement is false criticism—wrong answers to the wrong questions. The failure to recognize for example the instantaneous nature of painting. How does that garment hang on?

> It does not hang at all. Tis dropping. You catch sight only in an instant. So in running Figures, in a Horse full speed, the Gladiator Farnese. Who ever saw either of these Subjects precisely & distinctly in any such Attitude? So a Man falling from a Precipice. An *Angel, Mercury* flying. Michel Angelos natural attraction of his Resurrection Figures upwards. . . . All these *instantaneouse*. All is *Invention* (the first Part or Division of Painting.) *Creation, Divining*, a sort of *Prophesying* & Inspiration. The Poetical Exstasie & Rapture: Things that were never *seen*: no nor *that* ever *were;* yet feign'd. *Painter* as *Poet* a second *Maker.*[31]

This section is followed in the index by two others on the motives to and praises of art. There must be strong encouragement of the

30. PRO 30/24/27/15/93, r. and SC, 120.
31. PRO 30/24/27/15/22, v. and SC, 118–19.

creation of prints and etchings. Only thus will the eye of the public—injured by the French and Flemish taste—be restored. He returns again to the effect of art on those who are best able to afford it. Art not only smooths the manners, it forms and shapes. The beautiful beautifies, the gothic, gothicizes. Art is expensive, but if it ever needs to be sold, the owner will recover more than his original expense, providing he has purchased not according to fancy but by rules based on sound taste. Shaftesbury has great faith in the general consent of mankind as an index of what is generally true and beautiful. The general consent is not, of course, public opinion; rather it is a distillation of this, refined and tested by time. This is not so moving as the creative instinct he speaks of, but that is available only to a few. His own collection, strong in Poussins, would seem to show that, wherever his instincts came from, they were sound.

Throughout "Plasticks" Shaftesbury makes very circumspect references to himself and his works. In one passage we get some sense of how much art must have meant to Shaftesbury for relief in a life which was becoming progressively more painful, month by month: "With respect to *Self* (apologizing for it) This Recomendation of *Plasticks* &c. . . . That being *sick* and under Pains, Watches, *Insomnias* &c: as also disturbing Buisness or Affaires over-much for one in a low Habit &c: The Custome of viewing *the Forms* & raising these pleasing specters not only good, as *Chacers* Drivers away of other species & haunting Forms of Faces, Grimaces &c in weak stomachs, ·Indigestions, Head-Akes &c but in reality helping the Passions, calming, allaying"[32]—providing that virtuoso rules are followed; no flayings of martyrs and so forth are to be viewed.

From here on Shaftesbury's index seems to grow more miscellaneous until finally it descends to maxims and citations, though admittedly these seemed far more important to Shaftesbury than they will to his modern reader. It seems best, then, to take from the index what must have been the most important subjects to him, with a particular eye for those areas in which he has something fresh to say in relation to the works of those predecessors with whom he was most familiar. Three of these are most prominent: the book trans-

32. PRO 30/24/27/15/25, r. and SC, 122.

lated from the Latin by its author, the German-born philologist
Franciscus Junius (1589–1677), as the *The Painting of the Ancients*
(1638); Charles A. du Fresnoy's (1611–1665) *De arte graphica*
(1668), often translated; and a more or less negative source, Roland
Freart's (d. 1676) *An Idea of the Perfection of Painting*, translated by
John Evelyn in 1668. Shaftesbury seems also to have read one work
by Abraham Bossu (1602–1676), probably his *Le Peintre converty*
(1667). Much needs to be done on the sources of "Plasticks," a task
no one should envy.

One feature of all contemporary treatises of painting offers a good
opportunity to compare the four writers: the discussion of the five
parts of painting—invention, proportion, color, movement or sentiment, and collocation. The hasty notes for "Plasticks" are difficult
to compare with finished treatises, especially with so ponderous and
erudite a work as that of Junius, but almost everywhere that Shaftesbury does go into detail he seems fresher. For one thing, having the
moral analogy always at the back of his mind, he is more philosophical, more willing to go below the surface. Secondly, he has been a
keen observer of art for a quarter of a century and, perhaps on the
basis of this experience, he seems unwilling to accept something
which runs counter to his intuitions or to common sense.

The best example of this is the old saw about the analogy between
painting and poetry. Du Fresnoy begins

> Ut Pictura Poesis erit; similisque Poesi
> Sit Pictura; refert par aemula quaeque sororem,
> Alternantque vices et nomina; muta Poesis
> Dicitur haec, Pictura loquens solet ille vacari.

and the parallel is stressed by almost all writers on art until the publication of Lessing's *Laokoon* in 1766. Of all Latin writers, Shaftesbury was most influenced by Horace, but this key principle of the
Ars Poetica is referred to only twice in his "Plasticks," both times
negatively. Because poetry does not have the immediate impact of
painting, it can describe what painting cannot. A plague, the poet
can describe in detail; the painter has to be satisfied with faces
which reflect the agony of the plague sores; he cannot show the
sores themselves, without destroying decorum. This comes back to

Shaftesbury's notion that a painting is an instantaneous representation. Again, when the parts of poetry are compared to the parts of painting, the examples are completely unconvincing. "Comparisons & Paralels ran between Painting & Poetry (because of the Pictoribus atq. Poetis &c and the ut Pictura Poesis (vers. 361) allmost ever absurd & at best constrain'd, Lame or defective."[33]

One of Shaftesbury's freshest discussions is that of invention, the first part. He criticizes Freart for making collocation, the whole, an aspect of the first part as it is in poetry. Freart does not do so in my edition. Perhaps Shaftesbury did not have the book with him; as we shall see, he had other more compelling reasons for his bias against Freart. In poetry, the whole is part of invention because the poet speaks the same language as his reader; the manner of image making, of designation, is common to both of them. Invention in the painter is a fusion of the *materia plastica,* and his own forming or active part: "The good Painter (*quatenus* Painter) begins by working first *within.* Here the Imagery! Here the plastick Work! First makes Forms, fashions, corrects, amplifys, contracts, unites, modifys, assimilates, adapts, conforms, polishes, refines, &c. forms his Ideas: then his *Hand* his *Strokes.*"[34] This notion depends in some degree on the idea that what is most distinctive in a given painter is his "hand." Or in a very inexact parallel, if we assume that a picture has both form and substance, it is in the substance we must look to see the invention. This is why good models and fine etchings of the masters are so important. These are the materials which make the young artist inventive; to these he applies the fleeting forms between sleeping and waking, in what at first is an arduous process of continual selection. Finally, though, it becomes almost instinctive, as with the moralist. The ruin of young artists is to take the whole without question, not selecting, not gathering.

On the subject of the second part of painting, proportion, Shaftesbury tends to repeat his predecessors. Like all of these he naturally agrees that the only way to learn is to imitate the Ancients. This he feels is best done by the school of Rome, by Raphael (1483–1520),

33. PRO 30/24/27/15/38, r. and SC, 141.
34. PRO 30/24/27/15/8, r. and SC, 142.

Julio Romano (1499–1546), and Poussin (1594–1665), who have an unmixed, pure and simple grace, void of affectation. He points out that many of the members of this school learn by rote and do wonderfully; they know not why themselves.

On coloring, the third part, he has a great deal to say, which at first is rather puzzling because he does not in the long run regard it as one of the more important parts of painting. It is easy to forget that most of the really fine art that even someone of Shaftesbury's rank would see was colorless. The reason for his interest at this point becomes clearer when it is realized that the essay is more a warning piece than the others, and it is likely that he is reacting against some of the painting around him.

He begins with a simple paradox: "Thus in respect of Painting and the Art of Imitation by Colours, the least simple, sincere & genuine in the Cloth or Sum of Tablature are those which are the most simple, pure & absolute in themselves. These the true Art of Painting abhorrs. Nor wou'd *a Raphael*, a *Julio Romano* a Titian (the chief in this) indure such a Glare."[35] This is followed not by a simple injunction against bright colors but by a fairly subtle analysis of a large hypothetical outdoor painting with figures, to show how the sky and the earth dominate the coloring of various parts. "Strange Paradox but leading Maxim viz 'That in Tablature & Painting, Colours are in themselves Nothing nor have anything to do.'" Next he begins a remarkably mordant assault on the principle of *marriage des couleurs*—that aging improves colors. Ridiculous! When the paint is completely dry, deterioration sets in. So much for the false reverence of antiquity. He concludes with a discussion of the four modern colors and an approving discussion of the reigning tint, which he parallels to drawing a curtain of one color over the single entrance to a room.

Perhaps because he said so much on the subject in the "Notion," the fourth part, sentiment or movement, is very brief. He engages himself solely with his chief bugbear in this part, affectation, "An express'd Consciousness of Grace, which spoils Grace and its Sim-

35. PRO 30/24/27/15/87, r. and 88, r. and SC, 146.

plicity. An Attention to Self, to the Action, Movement or Attitude itself." This the Ancients rarely succumbed to.

The fifth part of painting is confined to a single topic, hyperbole, which Shaftesbury also makes the topic of a separate article. Hyperbole he defines as a voluntary and premeditated error from the rules of perspective, so that the first requirement for using it well is a very fine knowledge of perspective itself. This can be found in great paintings, as when Poussin makes a pointing finger in his Samaritan woman longer than the whole head, or even in a painter of less heroic subjects, though often the artist may not know why he succeeds. The greatest artist in hyperbole is Michelangelo (1475–1564), yet Shaftesbury feels that, despite his great knowledge of anatomy, his figures labor and toil without reason. On the other hand, if a painter is hyperbolic in the natural style, the result is farce. Raphael, he feels, is a perpetual instance of the happy medium. The discussion of hyperbole ends with an instance of its use in perspective, still visible when a Salvator Rosa (1615–1663), which he purchased from the estate of the Viceroy of Naples, is viewed in a counter light. Apparently Rosa had intended the landscape to be dominated by a huge rock, but when he began to decorate it with banditti, gypsies, and so forth, he went on to put larger figures in a cave, life-size in the foreground. Perceiving then that he had completely destroyed the hyperbolic effect of the rock, he seized a pencil and destroyed the cave and figures, leaving his rock majestic, terribly impending, vast and enormous.

Most of the remainder of what Shaftesbury has to say in "Plasticks" is conventional; as the table of contents reveals, moral and artistic maxims fill most of the final pages. The only question remaining is whether Shaftesbury sticks by his theories when he judges art in practice. I think he does in the treatise and as a practicing virtuoso, too. The only qualification necessary is that in writing the essay he is forced to pretend his tastes in art are less catholic than they are in reality.

It is difficult to say how often Shaftesbury had seen original paintings by Leonardo da Vinci (1452–1519). Apparently he did see *The Last Supper* on his first visit to Milan, but it was in such poor shape that there was nothing to be learned from it. In any case he regards Leonardo as the restorer of modern painting. Even though Raphael's career was brief, by the end of it he had proved himself the master of his generation and far superior to anyone who appeared since in his faithfulness to the Ancients. Michelangelo is the first sculptor. The Earl has his reservations about the frescoes in the Sistine Chapel yet he admires them so much that he will not let others attack them. One senses, though, that he always has Raphael in mind when he judges art of the sixteenth or seventeenth century. Guilio Romano, Raphael's student, also ranks high, but one senses that the association alone weighs for much in Shaftesbury's estimate.

Shaftesbury had an unfailing eye for the classical line. This is obvious in his opinions of painters of the manneristic and baroque periods; this shift must have seemed a calamitous reversal to him. Thus he is willing to forgive Annibale Carracci (1560–1609) for being theatrical, because he studied Raphael and ancient forms in reaction to manneristic excesses. The works of his disciple Domenichino (1581–1641) Shaftesbury looks upon even more favorably. The various cabals against him, led in one case by Spanaletto (1591–1652), could only enhance his standing. The classical manner is also responsible for the way he looks on his favorite seventeenth-century painter, Poussin (1594–1665). There is surely a touch of chauvinism in Shaftesbury's utter rejection of most of French painting. Poussin, an honest, moral man, was saved by going to Italy. Claude Lorraine (1600–1682), another classicist, also went to Italy, which explains why Shaftesbury admits to owning a painting by him. The figures in this painting are by Luca Giordano (1632–1705), whose studio in Naples Shaftesbury visited on his first trip to Italy. Finally, as we have seen, he admires Poussin's friend Salvator Rosa, who stands outside the baroque, indeed finally fled its capital, Rome. From Shaftesbury's point of view, it can have done him little harm that he was the enemy of priests and satirized the founder of baroque sculpture, Gianlorenzo Bernini (1598–1680).

When you look at those artists of whom Shaftesbury disapproves it becomes clearer how closely he ties adherence to the classical ideas to morality. When an artist who possesses great technical gifts consciously departs from the ideals of simplicity and wholeness, to prefer complexity and distortion, he not only misses the chance to improve morality, he depraves it. Thus when Shaftesbury exclaims, "Bernini is wicked," he means just that. And so it is with all practitioners of variance. Caravaggio (1573–1610) may be anti-manneristic but he also lacks classical idealism. To Shaftesbury he is false in the part of sentiment. One can never tell how much Shaftesbury's judgment in this case is colored by all the scraps of biographical information which he avidly collected.

The fusion of art and morality is quite evident in the judgment of Caravaggio's disciple Spanaletto (José de Ribera), whom he considered a villain for his treatment of Domenichino: "*Spaniolet . . . Bust Painter*, Half Figures, & of old ugly Figures, fierce Style (from M. Ang de Carravaggio) no drawing: the Antipody of Grace (witness his rival Picture to Domenichino's, in the Treasury of the great Church) horrid, monstrouse. is said to be well from Waste upwards, an *Executioner* from thence below. And indeed all his whole Figures, like himself barbarous and horrid."[36]

For baroque painters he has even less sympathy. Pietro da Cortona (1596–1669) is very weak in the part of color, and in the fourth part, sentiment, he is as grossly affected as Bernini. He is just the sort of painter Freart admires. As for Carlo Marrati (1625–1713), he is fashionable now but his work should never be compared to that of Raphael and Carracci. When he renders the latters' paintings they become theatrical—another synonym for affected. Indeed, he is fit only for beauty and soft action, so that when a cardinal commissioned both a tragic piece and a beautiful one, giving the former to Maratti and the latter to Rosa, Maratti's furies turned out to be angels, Rosa's angels became furies.

To conclude this discussion of *Second Characters* it is only necessary to return again to Shaftesbury's motives for writing it and insist that his moral impulses underlie the whole. As we saw in the account of his first tour of Italy, he was powerfully attracted by the art and architecture he saw, probably without thought of their further implications. Given his early conviction of the immediate impact of art, and his final beliefs on how taste evolved in the rational ob-

36. PRO 30/24/27/15/69, r. and SC, 133.

server, what would be more natural for him, then, to assume that art offered him a way to reach those whom he wished to change? Shaftesbury was not altogether honest with Micklethwayte about his avocation. These were not merely the entertainments of a man too feeble to do anything else. He was quite seriously attempting to construct a thoroughly moral aesthetic. This becomes quite clear when we turn to the account of his two final years.

To Naples
1711–1713

For the first few months of 1711 we have little more to go on than the bare record in Shaftesbury's almanac. The most important event of the year was the birth of his son on the ninth of February. As he records it, Lady Jane had abundant support in labor: from Bushey Hall her mother, sister Ann, and a servant; from Beachworth, Lady Ash, and, in addition to the midwife, four servants from Reigate. For the christening of the child with his own name, a month later, Shaftesbury chose only two godparents, Sir John Cropley and Lord Halifax, instead of the more common three who had been selected for him and his siblings. Cropley is an obvious choice, for he could be expected to watch over the son as he had the father, but why Halifax? Ideally the child should have at least one godparent who is both influential and bound by ties of blood, and as Shaftesbury points out to him in a letter, Halifax is related to both the father and the mother, and, secondly, he is a strong Whig and Shaftesbury's political advisor and associate. The intricacy of this genealogy tells us something of what *family* meant to the Earl and his peers.[1]

Apparently Shaftesbury also thinks Lord Halifax will provide sound political guidance to his son, since he feels it is likely that he himself will not be around to do so:

When he comes hereafter into the wider World, to learn his Part in it, 'twill be his highest advantage to be bred under You, and become Your

---

1. The simplest way is to go back to a common ancestor, Sir Edward Montagu (1532–1602). Through Edward, Baron Montagu of Boughton (1562–1644), a son by his second wife, Sir Edward was Shaftesbury's great-grandfather. Through Henry, Earl of Manchester (1563–1642), by his third wife, Sir Edward was great-grandfather to Lord Halifax, and great-great-grandfather to Lady Jane Shaftesbury. Given the distinction of the Montagus, the relationship was very significant.

Charge. 'Tis peculiar, my Lord, to your character to have a generous concern for the Youth in general: And 'twould be hard if such a Youth as this shou'd 'scape You, who if ever any was, may be said to be born to Liberty, & devoted to the Interest of those who are the Lovers & Defenders of it. For whatever Motives *other* Parents may have had; his (I am sure) had never met but in this view.[2]

In addition to Cropley and Micklethwayte, who stood for Baron Halifax, the mother of the Countess, her sister Ann, and Lady Ash were present; Edmund Bowyer and his other sister Frances, from Beachworth, and Coste were also there. Wheelock, who must have wanted to be there to see his dream confirmed, was, Shaftesbury notes, busy at St. Giles's House. Almost as an afterthought, Shaftesbury lists "Mr. Bird minister of the place."

At some time this winter they decided that if the Earl was to survive they must go to Italy, but since little Anthony's arrival was on time, his birth does not explain why Shaftesbury and Jane left England a good deal later than they should have. The best explanation is that Shaftesbury was not far enough along in preparing *Characteristicks* for its first edition, while at the same time he was at work on the second edition. For him this meant supervising every detail of an elaborately footnoted and indexed set. The first volume was not sent to Lord Somers until the thirtieth of March.

As Shaftesbury says in his letter which accompanied the book, the whole work should have been dedicated to Somers, "but there are Reasons again on the other hand, which your Lordship well knows, for suppressing this ambitiouse Forwardness & Zeal; that your Lordship may be no further dip't (as our modern Phraze is) than you are allready. For as in a Ship that goes with Wind & Tide & carrys us prosperously & to heart's content, we hear nothing but *steady! steady!* So is it with your *Character.* And so wou'd I have it *continue* that no noise be heard from any side but that of *steady!* Let others tack or shift their Sails as occasion serves. . . . 'Tis Joy to me to see you hold the helm as you still do." He still tends to lecture Lord Somers, but he is not at all worried, as he had been the previous May, about being known as the author of the ticklish essays on en-

2. The Earl of Shaftesbury to Lord Halifax, Reigate, February 23, 1711, in PRO 30/24/22/7/pp. 38–39.

thusiasm in the first volume. To these he refers only in passing: "By this 3d Volume of Chamber-Practice, your Lordship will find that if my *Good-Humour* be quite spent, I have *Courage* however left to attack & provoke a most malignant party, with whom I might easily live on good Terms, to all the advantages imaginable." Their religion has been frequently exposed; he hopes that *Characteristicks* will destroy their supremacy in letters.

> Their soveraignty in Arts & Sciences, their Presidentship in Letters, their *Alma-Mater's* and Academic Virtues have been acknowledged. . . . they who treated the Poor Presbiterians as unpolite, unform'd, without Rivall Literature or Manners, will perhaps be somewhat mov'd to find themselves treated in the same way; not as Corrupters merely of Morals & publick Principles; as the very Reverse or the *Antipodes* of Good Breeding, Scholarship, Behaviour, Sense & Manners.[3]

In the course of the letter he mentions that he will be ready to send a whole new set in sheets and on better paper in April, so that Somers can have it bound as he wishes. As it so often happens in publishing, the reality was something different. In his journal for June 3 there is the note: "Last of *Index* [to *Characteristicks*] and of the *Errata* went this day. Mr. Coste & Crelle in Town to finish it." Coste must have come into Shaftesbury's service this year. As we shall see, he planned to take him abroad. And he also warns his friends not to permit Coste to sell the annuity set up for him when he is gone to Italy.

That despite all of Harley's blandishments Shaftesbury remained true to his principles this year is evident when we look at the letters to Godolphin and Harley. In his last English correspondence the most poignant letter is that written on January 29 to Lord Godolphin. The date—the first on which there are any entries since the nineteenth of the previous August—suggests that Shaftesbury is telling the whole truth when he says he has been too ill too long to do much writing of letters, and it also suggests that this is the first opportunity he has had to condole Godolphin, who stepped down on the eighth of August. Shaftesbury's sympathy is warm; his loy-

---

3. The "most malignant party" is the Tory group. The Earl of Shaftesbury to Lord Somers, March 30, 1711, in PRO 30/24/22/4/pp. 153–56.

alty, which had progressively grown very intense, is undiminished. Speaking of himself, he says:

> What Thoughts Your Lordship may have of the worth of Mankind in general, I know not. For these are trying Times. But as long as you have in your mind a single Reserve, and can believe there is in your Nation one single Lover of its Interest; You may safely assure Your self, that tho' You Know not the Person, You have certainly a Friend full of Zeal and Indignation on your account. . . . In this Calamity, My Lord, You will have only your single share. But You have certainly been above all men bless'd, in having allmost all Mankind, and even your Enemys consciouse with You of the Good You did, and the Benefit, the World and the common Cause received under your Ministry. If Envy could have place where Honesty and a public Spirit prevails, Your Lordship might the soonest of all men be envy'd by the generous and good.[4]

The real key to reading the effusive letters of Shaftesbury's day is to look through what now seems a style of magniloquence and concern yourself with precisely what is being talked about in such lush terms. Doubtless, this is the way contemporaries read them, for if they are looked at this way, it soon becomes very easy to distinguish truth from flattery. Read this way, Shaftesbury's letters seem honest enough. Perhaps not even this caution is necessary in contrasting his letters to Godolphin and to Harley, now Lord Oxford, for to the latter Shaftesbury is blunt almost to the point of being uncharitable.

Only one letter to Harley has survived, but there may have been others, because the one we have is intended to thank the Lord Treasurer for helping him to get the necessary permissions to travel. Shaftesbury begins on a pleasantly nostalgic note; but when he turns from the pleasant associations of the past, to the present, his letter takes a peculiarly bitter tone, which no one, especially the man for whom the letter was intended, could fail to detect:

> What the natural Effects are of private Friendship so founded & What the consequences of different Opinions intervening your Lordship who is so good a Judg of Men & Things can better resolve with your self than I can possibly suggest. And being so knowing in Friends (of whom your Lordship has acquir'd so many) you can recollect how those Tyes

4. The Earl of Shaftesbury to Lord Godolphin, January 29, 1711, in PRO 30/24/22/7/pp. 33–34.

or Obligations have been hitherto preserv'd towards you; & whose Friendships, Affections & Principles you may for the future best depend on, in all Circumstances & Variations, publick and private. For my own Part, I shall say only that I very sincerely wish you all happiness, & can with no man living congratulate more heartily on what I account a real Honour & Prosperity. Your Conduct of the Publick will be the just Earnest & Insurance of your Greatness & Power. And I shall then chiefly congratulate with your Lordship on your merited Honour & Advancement, when by the happy Effects it appears evidently in the service of what Cause & for the Advantage of what Interest they were acquir'd & employ'd.[5]

And so he goes on, balancing the fact that the honour, probably Harley's advancement to the peerage, was merited, against just how much England will expect and deserve of him as Lord Treasurer. One wonders how many letters of congratulation which Harley received took this tack; from friends this long separated, not many, one would imagine. The odd thing about the letter is that Shaftesbury expects Lord Oxford to swallow his words, whatever they imply, for at the end he warmly recommends Micklethwayte, who works, of course, in the Treasury.

During the winter and spring most of Shaftesbury's energy and finesse in writing letters was devoted to getting him and his wife and servants to Italy. Had he been able to withstand the voyage directly to Italy, there would have been no problem, but, as it was, the only alternative to going through France in wartime would have been to retrace in part the route by which he returned in 1689. Even if his health had permitted him to survive much of this journey, he would have been forced to start long before he did.

To his journey through France, the English government seems to have made little objection. Except for one brief period, he had never gotten on with the Queen's ministers; on the other hand, they surely knew that of all her subjects he was the least likely to be subverted by the French. It is true that the earliest letter for 1711 accompanies a petition to Lord Dartmouth for a passport and it was some five months before he received it. However, it is possible that the pass-

5. The Earl of Shaftesbury to the Earl of Oxford, May 29, 1711, in PRO 30/24/22/7/pp. 57–58.

port was issued only when he needed it. He tells one correspondent early in March that the passport is assured.

On the other hand, getting a passport from the French could be another matter. In view of the gallant cordiality with which the French finally received him, it is hard to tell how well founded his fears were. Yet all his life he had been haunted by the thought that in traveling he might enable the French to get their hands on someone with his name. There is some indication that the letters he wrote were necessary, too. He had blithely assumed that he could take Pierre Coste with him across France. It was made clear to him that this was completely impossible because Coste was a French Protestant; indeed, Shaftesbury was forced to give his word that he would not do so. He did need someone fluent in French to manage his affairs, and finally decided to take a servant whom he had taught to speak some French along, until he could find a suitable Catholic in France.

We have some record of Shaftesbury's effort to obtain French permission for his trip after he had already begun working on the problem. The first letter is to William Herbert—as Shaftesbury styles him, Duke of Powis (d. 1745)[6]—thanking him for a testimonial he has given the French court. All of the letter is naturally delivered in flattering tones, the sincerity of which we have no reason to doubt. He would have been ashamed to apply in the first case to his Grace, had it not been known universally that he was in effect "a banish'd Man from Town," nor "has he in this or the previous reign ever engag'd in any Court interest." One statement is worth quoting, for though it is true enough of him, the Earl seldom expresses it:

> And I flatter my self with this Thought, that one whose Judgment and Knowledge of Men is with Justice so highly rated, and of such Authority as Your Grace's, can firmly answer for me, that what ever I may be, as an Englishman in respect of France, I have a Character I value more than that of Nation or Religion, and can on neither account resign that of *a Man of Honour*, or be capable of tourning the Favour

6. His father was elevated to this title by King James shortly after the abdication. Herbert's royalist ties kept him in continual trouble through 1715, but he was finally summoned to Parliament in 1722 as Marquess of Powis.

or Bounty of a Prince to his Prejudice, or disservice in any respect whatsoever.[7]

Shaftesbury was soon to have an opportunity to see how well this ideal applied to the French, too.

Probably more significant was another correspondence which began later this same month. At the battle of Blenheim in 1704 Marlborough had captured a marshal of France, Camille d'Hostun Tallard, later Duke of Hostun (1652–1728), who had thrown himself into battle in hope of rallying his troops. He was then conducted to London, as a French writer puts it, "comme une sorte de trophée." Apparently, Tallard settled in Nottinghamshire, for what turned out to be an eight-year wait, near Shaftesbury's relation, Scrope, Viscount Howe, who had married Shaftesbury's aunt, Anne. Shaftesbury, who considered Tallard a "great man of France" and knew that he retained his "high credit and influence" in their court, resolved on him as the best hope of getting passage through his country.

He wrote to Lord Howe near the end of March, and by the end of April was writing the Marshal to thank him for his favors. By early May Shaftesbury writes to Lady Waldegrave (1667–1730), daughter of James II by Marlborough's sister, Arabella, thanking her for obtaining the permission of her brother, the Duke of Berwick (1670–1734), for him to travel through France, and it seems likely that this came about through Tallard's intervention. The correspondence with Lord Howe and Marshal Tallard still goes on well into June, because the officer asks Shaftesbury if he will take along "one, or two horses" as his own, to be given to the Marquis de Torcy (1665–1746), Colbert's nephew. Shaftesbury took great pains to see that this commitment was fulfilled with precision. He sent his French-speaking servant, Bryan Wheelock, to Tallard in order to get his commands, though Tallard thought this unnecessary. Once the horses arrived in London, his own people took charge of them and their grooms, making sure that they arrived in France the same day Shaftesbury did, and he added a young horse of his own stock as part

7. The Earl of Shaftesbury to the Duke of Powis, March 14, 1711, in PRO 30/24/22/7/pp. 35–36.

of the gift to Torcy. Shaftesbury's friends had also been busy trying to get him a passport, so that in the Shaftesbury papers there are three passports of different dates, two directed to Crown officials and a third to the Count of Toulouse (1678–1737), Louis' military commander—his son by Madame de Maintenon.

Shaftesbury's party set off from Reigate to Dover on June 28. There were eleven of them. Besides the Earl and his wife, there were her gentlewoman Frances Whitney, Bryan Wheelock (d. 1735)—John's nephew who was to marry Frances in Naples—Mrs. Belle Skinner, Paul Crell, and five servants. Shaftesbury dated a letter from Dover on the second and that night his party arrived in Calais.

June had been a strenuous month for Shaftesbury, though the severe attack of asthma which he had suffered for weeks broke early in the month. There were innumerable preparations for the journey, including arrangements for funds abroad. And much of this had to be done just before leaving. John Wheelock's complete accounts had to be approved and the estate put in his hands. In addition to letters dealing with his English and French passports, Shaftesbury also wrote, he tells us, many letters to the ministry on behalf of both Micklethwaytes.

He took with him a very small private memorandum book, and in an envelope in the cover is a small ivory tablet on which he recorded his thoughts on philosophy and politics on the day of departing from England. Because of Shaftesbury's Stoic training, he never hesitated to make resolves, believing them morally efficacious as goals to be worked toward, rather than completely fulfilled either in reality or his anticipations of it. Viewed in this light, this resolution looks rather weak, as we might expect from a very ill man. It is a resolve to engage only in philosophy now and in the future, yet it is full of fears of being drawn back into politics by the pressures which constantly pull at him:

> Either one Part (Phil:) or the other (Politicks) Either wholly *in*; or wholly *out*. What if restor'd? Would it be well to engage anew in both Parts. How therefore, when such a weak thread left. Remember. Now Quarter from the Partys. Malice suspended of one (witness silence about Philol) Reproach over with the other. If not resist['d] whilst

abroad, How at St G:? How against New Parlement? How against
Friends, Sir John & c.? Faith and Solemn Promise given to W.[8]

Shaftesbury's party arrived in Calais on Monday evening and did
not leave until the morning of the following Sunday, the nineteenth
according to the new style. It is likely that the chief reason for the
delay was to give the Earl an opportunity to recover from crossing
the Channel. This we deduce from the time it took them to get to
Paris once they left Calais: seven days, down what must have been
one of the better roads in northern France, which would be about
twenty-two miles a day on the present roads, and could hardly have
been more than thirty, then.

Of course there was a good bit to be done in Calais. On Tuesday
four hundred pounds of luggage had to be unloaded from the ship,
carried to the customs house, and from there to the Silver Lion Inn
where the Earl was staying. The day before they left, all of this had
to be carried back to customs, where it was sealed and delivered over
to a hauler. There were also financial matters to be settled in order
that there would be money awaiting them along the road ahead. Paul
Crell seems to have had charge of the funds, but Bryan Wheelock
made most of the actual payments. There were great numbers of
these made at Calais to innumerable carters and porters, the captain
of the pilot boat and his crew, to "Harold an Irishman who was ser-
viceable upon the Key&c," and the barber for Shaftesbury, who was
wearing his wig.

At Calais Shaftesbury was much impressed by the kindness and
efficiency of the Chevalier de Molé, the commandant, who must
have had his orders. He and his wife apparently entertained the Earl
and his Countess grandly. Shaftesbury was so pleased that he wrote
Lord Dartmouth a letter for a friend of de Molé's who was going to
England. From Paris he wrote de Molé, wistfully: "Cependant, si
apres cette Campagne il plait à Dieu de nous envoyer La Paix, j'au-

---

8. PRO 30/24/46/83. The remark on malice over philosophy may refer to the reaction to his books on enthusiasm. "W." would seem to be Lady Jane Shaftesbury. Most
of the details on the party's travels across France and Italy and of the life of Shaftesbury's family in Naples are drawn from two almanacs, PRO 30/24/24/13 and 14, and
from Crell's meticulously kept accounts, PRO 30/24/24/15.

rois l'esperance de vous revoir, et même pour le reste de mes jours
. . . de vous rendre visite deux fois par an, à peu prés comme ces
Oiseaux qui vont et reviennent L'Automne, et Le Printemps."⁹

When they started forth the following Sunday morning, six in the
coach and five in the panier, they also had an outrider, Shaftesbury's
new manservant, a Catholic Frenchman named Durand, who was
waiting for them when the party arrived in Calais.¹⁰ They followed
the same patterns Shaftesbury had so many years before, a large dinner early in the afternoon and then supper at the inn. Shaftesbury
must have been struck by the number of the poor, to whom he gave
money; they were standing around the coach every morning and
wherever he stopped along the road. He followed the traditional
route down to Boulogne, then in a straight line through Montreuil,
Abbeville, and Beauvais to Paris, where they arrived the evening of
Saturday the twenty-fifth of July.

In Paris, where Shaftesbury lived for eighteen days, he stayed first
in the rue de Tournon, a short street which ends at the Palais de Lux-
embourg, where he apparently walked in the gardens. Before long
he moved to an apartment belonging to a family named Rousseau,
probably in the same quarter. Shaftesbury had a pathologic fear of
drafts, as well he might have. He paid glaziers all the way from Paris
to Naples to repair windows for him, and this could have been
enough reason for the move. Both places were rented for Shaftesbury
by a Monsieur Bussier, who may have been on the staff of his banker
Chabbert. What really made life as easy as it could be made was that
the staff of the Duke of Lauzun (1633–1723), from the steward Thi-
bould on down, was at his service, and he called on them frequently,
especially in arranging his travel further in France. Shaftesbury never
met the Duke, who must have offered his services shortly after the
party arrived. Just before he left Shaftesbury wrote him regretting

9. "Yet, if after this campaign it pleases the Lord to send us peace, I have the hope
of seeing you again, and even for the rest of my days to visit you two times a year,
rather like those birds which come and go in the Autumn and the Spring." The Earl of
Shaftesbury to the Chevalier de Molé, August 5, 1711 NS, in PRO 30/24/23/8/
pp. 6–8.
10. A panier was a basketlike container suspended from the front and rear of the
high stagecoaches of the day—the team itself being controlled by riders. Since it was
used chiefly for luggage, it could not have been a comfortable place to ride.

that it was impossible to begin to thank him for "cette Bonté que vous avez montre si genereusement, et d'une maniere si noble et dis-interessée à un Etranger, qui dans L'Etat où il se trouve, est si peu capable de vous rendre en recompense le moindre service."[11]

Shaftesbury had set out from England with the notion of proceed-ing directly on through France to Italy. When he reached Paris, how-ever, after so much suffering from asthma on the road, he wondered whether it would not be better to go directly to Montpelier or deep into Provence to get some immediate relief. One problem was Pierre Coste; the French were obviously making every effort to see that the Earl enjoyed his stay in France, but when he inquired again in Paris about Coste's coming there to travel on with him, the answer was still a firm no. It seems doubtful that Shaftesbury would have stayed anyway, although he was invited, because, as he told one correspon-dent, he was afraid the signs of peace were false, and he was unwill-ing to settle even for the winter in enemy territory.

Not long before he left Paris he received a number of letters through Furly, including one from Coste telling him that he was un-willing to come to Italy even by ship. He was most grateful for what Shaftesbury had done for him. Still, the state of his affairs and the large additional cost of the voyage to the Earl made it unwise to take the trip. After all, if well enough Shaftesbury intended to return in the spring and Coste might get to Italy only to find it was time to return to England. Shaftesbury was deeply disappointed; yet, every-thing considered, he took it well. Eventually he had reason to hope again for a visit from Coste.

We know of these letters only through the replies Shaftesbury made to them. One other, a long one to Thomas Micklethwayte, is worth looking at. He begins on a strange note: "If I have deserved of you 'tis you must serve me now and act for me and Family in your Turns, as I have acted for you and yours whilst able and even whilst *unable*, by which I may truly say with honest boldness and trust that I deserve your Care and love to continue even after my time

---

11. "That kindness which you have shown so generously, and in a manner so noble and disinterested to a stranger, who was in such a condition and is so little capable of requiting you with the smallest service." The Earl of Shaftesbury to the Duke of Lauzun, Paris, August 11, 1711 NS, in PRO 30/24/23/8/pp. 29–30.

to a Lord Ashley, the Pleadge I have left with you and under your Cares."[12] It seems likely that Shaftesbury also wrote to Sir John Cropley in these tones, though only the part in the letter book survives. Why was it necessary for him to write this way after such long friendships? It can only be the despair and the fear provoked by the thought of how slim his chances were of ever seeing England or his son again. He goes on to rejoice that so far *Characteristicks* has been well received. He may still be of use to his friends because "*Opinion of Power* . . . is in this case truly *Power*," and the letter closes on a sad note saying he grieved to hear that his "Apostate Disciple" Arent Furly, after ruining his health by "vitiouse Courses and Raking," has left Stanhope for another career.

Shaftesbury had every expectation of living a very retired life in Paris. Gradually, though, the warm air of the city began to revive him and he left his house more and more frequently. There are more chairs ordered for him, a coach for ten half-days near the end, and, one notes, bottles of Côte Roti and Hermitage became a regular part of his daily fare. By August 8 he felt well enough to travel to Versailles, so that he, Jane, and Mrs. Skinner could visit the Court.

Shaftesbury's party left Paris on the twelfth of August and arrived in Dijon on the eighteenth, going by Melun, Auxerre, Montbard, and Val Suzon. This is much better time than they had made from Calais, probably because the Earl was well, relatively speaking; at least he makes no entry in the diary where he notes such things. He does remark that from Paris they had "bad weather rain & cold all along." Durand left him on this part of the trip to return to Paris. Actually the only one of the lesser servants who made the whole trip with him is Harry, Henry Spencer, who is continually listed in the account books as needing something or other. Shaftesbury tended to hire local servants as he went along.

After two days at Dijon they headed south for a very long day's ride through the wine country to Chalon, where Shaftesbury's asthma returned to torture him. There they arranged to leave the roads and sail south on the Saône in what is described as a *coche*

12. The Earl of Shaftesbury to Thomas Micklethwayte, August 11, 1711 NS, in PRO 30/24/27/21. This is an original letter revealing that Shaftesbury's letter book is heavily edited, passages such as this, for example, often being removed.

d'eau, probably a barge of some sort. Even going downstream it took four oarsmen. The owner of the boat was paid for cleaning Shaftesbury's cabin and fastening the doors that separated it from the rest of the boat. They went ashore at Mâcon that night but apparently returned aboard to sleep. On the following day, the twenty-fourth, after paying the officer in charge of the chain at Lyons, Shaftesbury, his party, and their baggage were unloaded from the boat by water women, and they put up at the Three Kings.

Shaftesbury stayed in Lyons for eleven days, in part, as he tells a correspondent, to regain his health before the journey ahead; in part because he was now on the edge of a very active war zone and he had to be sure of clearance. The Intendant, or governor, of Lyons, Monsieur Meliant, sent a physician to him; from the apothecary a syrup of red poppy, containing hyssop water and licorice, was fetched, and later a *bain-marie* was purchased "for making my Lord's Viper broth." More windows were repaired, and the proprietor of the inn was given a sum to make sure that no one smoked near the Earl. With all this, Shaftesbury was still getting about the city when necessary and drinking his Rhone wines; Jane, however, did what sightseeing that was done.

Shaftesbury must have expected some word from home at Lyons. There was nothing, he notes in his diary. On the other hand there was a passport and letter from the Marquis de Torcy, for which Shaftesbury thanks him profusely. Most important was his correspondence with the Duke of Berwick. Unfortunately his reply of August 28 to a letter from the Duke saying he would have him escorted to the Italian border somehow went astray. Moreover, the Duke, thinking they had gone on to Grenoble, sent his letter there. When Shaftesbury finally found out that the Duke had planned on their being in Grenoble by that time, he waited only a day for further orders and left Lyons on October 6. His party was well protected from the cold and wet, even with umbrellas. They carried passports from the Duke and one from the Duke of Savoy, which Berwick had obtained for them. Because of his health and the treacherous road ahead of them, Shaftesbury himself was carried on a litter, and he explains to the Duke that this may mean that they will move quickly enough so that he will have the opportunity to thank him personally.

The party traveled southeast to Grenoble and arrived there in time for dinner on the eighth, not bad for a journey which on a modern road is about seventy miles. In Grenoble they had dinner with the president of the town and may have stayed the night with him. From here on, almost until they crossed the border into Italy five days later, they were in territories controlled by the Duke of Berwick, and he or his public officials provided many of their meals and sometimes their board. The next morning they set off abruptly northwest up the valley of the Isère in the general direction of Chambéry. Shaftesbury remained in his litter, the rest of the company now on horseback and the baggage carried by mules. Riding along as an escort was Captain Lacy, the Duke of Berwick's aide-de-camp, and a troop of dragoons.

Shaftesbury had a right to be worried about the movements of the military in the area. In one case he left his inn without paying the bill, just ahead of the soldiers. Who knows but the party might find themselves crossing actual battle lines? According to the Duke of Berwick's own account, the Duke of Savoy drove through the Mont Cenis pass early in July, but he was unable to force his way down the narrow valley of the Arc against Berwick's resistance. He then turned north toward the only other pass into Italy in that direction, the Little St. Bernard, where he would have the broader Isère valley to maneuver in and the pass to retreat by if necessary.[13] Berwick then moved back up to the head of the Arc, so while Shaftesbury was moving across the roughly west-east valley controlled by France, just to the north in a parallel valley were the troops of the Empire. The Duke's charge was to maintain a defensive line running irregularly from Geneva to Nice. Some of the country was so rough that a small band of troops could occupy a commanding position for a whole season without fear of being dislodged. Berwick held the line for four years.

Shaftesbury never told his friends how deeply indebted he was to the Duke of Berwick for so many services. In a little memorandum book he carried there are two pages filled with the names of Ber-

13. Marshal James Fitzjames, Duke of Berwick, *Mémoires du Maréchal de Berwick, ecrites par lui-même* (2 vols.; Libraires Associés, Switzerland, 1778).

wick's officers who helped him on his last days in France. Of course he sent his most profusely thankful notes to the Duke, saying among other things that the whole trip would have been unthinkable without his help and that of Lady Waldegrave. He did have the opportunity to thank him personally, too, though the Duke's army was at that moment engaged in very active maneuvers and counter maneuvers against that of the Empire on a front a hundred air miles, and hundreds of actual miles, long. For the tenth of September there is a note in the accounts, "At night treated by the D of B at Aigubello." We can be sure that a few years before Shaftesbury would have regarded this about as likely as sitting down with the Pope for food and wine. His embarrassment over the Duke's hospitality involves still another of his reasons for not staying in France; he did not want to be obligated to the French for anything more than passage through their country. Perhaps we can forgive this impassioned enemy of all things French and Catholic, that when confronted by the reality, he still sought to protect an ideal which may have been valid enough against the Sun King's dreams of hegemony. The trouble was that the Duke of Berwick agreed strongly with Shaftesbury's own comment to Marshal Tallard that there are some things more important than either nationality or religion, and reading his autobiography one senses that the Duke's world could not so easily be cut up into separate compartments as the world of the intensely idealistic Shaftesbury.

At no season would the journey from Aiguebelle up the tortuous valley of the Arc and over the seven-thousand-foot pass at Mount Cenis down to Susa on the Italian side have been safe for a person in Shaftesbury's condition. When he lay near death in Turin for several days, he had to admit he had waited too long. What must have been an exhilarating experience a quarter of a century before had brought him closer to the death that awaited him than he had ever been before. In parts, the gorge has been thoroughly scoured by glaciers leaving no soil anywhere, so that the precipitous sides are *sombre*, the favorite French term for the deep and twisting valley and its cliffs. Today one can stand in Modane and, if one's neck is sufficiently flexible, look up at fortifications so high that it seems a wonder that they were ever manned. At Lanslebourg at the foot of the final ascent, chairs were provided for the ladies. Somewhere during the climb the French troops were replaced by the Emperor's and the company proceeded down the eastern side, which rapidly becomes very sunny and open.

After a night at Susa, Shaftesbury and the ladies went on to Turin in a chaise, perhaps because it was necessary to get him in the hands of a physician as soon as possible. They arrived by noon of September 16. Because the Duke of Berwick did cross the passes to attack the Duke of Savoy's line of communications, Shaftesbury left none too soon. When the horses were sent back from Turin to Lyons, they had to return via the Great St. Bernard Pass and Geneva, almost twice as far as they had come originally.

The party remained in Turin for over three weeks while Shaftesbury recovered, treated by two physicians and bled—only once, fortunately—by a surgeon. Except for the occasional viper, his medicine was almost wholly herbal, syrup of poppies, ivy ground for juice, hyssop water, leaves from beets, parieter, violets, fresh almond oil, and so forth.[14] For food he depended largely on cock broth for the whole stay. There was one cheerful note in the visit. Forwarded by Benjamin Furly, mail arrived from England telling him for the first time since he had left Paris two months before that Lord Ashley was well. After twelve days he felt well enough to hire a sedan chair for a trip through the Valentine park, but though his health must have improved further, he did no more sight-seeing.

However ill Shaftesbury was, it must have been good to be in friendly territory again. One advantage was that he could use the services of English diplomats. The nearest to Turin seems to have been William Chetwynd (1685?–1770), later Viscount Chetwynd, the envoy at Genoa. The litter on which Shaftesbury had come over the Alps had been left behind in Susa, and Chetwynd had sent a litter and bardot, the latter probably some sort of cover, from Genoa with

---

14. It is possible to tell what the state of Shaftesbury's health is from the account books. Of all of his medicines, vipers are the most sensitive index of his physical state. Powdered viper can be used, but the best broth is made from a fresh one. The Italian viper is an exceedingly deadly snake, and the accounts show his servants buying boxes to hold them and tongs to handle them with. Almost every day on which his health incapacitates him from all outside and many inside activities another viper has to be bought.

its bearers, who carried Shaftesbury all the way to Naples. It is likely that he himself came to Turin; in any case someone made Shaftesbury known to the court of Savoy. Count Gallas (1669–1719), Envoy of the Emperor, arranged for a functionary named Eckersall to accompany the party as far as Florence and even one of the carriage drivers seems to have been in the service of the Queen of Savoy.

Aside from giving us a record of how much syrup of red poppies Shaftesbury consumed on the way to Naples, the account books are of little use to us below Turin. This is because the party is now traveling on the Italian system, the same one Shaftesbury had used on his last Italian journey, whereby a conductor is chosen for the journey and himself pays all the expenses, for which he is reimbursed at the end. There is no better example of how well the system worked than this one. Of the party, only the perilously ill Shaftesbury had any experience with traveling in Italy and the price per day was settled before departure with the aid of his banker in Turin. On the ninth of October Shaftesbury was again lifted into his litter and John Brun de Mondovy, the conductor, led them forth from the Auberge de l'Académie in Turin toward Milan; the rest of the party came in two caleshes, two-wheeled carriages with folding tops, and on horseback.

Although they did not go by Pavia, as Shaftesbury had in 1688, it still took them three days to reach Milan, where Shaftesbury tried some diplomacy on his own, despite his illness. As he explains it to Sir John,

> What I procured from Count Wratislaw was by my own boldness and assurance in accosting him as I did at Milan. He was surprised to hear of me there. 'Twas on the very day that the whole City was in an uproar, and drawn out in their Streets to receive the Emperor. The Count (as first Minister) holding his Court in his Great Palace, Laid up with the Gout, with his Princes and Grandees attending him. Late at night I sent him my message, which he receive'd so well that being wrap'd up in my Night Gown, just as I came out of my Litter, I was carryed in men's arms through his Antichambers and great Company and set close to him, where I had my Audience and a very friendly reception.[15]

15. The Earl of Shaftesbury to Sir John Cropley, December 29, 1711 NS, in PRO 30/24/23/8/pp. 78–83.

From there it took eight days to reach Bologna; apparently they could make only twenty miles a day with the litter. Surely his mind must have frequently returned to his youth, when he and his companions trotted their horses down this same road. Even when he spent full days looking at pictures and viewing the sights in Parma and Modena the journey did not take nearly this long. Regardless of time, how much longer must the trip in the litter have seemed? To make it worse, the evening air would be chilly now, and Shaftesbury was still behind the schedule he had planned on.

South of Bologna the mountains begin and they continue on the route the party had to take, until about thirty-five miles below Rome the road swings over to the coast where it stays until Naples. The mountains range up to three thousand feet high. And one can imagine what it would be to be carried in a litter through such a country, because even if the road dips into a river valley so that it runs level for a while it almost always rises up to the towns where one would dine or spend the night. This is where, according to the logic of both war and peace, inns had to be situated.

Arriving at Florence on the twenty-sixth, they spent two nights with Robert Molesworth's son John (1679–1726), later Viscount Molesworth, the English ambassador to Turin and Tuscany. He was the one resident in Italy most concerned about Shaftesbury's health, and according to Shaftesbury's grateful letters must have done much to make the trip go smoothly. Molesworth's own secretary had accompanied the party from Bologna to Florence. From there, now making only fifteen miles a day, they proceeded to Rome, down the familiar route through Siena and Acquapendente, in the Pope's territories Montefiascone and Monterose, which Shaftesbury had followed years before, and which most travelers continued to follow until the autostradas were constructed. They left Rome after only two days and arrived in Naples on the fifth, thirty-eight days from Turin. It had been over three and a half weary months and, on modern roads, fourteen hundred miles from Reigate.

Shaftesbury's bankers in Leghorn had urged him to find himself a house in Chiaia in the western part of Naples where the precipitous Vomero hill comes close to the bay shutting off the north wind, so that one gets the maximum benefit from the warm and sulfurous air. The day after they arrived Lady Shaftesbury went out to look over a house that their agent in Naples knew was available in the area; the Earl examined it the next day, and by the twentieth of November they were setting up housekeeping in the Palazzo Mirelli.

Palazzo is used loosely and does not always suggest what one might think, but this building was then grand enough to fit the word, so large that Shaftesbury could have needed, or maintained, only a small part of it—though he may have been the only tenant at the time. Imagine yourself in a boat offshore, first you would see a broad beach, then a wide boulevard lined with palazzi facing you on the Riviera, and not far behind towers the hill. At the intersection with the Arco Mirelli the facade of the palace stretches west for, say, over 150 feet, though the building is only about sixty feet tall, and it is not as deep as it is wide. The whole structure has a plain and squarish appearance; the stone ground floor is surmounted by two more faced in stucco. The profusion of horizontal lines is relieved by quoins on the corners and four similar stone pillars set in the face running from the ground to the slightly tilted, projecting roof. In the center of the ground floor is a very tall arch with columns, mirrored by three smaller arches on each side, and these are followed by a pair of rectangular windows in each corner. Above these in the stucco are two sets of eleven large, plain windows, each with its balcony. Through the portal one comes into an open courtyard with open stairs and galleries giving access to the rooms, and in Shaftesbury's day another doorway in the back of the courtyard opened into a large garden.

The palace was built in the seventeenth century for the Duke of Caivano Barile according to the plans of Cosimo Fansanga. A visitor to Naples in the 1630s, when it was still under construction, pronounced it the most magnificent palace on the Riviera, though Fansanga's plans were finally left incomplete. In any case, when the Riviera was paved near the end of the century, the palace received the highest assessment, some proof of its elegance. Frederick Calvert, the last Baron Baltimore (1731–1771), died there. It was rebuilt in the eighteenth century and finally came into the hands of the Prince Mirelli. Today the whole lower facade is cut up into shops, some of them with gasoline pumps decorating the curb. Yet on the

other side of the Arco stands the graceful French Consulate, a minia-
ture Pitti Palace, which still reflects the sort of grace which Shaftesbury's house must have had in its heyday.[16]

For good reason neither Shaftesbury nor his little family dwell on
the beauties of their home, and Lady Jane, "surely the Best Huswife
as well as Wife, Nurse, & Friend that was ever Known in her whole
sex," as he calls her, had a chance to show what she could do, for the
house was barely furnished. Everything from brooms to dishes to
liveries and wall hangings had to be purchased. There were calashes
to be bought, horses, hens, partridges, and an ass, so that Shaftesbury would have his milk. The cook must have chosen the complete
range of cooking equipment; the rest of it was Lady Shaftesbury's to
choose, and she seems to have purchased whatever she thought necessary and ordered the rest when the need became apparent.

One wonders when Shaftesbury discovered that there were no
fireplaces in the mansion except in the kitchen. Perhaps he remembered from his last visit, though it was then summer, that Neapolitans heated their rooms with braziers, as poor people there still
do today. In any case this meant that they had to have a chimney and
fireplaces constructed, and the natives do not seem to have been
very expert, for the one in his anteroom smoked. Furthermore, the
house was completely unglazed and windows had to be put into
some of the spaces. Apparently the poor were then poorer in Naples
than in other Italian cities, as they are now; almost every week for
months they discovered some door or cabinet that needed a lock in
the house or, perhaps a grating, such as was put up between the cellar and garden.

Jane theorized that it was this frenzy of activity which brought
them down with severe agues at the end of November—affecting
even the cook, who seems to be the same one who traveled with
them from Rome. Only Crell and Frances were spared. Most of them
responded to the quinine in Peruvian bark. Poor Shaftesbury, who

16. For details of Shaftesbury's last visit to Naples not available from his own papers, Benedetto Croce's presidential address to the MHRA, "Shaftesbury in Italy"
(Cambridge, n.d.), is invaluable. As an old acquaintance of Croce's once told me, he is
inevitably authoritative on Neapolitan matters. The address is in Italian, despite its
title.

had used the bark in Dorset, had subsequently discovered that it made his asthma worse. As Jane remarks in a letter to her sister, "he was so exceeding bad that I thought he cou'd never have come out of his fit. After near three hours being in the greatest Agonies that ever was felt, he fell into his feaver fit, which was very great and held 8. or 9. hours. He has begun to take Bark this morning."[17]

Poor Belle Skinner missed all this. Ever since Dijon she had been falling into "distracted Fitts" and became an additional burden for the travelers across the Alps and into Italy, all the more so because she had, as Shaftesbury says, a proud and violent temper. In Naples, Belle was desperate to go home and they put her aboard the first ship for England, the *Severn Galley*. Shaftesbury, fearing the ship might be taken by the French, sent a note with her saying that she was traveling under the protection of Louis XIV. He also wrote Wheelock to make sure that she was taken care of when she arrived in Bristol. Indeed, if she would put her affairs in Wheelock's hands, she was to be supported for life.

Late in December he writes to Cropley saying that the letters from Counts Wratislaw (1677–1733) and Gallas to the Viceroy, Count Borromeo (1657–1754), have arrived and there has been an immediate reaction. The Viceroy's physician now visits him regularly, yet refuses to accept any money. Shaftesbury knew how dependent he was on the good will of this officer. In Naples he was as close to Spain as he would ever get, and a previous Viceroy had made things very difficult for Protestants who decided to settle there. Sir John must see that high officials in England write to both the Viceroy and Count Wratislaw thanking them for their kindness. Cropley also receives, as Micklethwayte did, one of those painful lectures on his responsibilities toward Shaftesbury and the absolute necessity of being highly systematic in his correspondence—he was to specify the dates of letters received and so forth. By now his friends must have taken it for granted that Shaftesbury was incapable of seeing why everyone was not as meticulous in these matters as he was. There is no politics in the letters to Cropley or Micklethwayte, but

17. Lady Jane Shaftesbury to Mrs. Anne Ewer, November 30, 1711 NS, in PRO 30/24/23/8/pp. 56–59.

he writes to both John Molesworth and his bankers in Leghorn about secret negotiations and the dangers of an unjust peace. One wonders if he recollected how earnestly he had seemed to desire peace in his letters to French correspondents, from the Chevalier de Molé on, and whether he saw the inconsistency; probably not.

We can be sure that Shaftesbury's deep concern for Lord Ashley's welfare persisted, though for the most part we have little incoming mail abroad and very few original copies of his own letters—the only personal matters which the amanuensis recorded in the letter books were details on the publication of the second edition of *Characteristicks*, which Shaftesbury needed to keep notes on. Lord Ashley had been moved to Kensington, where his aunt, Anne, watched over him. Even from Rome, Shaftesbury writes to Wheelock speaking of the continuation of his line: "I Know your Affection for that Family & for him himself whom I saw (& since hear by every one) is so winning and engaging a Child. . . . Give Kisses from us to Lord Ashley when you come again to him next."[18] No doubt had we seen Shaftesbury with his nephew Ned this sentiment would come as less of a surprise in the letters of a man who when he writes is for the most part so formal and dignified.

By the end of December the household is well settled. Except for Shaftesbury's oatmeal and certain herbal medicines which must come from England, the family is fully Italianized. And locally, aside from maintaining their stocks and buying more and more locks, their purchases shift to luxury items, books and items for the Christmas season—materials for the cook to make sweet cakes, preserved fruits, and chestnuts. They hang draperies in the Earl's rooms to suppress drafts. Consul Fleetwood sends wine and the Viceroy, partridges. Pedro their footman, who was almost naked when hired, gets a sword; there are gifts to the Christmas boxes at Signor Moreau's, their agent, as well as at the Consul's and at the Viceroy's. There are also gifts to the latter's major-domo, for his German halberdiers, and for the drummers of the Regiment of Chiaia, who performed. Finally, Shaftesbury sends money off to the drummers of

18. The Earl of Shaftesbury to John Wheelock, November 6, 1711 NS, in PRO 30/24/21/143.

Prince Pio, who also performed on Christmas day, but they were thrown in jail for not seeking their master's permission.

The last year or so of Shaftesbury's life can be divided into four periods: the first months of 1712 when he is confined to the palazzo; a brief time from April through part of July when he gets out frequently and sees the city and its people; from July through November when he still hopes to survive the coming winter, though his health and the weather keep him more and more inside; and the final two months when he knows for sure there is no hope at all of surviving.

Especially in the winter Shaftesbury, like many of his contemporaries, is convinced that the state of his health has a precise, almost mathematical relation to the weather. When the air is harsh there is no venturing out. He is sealed in, with every draft shut out of his rooms and good fires blazing in what he often speaks of as the only fireplaces in Naples. By the new year, though, he begins to feel better, with the "soft, healing, cherishing, enchanting siren *Parthenope*" as he calls the breeze tinged with sulphur, which eases his asthma so that he can breathe more freely. His tertian fever, the swellings in his legs, and his cough decline, and by January his eyes are less painful, so that occasionally he can scribble a few lines of his own in a letter. By February he feels that winter is almost surely over, and he dreams of revisiting some of the scenes he saw a quarter century before. It is not until a sudden chill falls over the town in March that he admits the truth, that he must remain confined still more weeks. "This latter part has been the coldest Known in a long time in this Climate."

Oddly enough these first few months, and for that matter the whole year right up until his death, must be regarded as one of the most creative periods of his life. It is possible to see some of the reasons for this. His always powerful sense of mission is not blunted by the prospect of death, it is sharpened. He thinks now that through art he has found a way to fulfill his mission, if he can only live long enough to do so. This explains why his voluminous letters this year are such a mixture of optimism and pessimism, as he wavers between the hope he will succeed and the fear that he may not. His health rules all, but in a strange way he has been cured of any qualms relating to it, except for this fear involving his work. The Earl has been ill for so long and suffered so much that he now has learned to live from day to day. There is no end to illness, but there is real joy in looking back on a day when, despite his burdens, he has accomplished something tangible.

His first business is to complete the revision of a new edition of *Characteristicks*. This has nothing to do with whether or not another edition is called for. We may believe him or not when he says that his printer is merely another form of amanuensis, but he began revising for a second edition long before the first was out. Indeed, the first two volumes of the second edition were fairly complete before he left England, though in his hurry he forgot to bring a copy of them along, which he was to regret. The Earl is a perfectionist and he sees so many instances where changes are needed, largely in style and grammar. Apparently he read some of *Characteristicks* aloud to see how it sounded. In his copy of the 1711 edition with revisions, which has somehow found its way to the British Library, there is a typical note: "There was a kind of rhyming or leaping measure between *weak attempt* and *proper strength*." All these changes together add up to a vast amount of work and they sometimes result in long stretches in the book where there are alterations on every page.

Still another reason for a new edition of *Characteristicks* was that Shaftesbury now felt illustrations were necessary. There is some question whether these plates have ever been fully appreciated, even during the eighteenth century which was more familiar with the emblem tradition than we are, for they are very intricate, indeed.[19] Page numbers for the text of *Characteristicks* are given under each illustration, but they do not tell one much. All of the meanings are made clear enough by Shaftesbury's notes, however. Not counting the Ashley-Cooper coat of arms, which appeared over the preface in 1714, there are nine illustrations added: an illustration for the general title page of each volume and a headpiece for each individual

---

19. On this subject see Felix Paknadel, "Shaftesbury's Illustrations of *Characteristics*," *Journal of the Warburg and Courtauld Institute*, XXXVII (1974), 290–312. He is sound on their meanings. For his commentary on the "Judgment" he depends unfortunately on Rand.

treatise, all of these involving a central lapidary plate in a three-dimensional style, with detailed borders in a simpler style, which he calls grotesque. Some of the work had been done before Shaftesbury left England, but much of it was done abroad.

I suppose that Shaftesbury imagined that everything was very much as it had been on his first visit to Naples, but he seems to have been unable to find anyone who could follow his instructions in making the drawings. After firing one Neapolitan artist quite summarily, Shaftesbury wrote to a priest in Rome, the Reverend Doctor Fagan, who had greatly impressed Shaftesbury during his short visit there. Fagan was a correspondent of the Abbé Farely, whom the Earl had met in Paris and who worked for the Duke of Lauzun and was close to the Duke of Berwick and his family. Dr. Fagan made a number of suggestions as to artists and, after Shaftesbury had seen samples of their work, he decided on a Mr. Trench, an Englishman. The Earl gave Trench a carte blanche to buy books of reproductions of classical art. He was also to bring a list of engravers in Rome, presumably so one could be found to engrave the large plate of the Hercules. Trench's drawings and those of Gribelin from which he made the engravings for *Characteristicks* are in the Print Room of the British Museum.[20] Except for the plate to *The Judgment of Hercules*, which appears in some copies of the second edition, none of the plates carries the name of the designer. In one sense, however, Shaftesbury conceived that plate and all the rest too.

He reveals his motives in a letter to Micklethwayte, the first of them rather cryptically.

> I have a Noble *Virtuoso Scheme* before me, and design if I get Life this Summer to apply even this great Work (the History Piece bespoke, and now actually working) to the Credit & Reputation of *Philol*: But this is not the only View of Service which I ground on this chargeable and high Attempt. Our present Great Minister, or at least some future one may possibly have some compassion for the poor Arts and Virtuoso-Sciences which are in a manner bury'd here abroad and have never yet rais'd their Heads in Britain. It might be well for your joynt Interest and Sir John's as Friend to one another and to me if through your hands a

---

20. There they are all ascribed to Gribelin. Edgar Wind first distinguished Trench's work from Gribelin's. See his "Shaftesbury as a Patron of Art," *Journal of the Warburg and Courtauld Institute*, II (1938), 186–88.

Present should be made of a glorious Piece not only worthy of a Prime Minister but even of the reigning Prince, or of some Prince of the Royal Family, to whom the Piece itself may be a Council and Instruction— Pray lay this Saying up in your Memory. ffor I should hardly bestow my time and Pains with about fourscore Pistoles prime Charge and with so many consequent Expenses, for the sake of a Piece of Furniture meerly for St. Giles's or as a Meer Ornament to *Philol*.[21]

Art preoccupied Shaftesbury in other ways during the period when he had to stay inside the palazzo. It says something about early eighteenth-century English attitudes toward art that, despite the obvious decline of the Neapolitan schools, art enriches his life so much more in Naples than it did at home. At times he seems intoxicated by the experience. Not long after he arrived he met Paolo de Matteis, who was esteemed first among Neapolitan painters of the day. A copy of his *Galathea* was delivered to the palazzo late in January and by February Paolo is hard at work on *The Judgment of Hercules*.

Of course, the Earl is excited not merely by being close to the fountainhead of art; some of his gusto is due to the purposes for which he intends to use art, a subject which he is afraid to say much about in his letters home, lest his friends try to stop him from over-exerting himself. The passing comment on the "Noble *Virtuoso Scheme*" refers to his whole plan for improving men through art. Art is in decline throughout the Continent because of, among other things, the dominance of the baroque, a latter-day gothicism. In England, perhaps fortunately, art has not yet risen. There he hopes it will arise soundly based on classical principles. This is why Mr. Trench's commission involves copying classical sculptures and reliefs, but it also explains the care Shaftesbury took with the emblems in the second edition of *Characteristicks*. *Philol*, a term that often appears in Shaftesbury's later letters, sometimes refers to his study of morals; frequently, though, it refers more narrowly to the noble virtuoso scheme for the ethical use of art in paintings and in the art work for his books. In other words, properly executed, classical art is powerfully formative, or shaping, and this gives Shaftesbury a new vehicle for expressing his moral notions, all the more

21. The Earl of Shaftesbury to Thomas Micklethwayte, February 23, 1712 NS, in PRO 30/24/23/8/pp. 149–50.

effective because it works on the beholder without his being aware, at least at first, that it is doing so.[22]

While he was still confined to his chambers this winter, the Neapolitan intellectuals who were to make the last year of his life more agreeable began to visit him. Their lives were grouped around the aged Don Giuseppe Valetta, his library and his museum of antiquities. The library still survives and it is an awesome sight, displayed in a huge narrow room in the Biblioteca di Oratoriano, where the priests placed it after buying it when Valetta died in 1714. The light comes into the room very high and the walls are solidly filled with row upon row of ancient and modern books reaching up to a high balcony and then to the windows still further above. The selection of classical editions is very fine, but the real glory of the library is its collection of Renaissance philosophy and science from all over Europe, especially England.

Though Valetta was a far more influential man, there are a number of resemblances between his life and that of Benjamin Furly. The fact that it is no longer possible for polymaths such as these two to arise, apparently self-taught, from humble beginnings, should not obscure what an astounding performance it was in seventeenth-century terms. It is too easy to regard them as successful businessmen turned literati, where the truth of the matter seems to be that they were comprehensive geniuses. They needed wealth to fulfill

22. The history of the prints derived from the Hercules is complex. Apparently Shaftesbury envisioned two engravings of the "Triumph," a large one to be over a foot across, and the smaller one familiar to readers of *Characteristicks*, done by Gribelin. He hoped to have a Signor Arnoldo from Rome do the large one, but according to the catalog of de Matteis' works, the engraver was Guiseppe Malliar. This print may have been used by Gribelin in engraving for the smaller print. Shaftesbury also intended to have de Matteis make two copies of the painting, one of which was to go to Lord Somers and the other to Sir John Cropley. Later, he mentions only one copy, which is to be different from the "Judgment" thus making it an "originall." Shaftesbury's very interesting directions, under the heading "La Theorie et la practique doivent s'accorder" are in PRO 30/24/23/9/pp. 239–40. Sir John received the sole copy, and was told that if he wished he could keep it for his own collection and Shaftesbury would deduct £20 from the £200 given him to collect art for Cropley. If he did not want to do this, he could send the painting on to Lord Somers. Cropley kept it and it is now in the Leeds City Art Gallery. Despite rather frequent comments on how much *The Triumph of Hercules* cost him, Paolo de Matteis would have been satisfied with the 300 pistoles—about 60 pounds—rather than the 360 the delighted Earl pressed on him. The tenth Earl of Shaftesbury recently sold the family copy.

their dreams, and making money as a merchant in an intensely competitive world must have seemed no more difficult than becoming the competent classicists they were.

Valetta was a tailor's son, who ultimately became a jurisconsult and a doctor of civil law. Most of his writing is on legal and economic problems, but philosophically his interests ranged from the Epicurean thought of Gassendi to the quietism of Molinos. Most important for the persisting influence of such men is the way they used their savoir faire, their wealth, and their libraries—in a day when there were no public ones—to draw the best minds together so that there was a fertile exchange of ideas. In Valetta's case there were also disciples; according to authorities, he made scores of them in his long life. Benedetto Croce regards him as the link between Naples and the world, the motivator of her renaissance, civil and political, and says that he for "more than half a century dominated and directed Neapolitan culture."[23]

Shaftesbury is rather coy about his new friends at first. In January he remarks that though he is short of breath he is still capable of a little conversation "about Virtuosi and Painting," but it is not until March that he explains that he converses with "some few men of Art and Science, the Virtuosi of this Place, as in particular the family of the famous Don Josepp Valetta." The only other names mentioned in the letters are those of Valetta's grandson and Paolo Mattia Doria (1662–1746), a distinguished writer on civil government, education, and mathematics. Doria he must have known early, for in the account book for April there are two self-explanatory entries:

Mon. . 4 To Signor Dorea's Servant who came with a Present to my Lord of a Tame Deer. 1-0-0.
Tues. . 5 To a Porter helping Pedro with the Deer back to Signor Doreas & a Cord to tye it. 0-3-0.

23. There were a number of contemporary lives of Valetta. A brief modern life by Victor Ivo Comparato is "Giuseppe Valetta e le sue opere," in *Archivio Storice per le Province Napoletane*, 3rd ser., II (Naples, 1963). For a fine study of his intellectual life in relation to his later years, when Shaftesbury met him, there is Biagio de Giovanni, "Culture e vita in Giuseppe Valetta," *Studi sul Settecento Italiano* (Naples, Istituto Italiano per gli Studi Storici, 1967). See also the pamphlet by Benedetto Croce, cited above.

Shaftesbury must have felt gratified by the constant attentions of Valetta's circle and he did his best to repay their kindness. Naples seems to have grown more and more isolated from the intellectual world of the north as the war progressed, even though the viceroy in charge when Shaftesbury came was far more tolerant than his predecessor. Mails to and from England were especially chancy. Through his own postal system Shaftesbury was able to reestablish communications between Valetta's circle and that of Sir Isaac Newton. Considering the difficulties involved and the distance, this did not take him long, but of course he grew quite impatient that it went no faster.

The conversations with the Italian virtuosi must have been both pleasant and profitable, but for discussions of the more serious side of his work and what Shaftesbury calls the "Literate World" and his own role in it, he has only his correspondence with Pierre Coste. As he says, "You are my only Book-Correspondant." I have commented before on this oddly sorted friendship. Surely there was much which should have prevented it from becoming so close—politics, for instance. Once in 1712, when the Earl decided, temporarily it turned out, that Coste was not a suitable tutor for Lord Ashley, he remarks in a letter to Micklethwayte that there is "not a Tory in England, not even an Oxford or a Christ-Church-Colledge Proselyte . . . wou'd be found more true by far to Liberty and Property, and a National Constitution, than either poor C——— or the Best that ever was born and bred a French man."[24] Or there is Coste's destructive foolishness about money. Before he left England, having helped Coste obtain an annuity so that he would be free and never have to enter trade, the Earl found he had to intervene again, when he discovered that Coste intended to sell the annuity.

Yet the friendship remained warm up until Shaftesbury's death. The most compelling reason for this is probably the one hardest to see at this distance. They must have found they had that rare sort of rapport which permitted them to be completely candid with each

24. The Earl of Shaftesbury to Thomas Micklethwayte, April 12, 1712 NS, in PRO 30/24/23/9/p. 194.

other, in a society heavily bound by convention. That Coste was a creature of the Enlightenment, though from a completely different social and cultural background, could only have helped this aspect of the relationship. The fact that Coste had been Locke's secretary, yet was very much at home in Continental literary society, also seemed an attraction for Shaftesbury.

After the Earl was unable to arrange for Coste to come with him through France, the Huguenot took a job as bear leader for Thomas Hobart (1695–1756), later first Earl of Buckinghamshire, on his grand tour, and Shaftesbury vows to talk to him. The trip was postponed, and in January 1712 Shaftesbury received a letter from Coste, still in London, which is fairly typical of his later correspondence with the Earl. He will do everything he can to keep Shaftesbury up with happenings in the republic of letters. Le Clerc has published long extracts from *Characteristicks*—which Coste helped him choose. Leibniz (1646–1716) had previously asked for a copy of Coste's commentary on Horace, that is, Shaftesbury's, and he and Micklethwayte have decided to send Leibniz a set of *Characteristicks*. After reading this, Leibniz was to write his famous review of the book. Hester (b. 1675), daughter of Lady Masham, has written to tell Coste to thank the Earl for thinking of her. Finally, Coste gives an account of a visit he paid Lord Ashley in the company of Anthony Collins (1676–1729), which must have pleased Shaftesbury.

Shaftesbury replies right away because he has all sorts of ideas as to how Coste can make the Continent know him better. Coste could touch up his *Judgment of Hercules*, written in French, and have it published anonymously in the *Bibliothèque Choisie*. Thus Shaftesbury coyly hopes the public will come only gradually to realize that it is by the same author that wrote *Characteristicks*. Coste could also correct the lame translation of the *Letter Concerning Enthusiasm*, which with a properly annotated edition of the translation of *Sensus Communis*, Shaftesbury thinks would make a fine gift for a prince—he is probably thinking of the Electress of Hanover. Micklethwayte, perhaps anticipating the success of Le Clerc's extracts, has suggested that Coste translate all of *Characteristicks*, but Shaftesbury, remembering the problems with translating the *Inquiry*, rejects the notion.

Shaftesbury was to wait many months for an answer, because Coste himself had begun to travel and because the Earl's mails were so poor this spring. The Continental route was very circuitous, letters finally ending up in the hands of Furly, who sent them on to England. Mail sent by ship, it turned out, usually got there, but no one could tell when it would arrive. Shaftesbury fretted for two months this spring over when the Phenix Galley would dock in Leghorn. When it finally did so in late March, it had everything aboard he could wish for, except what he wanted most, copies of his partially revised version of volumes one and two of *Characteristicks*. These he needed so that he could work more accurately with the heavily cross-annotated book. Somehow the urgency of his request had not got through to Micklethwayte and Wheelock.

In April Shaftesbury began to try out his ability to get around out of doors, for the tardy spring had finally come. A calash, a lightweight carriage for four, probably with a folding top, is continually on hire, but Shaftesbury prefers the sedan chair, leaving the calash for the servants in bad weather. Sedan chairs were hired until the chair which was begun for him in the summer was finished. A coach should be used for longer trips or more formal occasions, and Shaftesbury began to think of renting one in April, but he never came to depend on them much, probably because they were draftier than chairs.

His favorite trip was up along the northern shore of the Bay of Naples to the volcanic regions, where at the Sulphaterra he could breathe all the sulphur-laden air he wished. These fumes often drifted down to Chiaia, and later when Vesuvius erupts, it is hard to tell whether he enjoyed the spectacle more, or the fact that the fumes which cleared his head came from both directions. This time we know that he experimented with putting a dog into the Grotto de Cane, for there is a note in the accounts: "To Pedro for a Shock Dogg." Another trip which he must have enjoyed was when he and Lady Jane were carried up in chairs to the peak of Mount Posillipo, where there is a magnificent view of the volcanic regions.

It seems inevitable that in retracing all these scenes from his youth and explaining them to his wife he would overdo it, and he did. By the twentieth of April he is again confined to the house and does not come out again until the second week in May. There was plenty to do inside in any case. Trench, the artist hired to do the actual drawings for *Characteristicks*, arrived from Rome this month, and was to remain until September. Living quarters were set up for him directly adjoining his master's, so that Shaftesbury could watch him work. Since the Earl's principal artist, de Matteis, often painted there, though he lived elsewhere, the palazzo must have had a decidedly artistic air about it. Contributing to this were Shaftesbury's own purchases of paintings, prints, and medals, both for himself and others. At times he did go out to view paintings which people wanted to sell him, but the usual procedure was for him to view them at home. The accounts are full of payments to porters for carrying paintings to and fro.

There was also still a lot to be done to make the palazzo comfortable. Given the Earl's obsession about drafts, more and more openings were blocked up and there were yet open windows to be glazed. Some walls were painted; in others handsome Neapolitan tiles were set; and many were covered with hangings to allay the chill from the heavy stone walls. A room was set aside as a picture gallery. And always new places were discovered where locks had to be installed to keep things from disappearing.

By the middle of May Shaftesbury began to feel better, and he started taking rather frequent jaunts which carried him up hill and down, along the rim of the Bay of Naples, from Portici a few miles to the south to the volcanic area in the north. In town or out, he sought whatever moved him in nature, antiquities, or art. Most of the art was of course to be found in churches or monasteries. For instance, there were at least two visits to the cathedral and the monastery of San Marino listed. Another time he went to the monastery of Mount Oliveto, where he seems to have purchased a painting through the agency of art dealer Signor Porchinaro, whose house he also visited frequently.

During the winter Lady Jane Shaftesbury's life had been full of chores and nursing, but it is wrong to think of her existence even then as a monotonous round. The short and painful lives that so many Neapolitans experienced were constantly punctuated by an elaborate series of holy days, at once both somber and joyous. Frequently the Countess went to the various festivals. Seldom did Shaftesbury have either the inclination or feel well enough to attend, though he shows a lively enough interest in other activities of the Church, including the miracles of Naples which he regards with discreet and restrained curiosity. His wife then often went forth only with her lady-in-waiting, Frances Whitney, and servants, though at night a halberdier or two was always hired to accompany her chair to and from the procession.

Shaftesbury's improving health gave Lady Jane still more time for herself. The trouble is that she knew only one woman outside of the palazzo who spoke English, and lack of Italian kept her from meeting Neapolitan ladies, which under the social system prevailing there would not have been easy in any case. She did chat and travel about frequently with Mrs. Howe, who may be a relation of Lord Scrope Howe, Shaftesbury's uncle. There were also many chores about the house which she did, simply because she liked doing them. She supervised the preserving of fruit and bought the crocks and the elderberries to make wine. One hopes too that she oversaw the plantings in the palazzo garden of her husband's favorite vegetable, asparagus. Jane also shopped more, buying fabrics for clothing and innumerable slippers and fans.

And festivals went on too. One can imagine her delight on the morning of Corpus Christi day in June. Pedro Rene, a servant who seems to be one of those Neapolitans who can rise to almost any occasion, awoke very early, bought new brooms to sweep the street in front of the palazzo and bales of flowers, then decorated the street with flowers in very elaborate designs, patterns which would be destroyed ritualistically by the feet of the marchers in the procession who bore the cross of the crucified Christ and other objects.

Most of what I have said about the recreations of the Earl and his Countess make it sound like they were visiting a slightly older version of what travelers to Naples see today, but for the English the town was full of perils. The whole temper of the town depended upon the attitude of the Viceroy. Gilbert Burnet speaks of the Viceroy in the mid-1680s, the Marquis of Carpio (d. 1687), as very en-

399

lightened, which translated means that he kept the Spanish in their place. Shortly, however, the strains of war were to be added to the dangers from the Inquisition. Cardinal Grimani (1655–1710), the Viceroy immediately before Shaftesbury's visit, was very repressive, so the English were daily insulted and abused in the streets. Only a powerful loyalty to either England or Mammon, depending on their vocation, could have persuaded them to continue living there. Grimani's successor, Count Borromeo, a member of the distinguished family from the Duchy of Milan, was again enlightened, yet he had to deal with a powerful pro-French party in what seems to have been a fairly Byzantine court.

As we have seen, the Count accorded Shaftesbury all the courtesies his rank entitled him to. In May he was able to go further. One of Shaftesbury's chief worries was the security and efficiency of his mails. The best he had been able to work out was for Furly to forward the mail from England to the English consulate in Naples. This did not mean that the mail traveled in some sort of equivalent of the modern diplomatic pouch; often it would lie around Naples for a long time before reaching the consulate. Because of his persecution complex and his illness, Shaftesbury suffered far more than the usual correspondent, whose lot was not a happy one. What Borromeo offered to do was to permit all mails for Shaftesbury to be directed by Furly to the Viceroy himself. On arrival the Viceroy's messengers then brought it to the palazzo. This completely solved the problem, and mail then often came in only five weeks. The arrangement had to be kept absolutely secret, so that at the beginning not even Micklethwayte knew to whom Furly was directing the letters. If Shaftesbury had any time alone with the Viceroy when he paid him a formal visit early in July, this arrangement must have been what he thanked him most for. Later, he was to have even better reasons for gratitude.

In July 1712 Shaftesbury entered a new phase which went on through October and was marked by increasingly longer bouts with illness. As autumn neared, the Jesuits' powder again appeared among the medicines, signaling a return of his fevers. Yet though he says that he is worn to skin and bone, the Earl remains essentially optimistic. Perhaps it is better to say Stoically optimistic. He still managed to turn out a volume of work which suggests that nothing is wrong with him.

One topic which is rarely to be found in his letters to England is politics. Prudence is the obvious reason why Shaftesbury would ignore a topic of such importance to him. Should a letter fall into the wrong hands, it might endanger his stay in Italy and perhaps the job of Micklethwayte, who still managed to hold on to his job despite the Tory government. This would seem to be proved by his letters to John Molesworth in Florence, which are filled with political commentary. This mail was more secure, and if it were seized, at least it would not fall into Tory hands.

His correspondence with John Molesworth starts out very amiably. He is grateful to him and seems delighted to have someone he can talk politics with. Later, though, when Robert Molesworth asks him to intervene in John's affairs, Shaftesbury bridles. Indeed, John's reaction to the whole state of affairs in England has not been to lie low, as might beseem a Whig ambassador, but to continue to live extravagantly, to rant against the more prudent Whigs, yet to fail to make peace with the Tories, in order to keep his post. The Earl replied when Micklethwayte asked him on behalf of Robert to write John: "Am I then to give ADVICE? Am I to be the *Monitor* and *Preceptor*? Am I to thrust myself thus between Father and Son?" But he went ahead and did so anyway.

As we have seen so many times, Shaftesbury was almost always a creature of principle. The Whigs may be depressed, but the Earl is not, so long as the war goes on. However, late in the spring of 1712, shortly after the Duke of Ormond refused to fight at the side of Prince Eugene, Queen Anne made plans to end the fighting, and when Shaftesbury finally heard of this, he despaired. The Grand Alliance which he saw as counterbalancing the power of France is collapsing: the Empire must abandon Spain, and Holland is betrayed. The Earl writes to Molesworth, "My Amazement has been such at the progress of Affaires in Brittain, that I am allmost at an end of *thinking*: much less can I either *speak* or *write* of them. In reality Matters are now push'd so far, that, an *Englishman*, who is truly such, can hardly make a single Reflection which is fit to trust to paper."[25] Later, when he is trying to convince John to change his ways, he is more explicit. After remarking that only Providence can deliver England, he is fair to Robert Harley, as he usually was:

> We are now at the mercy of one single Man; who has all Power in his Hands, and every Secret in his Breast. How Providence may dispose that Heart I know not. He has a Head indeed but too able. Nor have we had (in my opinion) a Genius equal to oppose to him. . . . You may ask me perhaps as a Friend, *What shou'd one do in such a Case?* especially one who is *a Minister abroad*, and personates *a Ministry*, such as it now stands *at home?* . . . I wou'd neither act so as to offend the present Ministry and be recall'd to sollicit all my Life afterwards for my Arrears. Nor wou'd I act so much to the Honour of my own Court and Nation as to encrease those Arrears by my expences in their behalf or for their credit. . . . Since I cou'd no way make that Figure I ought to do; I wou'd resolve to make none at all, but turn Economist with all my might.[26]

John had already retired to the country, and, after receiving Shaftesbury's letter, began to see some positive values in his retreat. He then dismissed most of his family and quietly awaited another day, which was not long in coming.

Although Shaftesbury still seems to hope that he can survive another winter, he knows that he cannot live much longer, which raises the question of his religious views at this stage. Has the truth that the end is not too far off caused any change? Does the creating spirit he now worships as God at all coalesce with conventional notions of the Deity? The answer would seem to be no. His sardonic descriptions of Christ written this year in the *Second Characters* would rule out any belief in the Trinity, any sacrificial God, any personal salvation. He reveres an ideal duality—the creating spirit and Nature. What does change in these final years and months is his attitude toward the religion of others. He is now confident enough of his own beliefs that pious closings, for instance, begin to appear in his letters for the first time: "God be with you" and the like. All this

25. The Earl of Shaftesbury to John Molesworth, August 2, 1712 NS, in PRO 30/24/23/9/p. 255.
26. The Earl of Shaftesbury to John Molesworth, August 30, 1712 NS, in PRO 30/24/23/9/pp. 272–74.

means, though, is that he realizes that many who correspond with him will look on his passing in religious terms.

Since he had always believed that faith is morally necessary for most men, this may be nothing new, but he does now realize that faith has still other purposes, whatever he may have thought once. In Naples he saw the power of ritual. Once during a violent eruption that shook all of Naples Shaftesbury began to wonder whether the whole town might be swallowed up, and he found the populace very calm for a change:

> [Our] Comfort, according to the assurance of whole People, both Gentry and Commonalty of the Place is, That our protecting Saint (the Saint Januarius) has perform'd his usual Miracle of the Liquefying of his Blood. This I assure You, confirms the People of all Degrees in such a manner that whereas the Least Shock, Eruption, or Earthquake at other time raises the outmost consternation; the Miracle being at present restored and the Saint gracious, there is little made of any Symptoms of this Kind. [An] Earthquake is endur'd with very great resolution: and the Conflagrations are beheld in cold Blood, and with great Tranquility. So superior is the religious miracle to any natural Miracle or Prodigy besides.[27]

Shaftesbury is well aware of the effect this might have on the commonality; what startles him in Naples is the universality of the response. Perhaps he had to settle in a Catholic country to learn this.

His anticlericalism remains as sharp as ever, especially when he looks homeward. In August of 1712 the Earl learns of the death of Mr. Horsey, parson of St. Giles's, and he immediately decides to replace him with Tom Hooper, brother to Lady Dorothy's husband, Edward. Tom has bowled many times with Shaftesbury, who comments, "I need not fear the Character of the *Gentlemen* shou'd be lost in the *Parson*, since he resolves to be one." At the same time Shaftesbury worries about Michael Ainsworth, whom he fears may defect even before he is appointed to a living. What defection means is not spelled out but one can guess. Shaftesbury's three commandments may seem easier to follow now than they were then. A recipient of one of his livings would have to be a solidly moral preacher

27. The Earl of Shaftesbury to James Harris, May 10, 1712 NS, in PRO 30/24/23/9/ p. 214.

showing no enthusiastic tinges, a gentleman, and a persistent follower of low-church doctrines.

There was other more disturbing news from home. In a way it was good that Shaftesbury had the opportunity to choose Tom Hooper as parson for St. Giles's, because he was trying to prove that despite Edward Hooper's weakness and complaisance, he was still loyal to him. Ned's error was to permit Lady Dorothy to borrow a coach and six horses from St. Giles's House to go to London. There she compounded her sins by going to the theater with her sister-in-law Katherine Ashley and gave final proof of her lack of responsibility by failing to visit Lord Ashley promptly upon her arrival to town. Thus she violated some of Shaftesbury's most intense prejudices. Shaftesbury's rank required him to have a coach; he used it most frugally, though, and continually bemoaned the expense of keeping it. For his sister with her much smaller estate to engage in this sort of conspicuous consumption was unthinkable. With regard to Katherine Ashley, Shaftesbury's estrangement from Maurice seems to have widened as time went on. His brother remained a solid Whig in his politics, yet one senses that his sympathies lie with a different faction. That he waited to marry until he had forced Anthony to do so must have increased Shaftesbury's feeling of personal betrayal. It hardly improved matters that he married a member of what must have been a very closely knit family which the Earl had come to regard as inveterately enthusiastic. Finally, we have seen how sensitive the Earl was about courtesy visits to his infant son. He even reproached most bitterly Lord Ashley's godfather, Lord Halifax, for delaying his visit.

There is something comic about this; on the other hand, it is also tragic. Shaftesbury has made so much progress in his philosophy that one would never think of comparing him to Samuel Johnson's lecturer on Stoicism in *Rasselas*; he is very wise in the ways of men and he becomes a better Stoic every day. Yet he is still the slave of his emotions in matters which seem trivial at this distance. Lady Dorothy certainly knew she was his favorite sibling. Perhaps she took too lightly the sort of gossip which relentlessly followed anyone of her class, yet everything she did was done openly and quite naturally.

Almost always Shaftesbury demands a lot more from his family than his friends. His distress over their unfaithfulness to some family obligation too easily outweighs his love and understanding of them. Yet he is always apologizing for Coste; Crell disappointed him by showing himself inept at handling the simplest financial affairs of the family in Italy, yet is forgiven, and Ned Hooper, who, according to the mores of the day, is wholly responsible for the conduct of Lady Dorothy, gets off scot free. If one thinks of the attack on his sisters that Shaftesbury wrote to Wheelock ten years before, it becomes clear that even Lady Gertrude, had she lived long enough, would have sooner or later run afoul of his impossible expectations. The problem troubled him from the beginning, when he was unlucky with John and unwise in handling his mother, so that it may go back to the disastrous split in his family. Perhaps in demanding so much of himself he expected others to do likewise, though every tenet of Stoicism would have warned him that they were unlikely to do so. Since the Shaftesbury Papers were preserved by the Earl as a record of his public personality and except for a few specific instances record the private man almost accidentally, it may be unfair to judge, but so far as the record goes, to see Shaftesbury in relation to his family is to see him at his worst.

The only exceptions to this rule are his child and his wife. Shaftesbury seems a typical parent, for example. To one who has read most of what little has survived and carefully watched his response to all news of Lord Ashley, it appears certain that Shaftesbury was intensely fond of the boy, not merely because he saw the child as someone to carry on the line, as he was conceived to do, but because he was the child's fond, easily flattered, and at times typically fatuous parent. It may seem unnecessary to make this distinction, but it is true.

Brother John is on Shaftesbury's mind when he makes plans for his son—as he was in his commentary on child raising in the Household Book. Everything must be done to make sure that the baby is not spoiled. For instance, Micklethwayte is bawled out for having reproduced in ivory a set of wooden alphabet blocks which Locke had given Shaftesbury as a child. It is also amusing to hear the Earl arguing with Sir John as to whether it is time yet for the baby to have his own coach. More seriously, Shaftesbury insists that Lord Ashley's governess, Mrs. Hern, should have absolute authority over the child so that no confusions will arise in his mind.

In another vein, he says to Cropley, "Nor need my Spouse or I regret the Loss of being Witness of the Little ones prettinesses, whilst we have so good a correspondent and such a Sharer as Your-self." And soberly he says to Micklethwayte, "Salute . . . The Kensington-Nursery and Nurseling, Your Play-fellow, whom I hope you will often play with, that you may the better be *seriouse* with him, when he needs it, and Sir John (who I know can hardly bear it) is out of the way." Or, finally, he writes in more formal style to John Molesworth: "Thanks for your Inquirys after Lord Ashley; who by what we hear, holds the same Character of Health, Strength and Humour: And receives many Encomiums from his Visitants, and Company whom he meets every Day in his Hide-Park-airings."[28]

As fall comes on, Shaftesbury is confined to the palazzo, where he speaks of walking from room to room with a stick, but the weather continues warm and he seems busier than ever. He continues dictating memorandums for "Plasticks" and decides to publish his own translation of the *Judgment of Hercules* in order to forestall Grub Street. The missing volumes of *Characteristicks* have arrived. One and three are finished, but two needs more work and the illustrations are not yet complete. Gribelin the artist has his faults but should not be offended; Darby the printer will need the attention of a hawk if he is to be kept honest. Shaftesbury still is very active in the art market and haggles incessantly over prices with Signor Porchinaro, whom he suspects, with some justice, of cheating him.

Inevitably there are problems with the servants. Crell, as we have seen, is worse than nothing if he is put to work on financial matters. Although Crell transcribes English well, when the Earl wants to make a point to him, he often has to speak in Latin or French. All of the work of the steward has descended on John Wheelock's able nephew, Bryan, who has begun coughing again and suffers from jaundice, too. Furthermore, he has been borrowed from the Ministry of

28. The Earl of Shaftesbury to Sir John Cropley, June 7, 1712 NS, in PRO 30/24/23/9/p. 233; the Earl of Shaftesbury to Thomas Micklethwayte, October 18, 1712 NS, in PRO 30/24/23/9/p. 297; the Earl of Shaftesbury to John Molesworth, March 29, 1712 NS, in PRO 30/24/23/9/p. 183.

Trade, where he holds a small post, and he has been given a deadline in February for his return to London, if he wishes to continue in his position. Shaftesbury feels that it is likely the deadline is directed at him by the Tories. Although he needs Bryan desperately, Shaftesbury's chief concern in the pages he devotes to the topic is the young man's welfare. Bryan leaves in November for the long trip home, carrying two volumes of the revised *Characteristicks* with him. His replacement is to be John Howard, the servant whom Shaftesbury taught French, but, though the Earl feels that his coming "must prove a considerable prolongation of my life, in which a few months is a great deal," Howard does not arrive on time, largely through his own negligence.

Coste had reported earlier that what he had thought would be an opportunity for leisurely travel and study has turned into a disaster. Hobart has proved to be a handful. He is very easily bored, he has no French at all, and he continually suffers from fevers. Shaftesbury also accepts this fall the truth that Coste is unlikely to help him with the French version of any of his works, that he only can be counted on to popularize the works on the Continent, which he does rather well. The Electress of Hanover has received through him a copy of *The Judgment of Hercules* and of the essay on *Enthusiasm*, which she approves, except for one passage. The Earl sends a copy of Leibniz' criticism to Coste, which he hopes can be printed in a Continental journal. Jane now insists that he tutor Lord Ashley. And the series of letters ends with the Earl still awaiting Coste's arrival in Naples.

This autumn General Stanhope was released from confinement, too late to carry on what Shaftesbury hoped for, a still more serious correspondence than the one that he carried on with Pierre Coste. The letters he did write from prison were lost when his servant was seized by the French. Stanhope had been captured on December 9, 1710, by a Spanish force under the Conde de San Esteban at Brihuega, about sixty miles northeast of Madrid. With Philip firmly restored to his throne, this was the last important campaign of the Peninsular War. For Stanhope it meant, as I have remarked, a long, long wait until the Tories ran out of excuses for not bringing back this vocal Whig member of the House of Commons. After the armistice he was exchanged for the Duke of Escalona and returned to London in August 1712.

He returned to an England so dominated by the Tories that the best tactic for strong Whigs was to lie low and wait. There was some triumph left to him, though: he received a congratulatory letter in the Emperor's own hand, he had an interview with the Queen, and he made a tour through the estates of the Whig nobility, which left Shaftesbury wondering at a distance whether he had been able to see Godolphin before Godolphin's death in September. Back in London he turned to the classics, having already translated part of *Characteristicks* into Latin, and he began promoting the book so actively that Micklethwayte claimed he was responsible for the sale of fifty sets.

As we have seen, Stanhope was closely associated politically with Shaftesbury as early as 1707, though most of the time it was through the Earl's agent, Sir John Cropley. It was possible for a military leader to wage war in the summer, then make it back to London in time for the opening of Parliament, though he might have to go back to war before the session ended. Shaftesbury showed his great faith in Stanhope's integrity and common sense when he made him an executor of his will in 1710. It would be good to say that when he had the opportunity, Stanhope became the sort of philosopher-statesman that Shaftesbury had in mind.

Actually Stanhope had too little life left for us to judge the influence his studies had on him. When the Whigs again came to power, by necessity his recreations were likely to be those of his class and time, centered on the banquet table. It does not seem he was as corrupted by them as Shaftesbury feared he might be. Certainly nothing he ever did politically would have displeased the Earl. He remained a staunch adherent of the principles of the Revolution, strongly anti-jacobitical. It was his remarkable candor which charmed Continental statesmen, and made him famed, as Basil Williams says, for looking at England's problems as a citizen of the larger European community. This, too, could hardly have displeased his mentor.

As he gets closer to the end, Shaftesbury becomes a more difficult person to write to, and no matter how fast the letters are coming now, the sheer distance involved also begets misunderstandings. For instance, Shaftesbury hears in April 1712 that toasts were being drunk to still another heir to the family on the way, a rumor which he suspects Maurice of starting. It is not until October that he makes it clear to everyone that he himself will announce Lady Jane's pregnancy, if it ever happens. The theatrical nature of Shaftesbury's last letters is no help, either; though how does one accuse a dying man of being theatrical? His correspondence is absolutely solid on everything that matters, but every month it is marked by more and more trivial anxieties. Thomas Micklethwayte, who is the Earl's chief correspondent and agent in England, is so vexed and harassed by these that in pique this fall he simply halves his letters to Naples.

In October 1712, Count Borromeo was forced by the pro-French group in his court to expel the English from Naples. General Stanhope may not have succeeded in his attempt to correspond with Shaftesbury in Naples, but his letters full of praise for the Earl did get to the court in Vienna, and when the English were driven out, Shaftesbury received only compliments from the Neapolitan officials. When he wrote to thank Stanhope through his English correspondents, he said that if he had gone with the rest he would not have lasted beyond Capua, a few miles to the north.

Late in November the Earl wrote to Coste that he was now confined to the house, but the state of his health "is so much better than what was expected in my Case, that my Spouse and Friends are very Joyfull at it." A week later he suffered an attack of asthma so severe that it stripped away all hope of surviving the winter. The optimism that had been at least faintly visible even in his darkest reports of his health before this time is utterly gone. He is now concerned only about his work and the state of his family on his decease. *Philol* is now almost completely revised and Shaftesbury is pleased with it. As to his virtuoso attempt to make men better in an easier way, the *Second Characters*, only two brief treatises are ready for the press.

With regard to the Earl's family, Lord Ashley had long before been committed to the best hands available; Lady Jane was his chief concern. Hardly any letter he wrote from Naples did not make some kind of reference to "the good Nurse, Governess, and Doctress," as he called her in a letter to the Abbé Farely. Even so he is reticent, because his marriage was more a matter of his own choice than most made in that day. Neither parents, wealth, nor beauty had much to do with it; pure fortune he can thank, and does, for giving him such an able and affectionate wife.

Typical of his care for her is the compact which he had her and his servants agree to on the first of December, 1712. First he had her make a solemn promise to him to return home without delay on his death, and then he had the servants sign this agreement:

> That we do engage Ourselves to My Lord (according to his positive Commands to Us) to put My Lady in mind of her solemn Promess made to My Lord before Us Vizt. That the Moment My Lord expirs She wou'd without Delay or hesitation apply herself to the Thoughts and Business of her sudain Removal hence in order to reach England, family and Friends the soonest possible Leaving his Remains together with Furniture and Houshold stuff . . . to be afterwards convey'd to England as Opportunity offers, but not so as to retard her Departure hence the Least moment, by minding any needless Ceremonys or Fashion. Also that to this End of greater Dispatch and Success in My Lady's removal hence, and for the preservation of her Life and Health, She will not give way to any Condoleances: receiving no Compliments of such Kind from others, nor offering to write by her own hand to any of her friends, but permitting Us to do it all for her as shall be necessary. Mr. Crell, De Roche, and even John Howard (if timely arriv'd) all to accompany My Lady together with Mrs. Frances and Harry, or whatever other assistance or Attendance necessary: but so as not to delay or make the Journey Less Expeditiouse.[29]

Lady Jane must have known that the chief purpose of this compact was not to speed her on her way, but to assure that she would immediately undergo the therapy of travel.

Thomas Micklethwayte first learned of Shaftesbury's certainty that he would not survive the winter in a letter of Crell's of November 29, 1712 NS. He replied after he had recovered enough to tell Sir John:

29. Agreement written by the Earl of Shaftesbury, December 1, 1712, in PRO 30/24/45/iv/80. The Earl's good intentions were defeated probably by the timing of his death. Lady Jane was still in Naples for some period after he died. In February it would have been impossible to begin a journey which would take her over the Alps without stopping in Italy to await the spring thaw. We do not know how she traveled, but she did arrive back in England at least two weeks before his Lordship's body, for which space had been reserved aboard a galley shortly after his death.

If that letter had not come as soon as it was due, & so gave me a Week's time to recover my self in some degree, I should have been very Unfit to have broke such a Sorrow in our Friend Sir John, but I have done it with some Art, which you know is necessary to him. . . . I can't but sincerely tell you, that if I lost you, I hope I should remain Honest, But it would Kill in me all Ambition for doing any thing Praise-worthy or really delighting in any thing.

He tries to make the rest of the letter as cheerful as possible. On Shaftesbury's son, for instance, he reports, "I saw Lord Ashley yesterday who is a very Thriving Lively Lad & talks very plain several sentences of 4 or 5 words. He Knows all his letters & a word that begins with each but N: is his Favorite, he allways crys out *Nurse* very loud when he comes to it."[30] The letter is marked "Recd Feb 11, 1713" in Shaftesbury's own hand—four days before his death.

Shaftesbury's last letters sent abroad are to Cropley and to Wheelock on January 10, 1713 NS. The longest passage in the letter to Cropley deals with his worries whether Bryan Wheelock will make it back in time to save his job, since he has been forced to follow the long route Shaftesbury followed in 1689. Cropley is begged to assist him. He also says, "My *bodily Offspring* (The Little-one) is that in which I doubt not of your assistances and cares after I am gone. But of my Brain-Offspring I doubt much."

The letter to Wheelock is full of injunctions to take care of the family. His friends "will be powerfull and considerable as they are affectionate tho only for the CAUSE's sake. But 'tis on YOU, YOU (Wheelock!) that I depend both for Councell and Service, Advise and assistance in all affairs both for my Wife, my Son and Family, as in my Will I have recommended in the strongest manner I was able." Personally, he says,

I now bid You *farewell*, and will here only say to You that setting aside your Services to me and Family, and my Regard for You on that account, I have all along had for You the most sincere affection of a Friend, thinking You one of the honestest of Men and the most cordially simpathyzing with me in the Love of honesty, Liberty, our Coun-

30. Thomas Micklethwayte to the Earl of Shaftesbury, December 23, 1712, in PRO 30/24/21/220.

trey and Mankind. This (Wheelock!) I hope You will at Length believe, and never think hereafter that I mistrusted You when I have all along so truly and affectionately Loved and confided in You.[31]

There are no famous last words. We have only the bare recital by Crell that the third Earl of Shaftesbury died at his house in Chiaia on February 15, 1713 NS. His body was embalmed, put aboard ship shortly, and according to the records, on June 27, 1713, the ever faithful John Wheelock went over to Salisbury to bring him back to Wimborne St. Giles for burial.

However, during the final days of his life, Shaftesbury sought to leave behind something far more important than dying words. Telling about it makes a fitting closing to the story of his life. We have three letters in French from the Earl to Paolo de Matteis dealing with a final commission, a commission which may seem a trifle bizarre in these times when men struggle so hard to evade certain realities of the process of dying. Yet no biographer could wish for a better example of his subject's chief thesis during his last years—the true relation of art to morality—or for better proof of his subject's adherence until death to his philosophic credo. The deaths of notable people had been and was to continue to be a popular topic for moral paintings. Shaftesbury commissioned Paolo to paint a picture of himself in explicit detail as a dying philosopher.[32]

As J. E. Sweetman remarks, there is some ambiguity if one depends on the letters alone, as one must, because there were drawings made and Shaftesbury and de Matteis must have talked over many of the details of the proposed painting. Yet there are so many details in the three letters that it is possible to get a clear view of what the last sketch must have looked like. The Earl was seen lying on his right side on a couch parallel to the plane of the picture, his head

31. The Earl of Shaftesbury to John Wheelock, January 10, 1713 NS, in PRO 30/24/23/9/pp. 320–24.

32. PRO 30/24/26/1/pp. 100–104. The letters are dated from the thirteenth through the seventeenth of January, NS. It is apparent from their texts that preliminary sketches were begun. One of the letters was noted by Edgar Wind in his "Shaftesbury as a Patron of Art," *Journal of the Warburg and Courtauld Institute*, II (1938), 186. For a fine article stressing the artistic significance of the commission, see J. E. Sweetman, "Shaftesbury's Last Commission," *Journal of the Warburg and Courtauld Institute*, XIX (1956), 110–16.

supported by his four fingers of his right hand, his left arm relaxed across his body, holding a book very loosely. His face shows the full, wasting effects of his disease, yet his expression is at once meditative, melancholy, and calm. Here is the emblematic reply to the letter we saw earlier in which Shaftesbury felt that Locke sounded like a dying Christian.

The attention of the spectator centers on the couch because all the rest of the portrait is in darker tones, except for a window through which one sees a distant outline of Vesuvius. As one knows, though, from reading Shaftesbury on art, every detail no matter how obscurely it is portrayed should relate to the central point. Behind his feet we can see the amanuensis at his table. The room itself is the cabinet of a virtuoso, ornamented with busts, antiquities, and drawings. A sketch of *The Triumph of Hercules* stands on an easel, and Shaftesbury's book on the subject is visible at the side. The Ashley Cooper arms are dimly seen in a tapestry.

This portrait is parallel in purpose to *The Triumph of Hercules*, so that the real action must be in the mind of the subject. It should be drawn so as to emphasize by a vital moment a shift in his thoughts. What is this change? The philosopher has been meditating, and the subject of his meditation is defined by the objects in the room; but according to the letters his attention is being withdrawn by something else. From the first letter it could be assumed that some thought had occurred to him that he wished the amanuensis to record, for his secretary is described with pen in hand, staring intently and expectantly at him, and in the first letter Shaftesbury is described as actually turned toward the secretary, as if he were going to say something. Probably when he saw the sketch Shaftesbury realized that this would not convey his point, because in the third letter he suggests that the subject's eyes rest on the spectator with an expression of languor and familiarity, as if he were being interrupted by someone he knew well who wished to speak to him softly. Who it is becomes clear from the last paragraph of the third letter, where the Earl specifies that a small book—Marcus Aurelius, one hopes—be put in his left hand, as if it were falling: "De sort que le Livre restera ainsi suspendu comme il feroit dan la Main d'un Mort." It is the specter of imminent death which has interrupted Shaftesbury's meditation.

Sweetman's analysis of the aesthetic implications of the scene is likely to remain definitive. He sees the portrait as describing the true function of the virtuoso—a virtuoso not elitist, but as an interpreter of art to the people. Perhaps it is well to stress *people*; Sweetman sometimes uses the word *masses*, which would have no meaning in Shaftesbury's day. Art then is interpreted not only as morally formative, but also to be valued for its own sake. The virtuoso promotes self-converse in the spectator of art. The true critic can be effective because he functions as creatively as the artist does. He informs his readers under the impress of the divine order, the realization of which has become habitual to him.[33]

These Platonic notions are likely to remain Shaftesbury's chief contribution to the history of ideas. He was all too successful in his attack on the morals of Hobbes and on Locke's ultimately theological ethic. Thus he remains a force in the shift from earlier ethics to one based on emotion—because of the nine English editions of his own rather expensive works which appeared by mid-century, and even more so through those who derived their thought from him or merely imitated him. When *Characteristicks* ceased to be published regularly, the chief reason was that nobody any longer questioned the rather simplistic moral ideas which Englishmen derived from it. And the rationalistic element which meant so much to the Earl was so little seen that were he still alive he might well have wished publication to cease.

As to the ideals of the Roman Commonwealthmen, they were in a sense passé when Shaftesbury inherited them and have long since become part of that sheaf of ideas out of which the builders of the British state have picked and chosen. The practical goals which he drew from these ideals and fought for all of his life have prevailed so far: the predominance of Parliament, the continuing development of the spirit of tolerance, and the principle that Europe should be governed by a balance of powers rather than by the hegemony of one.

Along with many of his notable contemporaries, Shaftesbury would deplore the overwhelming defeat of the Ancients by the Moderns, which also looks to us like a contest which it was foolish for

33. Sweetman, "Shaftesbury's Last Commission," 114.

him to have entered on. His support for the Ancients was encouraged by his belief in the cyclic theory of history. It has been a long time since the more acute thinkers of our own day abandoned that theory of inevitable progress which destroyed both the cyclic theory and the notion that the past must have been inevitably better. Let us hope, though, that modern developments will never prove the Earl right and force us into a gothicism far more barbaric that anything he could have imagined.

So far as his personal rather than public goals are concerned, his life was a remarkable triumph over adversity, or perhaps because of it. Setting aside his fretting over smaller matters and his exorbitant expectations of his kin—about which we may not know the whole story—to contrast the young man at twenty-two with what he was at his death two decades later reveals a remarkable growth in human understanding, morality, and wisdom.

It was later in the century that the cult grew up around his name, but even while he was alive it was being recognized that he had vindicated the name of Shaftesbury. The comments of the moderately Tory secretary of state Lord Dartmouth to John Molesworth are indicative of the way most Englishmen were beginning to think of him. He tells Molesworth simply to meet the Earl and assist him: "This is all that it is necessary for me to ask of you in his favour, for his Lordship is so great an ornament to his Country & so deservedly esteemed and beloved by all Englishmen, that as soon as you are acquainted with him, you will be desirous to render him all the services you can upon his own account."[34]

Some measure of his moral courage at death can be gained by returning for a moment to his last commission. Surrounded by ancient art and modern art in the classical style, meditating, book in hand, Shaftesbury here presents us with the perfect symbol of the virtuoso, yet the ultimate poignancy of the scene lies in the conception behind it. The reason for the continuing popularity of this genre of paintings is that it enables the artist to reveal a truth of the character of the subject as he sees it, never so clearly apparent during the subject's whole life. The moment of death gives us an insight into

34. The Earl of Dartmouth to John Molesworth, November 30, 1711 NS, in PRO 30/24/45/iv/55.

the real nature of anyone. This was true even before the Christian scheme of immortality gave the words of the dying the special quality of veracity they so long enjoyed in English law. But the picture Paolo was to paint is a real rarity, not an artist's conception, but Shaftesbury's own view of his death scene, with a message implicit for all. It is an intimate testimony to his faith in his own principles. He sees himself as melancholy because of the loss of family and friends, because of work left undone, but calm too, not in confidence of Salvation, but because he accepts unflinchingly his inevitable dissolution into the flux of the general scheme of things.

Bibliography

Principal Works of Shaftesbury Consulted

The Danger of Mercenary Parliaments. [1698]. With the collaboration of John Toland.

Select Sermons of Dr. Whichcot[e]. London, 1698. Includes a preface by Shaftesbury.

An Inquiry Concerning Virtue, in Two Discourses. London, 1699.

"The Adept Ladys or The Angelick Sect. Being the Matters of fact of certain Adventures Spiritual, Philosophical, Political, and Gallant. In a Letter to a Brother." 1702. PRO 30/24/46A/81.

Paradoxes of State, Relating to the Present Juncture of Affairs in England and the rest of Europe; Chiefly grounded on his Majesty's Princely, Pious, and most Gracious Speech. London, 1702. With the collaboration of John Toland.

The Sociable Enthusiast. A Philosophical Adventure Written to Palemon. [1704?]

*A Letter Concerning Enthusiasm, To My Lord *****.* London, 1708.

The Moralists, a Philosophical Rhapsody. Being a recital of certain conversations upon natural and moral subjects. London, 1709.

Sensus Communis: An Essay on the Freedom of Wit and Humour. In a letter to a friend. London, 1709.

Soliloquy: or, Advice to an Author. London, 1710.

"ΑΣΚΗΜΑΤΑ" ["Exercises"]. PRO 30/24/27/10. Written from 1698 to 1712. Edited by Benjamin Rand in 1900 in *The Life, Unpublished Letters, and Philosophical Regimen of Anthony, Earl of Shaftesbury.*

Characteristicks of Men, Manners, Opinions, Times. 3 vols. London, 1711.

Second Characters, or the Language of Forms. Largely written in 1712. Two works were completed of the four the Earl planned. We have no indication that anything was accomplished with the treatise that was to be third in order. Of the fourth of these, the largest and most significant, we have only the Earl's voluminous notes. Any ordering of the manuscripts is tentative.

A Letter Concerning the Art or Science of Design, written from Italy (on the occasion of Some Designs in Painting), to my Lord *****. MS in Virtuoso Copy Book, PRO 30/24/26/1. It appears in some copies of the 1714 edition of *Characteristicks*, and regularly from the 1732 edition on.

A Notion of the Historical Draught or Tablature of the Judgment of Hercules, 1713. First printed in French in the November 1712 edition of the *Journal des sçavans* as "Raisonnement sur le tableau du jugement d'Hercule, selon l'histoire de Prodicus." MS is PRO 30/24/24/18. The English translation is PRO 30/24/26/2, which was then in corrected form transcribed into the Virtuoso Copy Book PRO 30/24/26/1, whence it was printed. It is in some copies of the 1714 edition of *Characteristicks* and most later ones.

"Plasticks, or the Original Progress and Power of Designatory Art." The notes for this treatise are contained in a separate book. PRO 24/30/27/15.

All of these and a substitute for the third treatise were edited by Benjamin Rand. *Second Characters, or The Language of Forms*. Cambridge, 1914. A new edition is needed.

Characteristicks of Men, Manners, Opinions, Times. 3 vols. The second edition corrected. London, 1714.

Several Letters Written by a Noble Lord to a Young Man at the University. London, 1716.

Letters from the Right Honourable the late Earl of Shaftesbury, to Robert Molesworth, Esq. . . . with two letters written by the late Sir John Cropley. Edited with an introduction by John Toland. London, 1721.

Letters of the Earl of Shaftesbury. Collected into one volume. London, 1750.

Secondary Sources

Books and Monographs

Aldridge, Alfred Owen. "Shaftesbury and the Deist Manifesto." *Transactions of the American Philosophical Society*, n.s., XLI (Philadelphia, 1951), 297–385.

Arnold, E. Vernon. *Roman Stoicism*. Cambridge, 1911.

Barnes, Annie. *Jean Le Clerc et la république des lettres*. Paris, 1938.

Berwick, Marshal James Fitzjames, Duke of. *Mémoires du Maréchal de Berwick, ecrites par lui-même*. 2 vols. Switzerland, Libraires Associés, 1778.

Bevan, Edwyn. *Stoics and Sceptics*. Oxford, 1913.

Brett, R. L. *The Third Earl of Shaftesbury: A Study in Eighteenth-Century Literary Theory*. London, 1951.

Burnet, Bishop Gilbert. *History of His Own Time: From the Restoration of Charles II to the Treaty of Peace at Utrecht, in the Reign of Queen Anne*. London, 1838.

Carabelli, Giancarlo. *Tolandiana: Materiali bibliografici per lo studio dell'opera e della fortuna di John Toland (1670–1722)*. Florence, 1975.

Cartwright, James J., ed. *The Wentworth Papers, 1705–1739*. London, 1883.

Cassirer, Ernst. *The Platonic Renaissance in England*. Translated by James P. Pettegrove. Austin, Tex., 1953.

Clark, Sir George. *The Later Stuarts, 1660–1714*. 2nd ed. Oxford, 1955.

Comparato, Victor Ivo. *Guiseppe Valetta e le sue opere. Archivio Storice per le Province Napoletane*, 3rd series, II. Naples, 1963.

Coxe, William, ed. *Memoirs of John, Duke of Marlborough*. 3 vols. London, 1818–19.

Cranston, Maurice. *John Locke*. London, 1957.

Cudworth, Ralph. *The True Intellectual System of the Universe: The First Part; Wherein, All the Reason and Philosophy of Atheism Is Confuted; and Its Impossibility Demonstrated*. London, 1678.

Cumberland, Bishop Richard. *De legibus naturae*. London, 1672.

de Beer, Esmond S., ed. *The Correspondence of John Locke*. Oxford, 1976–

―――. *The Diary of John Evelyn*. 6 vols. Oxford, 1955.

Douch, Robert. *A Handbook of Local History: Dorset*. Bristol, 1962.

Downie, J. A. *Robert Harley and the Press*. Cambridge, 1979.

Fowler, Thomas. *Shaftesbury and Hutcheson*. London, 1882.

Gay, Peter. *The Enlightenment: An Interpretation*. 2 vols. New York, 1966–69.

Gibbs, Vicary, and others, eds. *The Complete Peerage of England, Scotland, Ireland, Great Britain, and the United Kingdom, Extant, Extinct, or Dormant*, by George Edward Cockayne. New ed. 12 vols. London, 1910–59.

Grean, Stanley. *Shaftesbury's Philosophy of Religion and Ethics: A Study in Enthusiasm*. Athens, Ohio, 1967.

Haley, K. H. D. *The First Earl of Shaftesbury*. Oxford, 1967.

Hicks, Robert Drew. *Stoic and Epicurean*. New York, 1910.

Holmes, Geoffrey. *British Politics in the Age of Anne*. London, 1967.

Horwitz, Henry. *Parliament, Policy and Politics in the Reign of William III*. Manchester, 1977.

Hull, William I. *Benjamin Furly and Quakerism in Rotterdam. Swarthmore College Monographs on Quaker History*, no. 5. Swarthmore, 1941.

Hutchins, John. *The History and Antiquities of the County of Dorset*. 4 vols. London, 1861–70.

Knox, Ronald A. *Enthusiasm: A Chapter in the History of Religion with Specific Reference to the XVII and XVIII Centuries*. Oxford, 1950.

Labrousse, Elisabeth. *Pierre Bayle*. 2 vols. The Hague, 1963–64.

Locke, John. *An Essay Concerning Human Understanding.* 2 vols. Oxford, 1894.
———. *Some Familiar Letters Between Mr. Locke and Several of His Friends.* London, 1708.
———. *Some Thoughts Concerning Education.* London, 1693.
Lysons, Daniel. *The Environs of London.* 4 vols. London, 1792–96.
Marsh, Robert. *Four Dialectical Theories of Poetry: An Aspect of English Neoclassical Criticism.* Chicago, 1965.
McCrady, Edward. *The History of South Carolina.* New York, 1934.
Mintz, Samuel I. *The Hunting of the Leviathan: Seventeenth-Century Reactions to the Materialism and Moral Philosophy of Thomas Hobbes.* Cambridge, 1962.
Molesworth, Robert. *An Account of Denmark.* London, 1694.
Newman, Aubrey. *The Stanhopes of Chevening.* London, 1969.
Ogg, David. *England in the Reigns of James II and William III.* Oxford, 1963.
Plumb, J. H. *The Growth of Political Stability in England, 1675–1725.* London, 1967.
Popple, William. *A Rational Catechism.* London, 1697.
Price, Martin. *To the Palace of Wisdom: Studies in Order and Energy from Dryden to Blake.* Garden City, 1964.
Rand, Benjamin, ed. *The Correspondence of John Locke and Edward Clarke.* Cambridge, Mass., 1927.
Redwood, John. *Reason, Ridicule and Religion: The Age of Enlightenment in England, 1660–1750.* London, 1976.
Rivers, William. *A Sketch of the History of South Carolina to the Close of the Proprietary Government.* Charleston, S.C., 1856.
Robbins, Caroline. *The Eighteenth-Century Commonwealthman: Studies in the Transmission, Development and Circumstances of English Liberal Thought from the Restoration of Charles II until the War with the Thirteen Colonies.* Cambridge, Mass., 1958.
Sachse, William L. *Lord Somers: A Political Portrait.* Manchester, 1975.
Salley, Alexander S., ed. *Commissions and Instructions from the Lords Proprietors of Carolina to Public Officials of South Carolina, 1685–1715.* Columbia, S.C., 1916.
———. *Records in the British Public Record Office Relating to South Carolina.* 5 vols. Atlanta, Ga., 1928–47.
Saunders, William L., ed. *The Colonial Records of North Carolina.* 10 vols. Raleigh, N.C., 1886–90.
Speck, William A. *Tory and Whig: The Struggle in the Constituencies, 1701–1715.* London, 1970.
Stoye, J. W. *English Travellers Abroad, 1604–1667.* London, 1952.
Sutherland, James R. *Background for Queen Anne.* London, 1939.

Toland, John. *A Collection of Several Pieces of Mr. John Toland.* 2 vols. London, 1726.

Tucker, Susie I. *Enthusiasm: A Study in Semantic Change.* Cambridge, 1972.

Tuveson, Ernest L. *The Imagination as a Means of Grace: Locke and the Aesthetics of Romanticism.* Berkeley, 1960.

Worden, A. Blair, ed. *A Voyce from the Watch Tower,* by Edmund Ludlow. Royal Historical Society, Camden 4th series, XXI. London, 1978.

Articles

Croce, Benedetto. "Shaftesbury in Italy: The Presidential Address for 1923–4." *Modern Humanities Research Association,* Cambridge, n.d.

de Giovanni, Biagio. "Culture e vita in Guiseppe Valetta." *Studi sul Settecento Italiano* (Naples, Istituto Italiano per gli Studi Storici, 1967), 1–47.

Hayman, John G. "The Evolution of 'The Moralists.'" *Modern Language Review,* LXIV (1969), 728–33.

Heinemann, F. H. "John Toland and the Age of Enlightenment." *Review of English Studies,* XX (1944), 125–46.

Holmes, Geoffrey, and William A. Speck. "The Fall of Harley in 1708 Reconsidered." *English Historical Review,* LXXX (1965), 673–98.

Marsden, R. G. "The Vice-Admirals of the Coast." *English Historical Review,* XXII (1907), 468–77; XXIII (1908), 736–75.

Meyer, Horst. "Ex Libris Shaftesbury: Die Bibliothek Eines Europäischen Aufklärers." *Wolfenbütteler Forschungen,* II (Bremen, 1977), 75–90.

Paknadel, Felix. "Shaftesbury's Illustrations of *Characteristics." Journal of the Warburg and Courtauld Institute,* XXXVII (1974), 290–312.

Robbins, Caroline. "Absolute Liberty: The Life and Thought of William Popple, 1638–1708." *William and Mary Quarterly,* 3rd series (1967), 190–223.

Robinson, Peter. "The Third Earl of Shaftesbury and Lady Anne Carbery in 1708." *Notes & Queries,* CCXXI (1976), 484–86.

Stolnitz, Jerome. "On the Significance of Lord Shaftesbury in Modern Aesthetic Theory." *Philosophical Quarterly,* XI (1961), 97–113.

Sweetman, J. E. "Shaftesbury's Last Commission." *Journal of the Warburg and Courtauld Institute,* XIX (1956), 110–16.

Tiffany, Esther M. "Shaftesbury as Stoic." *PMLA,* XXXVIII (1923), 642–84.

Voitle, Robert. "The Reason of the English Enlightenment." *Studies on Voltaire and the Eighteenth Century,* XXVII (Geneva, 1963), 1735–74.

———. "Shaftesbury's Moral Sense." *Studies in Philology,* LII (1955), 17–38.

Whitaker, S. F. "The First Edition of Shaftesbury's *Moralists." The Library,* 5th series, VII (1952), 235–41.

Wind, Edgar. "Shaftesbury as a Patron of Art." *Journal of the Warburg and Courtauld Institute*, II (1938), 186–88.

Wolf, Richard B. "The Publication of Shaftesbury's *Letter Concerning Enthusiasm*." *Studies in Bibliography*, XXXII (1979), 236–41.

Index